Praise for SERGEANT MAJOR

"The story of Sergeant Major Maurice Jacques is the story of a true warrior. With close to fifty months' combat in Korea and Vietnam, he's one of that rare breed, men who have looked the Devil in the eye—for a *long* time—and never blinked!"

—Lt. Col. Oliver North, USMC (Ret.)

Also by B. H. Norton
Published by Ivy Books:

FORCE RECON DIARY, 1969
FORCE RECON DIARY, 1970
ONE TOUGH MARINE

SERGEANT MAJOR, U.S. MARINES

Sergeant Major Maurice J. Jacques, USMC (Ret.),

and Major Bruce H. Norton, USMC (Ret.)

IVY BOOKS • NEW YORK

Ivy Books
Published by Ballantine Books
Copyright © 1995 by Maurice J. Jacques and Bruce H. Norton

ISBN 0-8041-1030-1

Manufactured in the United States of America

First Edition: July 1995

10 9 8 7 6 5 4 3 2 1

Sergeant Major, U.S. Marines is dedicated to my son, Bruce Hartley Norton, II. Though I pray he may never have to go in harm's way, if he should, then let it be with men as capable, as dedicated, and as brave as Sergeant Major Maurice J. Jacques, USMC.

Major Bruce H. "Doc" Norton, USMC, (Ret.)
October 1994

TABLE OF CONTENTS

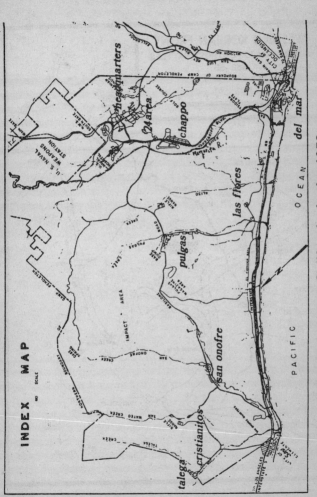

Camp Pendleton, California, in the 1950s

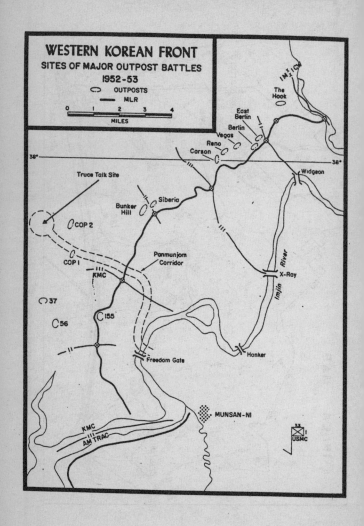

WESTERN KOREAN FRONT
SITES OF MAJOR OUTPOST BATTLES
1952-53

⊃ OUTPOSTS
— MLR

0 1 2 3 4
MILES

The Hook

East Berlin

Berlin

Vegas

Reno

Carson

38°   38°

Widgeon

Truce Talk Site

Siberia

Bunker Hill

COP 2

Panmunjom Corridor

X-Ray

Imjin River

COP 1

KMC

37

155

56

Honker

Freedom Gate

MUNSAN-NI

KMC
AM TRAC

1
USMC

OKINAWA

HEDO POINT

IE SHIMA

EAST CHINA SEA

Camp Schwarb

Camp Hansen

Camp Butler

NAHA

MCAS Futema

PACIFIC OCEAN

N

0   5   10   15

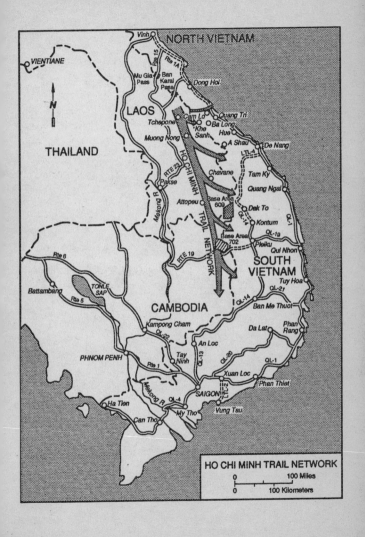

HO CHI MINH TRAIL NETWORK

0   100 Miles

0   100 Kilometers

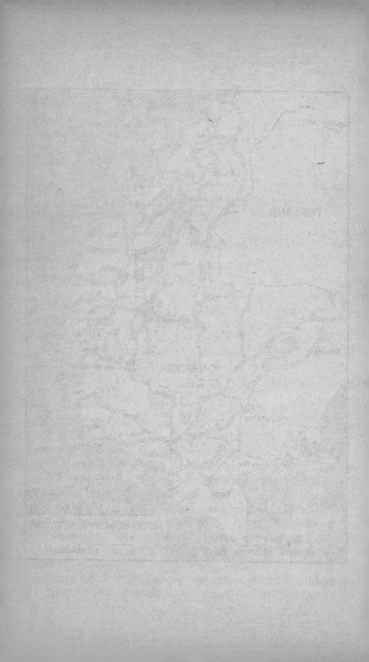

Introduction

I first met Maurice Jacques in the spring of 1970 in Vietnam. He was the first sergeant of 1st Force Reconnaissance Company, and I was a young navy hospital corpsman who had recently joined that unique organization. First Sergeant Jacques struck an imposing figure as he moved about our company area. Built like a heavyweight boxer, thick muscular arms adorned with large tattoos, and wearing a freshly cut high & tight, he personified the image of a professional Marine staff noncommissioned officer.

Jacques had been sent to 1st Force Recon by the 1st Marine Division's sergeant major to assume the position of the company's senior enlisted man, replacing the former first sergeant, a pathetic figure who had been accused, tried, and convicted of being a charlatan. By his own example, First Sergeant Jacques would—and did—correct the damage done to the reputation of the company by the thief. Jacques knew he had a difficult job to do, but he was sent to 1st Force Reconnaissance Company because he was the correct man for that job.

While I was in 1st Force Reconnaissance Company, First Sergeant Jacques became my scuba diving partner, and that was the beginning of a professional and personal friendship that has lasted more than twenty-five years.

I served with Jacques for the second time, but under much different circumstances, in 1975, when I was a second lieutenant platoon leader serving in Lt. Col. Alex Lee's 3d Battalion, 1st Marines. Maurice J. Jacques was our regiment's sergeant major: the senior enlisted man and the principal adviser to Col. Ed Snelling, the commanding officer of the regiment.

One day, late in 1975, I was selected to be a member of a meritorious promotion board—one of a dozen officers and senior enlisted Marines tasked with selecting, for promotion to the grade of sergeant, the best corporals within our regiment. Sergeant Major Jacques was a member of that promotion board. Each of us was given the opportunity to ask one question of each selectee, hoping their answers to our questions would provide enough information for us to select the best candidates. Each Marine's service record book was provided to the board as an additional source of information, but it was the Marine himself, his physical presence in uniform, and his ability to correctly answer rapid-fire questions, which, we hoped, would provide us with the "few good men" we were looking for.

The last man to ask a question of each Marine was the regimental sergeant major, and Jacques asked a dandy. "If you were leading a six-man reconnaissance patrol, and one of your men began acting a little crazy before you had reached your objective, and you were surrounded by the enemy, what would you do?" For as many Marines who stood before the board there were that many answers, guesses, and such honest replies as, "I have no idea of what I'd do, Sergeant Major." And though several of us on that promotion board had seen more than our share of close combat, no one could answer the question based on his experience: with the exception of Sergeant Major Jacques.

This book—this odyssey—traces Maurice J. Jacques's beginnings in Lawrence, Massachusetts, and follows him from boot camp at Parris Island to his first duty station on Guam, from Hawaii—where Col. Chesty Puller was his commanding officer—to combat in Korea, where only he and one other Marine in his squad survived the battle for the combat outposts known as the "Nevada cities."

As Jacques was promoted, his responsibility for providing leadership to his Marines multiplied. Jacques became a "teacher" of infantry skills and gained expertise as a combat engineer and a demolitions man. Promoted to staff sergeant, he completed two years of duty as a drill instructor at MCRD (Marine Corps Recruit Depot) San Diego before becoming proficient as a reconnaissance Marine, training as a parachutist, a scuba diver, and an anti-guerrilla small-unit leader. He went to Vietnam in 1965.

His combat record is exemplary. His first tour of duty lasted nineteen months. On one occasion, outnumbered more than ten to one, he and most of the Marines in his platoon survived a murderous night attack by a North Vietnamese Army battalion. Shot through the throat, Jacques remained in command, avoided capture, and led his men to safety over a two-day period. He recovered from his wounds and returned to the field three weeks later. He helped plan for, and participated in, the first combat parachute jump executed in the history of the Marine Corps.

As the first sergeant of E Company, 1st Reconnaissance Battalion, from 1967 to 1969, he continued to lead by example, patrolling against the North Vietnamese. By the end of 1970, First Sergeant Jacques had been fighting in Vietnam for forty-three months—completing three combat tours.

Promoted to the rank of sergeant major, Jacques served as the sergeant major of the 2d Battalion, 3d Marine Regiment, 1st Marine Brigade, located on Hawaii, from 1971 through 1975. By 1976, he had served as the regimental sergeant major of the 1st Marine Regiment, and in 1978, he had come full circle—retiring, after thirty years of service, as the sergeant major of the first Marine regiment he served with on Guam in 1948, "the fighting 5th Marines."

The Marine noncommissioned officer has been, is now, and will continue to be the backbone of our Corps. They are the individuals tasked with executing the orders that the officers appointed over them pass down. From 1948 until 1978, Maurice J. Jacques served faithfully and honorably and distinguished himself in the United States Marine Corps.

This biography—this extraordinary record of small discoveries—is my effort to accurately document the thirty-year career of a professional staff noncommissioned officer whose service to his Corps and to his country is embodied in the well-known phrase, "Once a Marine, always a Marine."

Major Bruce H. "Doc" Norton, USMC (Ret.)

CHAPTER 1

My Family History

My family's recorded history began in southeastern Canada when my great-grandfather, Belonie Jacques, was born in St. Frederic in 1830. He married his childhood sweetheart, Christine Gilbert, and they settled south of the city of Quebec in the rural township of Sacre-Coeur de Marie (Sacred Heart of Mary), where they raised eight children and worked a small farm. Their third child, my grandfather Georges Jacques, was very special to me. Born in Canada in 1856, he and his wife Lea Poirier, who came from Sacre-Coeur-de-Jesus, raised their family of six children and later immigrated to the United States through Durbin, Vermont, where they settled in Laconia, New Hampshire. My grandfather was a large, powerful man who worked first as a lumberjack in Maine and later as a farmer. He lived to be ninety-two years old, and my grandmother lived to be seventy-nine years old.

My father, Harmidas Jacques, who for some reason was nicknamed Meadow, emigrated from Canada to the town of Lawrence, Massachusetts, where he and his wife, Anntoinette, became U.S. citizens. They raised a family of four: me; my brother Francis, who was born when I was four years old; my brother Edward, born when I was thirteen; my sister Eleanor, who came into our family when I was fifteen.

My father worked as a truck driver, hauling heavy equipment around the six New England states. My mother kept an immaculate house, and though she did not work outside our home, she did have her hands full keeping track of the four of us.

I was born on June 17, 1931, and my earliest remembrances of growing up in Lawrence begin when we lived at 26 Adams Street, a place our family called the little house. The house had only four rooms, and I shared the attic with my brother Francis for eight years, until we moved to a larger house located at 11 Devonshire Street, a place we called the gray house, which my father bought in 1939, paying three thousand dollars to the man who had built it. Not long after we moved in, my father added a single-car garage to protect his car and tools from the weather. Like so many suburban New England homes, our house was a two-story, wood-shingled place, with hardwood floors in the front room and living room, linoleum covering the kitchen floor and the two upstairs bedrooms. The house had a forced-air heating system, and I can still recall many cold winter mornings spent with both feet placed squarely over the center of the large metal heating vent while I took my time getting dressed for school.

As a young boy, I was given household chores to do, probably not so much to reduce my mother's workload, as to keep me accounted for and continuously busy. It was my responsibility to empty the ashes from the kitchen's wood-burning stove, to cut, carry, and stack kindling wood inside the kitchen, and to feed our dozen Rhode Island Red chickens, which were kept in a small wooden coop, not too distant from the house.

As I grew older, my mother would hand me her printed shopping list, with just enough money to purchase the items on it, and send me to the local variety store. My greatest responsibility, though, was taking care of my younger brothers, making sure they remained close by and out of trouble. Watching out for them was never much of a problem, and as they grew older, I learned to enjoy their company. Our neighborhood had plenty of kids, and when

I was about ten years old, a group of a dozen of my closest friends and I formed a club. We were together all of the time. In the winter months, we played hockey from early morning until so late in the day that there wasn't enough daylight for us to see the puck moving across the ice. In the warmer months, we worked as a group and earned extra spending money running countless errands for neighbors and doing odd jobs after school. And when it was decided that we needed a clubhouse, we dismantled an "abandoned" workmen's shed, originally built by the WPA, and moved it, piece by piece, away from the railroad tracks and rebuilt it in an unused field closer to our neighborhood. We canvassed the area for old furniture, and we outfitted the clubhouse with a wood-burning stove, tables and chairs, an old crank-type RCA Victrola phonograph, and phonograph records. We held regular meetings there after school.

My first four years of grade school were spent at Sacred Heart Parochial School, a French-speaking Catholic school run by tyrannical nuns who maintained absolute order and discipline by wielding wooden batons, like those an orchestra conductor uses, to mete out punishment to those of us who broke their endless rules. I can still hear the "high notes" that came from those unfortunate souls being disciplined as they echoed through the long, empty halls of Sacred Heart school. Those sisters were definitely selective; I can't recall any girls having to be disciplined, but boys were never spared. My mother and father spoke fluent Canadian-French and they encouraged me to speak French, too, but I resisted. The nuns at school, who spoke only French, made my life miserable for my failure to speak their language, and because of this, I did not enjoy school at Sacred Heart. I transferred to Weatherby Public School for grades five through eight. There, at least I was allowed to speak English. At Weatherby, my favorite subjects were history and geography, and it was while I attended Weatherby that I became a member of first the Cub Scouts, and later, the Boy Scouts. Before I joined the Scouts, my grandfather, who had worked in a logging camp in Maine, had taught me many woodsman's skills: how to use an ax, build a fire, read a map and use a compass, and how to survive off the land. Because of what I had learned, I was able to earn quite a few merit badges during the years that I was in the Scouts. I enjoyed reading about foreign lands and people, and that was the beginning of my wanderlust; wanting to travel and see new and different places.

I remember the afternoon of the first Sunday of December 1941, as I sat with a group of friends on the front steps of our house and listened to the radio reports telling of the Japanese attack on Pearl Harbor. Our shock and helplessness were quickly replaced by a determination of the club members to somehow help to right that terrible wrong. That mood of patriotism grew stronger during the next five years. It may sound corny today, but even though we were too young to join up and serve our country, we pitched in and helped in every way we could. We collected aluminum pots and pans, nylon stockings, and old tires for the war effort, and we grew little Victory Gardens to help ease consumer needs across the nation. That kind of thing became a way of life and made us feel we were contributing to the national effort to win the war.

After completing the ninth grade at the age of thirteen, I decided to quit high school, simply because I was bored with it. That decision was not well received at home, and my parents made it quite clear I would not be allowed to "sit around the house and do nothing." I spent the summer of '44 working on a cousin's poultry farm. There, I learned basic carpentry skills, to drive a Ford flatbed truck, and to operate a steel-wheeled Fordson tractor, used for pulling stumps, plowing the fields, and spreading manure. I was able to split my time between the poultry farm and a vegetable farm, where I helped to truck fresh produce into Lawrence, but my father's idea of a real job was manual labor, and he advised me to apply for a full-time job at a local construction company.

The L. C. Cyr Construction Company built bridges, houses, and hospitals, and I was hired on at the age of fourteen to work as a common laborer at the rate of one dollar per hour. My first job was removing worn-out streetcar tracks from the main roads of Lawrence, Massachusetts. The workday began at 7:30, and despite my age, I was expected to do a man's job. I was the type of kid who liked to make money, and when I learned that the guy who operated the jackhammer got paid $1.25 per hour, I wanted that job. One day, the jackhammer operator didn't show up for work. I went to my boss, a massive Italian man, and told him that I'd like a chance to operate the heavy jackhammer. He laughed and said, "Kid, you won't last a full day behind that damn thing, but if you want to give it a try, then go ahead." I was determined to show him that I could do the job. I lasted out the day and was given the job, full time. In 1946, thousands of veterans were returning home, and they were looking for work. As a kid doing a man's job I had to demonstrate that I could be relied upon to always do a full day's work; that was the only way to insure that I kept my job.

One day, while working on a construction job at the Lawrence General Hospital, I noticed a cute candy-striper volunteer nurse who I wanted to ask out for a date. Eventually, my boss walked over to where we stood. He told me not to stop talking to the girl, and said, "Go ahead and keep talking, Jacques, and I hope you make a date with her, 'cause you'll have all the time you want, since this is your last day working here at the hospital." The next day I was sent to a job site at the Lawrence Gas Works. In those days, the natural gas used to heat homes was produced by burning chunks of coke, which produced a thick greasy film inside the gas filter tanks. It became my job to cover the walls of the tanks with wood shavings, shoveled in to "capture" the grease, then shovel the dirty shavings onto a conveyor belt which carried them outside, where they were dried before being reused as fuel. This was hard work, and when the time came to take a break, I looked forward to listening to a guy nicknamed Whitey talk about his days in the Marine Corps. His vivid recollections of the demands of Marine boot camp, island-hopping across the western Pacific, and experiencing the horrors of combat on the islands of Iwo Jima and Okinawa was the stuff of movies. His stories, and the feelings of patriotism I had experienced during the past five years, were enough to convince me that if I ever wanted to get away from Lawrence and see what the world had to offer, the Marine Corps could be my ticket to do so.

On 11 July 1948, I went by steam train from Lawrence to Boston, then walked to the Fargo Building on Summer Street and told the Marine recruiter that I wanted to enlist. I was given a physical examination, took a number of tests, and because I was only seventeen years old, returned home to have a stack of consent papers signed by my parents. I was told to return to the recruiting office the following day with my baptismal certificate as proof of my age. (Birth certificates were not as common then as they are today.) After I was sworn in with a dozen other Marine recruits, we were taken across the street to eat breakfast before being taken to the Chelsea Navy Yard. We spent the night at the navy yard, and early the next morning we went by bus to Boston's famous South Station, where we began a two-day train ride on the Pennsylvania Railroad that would deliver us to the home of recruit training on the East Coast—Parris Island, South Carolina.

A Marine reservist, a private from Boston named Bill McMann, was to make sure that our group of twelve made it safely to our destination. The route south took us through the cities of Hartford, New York, Philadelphia, Pittsburgh, and Charleston, West Virginia, while the number of recruits steadily grew, and ended with more than a hundred of us arriving in the farming town of Yemassee, South Carolina. From Yemassee, we boarded open-air railroad cars of the Southern Railroad that carried us to Port Royal, South Carolina. Private McMann had done his job of insuring that we stayed together by having us sit at the position of attention all the way from Boston to Yemassee, but as we pulled out of the train station and headed for Port Royal, we realized that he was not among us, and those of us who came from north of the Mason-Dixon line dared to comment on the terrible living conditions we were seeing in the deep South. When we arrived at Port Royal, we were met by a Marine master sergeant whose booming voice ordered us off the train and into a livestock corral. As our names were called out, we moved from the sweltering, unshaded corral to cattle cars owned and operated by the Marine Corps. Our final stop would be the recruit depot at Parris Island.

CHAPTER 2

Memories of Parris Island—1948

Every Marine who has ever undergone recruit training at Parris Island, South Carolina, remembers that precise moment, whether day or night, when he crossed over the two-lane bridge and onto the base, trading the creature comforts of the civilian world for the chance to earn the title Marine. For me, that moment came on a hot and humid Thursday morning in mid-July 1948, at 10:00 A.M, when the cattle car carrying me and seventy-five other recruits rolled to a stop at the front gates of the base. There stood two Marine sentries, allowing vehicles to come and go. Standing close beside each sentry was a huge German shepherd guard dog. Before this, I had only seen guard dogs in the movies, where "war dogs" were relentless in tracking down escaped POWs and were trained to bite everyone but their handlers. So, when I saw them, like so many who had come to Parris Island before me, I began to think, What in the hell have I gotten myself into? This place must be like some sort of prison.

The expressions on the faces of the other recruits who were seeing those sentry dogs added validity to my fears, and as our cattle car began again to roll forward there was not spoken a single word from the seventy-six of us. Passing through the main gate, and only entrance to Parris Island, we could see only endless swampland on either side of the road, and all thoughts of escape faded away as our cattle car continued meandering through the swampland.

The "hygienic unit" was our first destination. In those days there was nothing like the "receiving" barracks of today, where recruits are welcomed aboard for training, initially tested, and then introduced to their drill instructors, all accomplished with the highest degree of dignity, civility, and calmness.

In 1948, not only the theory, but the practice of keeping recruits shocked and scared to death was the driving force throughout our indoctrination. Within seconds of our cattle car stopping in front of the hygienic unit, the doors of the cattle car were thrown open, and the loud voices of a half dozen Marine drill instructors began to boom. "All right, get off that goddamn truck! Move it, move it, move it! You heard me, shitbird, move your ass. You there, stand right here, and don't you dare move a goddamned inch. You, stand right next to that man. Now don't you move." None of us had ever been pushed, pulled, shoved, or sworn at in such a manner, and the rapid-fire Marine commands only added to our confusion.

When we were finally assembled into an organized, standing herd, a young sergeant centered himself before us and announced, "You will now be getting Marine Corps haircuts. There are twelve barbers waiting for you inside. If any of you have a mole, scar, boil, or any type of open sore on your head, place your finger on that exact spot so the barber will not jam up his clippers with your flesh. Get in, and get out. There will be no talking. Following haircuts, you will be taken to the showers. Once it is decided that all of you are clean, you will strip yourselves of all civilian clothing and receive your first issue of Marine Corps uniforms."

No recruit's haircut took longer than twenty seconds from the time he sat in the barber's chair until he was tapped on the shoulder—signaling that his haircut was over—to move out. Within minutes, ankle-deep piles of hair formed a circle around the base of each of the barber's chairs, until some freshly shorn recruit was handed a dustpan and broom and ordered to sweep up the hair and toss it into a barrel. When the last recruit ran out from the barbershop, we moved to the shower building, where we were ordered to stand motionless, our feet on large yellow footprints painted on the floor, and then to strip.

The showers resembled a Spartan car wash—parallel sections of lead pipe, perhaps twelve feet long, with a dozen showerheads attached, greeted each of us as we passed like sheep through the wet mist created by the cold water. We were not given soap or towels to dry ourselves with, but were kept moving straight into another room where we passed along a clothing counter and were issued a utility uniform consisting of one pair of green boxer shorts, one pair of utility trousers, which had baggy pockets on each side and what was called a grenade pocket conveniently sewn across the seat. Then we each received one pair of low-cut work boots, called boondockers, one pair of green socks, one green T-shirt, and one utility cover. Still wet, we hurriedly dressed in our first issue, then returned to where we had stripped off our clothes and were ordered to stuff all our civilian clothing into individual laundry bags that were marked for shipment back home.

The ordeal at the hygienic unit lasted for nearly three hours, and never was any order given by a drill instructor in a normal voice. Any recruit who was the last one to perform any task was slapped, kicked, or so severely berated that he was reduced to tears, reminding the rest of us never to be too slow or the last one to do what was ordered. We were warned not to talk to one another. Once we were dressed and assembled, our names were read off, and we each ran outside, stopping directly in front of the Marine noncommissioned officers (corporals) who would lead us through recruit training: our drill instructors. Each drill instructor was immediately recognizable by his neatly pressed utility uniform, pistol duty belt, and pith helmet with the Marine Corps emblem of eagle, globe, and fouled anchor positioned in its center.

As each of us stood before the drill instructor, he placed

his hands on our shoulders, looked us squarely in the eyes, and said, "Stand right here." He did this to every one of the seventy-six recruits who were assigned to our platoon, until he had positioned us to his satisfaction, into four squads, then marched us away from the hygienic unit to the H-shaped barracks that would be our home for the next three months.

The first order of business—and all business was conducted at the double time—was to be assigned to our individual beds, forever after referred to as our racks, and then we were introduced to what was called a "rack drill."

Our drill instructor or his assistant, also a corporal, would run alongside each recruit and guide us into the barracks, where we picked up one cotton mattress cover, one thin mattress, one small pillow, two sheets, one pillowcase, and two green wool blankets, before being run back outside to rejoin the formation. Once every recruit had received a linen issue, we were run through the barracks again, and each of us was quickly shown how to properly make up his rack, first placing the mattress inside its cover, putting the sheets on the rack, complete with squared corners, and finishing the job with both blankets tightened over the rack.

Once our racks were made, we ran outside and resumed our places in ranks, until all seventy-six racks were complete. Then we were run back inside the barracks and stood in front of our assigned racks at the position of attention and watched in horror as the two drill instructors inspected our work and found fault with what we had done. They stripped the blankets and sheets from every rack and threw the mattresses onto the floor. "This is not acceptable, you shitbirds. We showed you how to properly make up your racks once today. You people have failed to do it right. Now you will do it again until you have it right." It took four trips in and out of the barracks, followed by four "failed inspections," before we passed rack drill. By that time, all of our sheets were soiled from having been dragged around, and the barracks floor was covered with dirt from our many trips to and from the outside formation.

That same afternoon, rack drill was replaced with learning the intricacies of barracks cleaning, known throughout the Marine Corps as "field day." Once we had removed our metal bunk-bed frames and wooden footlockers from inside the squad bay, we were taught to sweep the wood floor, renamed the "deck," in preparation for a more detailed cleaning using hot soapy water, scrub brushes, and toothbrushes. In the latrine, the copper pipes were to be polished to a brilliant shine, windows were made spotless, and the toilets and urinals were cleaned so thoroughly they would not produce "even the thought of dirt" beneath the fingernail scrape of any inspecting drill instructor.

Sometime close to 1700, we were marched to chow, and no mention was made of our having missed the noon meal. That first evening meal was a rushed event. Before entering the mess hall we were told, "Take all you want, but eat all you take." That was followed by the stern warning not to be the last man to finish eating, or risk paying the price; usually a slap to the back of the head or a well-placed kick beneath the pockets of one's trousers.

It was not until we returned to the barracks that our drill instructors introduced themselves. Ours was Cpl. John N. Henderson. He came from Florida and had already completed twenty-two years of honorable service. His assistant was Cpl. Richard D. Olsen, from Texas, who had completed twelve years in the Corps. Both were combat veterans of World War II. That first night, Corporals Henderson and Olsen wasted no time in teaching us the basics of how to survive on Parris Island. We were taught how to properly address not only them but any other drill instructor or officer we might encounter, and how to properly stand at the positions of attention, at ease, parade rest, and rest. By 2200, our first lessons inside the squad bay were over. Before lights-out, we were allowed ten minutes to make a brief head call. Within minutes of lights-out, I heard the sounds of young men crying and a few unanswered calls for "Mom" from the darkness.

Our first reveille, and a new battery of shouted threats, screams, and curses from the two drill instructors, came at 0300 the next morning. We were given only a few minutes to remake our racks before being run into the head to witness a demonstration of how to shave properly. One recruit was selected, and his face was covered in lather. Then Corporal Olsen produced a doubled-edged Gillette razor and, with skilled hands, removed all of the shaving cream from the "volunteer's" face without so much as a single nick. Razor in hand, he addressed us for the first time that morning. "Everyone of you shitbirds will shave every day. If you have never had to shave before, get someone to show you how. If I ever catch any of you needing a shave, I'll shave you myself, and then you can report to sick bay to get the shaving cuts sewn shut. Do I make myself perfectly clear?" Seventy-six voices shouted as one, "Yes, sir," hoping to convince Corporal Olsen that we would not forget to shave, ever.

The next day we received additional issues of clothing and equipment. We drew one tropical pith helmet, three sets of odd-looking green cotton skivvies, which had two lengths of string called "tie-ties" anchored at opposite sides of the waistband and used as clothespins. We got two sets of utilities, some men getting a World War II–style jacket with large cargo pockets, while the rest of us were given utility jackets that had two map pockets on each side of the front of the jacket. We were also issued a second pair of boondockers and one pair of brown leather dress shoes.

Once our clothing issue was complete, we were marched to a warehouse to collect what was called a "bucket issue." The bucket issue consisted, naturally, of a one-gallon, galvanized bucket for field-day use, filled with an assortment of items: a razor and one package of Gillette double-edged red blades; one tube of Barbasol shaving cream having the consistency of axle grease; one large bar of lye soap; one roll of tie-ties thick enough to last a lifetime; one wooden scrub brush; one wool swimsuit; one pair of leggings (to be worn laced up and over our boondockers); one pair of tennis shoes; a small sewing kit.

After drawing our bucket issue, we returned to the barracks and were given a short time to stow away the newly acquired gear in footlockers before receiving a class on the proper way to wash and dry our uniforms. Behind our barracks, and out of public view, were six stone-lined sinks called washracks, with a series of parallel clotheslines built close by and long enough to fit the needs of all seventy-six of us. There we watched Corporal Olsen show how our uniforms, underwear, and socks, were to be scrubbed, rinsed free of laundry soap, and properly hung (using tie-ties to keep them anchored to the clothesline with only a square knot). Our uniform during the washing of clothes was the blue-wool bathing suit, boondockers, and pith helmet, and once our clothes were hung up to dry, one recruit was assigned to "laundry watch" to guard the clothes until the South Carolina sun had dried every item hung on the line.

The issuing of the M-1 service rifle was a very special event. As a kid, I had shot both a .22-caliber rifle, and a 30-30 deer rifle, but there was no comparison between those rifles and the size, heft, and reputation of the nine-and-a-half-pound, combat-tested, M-1 Garand. All Marines considered the Garand a prize possession, and God help anyone who should drop his M-1 rifle at Parris Island. We would spend hours each day with the M-1, learning first how to disassemble and assemble the rifle, and how to properly move the rifle while performing the manual of arms and during the countless hours of close-order drill. The M-1 simply became a part of our lives.

The same day we were issued the M-1 rifle, we were introduced to the Marine Corps' two-pack system that would help carry our equipment into combat. That equipment, collectively called 782 gear, because that was the number of the receipt form, included one knapsack; one haversack; one waterproof poncho; a mess kit with knife, fork, and spoon; one half of a canvas camouflage-pattern, two-man tent, called a shelter-half; six tent pegs; two tent poles and two guidelines; one bayonet and scabbard; one first-aid pouch; a field jacket; one collapsible shovel (called an entrenching tool); a pair of belt suspender straps; one cartridge belt; one canteen and cup, and one combat helmet. These items tipped the scales at just over forty-five pounds, and were stuffed into a field transport pack. Of course there was only one way to wear any of that equipment—the Marine Corps way. The first-aid pouch was always worn on the cartridge belt, directly over a Marine's right rear trouser pocket. The canteen was placed on the cartridge belt and worn just behind the right hip with the two web flaps that held the canteen firmly in its pouch always crossed—just like our boot- and shoe-laces—left over right.

On the morning of our third day at Parris Island, Corporals Henderson and Olsen passed the word for all of us to fall in outside, and once assembled, took us on what was called a Cook's tour of Parris Island. This Cook's tour was, in fact, a long-distance run designed to serve a number of purposes. We ran from our barracks to the single causeway we had crossed three days earlier, stopping to catch our breath and listen as Corporal Henderson explained that the causeway was the only entrance onto and off of Parris Island. He pointed his walking stick at the distant bridge and shouted, "The swamp you are looking at is ten feet deep in some places and is home to some very big alligators. No recruit has ever been successful in managing to get off of this island by crossing through that swamp. That bridge is your only way out of here. Now, fall back in." From the causeway, we continued running until we stopped in front of the statue of "Iron Mike," an imposing bronze likeness of a Marine standing in triumph, .45 automatic held high in one hand, and a .30-caliber machine gun over his right shoulder. Corporal Henderson stared at the statue for a moment and then turned to face us. "That is what a real Marine looks like. I want all of you shitbirds to take a good look at it, so you'll never forget." Leaving Iron Mike, we resumed our run and when we were finally halted outside our barracks, there wasn't a single one of us who was not drenched in his own sweat and left gasping for breath. Ordered to stand at attention, our ranks still swayed, and Corporals Henderson and Olsen committed to memory the names of those who were badly out of shape and needed extra help. The rising heat and humidity of the day had brought out the biting sand fleas that Parris Island was famous for, and those of us who flinched at the tiny insect's bite were either slapped in the back of the head or struck on the top of the pith helmet, helping to drive home the idea that to move when ordered to stand at attention was a painful and costly mistake.

After the Cook's tour, we were never taken on another endurance run; it wasn't necessary because our drill instructors ensured that we received enough physical training each day to challenge even the most physically fit recruit. When we formed for PT each day, we didn't wear running shorts and expensive running shoes; our uniform was always the same; we wore only utilities and boots for all periods of physical exercise. Our PT program alternated, one day being dedicated to using the M-1 rifle while we exercised; the next day's session was spent running and doing calisthenics. Push-ups, side-straddle hops, and a particularly torturous exercise known as the squat thrust were the favorites of our drill instructors. Logs twelve feet long were made a part of our daily PT routine. We ran, holding the logs high above our heads and hoping we had the strength to keep them up. We did two types of sit-ups: those done in groups of six while holding the logs across our chests, and sit-ups done, not with knees flexed, but with legs flat on the ground. Push-ups were neverending. Strengthening every recruit's upper body was the DIs' goal, and the methods used were very successful. The heat and humidity of South Carolina, combined with a vigorous daily physical-training program, shed pounds from those who were too fat and put muscle on those who came to Parris Island without any.

The favored event of every recruit training day was chow, but that, too, was a much different event from what is experienced by today's Marine recruit. For us, chow was served "family-style," similar to the way meals are served at Annapolis and West Point, with our senior or junior drill instructor always seated at the head of one of our tables. After we entered the mess hall, we were handed a stainless-steel tray and cup and directed to a series of long dining tables. Placed on top of each table were plastic containers holding knives, forks, and large tablespoons; stainless-steel pitchers of ice water, powdered milk, and Kool-Aid (labeled panther piss or tiger's milk). Food was brought to the table in pans carried from the galley by recruits assigned to mess duty, and when a particular item was gone, its pan was held up in the air, retrieved by one of the messmen, and quickly replaced. During the meal, our drill instructors would ask questions about classes we had received during the day. Marine Corps history, infantry-weapons nomenclature, close-order drill, and first aid were learned then relearned during breakfast, the noon meal, and at the evening meal. The only person allowed to speak during chow was the drill instructor and the recruit who was answering his questions. When a recruit finished eating, he would excuse himself from the table, taking his stainless-steel tray and utensils with him, and head for a series of barrels located beside the scullery, where all garbage was collected and all dinnerware and trays were scraped clean before being placed in the appropriate bin for washing. The time allowed for any meal was fifteen minutes, but no one ever took that long; the price paid for being the last man done was always that well-placed kick in the ass.

As our training days on Parris Island matured into weeks, we became accustomed to the south's humidity, but the stifling heat reflected from the sloping area known as the "grinder"—the unshaded expanse of blacktopped drill field—was nearly unbearable. Periods of close-order drill, designed to sharpen every recruit's skill at marching and moving as one, were dreaded like no other event on our training schedule. Those who failed to pay attention or who failed to execute a command properly were struck on the top of their pith helmets by their drill instructors or whacked on the inner arch of the foot, leaving a throbbing reminder not to repeat the offense.

There were, unfortunately, individuals who, at some point during recruit training, came to the conclusion that life as a United States Marine was not for them. The Marine Corps had a particular response to them, called the "crazy suit." When the decision was made to send a failed recruit from Parris Island, it was not simply a matter of sending him on his way; the Marine Corps wanted those individuals, and all who saw them, to know they were being returned home because they were not good enough to be Marines. So they were sent from Parris Island dressed in an ill-fitting, light blue suit, a khaki shirt, with an outrageous tie, and wearing a Panama hat. Failures of Marine recruit training were made to look and feel ridiculous, but the very idea of having to return home while dressed like that was enough to motivate many recruits to remain and endure the hardships of boot camp.

Since our arrival seven weeks earlier, we had been stripped of our individuality and made to feel worthless and incapable of doing anything correctly the first time. We were taught the Marine Corps way of doing things, and any recognition of accomplishment was meted out ever so slowly by drill instructors who rarely, if ever, were satisfied. But rifle qualification was an individual event, and during it, for the first time, we were given the opportunity to demonstrate our abilities as individuals, not as members of the team.

The Marine Corps has always prided itself on the adage that every Marine is a rifleman, and to insure that the saying remained true, we packed all of our equipment into field transport packs, and with Private Bill McMann, the Marine reservist who had been held responsible for our safe arrival at Parris Island, carrying the platoon's guidon at the front of our platoon, we left our barracks and began the march to the rifle range for marksmanship training. During the time that we were assigned to the rifle range, our uniform was unusual; we wore utilities with canvas leggings, a shooting jacket, and—instead of wearing a utility cover—we wore a sharply creased garrison cover, commonly referred to as a piss-cutter.

Along the way, we marched past a farm that was run by Marines. The farm produced corn and watermelons, and it had dozens of pigs, which were fed garbage from the mess halls and later became hams, pork chops, sausage, and bacon served to hungry Marine recruits. When we arrived at the rifle range, we were billeted in personnel barracks or PB huts—unpainted wooden buildings, thirty feet long and sixteen wide, with tar-paper roofs—that would be home for the next three weeks. With a door at each end of the hut, a wooden partition divided our living area into equal halves for each section. And as we were not allowed to enter the front door of the PB hut, we had to enter the drill instructors' duty hut by scaling the plywood partition that separated us from them, and when dismissed, left the same way we had come in.

Only a few inches of open ventilation space separated the huts from the ground, so we learned after the first heavy thunderstorm that several inches of water could cover a hut's wooden floors for hours before slowly draining away into the porous limestone that made up Parris Island. We also discovered that the damp and dark PB huts were home to numerous large, black cockroaches (called Charleston racehorses by the locals), which used the hut's center beam as an expressway. During the night it was not uncommon to hear a scream of surprise from some recruit whose back had accidently become a cushioned drop zone for a fallen racehorse.

During our first week at the rifle range, called "snapping-in week," we were taught by our primary marksmanship instructors (PMIs) the various shooting positions we were required to master before ever firing a shot. The standing or offhand position, kneeling, seated, and prone were the four positions from which we fired at targets from two hundred yards to five hundred yards distance. Snapping-in began with each of us being issued a shooting jacket, a tight-fitting coat made from surplus Marine battle jackets. Then we were marched off to an open area near the rifle range, where we were shown by the PMIs not only how to get into the correct body positions for shooting but how to properly use the leather rifle slings and how to breathe, aim, and slowly squeeze the trigger for each and every shot.

I had arrived at Parris Island in what I thought was pretty fair shape, but in the ensuing weeks, I added additional muscle to my arms and legs, not realizing this would cause problems at the rifle range. For those of us who had difficulty in getting into the shooting positions demanded by our PMIs, we were force-joined to the "eight-ball squad" established for those recruits who would require additional instruction. The United States Marine Corps did not recognize any difference between right- and left-handed people, and since the M-1 rifle was primarily designed to accommodate right-handed shooters, all lefties had to learn the four firing positions and how to shoot as though they were right-handed. By the end of snapping-in week, those of us in the eight-ball squad were pronounced ready for the second week at the range, familiarization week, where we began to shoot the M-1. With the PMIs watching our every move and making immediate corrections, our rifle shooting began to be perfected.

By our third week on the range, after having fired hundreds of rounds, the novelty, innocence, and fun of learning how to shoot had worn off, and we began to grasp the seriousness of why we were shooting. The day before we shot for score was called "prequal day," and the atmosphere at the range suddenly changed. Scoreboards were brought out, spotting scopes and binoculars were on hand, and our drill instructors could be found nervously pacing behind us on the firing lines as we showed how well—or how poorly—we had applied ourselves to learning the skill of marksmanship. Any recruit who qualified as a rifle "expert" received an additional five dollars per month in pay and would leave Parris Island not only wearing the coveted Expert Rifleman's Badge, but also be promoted and wear the chevrons of a Marine private first class. Those who qualified in the lower-score category of "sharpshooter" received an additional three dollars per month, and those who qualified as "marksman," or failed to qualify, got nothing. At a time when a Marine private's monthly pay amounted to forty-eight dollars, a five-dollar incentive for shooting well was serious business.

The M-1 rifle course was not easy. Our shooting coaches and drill instructors were not allowed to stand near us while we fired, but their presence was surely felt. The first string of fire was eight rounds fired from a standing position, at a slow fire rate and at a range of two hundred yards. Then we fired another eight rounds from the kneeling position, slow fire; followed by two clips, or sixteen rounds of rapid fire from the kneeling position. Moving back to the three-hundred-yard line we fired eight rounds at slow fire, seated; followed by sixteen rounds of rapid fire. The final and most difficult string of our firing came at the five-hundred-yard line, where we were required to fire eight rounds from the prone position. When I had finished shooting I had scored a total of 324 points out of a possible score of 340, and was designated the high shooter of the week. For the first time in ten weeks I felt proud of myself, and even went so far as to risk smiling, knowing that I would leave Parris Island as a private first class.

After we left the rifle range, our platoon spent one week assigned to mess and maintenance duty, and as a reward for shooting well, I was given the job of platoon runner, spending those seven days carrying messages back and forth from the platoon's area to the battalion's headquarters at mainside. Since no recruit was allowed to walk anywhere while on Parris Island, running at a dogtrot soon grew old, and I welcomed the news that our platoon was moving to the field, following a detailed rifle and equipment inspection conducted by a sergeant assigned to our training company's staff.

Wearing utilities and standing at attention with our rifles in front of our equipment, we endured several hours of waiting motionless for the sergeant to determine that our rifles were clean and our 782 gear spotless and serviceable. We had spent hours in preparation for the detailed inspection; steam cleaning our rifles to rid them of any residue caused by corrosive primers, and cleaning equipment until stainless steel shined like sterling silver. The time spent in readying ourselves paid off when the sergeant informed Corporal Henderson that we "looked as sharp as any platoon he'd ever inspected."

We were marched several miles away to Elliot's Beach, where we spent several days being taught the basics of infantry tactics. There was no formal school for infantry training like there is today, and we were told that additional infantry training, particularly at the platoon and company level, would be taught at our next duty stations. In 1948, the Marine Corps relied heavily upon its noncommissioned officers, who had combat experience, to teach recruits the fundamentals of what was required of all Marine riflemen, and while we received formal classroom instruction on military subjects such as general orders, military law, and Marine Corps history, customs and tradition, taught by senior NCOs, the responsibility for teaching basic infantry skills was placed squarely on the shoulders of those Marines who not only knew their subjects well but had personal credibility for having survived in combat. Interestingly, we were shown Marine combat footage from World War II as a means of helping to strengthen the esprit de corps that is synonymous with the Marine Corps. Those unedited scenes of the horror, taken on the islands of Tarawa, Peleliu, Iwo Jima, and Okinawa left little doubt in any of us as to what demands would be made on us, once called upon to fight. Watching those films helped to build confidence while showing us the realities of war.

Before leaving Elliot's Beach, we visited the gas chamber and were shown how to wear a gas mask before being subjected to the effects of tear gas within the gas chamber. Once inside the gas-filled room, we had to remove our gas masks. Then we had to shout our names and service numbers, ensuring that each of us got to sample the debilitating effects of tear gas, and in turn, to appreciate the protection provided by our masks.

We returned to our barracks knowing that the only ordeals remaining before graduation day were our final close-order-drill evaluation and one last personnel inspection. Both events were considered a direct reflection not only of how well our drill instructors had taught us the basics but, more importantly, how well we had learned everything we could about being a Marine. We were marched onto the grinder by Corporal Henderson, and our best efforts to execute our drill instructor's commands, as sixty recruits moving like one, were evaluated and scored by a group of drill instructors from one of the other training battalions. They must have been impressed with what they saw because our platoon was given high marks, and we were designated the company honor platoon for graduation day. And as a reward for our having passed the company commander's personnel inspection and for having done so well out on the grinder, that night Corporal Henderson marched us to the base outdoor theater and allowed us the rare privilege of watching a movie.

When we returned to the barracks later that same night, Corporal Henderson read off the future duty assignments for every recruit in our platoon, and that was when I learned that I had been given orders "to the Pacific." For his final lesson, Corporal Henderson taught us one more trick of the trade; how to properly pack a seabag. He called for one recruit to bring his seabag to a table set up in the center of the squad bay, and using that recruit's complete issue of clothing, equipment, and M-1 rifle, he shared his knowledge. The heavy wool overcoat was the first item to go into the seabag to establish a solid foundation, followed by the galvanized bucket, centered on top of the overcoat. The bucket was used to protect the M-1, which was broken down into the barrel and receiver group, and all socks and skivvies were packed inside the bucket and around the rifle. As the sides of the growing seabag were unrolled, all remaining footwear, utilities, and all combat equipment were given a home, with the result being one tightly packed seabag, complete with each Marine's rifle, all of his uniforms, and his combat gear.

On graduation day, we were addressed as Marines for the very first time and congratulated by our company commander for having successfully completed recruit training, and then our platoon was dismissed for the last time by Cpl. John Henderson. Before Bill McMann and I boarded a chartered Greyhound bus destined for New York City, those of us with overseas assignments shouldered our seabags and carried them off to a warehouse where they would be stored until our return to Parris Island to begin a cross-country train trip to California. The weather was not in our favor on our graduation day, and by the time we reached the waiting buses, there was not a single Marine among us whose uniform wasn't soaking wet. For twelve weeks the importance of looking sharp had been driven into us, but on the one day when we wanted to look our very best, we boarded the buses looking anything but squared away. When our bus finally arrived at the New York City bus terminal, Bill and I were able to find a reputable tailor and press shop a few blocks away. With several hours to spare before boarding a connecting bus to Boston, we waited while one of the tailors sewed on my Pfc.'s chevrons and ironed new, sharp, creases into my khaki battle jacket. I wanted my parents to see me for the first time as a sharp-looking Marine, particularly because I was one of only five recruits in our platoon to have been promoted to the rank of private first class.

Bill McMann and I sat directly behind our bus driver, who we quickly learned was an old army veteran who had trained at Pearl Harbor's Schofield Barracks, and he went out of his way to make us feel comfortable during our five-hour trip. As we traveled toward Boston, passengers boarded and departed the bus, and many shook our hands and offered their congratulations to us for becoming Marines, and I have never forgotten how special those strangers made me feel that day. When we arrived in Boston's

North Station, I said good-bye to Bill McMann, and wishing him the best of luck, I headed off to find a train that would take me home for a brief stay in Lawrence.

During the time that I was home, my parents wanted every member of our extended family to see what the Marine Corps had produced. My mother and father were proud of me and insisted that I travel with them to visit every relative in town. My parents must have had my uniform cleaned and pressed at least a dozen times in five short days, but their feelings of pride were genuine, and my agreeing to be "paraded around Lawrence" was the least I could do to make them happy.

When my leave time came to an end, I said good-bye to my brothers and sister and watched my parents disappear from view as I began the long trip from Lawrence, Massachusetts, back to Parris Island, South Carolina, and to points west.

CHAPTER 3

From Parris Island to Guam

My return trip by Greyhound bus to Parris Island was for the most part uneventful. When I arrived in Beaufort, a Marine Corps truck picked me up for the trip back aboard the base and delivered me to a wooden barracks where I was billeted for two weeks while assigned to what was called the AT Unit, for those of us awaiting transfer to somewhere other than Parris Island. I was immediately put to work on the farm I had seen during our platoon's endurance run, nearly three months earlier. My work there ranged from visiting the base mess halls to collect garbage for the hungry pigs to the weeding and watering of the farm's numerous vegetable gardens. That farm was my first exposure to the concept of recycling. Unfortunately, it is gone, but for those recruits who had grown up in the city, it provided a brief taste of what life was like "down on the farm."

One morning, those of us assigned to the AT (Awaiting Transfer) barracks were gathered up and told we would be receiving our "spec numbers" and individual travel orders prior to leaving the base. In those days, there were none of the military occupational specialties (MOSs) which today denote a Marine's particular occupational field. Our spec numbers were typed into our service record books

(SRBs) and on our travel orders and were the recognized indicator of what that Marine was able to do.

As our names were called out, specific assignments were announced. Pfc. Bill McMann was pleased to learn he was headed for Sea School and future duty aboard ship, and sadly, that was the last time I ever saw him. Other Marines shouted their approval at learning where they were headed; a particular air-wing unit, an assignment close to home, or a choice duty station—most assignments based upon their having scored well on aptitude tests. For those of us who remained, an administrative clerk announced, "The rest of you Marines will be headed west, and will proceed to Marine Barracks at Treasure Island in San Francisco Bay for further assignment to the Pacific. Once you leave here, you will draw your seabags over at the supply warehouse and be taken by cattle car to Savannah, Georgia, for your train ride west." Our traveling group included a number of "characters" who had, for various reasons, been kept at Parris Island long after their graduation date. I recall a private first class named Pappy Gun who had come to Parris Island in 1947 and had yet to leave the base for his first duty station. There were also a number of U.S. Army veterans, now Marines, who had seen service in World War II and were headed to the Pacific with the rest of us.

The train station at Savannah offered little in the way of creature comforts as we waited to board our troop train. As each man's last name was read from the passenger manifest, he would respond, shouting back his first name and middle initial, ensuring that the correct body boarded the correct Pullman car. To ensure that "good order and discipline" would be maintained, a Marine noncommissioned officer was assigned to each Pullman car for the duration of our five-day two-thousand-six-hundred-mile trip. These Marine NCOs were themselves waiting to begin either drill instructor's school or shooting-coaches school, and with several weeks remaining before their formal schooling began, their services were put to use by bringing NCO supervision to our train. Also assigned to every car was a porter responsible for keeping the car's tiny lavatory clean and to make up the car's two dozen top-and-bottom pull-down beds. These porters actually had a pretty easy time of it with us Marines because, once they had shown us how our racks were put into position, we took care of ourselves and helped keep our cars clean and neat.

When we boarded our train at 1700 that afternoon, each of us was assigned to a rack and handed a bag lunch. To our dismay, every brown bag contained the same meal— one thinly sliced bologna sandwich, commonly referred to in those days as horse cock, one apple, and a small bottle of warm grapefruit juice. Only when we arrived in Mobile, Alabama, later the next day, were additional Pullman cars and several dining cars added to our train. From Mobile on, we were served all of our meals in the dining car closest to our coach.

As we traveled west without the comfort of air-conditioning, the increasing heat and humidity only added to our misery. No showers were available, and with only three small, stainless-steel sinks and one toilet to accommodate twenty-four men, the best we could do to comfort ourselves from the heat was to take a whore's bath; standing in front of one of the mirrored sinks and washing ourselves with a facecloth and cold water, followed by a good sprinkling of talcum powder, or liberal amounts of cheap aftershave we called "foo-foo" juice.

When we stopped in Baton Rouge, Louisiana, a surprise personnel inspection conducted by our Marine NCOs revealed a number of men who had failed to shave and some who had not kept their uniforms neat. Those offenders were dealt with quickly; those who hadn't shaved, had to, without the benefit of soap and water, and those whose uniforms looked less than squared away were made to do calisthenics until they reached the edge of collapse. With those discrepancies corrected, notice was served to the rest of us not to make the same mistakes.

While we waited in Baton Rouge, we watched as civilian cleaning crews boarded the train and changed the treated water in the men's-room holding tanks, while additional crews of railroad stewards brought the breakfast meal aboard in covered containers. When the train was clean, we were allowed to board and waited for the word that breakfast was served. Breakfast that morning was even more disappointing than the sandwiches we had received in Savannah—chunks of powdered scrambled eggs hidden beneath several inches of lukewarm, yellow water, and thick slices of canned bacon submerged in grease, were served with cold toast, which the stewards swore had been made the night before. We ate it all, without complaining.

To help pass the time until our next scheduled stop, San Antonio, Texas, we quizzed each other on Marine Corps history, weapons nomenclature, and how to conduct close-order drill. It wasn't long before we pulled into San Antonio station that rumors of another surprise personnel inspection began to spread from one end of the train to the other. But our NCOs had different plans for us. Once off the train, we were marched to an open area close to the station, and spent nearly an hour performing close-order drill. We must have done well, because we received a round of applause from the folks of San Antonio as we marched back to the train.

Out next stop was an early morning visit to El Paso, Texas, where, again, we fell out for an hour's PT, followed by a half-hour run. Our chanting must have woken up some of the local population as a number of El Paso's citizens came to the train station to "see the Marines who were making so much noise as the sun was coming up." Our fifth stop was Phoenix, Arizona, where we participated in another brief PT session before heading west. By the time we stopped in east central Los Angeles our uniforms had taken on the unmistakable odor of sulphur from the steady stream of smoke that the train's two coal-burning engines produced, and it was while we were in Los Angeles that our Southern Railroad cars were uncoupled and replaced by newer cars belonging to the Union Pacific Railroad.

We had been traveling nonstop for four days when we arrived in Oakland, California, and with ample time given to repack our field transport packs and change from our utilities into our best uniforms, we left the troop train wearing boondockers, khaki shirt and tie, khaki trousers, piss-cutter, and battle jacket. Our trousers had no back pockets, so we kept our wallets tucked inside our battle jackets or hidden in our socks. We were marched to navy buses, which took us over the San Francisco Bay Bridge and onto Treasure Island. During the ride, the bus driver provided us with a running commentary on the history of San Francisco and pointed out the island of Alcatraz, telling us Al Capone was still being held inside (he had died in 1947). He also told us the Marine Barracks at Treasure Island was a unique place; during World War II, the barracks had become a temporary home to many wounded servicemen, and served as an interim hospital for Marines and sailors awaiting further transfer to hospitals across the country.

When we arrived at Treasure Island, we were brought directly to our billets, but no stairs led into any of the buildings that made up the transient barracks, just long, concrete ramps built to accommodate wheelchairs and stretchers. Our open squad bay had once been a hospital ward, and the small room to which five PFCs and I were assigned had been used as a private room for the ward's critically wounded.

During the short time I was assigned to the Marine Barracks, I was joined to the rolls of Casual Company, the parent command of all transient Marines coming from and going to the Pacific. I soon learned that Treasure Island was also home to countless sailors of the Pacific Fleet, some assigned permanently, such as the naval hospital's pharmacist mates, while other sailors called it home for the six months they attended the navy's largest, western, radio-communications school. But Treasure Island was best known for being the shipping out place for those headed west, and once the number of incoming transients had reached a certain point, the navy would assign a ship to deliver its human cargo to the western Pacific.

In the meantime, work assignments were handed out, and I found myself assigned for several days to MP duty, helping to direct the heavy flow of early morning and late afternoon traffic, which jammed the island's main gate. I considered myself fortunate that my newly won Pfc chevrons had kept me from being made a member of one of the numerous transient working parties sent out each morning to keep the base clean. Being a Pfc, I also avoided the drudgery of fourteen hours of mess duty each day to which so many junior Marines found themselves assigned.

As every young enlisted man soon discovers, life as a transient is usually the worst of all possibilities. It was no different in October 1948. Each day after breakfast, we would assemble and listen to a sergeant from the administrative office read a list of names and their future assignments. Those whose names were read aloud then disappeared into the administrative abyss; those who remained uncalled were divided into groups, given to sergeants, and became members of menial working parties that lasted the day. The process was repeated the next day, and the next, until everyone had finally received orders.

When my orders came, I was excited to learn I was going to Tsingtao, China, for twenty-four months, to join one of the two Marine battalion landing teams (BLTs) that had remained there since the end of the war. Duty in China meant that I had to visit sick bay to have my medical records checked and then receive a series of inoculations against tetanus and yellow fever. Once done, I returned to the administrative office and had the dates of my shots stamped into the back of my circular, brass dog tags. With several days remaining before I was due to sail, I met several Marines who were headed home, having just returned from duty in China, and asked them to tell me about the Far East, but I was quick to learn that the price for their valuable information was not money but the one commodity that had been a stranger to them—ice-cold beer.

These Marines had enlisted as World War II was ending, but having volunteered for "the duration, plus two years" they remained in occupied China until their contracts had come to an end. Deciding not to reenlist, they stayed on Treasure Island for a few days of administrative processing before returning to the civilian world, but while they remained, I wanted to learn as much as possible and agreed to buy them beer as long as they told me the truth about what I could expect in Tsingtao. We even went on liberty in San Francisco's Chinatown, so that, according to them, I could experience "the feel of China." By the time I was out of money, they were drunk and out of information, so we parted company. I did learn several valuable lessons from the ordeal, the first of which was to be cautious of any Marine about to become a civilian.

Not all of my encounters with strangers in San Francisco were bad. On a whim, I walked into a Grant's five-and-dime store late one afternoon and met a salesgirl there who was my age. She told me she had grown up in San Francisco, and I persuaded her to meet me after work, and asked her to show me around. As we walked from Market Street to Nob Hill, she told me the history of the city, pointed out where the great fire had consumed city blocks, and where the earthquake of 1938 had done its damage.

It was also during this time that San Francisco was celebrating its centennial. So, with free events scheduled for the public every night of the week, we took advantage of the fun. Though we went out several times while I was on Treasure Island, sightseeing within the city was as far as our relationship went, but I am still grateful for the kindness she displayed toward me as a stranger in her city. On the evening of my fourteenth day on Treasure Island those of us billeted in the transient barracks who had been assigned overseas were told to have all of our gear "packed and stacked" outside at 0500 the next morning and be ready to board the navy buses chartered to take us from the island, back across the Bay Bridge, and to our waiting ship, named in honor of the Confederate States Army General John C. Breckenridge.

Under the gray-gold sky of dawn, we stacked our sea-bags in the rear section of a bus and became part of a long convoy of navy buses that took us to San Francisco's waterfront and into a huge warehouse next to the *General Breckenridge*. After we had taken our gear from the back of the bus, we assembled inside the warehouse and waited patiently as, again, each man's last name was read aloud from the ship's manifest before he was allowed to board. At least two thousand Marines boarded the ship which would, eventually, take us first to Hawaii, then continue on to the islands of Midway, Wake, Kwajalein, Johnston, and Guam, before sailing farther west to Chi-Chi Jima, Saipan, and to China.

To help keep confusion to a minimum, members of the ship's crew had been assigned as guides and led us down to our living compartments. I was assigned to a small compartment, three decks down from the ship's main deck. Our racks, stacked four high and separated verti-cally by eighteen inches of space, would be home for twenty-four men, and remembering the advice given to me by Marines who had spent time aboard navy ships, I quickly claimed a top rack as my resting place because I'd notice less traffic passing by than from the lower racks, and it would spare me the obvious danger of sea-sickness from above. After we had tied our seabags to the foot of our racks, our ship's guide told us to take a life jacket from a pile of them and make sure that we tied it securely to our rack, too, making it easy to find if the ship's internal lighting system should fail. Before leaving our compartment, the crewman reminded us that we would be required to wear our life jackets during the man-overboard and abandon-ship drills that would happen soon after the *Breckenridge* cast off her lines. He told us that we were free to leave our living area, but were warned not to get in the way and to stay out of the ship's working spaces.

Following his instructions, we each grabbed a life jacket, only to find that they had absorbed stains from standing water and oil and were thoroughly impregnated with the stench of vomit. Having already fouled the air inside our compartment and with several hours remaining before we sailed, we climbed to the main deck to find fresh air, and began to explore more of the huge transport ship as we got under way. As we passed under the Golden Gate Bridge, I stood on the ship's main deck and took several photographs as a reminder of what would be my last visual contact with the United States of America for the next two years.

Not long after that, a series of short horn blasts came over the ship's speakers; the promised ship's drills were in progress. Wearing our life jackets, we ran to the assigned positions next to our lifeboats and watched as crewmen lowered several boats. A new signal, eight short horn blasts, meant "man overboard," and we responded by returning to our compartment and taking a muster of all hands. The written musters were collected by the crew and run up to the ship's bridge, ensuring that all crew members and passengers were accounted for. They were not; our ship's captain had taken a crewman as his "prisoner," but his cabinmates had not reported him missing, so the captain repeated the drill two more times until the "captive" sailor was finally reported missing. Once satisfied that the important ship's drills could be conducted properly, the daily routine resumed.

As we headed west, the weather grew progressively worse. The cold forced everyone inside, and with land still in view, the rocking motion caused by the ground swells began to take effect. We could hear the *chug-chug-chug* of the ship's huge twin screws when they broke the surface of the water as the *Breckenridge* rocked, dipped, and swayed. Within a very short period of time, our ship, which we had found spotless when we boarded, became a bucket of vomit. Marines were spread out over the entire ship; many were in fetal positions, clutching their stomachs; others could be found throwing up wherever they found a private place to be sick.

Feeling seasick for the first time, I went to the head closest to our compartment and witnessed how dehumanizing seasickness could be. Inside, one seasick Marine, looking much older than his years, was seated over a trough of sloshing seawater designed to remove human excrement from the ship. With his head on his chest and eyes closed, he began to heave violently while he shuddered and moaned. Suddenly, he stood up, spun around, and wrapped his arms around his stainless-steel toilet seat, retching his guts into the open metal trough. His strength was sapped completely, and his right arm fell into the water and was quickly covered with vomit and feces. Appearing unable to throw up anything else, he struggled to stand, pull up his trousers, and adjust his belt. As he brushed his hair away from his eyes and tried to wipe the clinging strands of mucus from his nose and mouth, he succeeded only in smearing excrement across his face, and when he gazed up into the large mirror that hung above the row of sinks, the sight of his own pathetic image made him fall down and retch again. Realizing that to remain in the head was not the solution to my problem, I returned to my compartment. But it, too, smelled terribly. After climbing up into my rack, I tried to hold my breath and equalize my ear pressure, having been told by one of the old salts back on Treasure Island that keeping pressure on the inner ear was the secret to controlling seasickness. His remedy seemed to work, but I had the constant sensation of butterflies in my gut while trying to suppress the persistent urge to throw up.

Later in the afternoon, a private named Finnley who had been in the merchant marine and was a member of my platoon at Parris Island, suggested that we go down to the messdecks and get something to eat, arguing that it was better to have something to throw up than to suffer the pains of dry heaving. As the *Breckenridge* continued to rock and roll through the ocean, Finnley and I moved down to the messdecks and joined with other Marines who thought that eating something might help. The mess-decks had been set up to combat the ship's constant pitching and rolling; our tables were adjustable, fitted to pipes that allowed the tables to be raised during foul weather. Of course, we had to stand up while we ate. Nevertheless, taking our trays and silverware in hand, we moved slowly down the serving line and were surprised to see that our meal was turkey a la king and what was ladled out onto our trays looked very much like what we had just cautiously stepped over in the ship's passageways. Deciding to pass on eating the main entree, Finnley suggested we eat only the saltine crackers placed in large tins on every table, and as we stood eating salted crackers, we also filled our jacket pockets with them, insuring that we would have something to eat during the long hours ahead.

The storm that had greeted us as we sailed from San Francisco lasted for three days, and with the appearance of the sun and a calmer sea, Marines who had remained hidden below in their compartments emerged from hiding and began to regain their strength.

Not missing the first opportunity to get his ship squared away, the captain ordered a complete field day of the *Breckenridge*, and I was assigned to make sure that the head next to our compartment was made spotless. Our head had three faucets; two for hot and cold salt water, while the third produced cold freshwater, which was made available at the discretion of the captain. Our showers were usually taken using salt water, which rendered all bar soap nearly incapable of producing lather, but when freshwater "navy showers" were allowed, the rules for bathing changed, too—get in, get wet for fifteen seconds, wash and shampoo, then rinse away any soap for fifteen seconds, and use a clean facecloth as a towel. Using no more than thirty seconds' worth of the ship's freshwater each allowed all hands the rare opportunity to feel clean, but if the ship's engineering officer reported that the freshwater level had dipped too low, all freshwater showers would be suspended.

As the weather returned to normal, so did the ship's

daily routine. The bugle notes for reveille were sounded at 0500, followed by a ship's loudspeaker announcement for a "clean sweep down, trice up," meaning that the three lowest racks in each compartment were to be raised, then secured in an upright position so the compartment's deck could be mopped clean. All personal equipment was placed on the fourth rack until the compartments were inspected by a member of the ship's crew, accompanied by a Marine NCO.

By the end of the fourth day the *Breckenridge* was considered shipshape, and new work assignments began. The Marines in our compartment were handed over to a first class petty officer, a boatswains mate, who was responsible for managing a paint-chipping detail on the ship's fantail. After we had mustered at the rear of the ship, the boatswain's mate showed us how all of the gray paint was to be chipped from a large boom. Wearing goggles, gloves, and kneepads, and using chipping hammers, short lengths of chain, and electric grinders, we removed the old paint and rust until we exposed bare metal. Our work detail lasted for several hours before we were allowed to go to chow, and by 1430, we were nearly finished, our last duty being only to repaint whatever we had chipped away, but the boatswain's mate treated us well. He was a veteran of World War II and considered the navy his home. He took the time to teach us about shipboard life and did his best to make the remainder of our time aboard "his ship" a tolerable experience.

On our fifth day out, we saw land for the first time when the island of Hawaii loomed into view. We sailed past Diamond Head and past the white sands and palm-lined beaches of Honolulu, noting that there were only two large hotels on the shore of Waikiki—the Mawana Hotel and the Royal Hawaiian. As we sailed into Pearl Harbor, many of us were surprised to see the long, sixteen-inch, coastal artillery guns of the army's shore batteries that for years had protected Pearl Harbor. Suddenly, the commands, "Attention on deck" and "hand salute" were broadcast over the ship's intercom, but even as the orders were executed by all hands, we were not sure what it was we were honoring, but as we sailed past the hulk of the USS *Arizona*, a ship's announcement made it clear. At that time, no war memorial had yet been dedicated to the thirty-five hundred Americans who became the first casualties of war on December 7, 1941, but the wreckage of the war was still visible in the water, and Japanese bullet holes served as silent reminders of Pearl Harbor's violent past.

Once the *Breckenridge* came to rest alongside its pier, all Marines shouldered their seabags, disembarked, and gathered in front of a series of Marine Corps cattle cars pulled by International Harvester trucks (called M-5s) that towed us down Dillingham Boulevard, past the headquarters of FMFPAC, (Fleet Marine Force Pacific) and on to Camp Catlin for additional administrative processing. We were billeted at the camp in H-style barracks for two days without being assigned to any working parties, but without enjoying the privilege of liberty, either. While I was at Camp Catlin, I learned the disheartening news that Marines assigned to China were now being reassigned in accordance with new Marine Corps policy. Marines who were seventeen years old were not allowed into a designated "combat area," and because of the increase of violent incidents by the Chinese Communists in China, Shanghai had been designated a combat zone. I was crushed. I had my heart set on seeing mysterious China, and it was a shock to learn that, because of my age, I had been assigned to duty with the 1st Provisional Marine Brigade on Guam.

Returning to the *Breckenridge*, we discovered that we had lost to duty in Hawaii nearly half the Marines originally assigned to our compartment, and although we would enjoy having the luxury of twice the living space, we now had only half the workforce to keep our area clean.

We left the beauty of Pearl Harbor and headed for Guam, which was thirty-nine hundred miles and five sailing days away. On the morning of our third day out, the command to "battle stations" sent sailors running, and us Marines down to our compartments and locked behind watertight doors. A free-floating Japanese mine had been spotted drifting toward the ship, and the crew responded by bringing out a .50-caliber Browning machine gun. They sandbagged it to the deck and tried in vain to hit the bobbing mine. They finally gave up in disgust, and the mine's position and direction were radioed back to Pearl Harbor.

As we traveled on to Guam, a noticeable change in climate made the ship's deck so hot that no one could bear to sit on the exposed steel. All paint-chipping details and other outside ship's work were canceled, and we became more like baggage than passengers. The heat and humidity were terrible; our uniforms were dark with sweat, and as there was no air-conditioning on the *Breckenridge*, we salted our food with our own perspiration while we ate.

We spotted land early on our fifth day at sea and sailed north of Orote Point and into Apra Harbor, on the western side of Guam. Soon, navy Mike boats came alongside the *Breckenridge*, and the two hundred of us assigned to duty on the island climbed into the waiting boats and were shuttled to shore where, again, we transferred our seabags into waiting cattle cars that took us first to the Marine Barracks on Orote Point before delivering us some twenty miles inland, to the headquarters of the 1st Provisional Marine Brigade.

Known as Camp Witek, it was named in honor of Pfc. Frank Witek, a native of Derby, Connecticut, who, while serving with the 1st Battalion, 9th Marines, 3d Marine Division, during the battle of Finegayen, had won the Medal of Honor, awarded posthumously by the president in the name of the Congress, for single-handedly killing sixteen Japanese soldiers and for knocking out an enemy machine-gun emplacement before Private First Class Witek was killed on 3 August 1944.

When we arrived at the Marine Barracks, the commanding officer of the brigade, BGen. Edward A. Craig, was waiting to greet us. To be personally welcomed by a

Marine general officer was one of the more memorable experiences that I can recall as an impressionable young private first class. The general waited until our group assembled, and I still recall his opening remarks. "First, I want to welcome you new Marines to Guam and to let you know that we are glad you are here. You men are about to join the 1st Provisional Marine Brigade, of the 5th Marine Regiment, the most combat-ready organization in the Corps at this time. I am proud of every Marine in this brigade and hope that you will find your time here rewarding and a real challenge." The general told us briefly about the brigade's history, how the Marines had fought to retake Guam from the Japanese, and he tried to make us feel welcome as new members of his command. It was a great beginning to my first tour of duty in the Marine Corps.

CHAPTER 4

First Duty on Guam

By August 1945, the United States Marine Corps had reached a peak strength of 485,053 Marines, comprised of two corps, six divisions, and five aircraft wings, but with the war's end came the rapid demobilization of the Fleet Marine Force and the execution of plans for the redeployment of the Corps' major units in the eastern Pacific and the United States. President Truman now sought a unification of the armed forces and wanted all services to be merged under a single Department of War, with a single chief of staff and a national general staff. Plans were put in motion to rapidly reduce the size of the armed forces. For the Marine Corps, that meant that there would be a Fleet Marine Force Atlantic as well as a Fleet Marine Force Pacific, each with a division and a wing, plus supporting combat and combat service units. Congress then set the peacetime strength of the Corps at 107,000, and forced reductions began.

The responsibility for the military occupation of Japan went first to the 1st and 3d Battalions of the 4th Marine Regiment, a fifty-four-hundred-man force that went into Tokyo, while the 2d and 5th Marine Divisions were sent to occupy Kyushu, Sasebo, and Nagasaki. Finding the Japanese as docile and cooperative in defeat as they had been fanatical and intransigent in battle, the 5th Marine

Division left for home in December 1945, while the 2d Marine Division stayed on in Japan until June 1946. The Marines of the 1st and 6th Divisions of the III Amphibious Corps were sent, temporarily, to occupy north China, with the Marines of the Corps' 3d Division spread across the islands of the western central Pacific. By July 1946, the strength of the Marine Corps had been reduced to 146,000, and one year later had dropped to 92,000. When I enlisted, in 1948, the Corps consisted of only *75,000 Marines* spread thinly around the world in only *eight infantry battalions* and twelve aircraft squadrons. As one of those 75,000, I welcomed the chance to serve.

After being processed into the brigade, I was assigned to the 2d Platoon of Baker Company, 1st Battalion, 5th Marine Regiment (B/1/5). My platoon sergeant was named Roy Pitman. Roy was a combat veteran who had been with the 4th Marine Division during the fighting on Iwo Jima. He assigned me to the platoon's 3d Squad, led by a corporal named Robert J. Mesa, a citizen of Monterey, Mexico; he, too, was a veteran of Iwo Jima. Both Marines were highly respected, and I was pleased to be in their company, realizing that I would begin learning the complicated trade of an infantry Marine from professional noncommissioned officers who had great credibility.

My memories of duty on Guam begin with recalling the routine of garrison life within our rifle company. Chow on Guam was unique, to say the least. We ate prepackaged food called Alpha rations, as there was little refrigeration available on Guam to keep any vegetables, meats, or dairy products fresh. We were usually served powdered eggs at breakfast, but on a special occasion such as Sunday mornings, real eggs, purchased on the local economy, were taken out of the mess hall's cold storage unit and placed on the chow-line grill to be cooked as ordered. The cooks would select an egg, crack it over the grill, and if the egg yolk was green, they would place the broken shell on top of the yolk as a quick reminder not to serve it, and they'd continue to crack open eggs until they got lucky. All the rotten eggs topped with white shells were tossed into the garbage. There was no fresh milk on Guam; that, too, came to our mess hall as a powder. Nearly all our vegetables were canned, as were the majority of our meats. It took some getting used to, but that was the best we could expect, and complaining about it did little good. Holidays, however, were treated differently, and particular attention was given to improving what was served in our mess hall.

My first observance and celebration of a Marine Corps holiday was on 10 November 1948; it was the Corps' 173d birthday and observed throughout the Corps as a "holiday routine." At our battalion's morning formation that day, the traditional birthday message, written in 1924 by the Corps' thirteenth commandant, Gen. John A. Lejeune, was read aloud. That was followed by the reading "to all Marines" of a message from Gen. Clifton B. Cates, our nineteenth commandant. In part, General Cates's message reminded us that because our Corps had been so greatly reduced in size, to be a Marine was an honor and a privilege; only "a few good men" could serve.

Those messages and the pride that was exhibited by our company's noncommissioned officers made us proud to be United States Marines. As we marched away from that morning's formation, we stood a little straighter and moved a little sharper to the notes of the "Marine's Hymn." At noon chow, we enjoyed a meal of canned turkey and were each given a cigar before marching to the battalion's athletic field to watch one of the more innovative field meets I ever saw.

The first event was a greased-pig chase: Three small island pigs, covered with a generous coating of axle grease, were released within a fenced area. As individual Marines chased, dove, and grabbed at the screaming little pigs, they managed to cover themselves in mud, grease, and grass stains. Only those Marines who went after a pig as an organized group succeeded in capturing one, and that was the purpose of the event—to show us the importance of teamwork. Other events, such as tugs-of-war, which pitted one rifle company against another, and relay races, where the disassembly and assembly of light and heavy machine guns, Browning automatic rifles, and even Colt automatic pistols, served the same valuable purpose.

We trained six days a week. Because of the high heat and humidity, our daily routine in garrison started at 0430 each morning and ended by 1600. Following reveille, we would "shit, shower, and shave," conduct a quick field day of the barracks, and be ready for training by 0630. Sunday was not a scheduled training day, but to keep us occupied, organized athletics were a major part of every Sunday afternoon. Collegiate-level sports were a significant factor in Marine Corps training. Encouraged and supported at nearly every level of command, the Corps' athletic program rivaled many colleges and universities.

In late 1948 our brigade had the best military football team in the Pacific. Having beaten Guam's U.S. Naval Air Detachment (NAD) team, they also defeated the navy's first-place team, flown in from Hawaii, and were later flown to the West Coast to play in the armed forces championships.

Infantry training within the brigade was conducted much differently than the way it is conducted today. First we were taught everything there was to know about the weapons that were organic to a Marine infantry battalion. Our NCOs demanded that we know not only how to fire the M-1 rifle, the BAR, the carbine, and the Colt .45 automatic pistol but also that we were proficient with any and all of them. We learned how the weapons functioned and were taught how to remedy the problems associated with the breakdown of each of them. It was not enough to know only how to load and fire a BAR; we were taught how to take it apart, put it back together, and to name each piece of the weapon when we touched it. The same was true for the other rifles and the pistol. The term "mastery" was used to denote the degree of understanding which all infantry Marines had to achieve in order to satisfy their veteran squad and platoon leaders. If a Marine was assigned to a weapons company, he had to know all there was to know about the 60mm and 81mm mortars, the light, air-cooled .30-caliber machine gun, the flame-thrower, and the 2.36-inch rocket launcher, known as the bazooka. But, all the rest of us were required to know how those weapons were employed and the cycle of maintenance that was required to keep the weapons in proper working order.

Our physical training was also different than today's. An infantry Marine's overall endurance, not just his upper-body strength, was considered to be of greater importance. To be able to get to the objective and arrive ready to fight could not be stressed enough. On Guam, we ran, or were marched on the double, to every training site and firing range. We didn't have the luxury of vehicles to carry us around, and by definition we were "amphibious" and would not experience the luxury of riding into battle. As an example, we were scheduled to fire our battalion's weapons at a known-distance range one day, near the Marine Barracks on Orote Point. Our NCOs used this opportunity to enhance our training so the twenty-mile march was treated as a movement to contact. We were issued one day's rations and water, humped to range, fired all our weapons, and marched back to Camp Witek, arriving back home close to midnight.

Field training within the brigade presented a problem because of the obvious shortages of personnel, compounded by the limitations on fuel, ammunition, and spare parts. Our tactical training consisted of learning how to conduct squad-size patrols, combat and reconnaissance and learning the complexities of how to attack fortified positions. The Pacific war was fresh in the minds of many squad and platoon leaders—veterans of Peleliu, Iwo Jima, and Okinawa—and they shared their experiences with us. Beginning at the squad level, and progressing to the platoon and company levels, tactical training was always a challenge and always fun.

Not surprisingly, dry-net and wet-net training were always a major part of the training schedule, and I don't remember a single week going by where we did not practice on those nets. For dry-net training, using a ladder, we'd climb to the top of a thirty-foot wooden tower, and wearing packs and carrying rifles, we'd use the nets to climb down into the hull of an old "Papa" boat positioned at the base of the tower. We learned how to lash heavier gear, such as machine guns, bulk supplies, and ammunition boxes, and how to lower the weapons and equipment into the boat.

Wet-net training took place on Guam's western side, in Tumon Bay, where the wet-net tower was positioned so that Mike boats could come alongside. And while we practiced on the nets, the navy's boat handlers benefited from our training, too. Many times, Marines learned the hard way about judging their distance from the net to the boat and unfortunately ended up in a heap on the floor of a bobbing Mike boat. It was during our wet-net training that we were introduced to classes titled "Troop life aboard ship" and learned about the configurations of the amphibious ships that we would use, and how to conduct ourselves while aboard them.

The company's amphibious exercise was the high point of our training in late 1948, and began with us using a Jacob's ladder to climb aboard the navy's LST 800, an aging relic left over from World War II, anchored in Tumon Bay, and then sailing to Pagan Island, located in the Mariana Island group. Old LVTs (landing vehicle tracks), which had been stowed aboard the LST, took us ashore, and we conducted company-size training on Pagan Island for ten days before returning to Camp Witek. Interestingly, at the time, amphibious assaults against fortified beaches had been written off by many military experts as a nuclear-age improbability and General Omar Bradley, then chairman of the Joint Chiefs, gave his opinion to the House Armed Services Committee that amphibious operations "were a dead letter" and that there would "never again be another amphibious assault." Fortunately, General Bradley's message failed to reach us on Guam, and we continued to practice ship-to-shore movement.

Just after our return from Pagan Island, we began to hear stories about "Screaming Willie," the name given to either a Japanese holdout or a battle-crazed Marine left over from the fight to recapture Guam, who let his presence be known by screaming at the top of his lungs while hiding in the jungle that surrounded Camp Witek. One night, I was awakened by the same distant bloodcurdling scream that woke up half a dozen other Marines in our barracks. At first we thought that it was a practical joke. The man's screaming, which carried well through the jungle, came from at least one thousand yards away. A security patrol was sent out to see if they could find whoever, or whatever, was screaming, but nothing was ever found. Even so, many Marines who served on Guam after World War II will attest to the story of the mystery man known as Screaming Willie. And there were Japanese holdouts—as late as October 1965, four Japanese infantrymen who had remained hidden since the end of the war surrendered themselves on Guam. And in the spring of 1974, Second Lieutenant Onoda of the Japanese army made world headlines when he emerged from the Philippine jungle after a thirty-year ordeal.

Life on Guam was not all work and no play. We received mail on a regular basis, brought in by a navy seaplane, but packages were brought to Guam via ship, and it was not unusual for a Marine to open a package of home-baked cookies that had been made three months earlier. One Sunday, I was able to catch a ride all the way to Tumon Bay and met up with a couple of friends who had been with me at Parris Island. One of them suggested that we take our M-1 rifles with us in a boat to see if we could hit the sharks that swam in the shallow waters of the bay. Before long he was able to shoot and kill a huge tiger shark that cruised by the boat. We tied a rope around its tail, got it back to shore, and took a few pictures, then presented the tiger shark to a group of local residents who used their machetes to transform it into shark steaks.

In February 1949, a new rumor began to spread through the brigade—we heard that the brigade would be heading for Camp Pendleton, California. And it wasn't long before rumor became fact. But in March 1949, I and about twenty other Marines received orders directing us to join the Marine Barracks at Pearl Harbor. Since we'd spent only six months overseas, we were not eligible to return to the States, so our reassignment to the Barracks would be for eighteen months. On March 15, we loaded ourselves and all of our gear into a navy seaplane that took us on a five-hour flight back to the Territory of Hawaii, and to the island of Oahu, where we landed at Keehi Beach, next to what is now the Hawaiian International Airport. We were then taken by truck to the Marine Barracks and to meet our new commanding officer, Col. Lewis B. ("Chesty") Puller, USMC.

CHAPTER 5

Marine Barracks, Pearl Harbor

After unloading our gear from the truck and stacking our seabags on the sidewalk, we were taken into the Marine Barracks headquarters building where a staff sergeant ordered us to form into three files. We stood at ease until the command "Attention on deck" alerted us to the arrival of Col. Lewis Burwell Puller, commanding officer of the Marine Barracks and a living legend in Marine Corps history. Among his numerous decorations, Colonel Puller wore four Navy Crosses he'd won for extraordinary heroism during his colorful career.

Standing in front of our small formation, he welcomed us aboard and said he was glad to learn that we had enjoyed a safe flight. As he moved down our ranks, carefully looking at each of us, he learned something about each of us through a handshake. As the colonel spoke to individual Marines, we could hear his remarks and knew we had joined a spit-and-polish unit. The dynamic officer from Virginia had a reputation as a man who held his enlisted Marines in high regard and treated them with respect. Before departing the quarterdeck, he promised that he would quickly come to know us by face and by name, and said he hoped we would enjoy our duty at the Barracks.

In truth, the Marine Barracks was probably one of the

most scattered units in the Pacific. In addition to three Marine detachments on Oahu, there was a detachment on Midway, Samoa, and on Wake and Johnston islands. Marines from the Barracks went to Midway for a three-month stay before they rotated back to Pearl Harbor, and there was no lack of volunteers because the Marines there maintained the security of the island, operated the movies, and ran the rifle range.

Marine Barracks, Pearl Harbor, was organized into Headquarters and Able (A) and Baker (B) Companies for the 620 officers and men who made up the command. While Headquarters Company Marines saw to all of the administrative needs of the Barracks Marines, including those assigned to the small detachments on the distant Pacific islands, it was the Marines of A and B Companies who labored the most on Oahu. Both letter companies split the duties of interior guard, base security patrols, and gate guard. In addition, A Company maintained the rifle range, while Marines in B Company were charged with running the naval brig. Each company consisted of three guard platoons that made up the four-section watch. I was assigned to the A Company's 2d Platoon and was quickly introduced to the life cycle on guard duty. Once posted, we remained on guard duty for twenty-four hours, then, on the second day of duty, we were assigned to working parties. On the third day we prepared uniforms and ourselves for the next day's guard duty. Neatly pressed and heavily starched khakis, with spit-shined shoes, was the guard uniform of the day, and each member of the detail was inspected and thoroughly briefed by the corporal of the guard before being posted. As a member of the guard, my duties ranged from patrolling the fence line around the navy's highly sensitive Wahiawa radio station, to walking countless miles around the not-so-glamorous Marine Corps supply depot's dry docks.

Even off duty, Colonel Puller saw to it that there was little wasted time at the Barracks. Not long after assuming command in July 1948, he announced that he wanted a baseball stadium for his Marines but was told that funds and manpower were not available for such an extravagance. Unwilling to accept that explanation, Puller put the entire off-duty guard force to work, built the field, and then challenged all comers to play ball.

Eight years after the attack on Pearl Harbor, I was surprised to see the extent of the damage that remained visible around our barracks, which were still pockmarked with bullet holes. They were one of the few places from which Marines had fired at attacking Japanese dive bombers. When I arrived at Pearl Harbor our three-story barracks were considered unsafe, but not long afterward they were repaired and, following a brief rededication ceremony, those of us assigned to A Company moved into the top deck, the second deck became home to B Company, and the first deck was used as the office space for the commanding officer; the Barracks executive officer, LtCol. George Newton, and our Barracks sergeant major. The mess hall was located in the center of the building and run by a mess officer named Yewzerski who had been a chef in one of the larger hotels in New York City. He and his crew of messmen provided us with the best chow any of us had had since joining the Corps. At this time, Colonel Puller endeared himself to us by turning our old barracks into three separate clubs; for staff NCOs, NCOs, and nonrates. Each had a dining room, snack bar, and a dance floor. The club rooms became the principal gathering places for Marines and their dependents and boosted morale for all of us.

Sightseeing on Oahu didn't take very long because at the time there were only two major tourist attractions on the island. Most people went to Mount Pali and looked from a cliff there to the other side of the island. That spot, revered by local Hawaiians, had achieved a certain notoriety long ago, when King Kamehameha was said to have thrown several thousand natives over the sheer face of the mountain. Departing Mount Pali, visitors could follow a winding road which led around the southern tip of the island and to a blowhole, a rock formation that shot a stream of seawater into the air. Depending upon the tides, sometimes it worked, other times it didn't. After seeing the blowhole, tourists would continue along the same road leading directly back into Honolulu. All that might not sound too inviting, but the island's beautiful vegetation, flowers, and the civilian residences formed a radiant picture.

Looking out from the barracks, I could see Ford Island and the skeletonlike superstructures of the sunken battleships *Arizona* and *Utah*, and over a period of weeks, I watched as dozens of welders finally reduced the once proud ships to scrap metal. As I became more familiar with Pearl Harbor, I was able to travel around Oahu and see more of the results of the war. At the navy's submarine base in Pearl Harbor, a Japanese two-man submarine, captured during the early morning hours of December 7, 1941, was on display, and the airplane hangars at Hickam Air Force Base still bore the scars from the surprise attack. The numerous long guns of the army's coastal artillery positions, which had once defended the island, still pointed seaward, but were covered with thick, creeping vines and were left to rust beneath the tropical sun.

For all Marines below the rank of corporal, liberty ended at midnight, without exception, and most Marines who walked out the main gate headed for Hotel Street to drink beer at the Anchor Bar, Bill Leader's Bar, or another well-known watering hole called Sad Sam's, which was owned by a Japanese gentleman named Ichinoza, who endured the nickname of Itchy-nose. At the time, draft beer cost ten cents per glass, with Royal and Primo beer being the island's two favorites. Unfortunately, in 1949, the drinking age in the Territory of Hawaii was twenty-one years old, and any Marine who was not old enough to drink had his armed forces identification card stamped with the word MINOR in bright red letters on the front, directly beneath his photograph, which was connected to the ID card by a metal grommet making alteration of the card almost impossible. The enlisted clubs aboard the base, called slopchutes, did serve beer to Marines under twenty-one years of age, at a cost of five cents per can, with no restriction on the number of beers a Marine could buy. Common sense was the rule, and if a Marine appeared to have had "one too many," he was simply cut off and told to leave the club.

The Barracks routine was similar to that on Guam, requiring a six-day work week, and come hell or high water, Saturdays were always used for inspections, with either Colonel Puller or Lieutenant Colonel Newton doing the inspecting. No two inspections were the same, and though we thought Colonel Puller might be the more difficult of the two, we soon found out we were wrong. Since the Barracks executive officer wore only a few ribbons above his left breast pocket, we assumed he had seen little, if any, action during the war. In fact, Lieutenant Colonel Newton had been a member of the 4th Marine Regiment, the defenders of Corregidor, until he was taken as a prisoner of war. He survived the Bataan Death March and more than three years of imprisonment as an involuntary guest of the Japanese Imperial Army. He knew the importance of Marines' maintaining their equipment and could not be fooled by halfhearted attempts at cleaning combat equipment.

At the beginning of each week, a notice was posted in the barracks indicating exactly what type of inspection would be held on the following Saturday morning, and thereby eliminating any excuses for not knowing what was expected. On some inspections, we were required to fall out wearing our field marching packs, and on the command to "open ranks," we would display all of our combat equipment. The following week might be used for a detailed rifle and personnel inspection, or to "form for shelter halves" to demonstrate our abilities to quickly construct our two-man tents. Clearly, monotony was not a part of Colonel Puller's inspection process, and in the rare event of rain, we laid out our gear on our racks inside the barracks. These detailed inspections, nicknamed "things on the springs" or "junk on the bunk," always took up half of any rainy day.

Our uniform of the day was fresh, starched khakis, a

long-sleeved, open khaki shirt, starched khaki trousers, spit-shined brown shoes, and a piss-cutter. The only exceptions to this rule was when we were sent to the rifle range and wore our utility uniform, or when we were assigned to patrol the dry-docks area and were allowed to wear boondockers instead of our dress shoes. Unfortunately, some unknown Marine, who must have gotten bored on post, decided to rub smooth the roughed-out suede of his boondockers and spit shined them. This fad caught on and Marines began to "bone" their boondockers, using either a Coke bottle or a hard plastic toothbrush to make the rough boot leather shine before they applied spit and polish for the desired look. I can't say that the practice of spit shining boondockers began at Marine Barracks, Pearl Harbor, but it was a common practice, one that most of us resented. We did, however, consider ourselves fortunate to have a base laundry that charged only one dollar for every twenty-five pieces of laundry. It was picked up at the barracks each Monday morning and returned each Friday afternoon, starched and pressed, bound by string, and wrapped up in heavy brown paper. Since monthly pay for a private first class with less than two cumulative years of service was less than one hundred dollars, any chance to save money was most welcomed.

We had been told that when Colonel Puller arrived at Pearl Harbor he found the training of the Barracks Marines lacking, so he immediately demanded a new training schedule, one designed to increase weapons familiarization firing for all machine gunners and mortar men, saying that he would not let history repeat itself. In July 1926 when then 2d Lieutenant Puller arrived in Hawaii for the first time, he was ordered to familiarize himself with the defense plans of the Hawaiian Islands. The plans showed that, in the event of activation, the island's small six-hundred-man Marine detachment would be used as a machine-gun battalion. When Puller asked to see the machine guns he was told by a quartermaster captain that they were "in storage and in good order." Unsatisfied with the captain's reply, he investigated and found "there were no water cans, no hoses—not a single tool, and no ammunition belts or asbestos gloves, not even a loading machine for the ammunition."[1] When the necessary equipment finally arrived, Puller became the battalion machine-gun officer. Twenty-three years later, the colonel was still interested in inspecting his machine guns.

Going to the rifle range at Pearl Harbor was a welcome break from the monotony of guard duty. The rifle range was well run. Its firing lines were made of crushed lava rock, which made for stable firing positions at all range distances. The impact area, called the butts, was positioned facing the ocean, and while firing was in progress, a navy picket boat was positioned offshore to warn away fishing boats and swimmers. Near the rifle range was a string of unused coastal gun sites, which were surrounded by dense jungle. In the years following the war, Marines had built a swimming pool out of one of the concrete gun tubs, using planks to shore up the entrance and then caulking the wood to make it watertight. Once flooded with cool water, the pool made for a very relaxing place to go following a full day of shooting under a hot tropical sun. The small mess hall at the range planned its serving schedule around each firing detail, which made our lives much easier during the two weeks we were assigned to the rifle range.

On October 15, 1949, I was standing in morning formation when my name, and many others, were read from a roster by our company first sergeant. We were told to return wearing our best-looking uniforms and meet outside of the Barracks headquarters building before going inside to be promoted by Colonel Puller. My proficiency and conduct marks had been good, and I had not gotten into any trouble, but had no idea I had been considered for promotion to corporal. Once assembled, our group of nearly thirty Marines was marched onto the quarterdeck and waited for the arrival of the commanding officer. As

---

[1]*Marine! The Life of L.T. Gen. Lewis B. (Chesty) Puller* by Burke Davis. 1962, Little, Brown, and Company, Boston, Mass. Chapter IV.

we stood at attention, our warrants were read aloud. It was a significant moment; our promotion warrants actually meant something, and they were worded so that all Marines could understand the significance of the advancement in rank and know what was expected of all promotees.

My warrant read:

By the direction of the Commandant of the Marine Corps, Maurice J. Jacques is hereby appointed a Corporal in the United States Marine Corps, and he is therefore enjoined to diligently discharge the duties of that rank by displaying in himself a good example of subordination, courage, sobriety, neatness, and attention to duty. He shall aid to the utmost of his ability in maintaining good order, discipline, and all that concerns the efficiency of command. He shall further observe and obey such orders and directions as he shall receive from his commanding officer or other superiors set over him, according to the Articles for the Government of the Navy.

My warrant to corporal is dated 9 September 1949 and is signed by "L. B. Puller, Colonel, USMC." It is one of my most valued possessions.

Using the example of outnumbered Marines storming the Mexican castle at Chapultepec in 1847, and citing the eleven principles of military leadership, Colonel Puller shared his thoughts with us as to what he believed it was that separated Marine noncommissioned officers from their subordinates. He used three of the principles of leadership to make his point. "First, be technically and tactically proficient. Young Marines expect you, as NCOs, to know all there is about weapons, equipment, and tactics. Secondly, know your Marines and look out for their welfare. Your Marines have strengths and weaknesses, and you can maximize your strengths and work to improve your weaknesses. As NCOs, you are leaders and will have to deal with followers, peers, and seniors. You will have to motivate the people who support you and understand them in order to develop a disciplined and well-trained unit. That is the job of the Marine NCO. Thirdly, and most importantly, as a Marine NCO, you must set the example. If you show your subordinates how to act, you are teaching them at the same time. When you follow regulations, you show your subordinates that you expect regulations and policies to be followed. You also prove your own degree of self-discipline. Today, your lives have changed forever, and it will not be easy to separate yourself from your friends, but that is what is demanded of you as noncommissioned officers in our Corps. If you will remember these three things, you will do well as NCOs." Colonel Puller's tip really hit home, and I promised myself that I would carry his good advice with me for as long as I remained in the Corps.

We celebrated our promotions with a party in the Barracks slopchute. Wearing corporal chevrons for the first time was wonderful, but it didn't take long before reality set in. Suddenly, I was no longer just a Marine, I was a noncommissioned officer and was required to move out of the open squad bay and share a room with the other NCOs of the platoon. I was assigned as one of the corporals of the guard and was held responsible for ensuring the Marines assigned to the guard force knew their general and special orders, looked squared away, and came to duty feeling motivated, ready, and able. But I didn't like what was happening. I felt that I was under the gun, and with the sergeant of the guard and the commander of the guard being seasoned veterans of World War II, they must have thought that a few new corporals of the guard would make their lives much easier. The commander of the guard was Red Lambert, technical sergeant (E-6), a veteran of Guadalcanal, and one tough individual. He had to be; his given name was Pershing, in honor of the army general, and with a handle like that, in an antiarmy environment, he said he'd learned to fight from the first day he'd joined the Corps. By saddling us with a very demanding list of responsibilities, he and the sergeant of the

guard made our lives miserable, as we were held accountable for everything that happened on guard duty. It was
then that I began to learn that not all NCOs had my best
interest at heart.

It was inevitable that I would run into Colonel Puller
during the time I was stationed at the Barracks, and I can
recall at least two humorous incidents that involved the
colonel and me. I was posted as the corporal of the guard
one afternoon when I was told by the sergeant of the
guard to take two Marines to Quarters #1, the commanding officer's home. When we arrived, we were greeted by
the quarter's maid and Colonel Puller. While the maid
held a handkerchief to her face, the colonel lit up a corn-
cob pipe and explained the problem. "I sure do hate to
have to use Marines for this, boys, but it seems that a
damned cat has chosen a place beneath our porch to die.
I need to get that animal and its stink out of here, or Mrs.
Puller will have my head." Of course the colonel's wish
was nothing short of an order, and the cat's body was removed and taken away immediately.

The second time I "helped" the colonel was when I
tried to help teach his son, Lewis, Jr., to swim. The Puller's home was located close to a swimming pool, and the
colonel had exhausted himself trying to convince his
young son to get in the water, but Lewis, Jr., would have
none of it, refusing every one of his father's suggestions.
In desperation, Colonel Puller told his son to get dressed
and meet him in front of his green Plymouth staff car.
Then the colonel, with Lewis, Jr., standing up beside him
in the rear seat, had his driver take them to the base brig.
Explaining to his son that "Marines do not disobey orders," the colonel had Lewis "locked up" until he changed
his mind about swimming. Lewis, Jr.'s total brig time was
only about ten minutes, but the colonel's plan worked, and
Lewis, Jr., became a regular at the pool.

I tell of these incidents because it's necessary to mention the relationship between officers and enlisted men in
1950. At that time, privates did not talk to NCOs unless
they were spoken to, and NCOs observed the same cour-

tesy with staff NCOs. Only the most senior enlisted men spoke freely with officers. There was a very distinct caste system in the armed forces then, particularly in the Marine Corps, and those barriers which separated enlisted men from officers were not broken, ever.

One day while I was off duty from the guard, since I enjoyed working out from time to time on the heavy bag, I went to the gym and asked for a pair of hand wraps. My request for boxing gear drew the attention of a staff sergeant named Marcelli, who asked me if I was interested in trying out for the Barracks boxing team. Little did I know that by agreeing to try out for Marcelli's six-man team that I would be accepted, relieved of my duties as corporal of the guard, transferred to HQ Company, and become a punching bag for a huge private named Joe Collins.

A Private First Class Jennings and I were the only two who could spar with that guy, who prided himself on being a knockout artist; we learned how to box out of necessity. During our training day, we'd split up, two guys sparring in the ring, one on the rope, and one on the speed bag, and the remaining two sparring outside the ring for three-minute intervals. The other Marines on the squad, MacBee, New, and Gribble, helped fashion a pretty fair boxing team. We boxed in AAU tournaments in Hawaii, against the Honolulu Kameeki Eagles, and against a stable of young boxers managed by Mr. Sam Ichinoza, the owner of Sad Sam's bar. Every Friday night was fight night at the Honolulu Arena, located outside the main gate, and Colonel Puller attended nearly every fight, always sitting in the front row and cheering on his Marines. The arena was always packed with Marines, sailors, and the local Hawaiians who loved all contact sports.

Although I had a pretty fair record, I wouldn't say that I was a contender, but I did fight in the Honolulu Golden Gloves, the All-Navy boxing tournament, and managed to get as far as the AAU finals. I had good training, gained about ten pounds, and went from a middleweight to a light heavyweight. My biggest problem was that I was a bleeder. To cope with that, I was told by our coach to inhale crystallized Epsom salts, which would help toughen the lining of my nose and prevent bleeding. This old trick helped to reduce my bleeding, but it turned the tissue lining in my nose into something akin to shoe leather.

Within six months of joining the boxing team, I decided that boxing was not the reason I had joined the Corps, and I hung up my gloves, only to be assigned to help run the Barracks maintenance section. It happened that a corporal named Doc Barrington had reported in at the Barracks, and during an encounter with Colonel Puller, he explained that he'd been a tree surgeon before joining the Corps. He thought that he could do some good for the trees on the Barracks grounds and Colonel Puller agreed. Corporal Barrington and I became part of a tree-maintenance section, and he taught me more about trees and landscaping than I ever wanted to know, but he made our work section a valuable addition to the Barracks.

During the period that Doc Barrington and I were trimming a stand of trees near the brig, an investigation was ordered that drew a great deal of attention to that ominous place. The naval brig at Pearl Harbor was considered a "red line" brig, where punishment was meted out to prisoners by their Marine guards in an attempt to correct any and all disobedient behavior. But when several sailors were released from confinement and returned to their ships with stories of maltreatment at the hands of their guards, an immediate investigation was ordered. The sailors said that while they were in the brig their guards punished them, dragging them into the head, hanging them beneath a running shower, and had administered several dozen lashes with a wet swab. No marks were left on them because of the running water, but their stories were believed, and naval officials asked Colonel Puller to investigate their allegations. As it turned out, the story was true, and three Marine guards were found guilty of abusive treatment of navy prisoners and were themselves swiftly punished. All three were reduced to the rank of private, confined for thirty days, and put on a diet of bread and water during the entire time of their confinement. As soon as they were released, they were transferred from Hawaii to the "garden spots" of the Pacific; one to Midway, one to Kwajalein, and the third to Johnston Island.

The investigation of maltreatment brought about several changes in brig policy. Prisoners wore a blue navy uniform consisting of a dungaree jacket, a blue shirt, and blue navy trousers with a large letter P stenciled in white on the back and front of all their clothing. The daily display of prisoners being marched to and from each meal, wearing their distinguished P uniforms, was a sobering sight and was meant to be a visual reminder of what would happen to those who chose to break the rules pertaining to good order and discipline. As an additional reminder of what could happen to those who misbehaved, each time a court-martial was adjourned, the offending sailor or Marine was marched out to stand before the flagpole in front of our mess hall while the officer of the day read the charges and the imposed sentence. I recall standing in formation when a Marine who had been in the brig and on bread and water for thirty days, decided to attack a guard. He was tried again, and as he stood before us a groan could be heard coming from our ranks as he was sentenced to an additional thirty days on bread and water.

On June 25, 1950, eight divisions of the North Korean People's Army (NKPA), drove south across the 38th Parallel and began a campaign to unify Korea as a Communist state. This event changed the life of every Marine at the Barracks, from our commanding officer to the newest private. It was rumored that Colonel Puller had paid his own way to fly from Hawaii to Washington, D.C., in an attempt to get a rifle regiment into combat in Korea. The Barracks was not unlike a small town, where nothing was secret. In fact, it was the colonel's driver who kept us informed as to what was really happening in Korea and to the likelihood of possible Marine involvement. He told us that Colonel Puller believed he was on "twilight tour of duty," but the war in Korea was an opportunity for Marines to fight, and that was what Puller had joined to do. He sent numerous telegrams to the commandant, to the assistant commandant, and to the commanding general of the 1st Marine Division, pleading with them for an opportunity to command. And then his wish came true.

When I heard the 1st Marine Brigade had been ordered to Korea, I felt badly that I was not with them. I had served with many of them on Guam and could see my one chance of going into combat going up in smoke. In August, when the division came through Pearl Harbor, the presence of a Marine amphibious unit heading into combat proved too enticing for some Marines. When the navy's carrier *Philippine Sea* came into Pearl Harbor, a friend of mine, Cpl. R. B. Isley, and another Barracks Marine packed their gear and stowed away on board the ship. When the two Marines were discovered, two days out from Pearl, it was learned that Isley had a hometown friend on board who had helped them stow away. Messages were sent from Vice Adm. Arthur W. Radford, the Pacific Commander, to Headquarters Marine Corps, and to the surprise of many, the question of what to do with Isley and his buddy was answered with the reply: "grant their wishes." That caused our company first sergeant J. B. McGinnis to hold an unscheduled company formation out of fear that he was about to face a mutiny. He stood before us and said, "I guess you people have heard what happened to Isley and his idiot buddy. Let me make this perfectly clear; there will be no more acts of stupidity performed by Marines in this company. You will get a chance to go to Korea only when your tours of duty are finished here. Do not ask me to help you get off of this island any sooner. Dismissed."

Despite the first sergeant's warning, I made a nuisance of myself trying to ambush him in the hallways of the barracks so many times that when he'd see me, he'd head in the opposite direction. I realized that I had made a mistake by trying out for the boxing team. By doing so, I had become "indispensable," not to be used for anything other than boxing. Now, with a war on, and being assigned to

Headquarters Company, I stood less chance than ever of getting into combat. To add insult to injury, it was not long after our first sergeant had warned us about leaving that a draft of replacements was made up from Marines in A Company, and those Marines were flown directly to Korea.

My enlistment was due to end in July 1951, but President Truman extended all enlistments by one year and increased my chances of going to Korea. That was fine with me but others did not take kindly to their extension, saying they were not happy in having to serve out their "Truman year."

In July, Colonel Puller was given the orders he desired, and left Marine Barracks, Pearl Harbor, for Camp Pendleton, to command the 1st Marine Regiment, and as Colonel Puller and his Marines prepared for war, those of us who remained at the Barracks stood at attention and listened as Col. R. M. Victory, the new commanding officer, said that no more Marines would be leaving Hawaii for Korea and that he would not tolerate anymore administrative assistance (AA) forms from Marines requesting orders. From that moment on, I swore to myself that for as long as I remained in the Marine Corps, I would never consider any Marine as indispensable and stand between him and a chance to fight.

In March 1951, I received orders back to the States and boarded the USS *General Mann* for a five-day sail to San Francisco. I stayed on Treasure Island for only two days before boarding a Union Pacific train that took me east to Chicago. The cost of flying coast to coast was out of the question, as was the price for a Pullman sleeper car, but I was happy to have the company of several Marines I had been with on Parris Island, who had just returned from Korea, and as we traveled along, they told me about their experiences in combat.

Upon reaching Chicago, we said good-bye to one another, and I walked to the La Salle Street Station where I transferred to a New York Central train that took me through upper New York, eventually arriving in Boston.

From the state capital, it was only a matter of one short train ride on the B&M railroad, back to Lawrence, where I was able to spend thirty days at home with my parents, brothers, and sister.

The high cost to travel home had depleted my savings, and not wanting to ask my parents for any money, I spent part of my leave caddying at the Andover Country Club, where carrying a double set of golf bags for eighteen holes paid only five dollars a day. When my leave was up, my father suggested that he and the rest of my family would be happy to drive me from Lawrence to the Marine base, at Quantico, Virginia. We loaded up my father's 1948 Dodge with my seabag and their luggage and made the six-hundred-mile trip in two days, passing through New York City, Baltimore, and Washington, D.C.

Not wanting to have my parents drive me all over the base—I was a corporal after all—I thanked them for bringing me to Virginia, said good-bye again, and shouldered my seabag as I walked toward Quantico's main gate.

CHAPTER 6

Marine Corps Base, Quantico, Virginia

I was given directions to D Barracks by one of the sentries at the main gate. The transient barracks were not too far away. When I arrived at the barracks, I presented my orders to the duty NCO, a sergeant, and was escorted by his assistant, a corporal, upstairs to a rack in an open squad bay for NCOs. The uniform of another corporal, who I was told had gone to evening chow, was laid out on the lower bunk, making the upper rack mine. And, wanting desperately to wash off the effects of the long road trip and my hike to the transient barracks, I unpacked my seabag and went into the head to wash. When I returned to the squad bay I was stunned to see none other than Cpl. R. B. Isley, the Marine from Pearl Harbor who had stowed away aboard the Korea-bound carrier *Philippine Sea*, sitting on the bunk's lower rack. Corporal Isley had not only survived the war, participating in the retaking of Seoul, he had endured the terrible winter ordeal with the 1st Marines at the Chosin Reservoir. He had arrived at Quantico just a day earlier than I and had been assigned to Camp Goettge to help run a boiler plant that provided steam to the outlying camp's busy mess hall.

I spent the rest of the evening listening in fascination as Isley talked about how difficult combat had been, particularly during Korea's harsh winter months, and I went to bed wondering if and when my turn might ever come. The next morning, I began checking in and was assigned to a command known as Marine Corps School's Training Battalion, headquartered at Brown Field. This organization was structured like a reinforced battalion of Marine infantry, complete with artillery, tanks, engineers, amphibian tractors, and trucks, whose mission it was to support Quantico's schools, testing and evaluating equipment and techniques, and teaching and training officers. Since World War I, Quantico had been recognized as the principal home of formal schooling for Marine Corps officers and enlisted men, and those Marines assigned to the school's training battalion were an integral part of the forty-five-hundred Marines and sailors stationed aboard the base.

While I was going through the checking-in ritual, a chief warrant officer happened to notice me waiting in line. He walked over and asked, "Corporal, do you know anything about explosives?" I snapped to attention, and without thinking, looked him dead in the eye and said, "Yes, sir, I sure do." He motioned me to follow him, and we were joined by another Marine he had spoken to earlier. In the quiet of an unbusy hallway, Chief Warrant Officer Eldridge introduced himself to us, and congratulated us on having joined the demolitions section of the school's Troops Section. I didn't have the nerve to tell him I was not any more familiar with high explosives and demolitions than any new recruit, but it was just as well that I managed to keep my mouth shut because I had just volunteered for duty in a well-run outfit.

CWO-4 Eldridge had lost one finger of his right hand and a portion of another while fighting on Guadalcanal and Tarawa, but despite the obvious dangers of what he referred to as "risky business," he was an outstanding officer who knew his job and took care of his men. The manner in which he welcomed us into his section was similar to his character. "I don't really care if you new guys are booze hounds, or liberty hounds, but what I do expect is you to be ready to go to work each morning.

During the next few weeks, you'll be taught how to handle explosives in a safe and correct manner, working in two-man teams to insure each other's safety. If you have any problems at all, I expect you to come to me first."

Our section, called the Range Section, was made up of only seven Marines, including the gunner (warrant officer) and was billeted in our own Quonset hut at Camp Barrett, a newly constructed area built to meet the needs of an expanding officer population destined for Korea. As the gunner had mentioned, we were divided into pairs, and I was assigned to work with a veteran corporal named Robert Bender. A native of Alabama who had joined the Corps at eighteen years old, was baptized in combat as a demolitions man serving with the 2d Marine Division, first on bloody Tarawa and later on Saipan and Tinian, Bender was a retread. He left the Corps at war's end, but finding nothing back home in rural Alabama as exciting as the Marines, he came back in as soon as the shooting had started in Korea.

Our job was fairly simple. Following an 0430 reveille each morning, we'd square away the Quonset hut before heading off to chow and then report to the Range Section to pick up our daily assignments. We were responsible for placing explosive charges inside the demolition beds on the numerous ranges used to teach infantry tactics to the lieutenants attending the basic school. We did not teach them the use of demolitions, but ensured that when they arrived at a particular range to observe tactical demonstrations or simulations, the required explosives were set up and ready to be fired at the flip of a switch.

Upon arriving at a range, our first order of business was to use an ohmmeter and check the electrical trunk line, making sure we had good electrical contacts inside each demo bed. Then, using electrical blasting caps, we connected them to quarter- or half-pound blocks of TNT, simulating artillery rounds, mortar fire, or the explosion of bangalore torpedoes to add realism to the tactical situation. Once we had set up the explosives, we'd hand over a set of keys to the padlock that kept the electrical switchboard secured. When the switchboard keys were placed in the hands of the range officer, our job was done, but we'd stay at the range until all explosives had been detonated before moving on to another assignment.

Corporal Bender was an expert instructor. He took his time and explained to me every move he made. More importantly, he never dodged any questions, no matter how ridiculous or complicated, and because of Bender's helpful attitude I felt confident in myself, having learned about explosives from a professional.

Chief Warrant Officer Eldridge would visit each of the ranges daily, checking to see if there were any problems and lending a hand when needed. There was no range he was not familiar with, but there was one particular monthly event in which he took particular interest—the atomic bomb simulation. Combining the explosive effects of one M-3–shaped charge (designed to crater roads or runways) with two thirty-five-gallon drums of gasoline and fifty pounds of mess hall flour, the gunner created his fireball by wrapping several hundred feet of detonation cord around the cratering charge and the gasoline drums. The mushroom cloud came from the flour. It usually took several days for him to set up the affair, but the event was always a great hit with those who observed it.

Summertime at Quantico also meant afternoon thunderstorms, and with the first audible rumble, we would separate ourselves from our explosives work as rapidly as possible and shut down operations for the rest of the day. Premature detonation of explosives caused by a sudden change in local electrical conditions was something we were constantly warned about, and though it would not be until years later, in Vietnam, when I would witness such an event, I learned at an early age the first rule of demolitions work was that safety is always paramount.

On the morning of 1 July 1951, I was told by Gunner Eldridge to take the Marines of our section to Brown Field to attend a battalion personnel inspection. When we arrived, we were met in the battalion's parking lot by the gunner, who informed me there was no personnel inspection. I was there to participate in a promotion cere-mony—my own. And for the second time during my rel-atively short career, I was surprised to learn I had been se-lected for promotion. Making the occasion even more memorable, my old pal, Cpl. R. B. Isley, was not only present, but stood beside me, as he, too, was promoted to the rank of sergeant of Marines. I was now also allowed to wear one red stripe, a hash mark, indicating three years of service on the lower sleeve of my dress uniform.

With my promotion to sergeant came not only an in-crease in responsibilities and an increase in my monthly pay to $129.95 but the financial ability to purchase an au-tomobile and expand my horizons past Quantico, Virginia. Having learned from my work experiences as a kid, and by having faithfully put money into a savings account each payday, I had managed to save enough money to pay cash for the kind of car I wanted, a 1946 Ford. Corporal Bender suggested we visit a friend of his who sold cars in Alexandria, Virginia, to make my dream come true. He reasoned we had walked long enough the unimproved dirt roads which led on and off of Quantico, covering our shoes and soiling our uniforms with the fine dust of Vir-ginia's red-clay soil. And, filled with visions of driving around Washington, D.C., and all points north in style, we hitched a ride to Alexandria and returned to Quantico in a 1946, maroon, two-door Ford coupe. The car had been kept in fine shape by its original owner and showed only twenty thousand miles on the odometer. It looked great and needed only a few improvements to enhance its over-all appeal. Bender and I went to Western Auto Store and purchased a can of tire paint and painted whitewalls on the car. Soon after, I added a sun visor above the wind-shield, added a pair of brand-new seat covers, and un-knowingly began traveling the road to what nearly became my own destruction.

At first, I used every excuse I could to jump behind the wheel of that Ford and drive just for the sake of driving. I visited Washington, D.C., and drove south of Quantico, to Fredricksburg and Spotsylvania, but soon tired of day trips. I decided to use the car only on weekends, and to make long trips to places I had only read about. A number of times I took one of the sergeants in our section to his parents' home in the Bronx, and once, while we were in a variety store buying eggs for his mother, we met the great boxer and local legend, Jake "The Raging Bull" La Motta. He'd been one of my boxing heroes, and after being introduced to him, he wished us luck and said goodbye as he got behind the wheel of a jet-black Buick Roadmaster and drove away. During our two-day visits to New York City, we became familiar with Garden City Park on Long Island, and Coney Island amusement park, but we always managed to return to Quantico by 0430, on Monday mornings.

I began to risk longer drives, traveling home to Massachusetts several times, but once there I spent more time away from my family than with them, and it was not long before I began to feel I was not as welcome at home as I thought I'd be. Not long after I had driven with some Marines as far west as Michigan City, Indiana, I realized I was not only wasting my time behind the wheel of the car, but wasting the money I had worked so hard to save.

I hadn't lost my desire to go to Korea, so I went to see our company first sergeant and asked him for a little help. His attitude was the opposite of what I had experienced at Pearl Harbor. The first sergeant told me that although there was nothing he could do for me in the way of getting orders until I had at least six months at Quantico, he did agree to submit an AA form to Headquarters Marine Corps on my behalf and said he would not stand in my way of going to Korea. He told me to be patient, that my orders would come, eventually.

As I continued to work in the Range Section and wait for orders, I happened, one day, to stop by a small country store located along historic Quantico Road near the town of Ruby, Virginia, not far from the western boundary of the base at Independence Hill. The place reminded me of the one-room stores I had visited as a boy in New

England, so I went in to take a look and found a group of old men seated around a potbellied stove, trying to keep warm while telling stories about hunting for deer and turkey. A stranger, I was asked my name, and when I mentioned I was from the base, the oldest of the men asked me to sit down and join them next to the stove. That old gentleman was named Mr. Ruby, he was one of the descendants of the people who had first settled in the area, and he told me he used to have a huge farm in Ruby, "until the government bought up the land so the damyankee soldiers could train in the woods." I thought he was referring to the Union soldiers who had actually fought on his family's property back in 1861, until I realized any man who didn't speak with a southern drawl was considered by him to be a damyankee.

Mr. Ruby's store was a wonderful place to visit, although he didn't try to make everyone feel as welcomed as he had me. He had electricity coming into his little store, but no refrigeration other than a small icebox, and anyone asking for a drink of water was handed an empty soda bottle, which was dipped into a wooden barrel of clean well water. Any stranger asking to use the "facilities" was pointed in the direction of a distant two-hole outhouse.

During one of my visits to Mr. Ruby's store, talk around the woodstove turned to a discussion about finding artifacts on the nearby Civil War battlefields. Interested in how easy it was to locate buttons, bullets, and bayonets lost nearly ninety years before, I returned to the base and convinced Sergeant Isley to join with me to hunt for lost artifacts on our off-duty weekends. Before long Isley and I, and a number of other Marines interested in local Civil War history, had launched our own campaign to visit as many of the local battlefields as possible. While we became familiar with such distant places as Bull Run, Fredricksburg, the Wilderness, and Richmond, we also learned about the encampments that had been in Garrisionville, Dumfries, and on the base at Quantico. The

Aquia Harbor Episcopal Church, only a few miles south of the base, boasted a Union cannonball still embedded in one of its walls.

With the help of a mine detector we borrowed from Gunner Eldridge, over the months we were able to find a Confederate soldier's belt buckle, a section of rifle barrel, and so many lead bullets I kept them in the trunk of my Ford as extra weight for traction during the snowy winter months. As we continued to visit the battlefields and to learn about the tactics, weapons, and history of the Civil War, our understanding and appreciation of our own military history and heritage grew considerably.

The weeks just before Christmas were traditionally a quiet time at Quantico, and those of us in the Range Section who had not requalified with the M-1 rifle were assigned to a detail that would ensure our having fired for record before the end of the calendar year. I requalified with the rifle, for the first time having to shoot while it was snowing. Despite the snow, I managed to qualify as an expert rifleman.

On June 22, 1952, following a day of hunting for relics, two friends and I made the mistake of sampling a batch of white lightning before returning to Quantico well after dark. I was driving up a hill when I slammed into the back of a trailer truck that had no working rear lights. With no seat belt to restrain me, the impact of my Ford hitting the truck sent me crashing into the windshield. I received a three-inch laceration across my head, a two-inch cut across my mouth, and I suffered internal injuries from crushing the car's steering wheel with my body.

The truck driver never stopped to see if we were all right, and he disappeared into the darkness. Luckily, my two companions received only a few superficial cuts and bruises and thought they could make it back aboard the base without any difficulty. I, too, wanted to get away from the scene of the accident as quickly as possible, but incapable of thinking clearly, not only as a result of the accident, but due to the effects of the 110-proof thoughts lingering in my head, I tried to hitchhike back to Camp Barrett.

If it had not been for the thoughtfulness of strangers, I would probably have died. A couple who happened to be driving along Route 1 stopped and offered me a ride. I thanked them by passing out in the backseat of their car. They took me to the emergency room at the base hospital where navy doctors Cdr. G. O. de Tarnowsky and Lt. J. L. Sawyers sutured up my lacerations and performed a laparotomy, closing a deep tear and perforation to my intestines, which prevented me from bleeding to death internally.

I was hospitalized for more than a month, and at one point during my convalescence, a nurse asked me if I felt well enough to see a Marine private first class who had stopped by to see me. I was surprised to find that the visitor was my younger brother, Francis, who had enlisted in the Marine Corps without telling me, and following his boot camp leave he'd stopped in at Quantico to say hello. The surprise was on him when he learned I was recovering from the automobile accident, but his visit was the one bright spot of the entire ordeal.

Ironically, as I was about to be discharged from the hospital, my orders to Korea finally arrived. However, I made the mistake of telling one of the nurses that I would soon be headed overseas, and she alerted my doctor to this interesting news. The doctor came to my room and informed me he had not opened me up "from my gut to my neck" just so I could get myself killed in Korea. It was his opinion it would take "a full year" for me to recover from surgery, and although he would approve my discharge from the hospital, he would not find me fit for full duty. Angered at what the doctor told me and realizing my four year enlistment was just about up, I felt that if I was not fit enough to go to Korea, then I was not fit to stay in the Marine Corps. I asked to be discharged.

During the spring, I had befriended a girl whose uncle owned a moving company that carried cargo for Allied

Van Lines. As soon as I was handed my discharge papers, I went to Hagerstown, Maryland, to see her and to ask her uncle for a job as a truck driver. I felt badly about leaving the Marine Corps so suddenly, and I certainly had no desire to return home and explain myself, so I planned to distance myself as far as possible from my family, friends, and Quantico.

After passing a truck-driving test, I was given a Class 1 vehicle operator's license and was introduced to my partner, a truck driver headed for Alameda, California, with a trailer truck full of furniture. But what might have been a promising future soon deteriorated into a bad experience. The truck driver looked on me as a kid and tried to take advantage of me, asking me to drive the truck when he should have been behind the wheel and committing the cardinal sin of telling fellow truck drivers that I was a former *soldier*, recently discharged from the army!

By the time we hit Kansas City, Missouri, I had decided to end my career as a truck driver, particularly because of an idiot who never did understand the difference between a Marine and a soldier. Correcting his ignorance did no good as he really didn't care to listen to me explain the difference between the two services.

We had just pulled into a truck stop for breakfast when I told him I had decided to quit. He thought I meant to quit the job after we'd reached California, but he began to put two and two together when I asked our waitress if she knew where the closest Marine Corps recruiting office was located. She knew because her brother had enlisted in the Corps a week earlier, and after she gave me directions, I told my partner to go to hell and left the truck stop.

A master sergeant named Bennett ran the local recruiting office. After I explained my story to him, he made a few telephone calls, typed up the necessary paperwork, and asked me if I wanted to get something to eat. By 1400 that afternoon, on 18 August 1952, I was reenlisted in the Marine Corps, having been a civilian for only thirteen days, and allowed to keep my rank as a sergeant. I was a handed a set of orders and a train ticket that would take me to Oceanside, California, and to duty at Camp Pendleton.

CHAPTER 7

A Short Tour At
Camp Pendleton, 1952

Four days after reenlisting in Kansas City, Missouri, I arrived in California, and as my train slowed to a crawl entering the seaside town of Oceanside, I saw dozens of canvas tents lining the beach of Camp Del Mar, home to the men of the 3d Marine Division, which was building up at Camp Pendleton. I left the train station and had walked only a few blocks up to North Hill Street when I spotted a Marine Corps truck with several men riding in the back. My shouting to the driver caused him to stop and guaranteed me a ride onto the Corps' second largest base. I was wearing only a pair of issue khaki trousers and a green T-shirt, and carrying a ditty bag, which contained my shaving kit and a couple of dirty shirts, so I must have looked a little suspect to the driver, but he didn't ask any questions other than where I needed to go.

The sprawling base was divided into a number of isolated areas and camps, but my orders to Marine Corps Base, Camp Pendleton, meant that I needed to find the base headquarters located in the 24 Area and begin checking in for duty. Upon my arrival at the headquarters building, I presented my orders to one of the administrative clerks, and after a short wait was told to report to Range Company, headquartered several miles away in the 14 Area. A truck ride brought me to the Range Company's office, where I told the company first sergeant my story. He made every effort to make me feel welcome and assured me he would help me to get "back in step" as quickly as possible and initiated the paperwork for me to receive a new issue of uniforms since all of my uniforms had been put in storage while I was hospitalized at Quantico.

I was temporarily assigned as a rifle range coach at one of the rifle ranges known as Chappo Flats, and for the first time in weeks I felt at home. I had made the right decision in rejoining the Marine Corps.

Because of the war in Korea, the pace of activity at Camp Pendleton in August 1952 can only be described as nonstop. Every effort was made to get Marines trained for combat and shipped out as rapidly as possible. And though I had explained to my new first sergeant my desire to get to Korea, my orders as a rifle-range coach were to be carried out before any consideration would be given to my request for duty overseas. The range at Chappo Flats was dedicated to getting Marines qualified as riflemen before they sailed for Korea, and to meet the demands of hundreds of shooters, long work hours were inevitable. Reveille for range personnel was sounded at 0400 each morning, and only by getting up so early could those of us assigned to help run the rifle ranges ensure the first round could go downrange with morning's first light. Looking like characters from a horror movie, those of us assigned as rifle coaches would arrive at the range by 0530, and trudge through the early morning fog down a narrow trail that ran perpendicular to the range, which was lined with burning smudge pots designed to be used by shooters to blacken their rifle sights before shooting.

I had not been at Chappo Flats for more than a few weeks before I was called in to see the company first sergeant who offered me a new assignment. One of the rifle ranges located near Camp San Onofre required an NCO to run the target end of the rifle range, the butts, and my name came up as a candidate. What really was required was a Marine NCO to keep half of the Marines assigned to a range detail busy working in the butts, either making dozens of targets, pasting up bullets holes, or scoring those targets which were being fired upon. I accepted the first sergeant's offer and prepared to move to the northern end of the base.

My new home was called Tent Camp #2 and consisted of dozens of Quonset huts and hundreds of canvas tents for the permanent personnel. Life within the camp was Spartan living, at its best. Our Quonset hut was used only for sleeping, and the community head, located several yards away, produced only enough hot water for the first six Marines who got there. It was comical to watch as Marines, wrapped only in woolen overcoats and wearing pointed-toe Korean shoes, called "iddy-wa" slippers, dashed from their tents to the warmth of the showers. We ate our meals in a chow hall that had a notice posted outside that said, "To eat here, bring your own meat can, meat can cover, canteen cup, and knife, fork and spoon." Every Marine who went to that mess hall had constructed a wire "safety pin" fashioned from a coat hanger on which he hung his mess kit and cutlery and sanitized his mess gear, before entering the mess hall, by submerging them into a drum of boiling water.

Our slopchute had once been a huge warehouse, but a welder had transformed it by using his torch to cut out several sets of double doors. Inside, Marines paid five cents to choose from half a dozen trash cans full of Lucky Lager, Pabst Blue Ribbon, or Schlitz beer. To insure there was never any trouble, the club was patrolled by Marines assigned to the area's interior guard. At the end of the evening, a fire hose was used to wash down the walls and floor before the doors were locked at 2030.

While I was assigned as the NCOIC (noncommissioned officer in charge) of the butts, my boss was a first lieutenant named Lang who, with the help of a staff sergeant named Brown and an assistant named Guenny, ran the range. Working six days a week, getting Marines on and off of the range as qualified shooters, made my time there seem to fly by. After less than a month of working at

Range 214, I was informed by the lieutenant that my long-awaited orders for duty in Korea had finally arrived. I was to transfer directly to the T&R (training and replacement) Command, located at the northern end of Camp Pendleton, at what today is known as Camp San Onofre.

T&R Command was a "paper tiger" organization made up of base permanent personnel—officers and enlisted instructors—who prepared Marines for combat duty in Korea. To help distinguish T&R instructors from their students, color-coded helmets were used—tactics instructors wore a fiberglass helmet liner rimmed with a yellow stripe, while troops handlers wore helmet liners with a white stripe.

As soon as I checked in at T&R Command, I became a member of the 26th Draft Replacement Battalion, approximately eighteen hundred Marines divided into four companies: M, N, O, and P, each with four platoons and four squads per platoon. I was assigned to the 1st Platoon of Nan (N) Company as the 4th Squad leader. Our battalion was assigned to Tent Camp #2, and we began five weeks of infantry-skills training immediately. The first week began with classes on basic infantry formations, small-unit offensive tactics, demonstrations of mines and booby traps, and organic infantry weapons and fire support. The second week was dedicated to platoon-size defensive tactics and with classes on day and nighttime patrolling and radio communications. Particular emphasis was placed on noise and light discipline. Our third week was spent in the conduct of company-size operations and culminated in our fourth week, which was spent in the field in a five-day war that pitted us against demonstration troops. We were to take ten objectives during those five days and nights.

Our four weeks of infantry training were made to be as realistic as possible, and no matter what a Marine's background, everyone, from the most senior officer to the newest private, was treated as though he were going through infantry-skills training for the very first time.

Reveille was sounded at 0430 each morning, and we fell out at 0600 each morning, wearing packs and carrying newly issued rifles, ready for the day's training. Our noon chow came to the field in brown paper bags we called khaki sacks. Usually they held not much more than a bologna sandwich and a stale piece of fruit, to be washed down with warm water from our canteens. Our outdoor classrooms and demonstration areas were located on hilltops, often separated by several miles, and to help develop stamina, we ran from one class to the next. The terrain surrounding our training area rose from sea level to steep hills in excess of eight hundred feet, and our daily conquering of those hills with pack and rifle guaranteed we were in good physical condition by the time we entered our fifth week of training at the Marine Corps' Mountain Cold Weather Training Center, in the Sierra Nevada range, near Bridgeport, California.

Before leaving Camp San Onofre, every Marine in our draft replacement battalion drew a complete issue of cold-weather gear, which included several pairs of wool socks, long johns, wool shirts, leather gloves, a full-length alpaca-lined overcoat, and one pair of heavy, felt-lined shoe pacs. Each of these items was held aloft and inspected for proper fit and serviceability by us NCOs before it could be stuffed into a seabag. Marines were also issued packboard frames on which they lashed extra equipment, and green satchels called "willie-peter" bags were issued, which provided waterproof protection to our sleeping bags. The weight of a Marine's cold-weather pack, including his service rifle, averaged nearly seventy pounds.

We climbed aboard our Greyhound buses and left Camp Pendleton at 0230 on a Saturday morning and began the ten-hour ride to Bridgeport, traveling first through rural Fallbrook before we turned north onto Route 395 and passed through the Riverside and San Bernardino counties before making our first pit stop at George Air Force Base, located outside of the town of Victorville. Our second stop was an even more remote spot called

Lone Pine, an abandoned airstrip, which allowed room for our buses to park in a huge circle. After being fed C rations for lunch, before we left, we were given enough time to put on cold-weather clothing. Then we traveled on past Lake Crowley and through the little towns of Bishop and Bridgeport, before finally arriving at the mountain training center.

The training center was designed to prepare Marines for combat duty in the cold weather. Classes and tactical problems were conducted year-round by the base's permanent personnel, who doubled as an aggressor force during tactical problems. As soon as we had unloaded the gear from our buses, we began a slow march from the lower base camp known as Pickle Meadows and moved to higher ground several miles away, Summit Meadows. At Summit Meadows, we saw only a few large general purpose (GP) tents in an open area, and learned they were to be used as our mess hall, a sick bay and as warming tents. There were no billeting tents; we were told we would not be given the luxury and protection of canvas squad-size tents during our stay, but would find shelter in two-man shelter halves—and only when that was allowed.

A few classes on cold-weather survival were given by our instructors, who were eager to start. They told us the purpose of the course was not only to teach every Marine to survive but how to fight and win in the cold-weather conditions of higher elevations and difficult terrain. Our first class lasted no more than an hour, but it was an important one, used to teach us the basics of cold-weather survival—how to conserve body heat by keeping clothing and equipment clean, avoiding overheating, wearing cold-weather clothing in loose layers, and by trying always to keep dry. The rest of the afternoon was spent forming our platoons into two-man teams and constructing shelter halves while trying to get acclimated to the higher altitude.

Each Marine carried in his pack one shelter half, six tent pegs, two sections of wooden tent poles, and several sections of guideline to construct a shelter. When properly assembled, the shelter halves would combine to serve two men with protection from the cold and snow, with interior warmth provided by the body heat of its shivering occupants.

Most of our instructors were veterans of Korea and knew what would be expected of us there, so they made our training as realistic and demanding as possible. They wanted us to learn not only how to survive in the cold but how to be successful in cold-weather combat. Even Mother Nature lent her helping hand toward realism—the cold clear weather we had found when we first arrived had changed by late on our second day, and it began to snow heavily. Marines were posted to brush the snow off our shelter halves to prevent them from collapsing, but by the time the snowstorm had passed, nearly a foot of wet snow blanketed the ground. Our final classes were lessons in first aid, prevention of frostbite, methods of cold-weather survival, and on how to lubricate our weapons in sub-zero conditions, all in preparation for our final tactical problem: the three-day war.

Before the tactical problems began, we were told we would not be allowed to use shelter halves for protection from the cold. Instead we would demonstrate our newly acquired abilities and construct makeshift shelters while we were in the field. Warming tents were set up in specified areas for only those Marines who had fallen into icy streams or who dropped through the snow-covered ice on the few ponds that dotted the training area. Using blank ammunition, we attacked and defended against a company of Marines of the aggressor force, part of the two hundred permanent personnel at the training center, who had the advantage of being intimately familiar with the local terrain.

The three-day war of company-level tactics was not designed to see only who could win and who could lose, but what it also revealed, an even more important issue—who could be trusted not to fall asleep on post, who exhibited common sense and leadership, and, of course, who among us was selfish and could not be trusted. These were all a

SERGEANT MAJOR, U.S. MARINES　　87

part of the lessons learned while we were training under conditions made much more difficult by the cold weather. We learned how demanding it was to survive in the cold while moving steadily through snow and carrying heavy packs. As a team, we learned to overcome such difficulties, and those lessons would help us through the most trying of times because they were the hard lessons that we would take into combat.

When the three-day war was over, we received word to move down to the lower base camp at Pickle Meadows, then climbed aboard the buses, which returned us to Camp Pendleton. I cannot recall ever being as cold as I had been while I was at Pickle Meadows, and the news that the buses had finally arrived was welcomed, but as we climbed aboard and settled in for the long ride back to Camp Pendleton, we knew each day brought us that much closer to our leaving for Korea.

We returned to Camp San Onofre on Sunday morning, and after being given only enough time to unpack our gear, we went directly to the rifle range and zeroed in our rifles for the last time. Every Marine's rifle was checked by a group of armorers, and if a Marine was not pleased with his weapon, every effort was made to give him a rifle which would make him feel a little more comfortable.

That night, on November 1, 1952, just before 0200, hundreds of Marine Corps trucks and buses lined up on Basilone Road, and as our serial numbers were called out, we boarded the vehicles that took us away from Camp Pendleton, down Highway 101, and deposited us at the foot of the Broadway pier in San Diego at 0500. There we were joined by several hundred Marines belonging to the 1st Marine Air Wing and several companies of navy Seabees and beachmasters—the men responsible for offloading personnel and equipment ashore, and we boarded the USS *Brewster*. The *Brewster* was the sister ship to the USS *Breckenridge* and the USS *Mann*, the very ships that had carried me to Guam and then home from Hawaii, respectively. I can still recall standing on the ship's main deck, close to noontime, watching as we sailed west, past

Point Loma, and headed for Korea. And though I was a sergeant, in the company of two thousand fellow Marines, many of whom I knew well, I had never before felt so very much alone.

CHAPTER 8

Early Lessons:
December 1952–February 1953

It took thirteen days for the USS *Brewster* to sail from San Diego to Kobe, Japan, but this time at sea proved to be a far better experience than the miserable time I'd suffered when I sailed west to Guam. Daily shipboard life was for the most part boring, and most of the junior Marines were assigned to a few of the ship's working parties or to duties in the galley; the rest of us were considered by the crew to be not much more than living baggage, and we spent our time cleaning and inspecting weapons, participating in organized PT, writing letters, playing cards, waiting endlessly in line for chow, and at night watching old movies shown on the open deck. As we got closer to Kobe, endless rumors began to spread of the possibility that we would be granted liberty in Japan, but only those Marines aboard the *Brewster* who were assigned to the division's air wing, along with the Seabees and beachmasters, would be allowed to disembark.

When we arrived in Kobe, sometime close to 0100, those of us who were still awake wished good luck to those Marines and sailors we had come to know under close-quarter living conditions, then stood against the steel railing on the ship's main deck and waved good-bye as they moved down the gangway and disappeared into the darkness of the busy port. No time was wasted in the off-loading of equipment, and within several hours, we departed for Korea. In preparation for our arrival there, the ship's captain announced over the ship's intercom system that in less than twelve hours we would be off-loading at Inchon Bay, which had been made famous two years earlier when Marines accomplished their surprise amphibious landing against the North Koreans.

The captain explained that because of the tidal range at Inchon—about thirty-two feet—the racing tides caused currents to run constantly between four to seven knots; all Marines would be called topside according to their living compartment numbers and then be ferried ashore by a variety of navy landing craft.

First to arrive alongside the *Brewster* were the LCMs (landing craft, mechanized) whose mission it was to land heavy vehicles, equipment and personnel. With a length of seventy-four feet, a beam of twenty-one feet, and a draft of only five feet, these boats could do nine knots and carry 150 combat-loaded Marines and sixty tons of cargo on each trip to shore. The larger LSUs, (landing ship utility, now designated LCU) were even more remarkable: Designed and built during World War II for the purpose of landing tanks, these landing craft had a bow ramp and a hinged stern gate aft, which permitted passage of vehicles thirteen feet or less in width. With an overall length of 135 feet, a beam of 29 feet, and a shallow draft (only 3.5 feet), the LCU was capable of a speed of eleven knots, while carrying four hundred combat-loaded Marines and 168 tons of cargo ashore.

When we arrived on cold Korean soil, we reformed into companies and boarded waiting U.S. Army trucks, then were taken by convoy six miles inland, to a onetime U.S. occupation forces supply depot called ASCOM City (Army Service Command) for further assignment. At ASCOM City, we were again herded into a holding area and remained outside, shivering in the cold, while Marines with specialized occupational ratings were called out from our ranks. This processing system went on for several hours until only Marines with infantry MOSs remained.

We reformed into rows of ten men and watched as a master sergeant marched across the front of our formation, and gesturing with his right hand, shouted, "From this rank down, 1st Marines. From this rank down, 5th Marines. The rest of you will join the 7th Marine Regiment."

As luck would have it, I was standing at the end of the last file of men selected to join the 5th Marine Regiment and was overjoyed in knowing I would be joining the same regiment I had been assigned to on Guam. My happiness, however, was short-lived when, out of curiosity, I asked a staff sergeant why so few men from our group had been assigned to the 7th Marine Regiment. His response was curt. "The 7th Marines are now in reserve, and we need to bring the other regiments up to strength because of the high number of recent casualties."

Those of us assigned to the 5th Marine Regiment were met by NCO representatives, and I was assigned to duty with the 1st Battalion, 5th Marines. We spent several hours unpacking our gear and rebuilding our combat packs, taking only our rifles and essential items of clothing and equipment we would need for life on the lines. Extra clothing we stuffed into our seabags and placed in a warehouse where, we were told, we could reclaim them twelve months later. We spent our first night in Korea at ASCOM City, as no traveling was permitted during the hours of darkness, and those Marine NCOs who had represented each of the three battalions of the regiment remained there with us to serve as our guides.

The next morning, following chow, we shouldered our packs and rifles and were led by the guides to our battalion's command post and from there to our further assignments at the rifle-company level. Along with a dozen other replacements, I went to C (Charlie) Company, where I was assigned as a squad leader in the company's 2d Platoon. I recall that little time was wasted on introducing NCOs to the Marines who ran Charlie Company. Our company commander was a captain named Mathews, who happened to be attending a briefing when we checked in. We were introduced to the company executive officer, 1st

Lieutenant Workman, who welcomed us aboard and, in turn, introduced us to our platoon guides. A sergeant named McCarthy who, I later learned, came from Lynn, Massachusetts, and was the 2d Platoon's guide, told me to follow him as we went on to meet our platoon commander, a staff sergeant and veteran of World War II named Stout. When we arrived at the platoon's position, Staff Sergeant Stout looked me over quickly, shook my hand, and told me to drop my gear and follow him into a heavily sandbagged bunker, where he began to orient me as to what was going on, saying something like, "Welcome to the 2d Platoon, Jacques. I'm glad you're here, and after I get done with you, Sergeant McCarthy will take you to meet Corporal Higgins, the acting squad leader. He'll tell you a lot more about what goes on around here, but for now, just relax, get accustomed to the occasional sound of artillery fire, and listen to what I tell you." During the next half hour Staff Sergeant Stout explained in great detail not only how our battalion had come to occupy its position but of Charlie Company's future plans in support of the battalion's mission.

In early and late October 1952, Chinese Communist forces had maneuvered to take five hills of critical terrain on the flanks of the 1st Marine Division. This action later became known as the Battle of the Hook, and ended with the Chinese having gained six combat outposts—three in the Korean Marine Corps sector and three to the north of our regimental line. This MLR (main line of resistance) was code-named the Jamestown line and ran west from Seoul, thirty miles east to the Samichan River. South Korean Marine forces were on our division's left flank and our right flank was protected by the soldiers of the U.S. Army's 25th Infantry Division. The responsibility for the center section of the Jamestown line, which was nearly five miles long, was given to the 1st Marine Division, commanded by MGen. Edwin Pollock, with the left half of the sector occupied by the 1st Marine Regiment, commanded by Col. Walter F. Layer, and the right half of the sector occupied by the 5th Marine Regiment, commanded by Col. Lewis W. Walt. The 7th Marine Regiment, commanded by Col. Thomas C. Moore, was in reserve. This two-up-and-one-in-reserve concept was used from the division level down to the platoon level, so it was not surprising to learn that while the 1st Battalion, commanded by LtCol. Jonas M. Platt, and the 2d Battalion, commanded by LtCol. Oscar F. Peatross, were in place along the Jamestown line, the 3d Battalion, 5th Marines, commanded by LtCol. Robert J. Oddy, was held in reserve behind the MLR.

Staff Sergeant Stout explained that officer platoon leaders came and went so fast in the company that Marines within the platoons hardly had enough time to learn their names before they were replaced because of wounds, reassignment to new and perhaps safer jobs, or death. Stout had been the platoon leader of the 2d Platoon for nearly two months, and I was one of the first sergeants to join the platoon in as many months. To become a rifle squad leader in combat was a great responsibility, and I looked forward to getting started. With the help of a Corporal Higgins, who had been assigned as the 3d Squad leader, I was able to do so.

The 3d Squad was made up of eleven Marines, not counting myself, formed into three fire teams. Each fire team had a designated Browning automatic rifleman. Corporal Higgins was now the first fire team leader and had DeLuca and Fuller (a BAR man) with him. My second fire team leader was a private first class named Augire, who had with him Davis, Burns, and Fry, the second BAR man and a trained flamethrower operator. The third fire team consisted of Marines Lopez, Butler, Signoski, and Sutton, the squad's third BAR man. The twelve of us occupied one reinforced bunker and four two-man fighting holes within a sector of the 2d Platoon's area of responsibility, which extended nearly three hundred yards along the company's linear frontage.

It was here, along a rocky, frozen ridgeline not more than one hundred and fifty yards above sea level, a place I would walk over at least a dozen times each day and night, that I became intimately familiar with every rock, stone, and hole in sight and began to practice the trade of being a Marine squad leader in combat. As I walked the ground assigned to the squad, along with Corporal Higgins, I introduced myself to each member of the squad, climbed into and inspected their primary and secondary firing positions, and inspected every man's weapon. I recorded, in a small notebook that I kept in my overcoat pocket, all that I observed. It was obvious that Corporal Higgins had done an exceptional job as squad leader, and I am sure he resented my assignment as the new squad leader, but I am equally convinced he was relieved in relinquishing the responsibility for the lives of ten Marines to me. Thanks to him, I inherited a squad of combat-veteran Marines who were as ready to help me as I was eager to lead them. As I saw it, we had only two enemies—the Chinese Communists and the extreme cold.

My first days spent on the MLR were cold, unhurried, but never boring—a squad leader always has something to do. There were no large movements along the MLR as orders from above had been given to cease all offensive actions in December, but those Marines who had heard of "truce-talk" knew the Chinese Communists would move against us whenever and wherever they thought our guard was down. We were cautioned that renewed negotiations to bring an end to the war were not to be believed, and we prepared ourselves for new assaults along our line of defense. Although in more genteel circles, life on the line was known as "positional warfare," to those of us who occupied the two-man fighting holes it was nothing more than trench warfare.

* * *

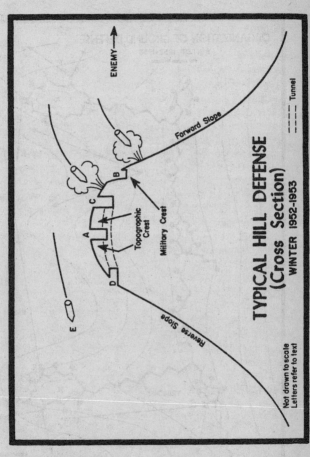

TYPICAL HILL DEFENSE
(Cross Section)
WINTER 1952-1953

Not drawn to scale
Letters refer to text

----- Tunnel

ENEMY

Forward Slope

Reverse Slope

Military Crest

Topographic Crest

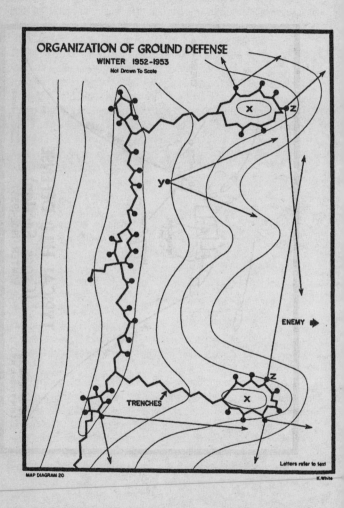

ORGANIZATION OF GROUND DEFENSE
WINTER 1952-1953
Not Drawn To Scale

x

z

y

ENEMY ➡

z

x

TRENCHES

Letters refer to text

MAP DIAGRAM 20

K. White

During the winter months of 1952–1953, the 1st Marine Division modified the organization of its tactical defense, although it retained the basic concept of the combat outpost system as the backbone of the MLR defense. Development of much of the Kansas line, a secondary defense line, and parts of the Marine MLR during this period reflected several new ideas on how the ground defense could be better organized. Recent experience during Communist attacks had shown defensive emplacements and positions could be dug deeper and belowground to withstand massed enemy fire. Contrary to traditional concepts, it had also been found that centering the defense on the military crest of a hill, that point along the slope of a hill at which maximum observation up and down the hill can be obtained, was not always the best procedure. Emplacement of machine guns downslope or in low firing positions to cover draws or flat ground was not entirely suitable to the Korean terrain, enemy, or nature of positional warfare.

Altered defense concepts, beginning late in 1952, took on the following form:

(1) The trace of defensive positions followed the topographical crest (A) rather than the military crest (B) of key terrain features.

(Map diagrams 1 and 2 illustrate these changes.)

(2) Fighting positions and emplacements were dug a short distance downslope (C) from the topographical crest.

(3) Trenches on the topographical crest permitted easier, faster, and more protected access to fighting positions from the reverse slope and support area (D).

(4) Positions on the topographical crest were less vulnerable to enemy artillery because it was more difficult for the enemy to adjust his fire on these positions than on trenches dug along the military crest. Many shells simply passed over the top (E) of the hill.

(5) Certain hills and noses were selected and organized so that trenches and gun emplacements, encir-

cling the crest, would form mutually supporting positions (X).

(6) Machine guns were moved from the draws (Y) to hilltops and noses (Z) where better long-range observation and fields of fire existed.[1]

Another change in the improvement of field fortifications came into use during the winter months. A different type of barbed-wire obstacle, called "Canadian," "random," or "double-apron" wire, began to find favor with Marine infantrymen. Canadian wire consisted of two parallel rows of three-strand barbed-wire fencing, erected about three feet apart. The void was filled in with additional barbed wire, placed at random, but connected to the parallel fences. Besides being simple and fast to emplace, Canadian wire became more entangled by artillery shelling, which quickly ripped apart the standard double-apron barbed wire previously used in COP (combat outpost) slope defenses. And, in preparation for things to come, my squad, as part of a company-size operation, began to prepare for a series of day and night ambushes and raids against known Chinese Communist positions, located not more than several hundred yards distance from our own positions.

During the morning of my third day as squad leader, I was summoned to Staff Sergeant Stout's bunker and learned our platoon had been selected to conduct a night ambush. We would leave our positions late in the day, make our way to a planned ambush position nearly four hundred yards forward of our lines, then lie in wait for a Chinese patrol to wander into the kill zone. Recently there had been an increase in the number of enemy patrols sighted, and it was explained to all squad leaders that Colonel Walt now wanted more night ambushes so his Marines would become more familiar with territory not only

---

1. Lieutenant Colonel Pat Meid, USMCR, and Major J. M. Yingling, USMC, *US Marine Corps Operations in Korea 1950–1953*, Vol. 5, *Operations in West Korea* Ch. 6, p. 251.

to our front but on our flanks, as well. In preparation for the night's patrol, I gathered up my fire-team leaders and told them what I wanted accomplished by 1400 that afternoon. And, based on the information that I had received from Staff Sergeant Stout, on the ground outside of our bunker I prepared a sand table of the area in which we'd go and studied for my first venture into combat.

At 1500, I inspected the equipment and weapons of each member of my squad. Dressed in cold-weather clothing and wearing a helmet, insulated "Mickey Mouse" boots, and armored vests, each rifleman also wore a cartridge belt and suspenders and carried ten eight-shot clips of rifle ammunition, two M-2 fragmentation grenades, a bayonet, one first-aid pouch, and one canteen of water. Using the terrain model and a map, I indicated the three checkpoints where we would stop and passed along the night's challenge and password, which would be used by all members of the platoon as a recognition signal whenever we halted and when we returned through friendly lines. Satisfied that every member of the squad knew his position in the line of march and what our squad's specific mission was during the ambush portion of the patrol, I dismissed the squad, telling them to return to my position at 1950 that evening for one last inspection.

Carrying three .30-caliber BARs, my squad took its place in the center of the platoon, and we began a single-file move east, away from Charlie Company's lines and toward the company's right boundary. As we moved cautiously downhill, the single strand of communications wire that linked us with the company commander's headquarters element was covered with snow, making it all but invisible. Staff Sergeant Stout, located near the front of the platoon with the 1st Squad, had his primary radio operator behind him. At the rear of our column, moving with the 2nd Squad, was Sergeant McCarthy, the platoon guide, with a secondary radio operator following close behind.

Our challenge for the night was the phrase "cake walk," and because of the difficulty that Orientals have in pronouncing words which contain the letter *L*, the proper whispered response was "long life." And in the event any response to a challenge should be returned sounding like "wrong rife," our instructions were to answer with a well-placed hand grenade.

Nearly an hour after leaving our company's lines, we arrived at the first checkpoint and received the hand and arm signal to stop and rest. This was not done by simply flopping one's ass down in the snow, but with each Marine slowly lowering himself into a comfortable sitting position and facing in a predetermined direction to protect the body of the platoon, while still being able to remain silent and watchful, ready to respond quickly in the event we might encounter an enemy patrol.

After the first checkpoint, our next stop would be the selected ambush position, where the 1st Squad would set up on the left flank; my squad would be dispersed across the center of the kill zone, and the 2nd Squad would protect the platoon's right flank and rear.

When we arrived near the ambush position, we stopped and waited until the two security teams moved into position to protect our movement forward, and then I moved my squad into place. Our movement to the ambush site had been deliberate and painstakingly slow, but I was pleased no one in the squad had coughed, farted, fallen down, or otherwise alerted the Chinese to our progress into their territory. Now, it would simply be a matter of our sitting and waiting in the freezing cold for the opportunity to surprise the Chinese at doing what we had just accomplished.

With the help of a weak but illuminating quarter moon occasionally made visible through passing dark clouds, I studied the rocky open area in front of my squad and began to familiarize myself with the irregular forms of large rocks and brush outlined by the snow. Less than a hundred yards to my left, a small finger ran from a hill down to a cluster of dark objects. I wasn't sure what I was looking at, but assumed it was nothing more than a patch of waist-high perennial bushes. But the more I scanned the area, the more my eyes returned to the same object, and

I was soon concentrating on only that object for what seemed to be a very long time. When the moonlight drifted across our front, I was sure the object had moved, and not wanting to give away my position to a Chinese sniper by moving or speaking to alert my squad to his presence, I continued to focus on the enemy soldier, straining my eyes until I could positively identify his outline against the snow-white background. He must not have seen us, so when the wind picked up and he began to sway slowly back and forth, I carefully raised my M-1, found his outline in my rifle sights, and pressed my gloved index finger against the firm steel trigger. I gradually took up the slack until the hammer fell, and I lost sight of him from the recoil of the shot.

Within seconds I was joined by Staff Sergeant Stout. "What the hell did you fire at, Jacques?" he demanded in a whisper.

"There was a Chink out there at the end of that finger," I said. But no one else had joined my firing, and I knew at that moment that the first enemy target I had engaged in combat was a Korean bush.

We remained in our positions for hours, and whether or not Staff Sergeant Stout did so hoping to attract a Chinese patrol made curious by my stupidity, or by his not wanting to risk walking into a hasty Chinese counterambush, I'll never know, but while we remained at the ambush site, feelings of guilt washed over me, and I began to feel humiliated. As dawn began to crawl over the eastern hills, our platoon snaked back through the safety of Charlie Company's lines without incident. Before I dismissed the members of my squad, telling them to get some rest, I instructed them to return to my position for a brief meeting at 1300 that afternoon.

Corporal Higgins woke me just before 1300, saying that the squad was assembled and waiting. From when we left the ambush site until we had trudged back to Charlie Company's area, I had mulled over, countless times, what I wanted to say but those thoughts had been lost during hours of deep sleep. I grabbed my rifle, walked up to where the squad was seated, and as they gazed up at me I began to speak. "I want to apologize to all of you for what happened last night. I was convinced that I was looking at a Chink sniper, and I wanted to get him before he got any of you." But before I could say another word, the men of the squad stood up, and I was uncertain for what reason, until I heard a voice from behind me tell the squad to sit back down. Accompanied by Staff Sergeant Stout, Captain Mathews, the company commander, had been walking up behind me and heard what I said.

The captain stepped up beside me and said, "Sergeant Jacques doesn't have a damned thing to apologize for. He might think that he made a mistake last night, but in my book, what he did was reasonable. I'd rather have Marines with me in this outfit who are not afraid to fire their weapons than have Marines who would hesitate and allow a Chink to get in close enough to throw a couple of grenades. Every one of us knows how easy it is to let our imaginations play tricks on us, especially at night. It's happened to me, and if it hasn't happened to any of you, just wait, 'cause it will. Sergeant Jacques, you and your men did a good job out there last night. Now, dismiss your squad."

The weight of the world seemed to have been lifted from my shoulders by the captain. I knew that I had been forgiven by him, my platoon commander, and by the members of my squad. All that remained was for me to forgive myself.

During January, February, and March of 1953, the battle of patrols and enemy probes began to increase sharply, and our company participated in numerous raids to ambush Chinese Communists, snatch prisoners, and to tear up tunnels, trenches, and bunkers. My inexperience as a squad leader was short-lived. By mid-March I had participated in dozens of patrols, ambushes, and platoon-size raids. I learned quickly, and the Marines in my squad and I survived.

CHAPTER 9

The Battle for the Nevada Cities

Background

As the 1st Marine Division continued to revamp and strengthen its primary defenses, a change of pace on the battlefront was gradually being felt. Only a few major raids had taken place during November, December, and January, and these involved no transfer of real estate. Casualties had been light. Artillery rounds, both incoming and outgoing, had dropped substantially. By February, however, it became apparent the period of winter inactivity was nearing an end.

Taking the initiative in the renewed action was the 5th Marines, occupants of the right regimental sector of the MLR since 25 January. The next month, the regiment conducted three successful daytime raids against fortified positions. Targets for the initial action, on 3 February, were two consistently troublesome hills, 31 and 31A in the Ungok hill mass, north of the left battalion sector.

Since all battalions of the 5th Marines were to be involved either directly or indirectly in Operation CLAMBAKE, the initial planning and actual raid was to be carried out by the regimental commander, Colonel Walt. CLAMBAKE required especially thorough coordination of the heavy fire support since it was to be launched with a tank-artillery feint against several CCF positions (Hill 104, Kumgok, and Red Hill) generally west of the Ungok objective area. The two target hills were to be assaulted by reinforced platoons from Company A (Capt. Don H. Blanchard) of the reserve battalion 1/5, commanded by LtCol. Jonas M. Platt, who was responsible for the later planning stages of the raid. It was anticipated intensive air and artillery preparation on the feint objectives and the movement of gun and flame tanks during the diversion would gain the element of surprise for the assault platoons. Thus, the Marines hoped to take prisoners, the main purpose of the raid, and to kill enemy troops and destroy their defenses.

During the five weeks of preparation, every aspect of the maneuver was thoroughly reviewed and rehearsed. All participating units took part in the planning conferences. Routes were reconnoitered, mines cleared, and fire concentrations plotted and registered. Marine Air Group (MAG) 12 pilots studied the target areas from the nearby MLR. Six rehearsals, including practice in casualty evacuation, uncovered potential problem areas. Final rehearsal was held 1 February, with artillery and air preparation made against feint objectives. Four close-air-support strikes were conducted that day and the next as part of the plan to divert enemy attention from the CLAMBAKE destruction mission.

Shortly after first light on 3 February, three platoons of tanks rumbled across the MLR to assault the feint area. A heavy "false" artillery preparation by 1/11 (1st Battalion, 11th Marines) was also placed on the three western enemy hills as well as direct fire from gun and flame tanks. The two Marine assault forces, one against each hill, moved out, armed with flamethrowers, 3.5-inch rockets, machine guns, grenades, satchel charges, bangalore torpedoes, and automatic weapons. Enemy forces occupying the positions made three separate counterattack attempts, which were blunted by Marine supporting arms. During the infantry attack, friendly air hovered on station, and artillery fired continuous counterbattery and countermortar fire.

With the exception of the change of withdrawal route of one of the assault teams, the 5th Marines reported the operation was carried out according to plan. Company A tanks had swung left across the frozen rice paddies to provide left-flank security for the infantry and to interdict trench lines which connected with the Ungok objective. Intense enemy fire lashed the armored vehicles as they approached Kumgok and Red Hill as well as those supporting tanks which remained on the MLR. Air, artillery, infantry, and tanks produced an estimated 390 Chinese casualties (including 90 known KIA) in addition to damaged or destroyed trench lines, tunnels, caves, bunkers, and weapons of the enemy. Marine losses were fourteen killed and ninety-one wounded. One flame tank was lost.

As in the case of the 1st Marines WAKEUP raid in November 1952, CLAMBAKE was important not so much in accomplishing its primary mission (actually no POWs were taken) as in lessons learned. One of these was to reemphasize the fact that thorough preparation helped to ensure smooth coordination of infantry and supporting arms. In his report of the operation, Lieutenant Colonel Platt wrote, "minute planning to the last detail along with carefully executed rehearsals are basic to success in actions of this type." He further noted "confidence and enthusiasm stimulated by the rehearsals are assets which cannot be overlooked." The battalion commander also commented on the importance of planning for both troop withdrawal and maintaining a flexible schedule of fires by supporting arms. Air, artillery, and tanks all employed fire plans which could be readily adjusted to meet the changing tactical situation.

On the ground, flame was found to be the best weapon for neutralizing the well-fortified CCF caves. From Company A, 1st Tank Battalion, came information about Chinese 3.5-inch rocket-launcher teams used in antitank defense. Several of these tank-killer teams had run down the trench line, holding small bushes in front of them. The enemy then boldly advanced through a hail of bullets to within fifteen to twenty yards of the Marine tank before opening fire with their rockets. Short bursts of flame from headquarters tanks soon caused even the most intrepid to beat a hurried retreat.[1]

Concluding his after-action report of CLAMBAKE, the regimental commander, Colonel Walt, observed:

> In addition to inflicting large numbers of casualties and destruction upon the enemy, the operation served a secondary purpose, none the less important. It provided excellent training and experience for the various infantry and supporting arms staffs involved, helping to develop them into a smoothly functioning infantry-air-artillery-tank team.[2]

Shortly before the end of the month, the 5th Marines made another major assault. As in the earlier CLAMBAKE, this raid was again in two-reinforced-platoon size and made during the early daylight hours of 25 February. This time the objective was a single height, Hill 15 (Detroit), two miles east of the CLAMBAKE objective. LtCol. Oscar F. Peatross's 2/5, manning the extreme right sector of the division, gave the assignment to Company F, then under Capt. Harold D. Kurth, Jr. Planning for Operation CHARLIE, a standard-type kill-capture-and-destroy raid, was carried out in much the same detailed manner as the earlier 1/5 raid.

Operation CHARLIE differed somewhat in concept in that the 2/5 operational plan attempted to gain surprise by launching the attack during the BMNT (Beginning morning nautical twilight is the period before sunrise or after sunset when visibility is limited to approximately

---

1. Lieutenant Colonel Pat Meid, USMCR, and Major J. M. Yingling, USMC, *US Marine Corps Operations in Korea 1950–1953*, Vol. 5, *Operations in West Korea* Ch. 6, pp. 255–258.
2. 5th Marine ComD, Feb 53, APP6, dtd 20 Feb 53, p. 3.

three hundred yards.) period as well as in use of smoke to screen enemy observation. Supporting arms preparatory fires had been carefully plotted, including the precise destruction aerial bombing which had proved so effective in the CLAMBAKE assault. In actual execution of CHARLIE, however, bad weather prevented the use of almost all of the planned pre–D day and D day air strikes. Upon reaching the Detroit objective area, assault Marines "found the majority of enemy installations were relatively undamaged, even though subjected to heavy bombardment by other supporting arms." Artillery preparatory fires had been employed successfully to isolate the battle area, and howitzer and tank missions supported the raid. (In nearly three hours of firing, the 11th Marines and its reinforcing and attached units, including the 1st Royal Canadian Artillery, expended 11,881 rounds.)

Between the time of CLAMBAKE and CHARLIE, a series of Marine and enemy small-unit actions erupted, which were soon to become a way of life for the MLR combatants. By mounting sporadic outpost attacks and increasing their use of artillery, the Chinese were beginning to demonstrate a more aggressive attitude than in recent months. On the night of 12–13 February, a CCF platoon, supported by mortars and artillery, probed COP Hedy (Hill 124), in the right battalion of the center regimental sector, held by Lieutenant Colonel Barret's 3/7. On the next night, it was the Korean Marines who turned aggressor. Two of their platoons raided Hill 240 on the west bank of the Sachon, nearly three miles north of the mouth of the river. The following night, a 7th Marines patrol, moving into ambush positions, was itself stalked by a large CCF patrol. When reinforcements, including armored vehicles, moved out from the MLR to support the Marines, the Chinese hastily withdrew.

Three more contacts were made before the end of the month along the division front. On 19 February, CCF soldiers, in two-platoon strength, engaged KMC sentries forward of COP 33, located about a mile east of the action the previous week. After the initial exchange of small-arms fire, the Koreans moved back to the outpost and called down supporting fires on the Chinese. Artillery and mortars tore into the attackers, causing numerous casualties and forcing the enemy to withdraw. On the morning of 22 February, a raiding party from the 5th Marines assaulted a smaller enemy force at Hill 35A, approximately one thousand three hundred yards southwest of the Ungok hills. In this second raid staged by the 5th Marines that month, assault troops of H/3/5 used flamethrowers in the early stages of the action to help clear enemy trenches of hostile grenade throwers.

Late the next night a 7th Marine unit, consisting of a reinforced platoon and four M-46 tanks, set out to raid Yoke, located near the peace corridor five miles north of Freedom Bridge. The assault against the position never happened. At 2137, as the B/1/7 platoon moved into preliminary positions on Hill 90, north of the ultimate objective, a Chinese company ambushed the patrol from three sides. When the Marines closed with the enemy in hand-to-hand fighting, a support platoon was sent from the MLR. After an intense thirty-minute firefight, the CCF began withdrawing at 0138. Enemy losses were listed as forty-five counted KIA, thirty-three estimated KIA, and thirty-five estimated WIA. As a result of the assault, orders for the 7th Marines raid on Yoke were cancelled. Marine casualties numbered five killed, twenty-two wounded.

Where February was characterized by a marked increase in ground contacts between Marines and their CCF adversaries, during the first part of March they again assumed an inactive posture. Marine patrols reported few contacts. Except for a KMC raid on 3 March, little action that could be considered a sizable engagement took place until after midmonth. On the sixteenth, there was a brief skirmish involving a 5th Marines combat patrol near Reno and a short firefight between Carson defenders and an enemy squad. The next night, a Chinese platoon, waiting near Vegas for a Marine patrol to pass by, was itself put to flight by the patrol.

Two encounters with the Chinese Communists on 19 March marked the heaviest action yet of the month. Early that morning a predawn raid was staged by B/1/5, commanded by Capt. Theodore J. Mildner, at Hill 31A, one of the Ungok twin objectives in CLAMBAKE the previous month. The March Item Company raid employed 111 Marines. One platoon was to make the assault, the second platoon to support the operation and assist in casualty evacuation. Following a series of nearly a dozen air strikes on the objective and artillery preparation, Captain Mildner's two assault platoons jumped off from the MLR checkpoint at 0518. As usually happened in such operations, the preliminary fire drove the Chinese to reverse-slope defenses. No enemy POWs were taken, and at 0700, the Marine units disengaged due to casualties sustained from enemy shelling and machine-gun fire. (Prior to this raid, various combinations of flamethrower fuels and pressure were extensively used. The purpose was to determine the maximum effective range of the flamethrower teams in order to "neutralize the hand-grenade throwing potential of the enemy, this being one of the major problems confronting assault elements on other raids.")

Earlier that same day, two attacks had been made simultaneously by the enemy on outposts in the center regimental sector where the 1st Marines had relieved the 7th on 10 March. At 0105, one CCF company struck in the vicinity of Hedy while a second lunged at Esther, about 1.5 miles east. When a G/3/1 reconnaissance patrol operating forward of COP Esther observed enemy movement, the Marines pulled back to the outpost, alerting it to the impending attack. After a heavy incoming artillery barrage, the enemy assaulted the outpost, but when a three-hour effort failed to carry the position, the attackers withdrew. By that time, the Chinese company which had hit COP Hedy had also broken off the attack.

Actually the fight in Capt. Carl R. Gray's Company H sector, to the rear of Hedy, was mainly at the MLR, for the Chinese indulged in merely a brief firefight at the latter outpost, bypassing it in favor of a crack at Jamestown. The main line of resistance failed to yield to the enemy thrust, which was supported by twenty-four hundred rounds of mortar and artillery fire along the MLR and outposts.

After being thwarted by Hedy-Esther defenses, the enemy shifted his efforts westward to the 1st KMC area. The Korean regiment received the brunt of the enemy's minor infantry probes immediately preceding the Nevada cities battle. Late on 25 March, a series of skirmishes broke out in the 1st Marines sector between one- or two-platoon-size Chinese infantry forces and Marine outpost defenders. Following a quiet daylight spell on the twenty-sixth, the Chinese resumed the offensive with a probe at COP Dagmar. This coincided with what developed into a massive regimental assault unleashed against Carson, Reno, and Vegas, outposts in the 5th Marine sector to the right. There Colonel Walt's regiment would shortly be the target of *the bloodiest Chinese attack to date* on the 1st Marine Division in West Korea.[3]

The semicircular hill mass that made up combat outposts Carson, Reno, and Vegas lay just below the 38th parallel and was situated only fifteen hundred yards north of the MLR, sitting squarely in the middle of the ancient invasion route to Seoul, just thirty miles to the south. These three hills offered the Chinese a commanding view of the land they so desperately wanted, and with their advance south having been held in check since October, gaining the three prominent positions located so close to

3. Meid and Yingling, Ch. 6, pp. 255–261.

the MLR would not only be a great military victory but a psychological triumph as well.

On the morning of 23 March, our reinforced platoon was relieved in place, and we returned to occupy defensive positions along the MLR, following a ten-day stay out on Reno. The outpost was dug in on a ridgeline that fronted enemy Hill 25A, also known as Hill 150, directly to the north. Reno was also the one most distant from Marine lines. Two main trenches led into the outpost, a reverse slope fortification. The forward trench, perpendicular to the ridgeline fronting the position, was approximately twenty yards long and eight feet deep. The second, to the rear, and about the same length, traversed the outpost from east to west. Approaching from the entrance, or "gate" of the MLR, the two trenches joined on the left, forming a ninety-degree angle. A cave, located in the arc between the trenches, provided overcrowding living quarters where personnel slept on the dirt floor or atop sandbags, since there were no bunkers on Reno. The ammunition supplies, as well as the corpsman's first-aid facilities, were cached in the cave. Sanitation was a problem as the area within the perimeter of the outpost smelled terribly; months of use contributed to the heaps of garbage, rotting C rations, and the stench of fecal waste.

A major blocking position one hundred yards south and to the rear of Reno was covered by Marines posted in the trench line. Left of the forward trench, protective wire was placed across the topographical crest. This left finger had good observation to Ungok and Arrowhead, but also served as an approach to Carson. Twenty-four-hour security at Reno included an automatic rifleman at the gate, at post 1, on the forward trench, and post 2, which was at the extreme right of the rear trench. Ten machine gunners were also detailed as night watch on the guns. During the daytime, they were responsible for maintenance of ammunition and weapons, which consisted of eighteen M-1 rifles, six BARs, five A-4 light machine guns (LMGs), two flamethrowers, one carbine, and seven pistols.

The biggest defense problem at Reno stemmed from restricted fields of fire. Able gun, for instance, covered the rear of the topographical crest and Hills 31 and 67, on the left. But dead space masked its effectiveness practically from the base of Hill 67 to the gun itself. The Baker gun, protecting the reverse slope, had a lateral firing range of from ten to thirty feet. Charlie gun maintained an unlimited sector of fire, approximately 180 degrees, and Dog gun covered the rear. As there were no prepared machine-gun positions, they were fired from the parapet protecting both the fighting holes and firing positions in the trench line. The two fighting holes were manned by BARs, and two were used as machine-gun posts.

Customarily forty to forty-three men were on duty at COP Reno. In fact, this number had been viewed dubiously as being "far too many to man defensive positions at any one time," by the commanding officer of the 1/5 Weapons Company during a survey earlier in the month, noting that "about 20 could adequately defend the position."[4] A six-man force was detailed as a permanent working party for the improvement of fortifications; sound-power phones linked all positions, and field phones connected the forward observer with gun positions. Overall, for proper defense, Reno depended heavily upon support fires from Carson and Vegas, on its right flank.[5]

As we set about cleaning our weapons and equipment and improving our former positions, we knew we'd been very lucky not to have been the objective of the creeping tactics used by the Chinese to test our defenses during the past ten days and nights. From where we were, looking north from our sector on the western (left) part of the regimental line, Carson was 1,000 yards to our left front; Reno was 450 yards to the right and forward of Carson, and Vegas, at 550 feet the tallest of the three hills, was located 1,000 yards to the right of Reno. Only five hundred yards forward of our platoon's position on the MLR, and

----

4. 1/5 ComD, Mar 53, Inspection of COP Reno, by Capt. H. A. Checklou, dtd 12 Mar 53, p. 4.
5. Meid and Yingling, Ch. 7, p. 275.

directly behind Reno, was a small hill called Reno Block, used as a supporting defensive position and manned by a reinforced squad to help protect Reno from the possibility of enemy attack from behind.

I recall late in the afternoon of Thursday, 26 March, our platoon was notified we would be providing cover firing for a reinforced squad from Charlie Company as they moved up to occupy their position on Reno Block. Having lost Corporal Higgins and Private First Class Burns to their rotation dates back to the States, I now had nine Marines in my squad. Alert and ready to respond to any trouble, we were peering out in the direction of Reno Block when, exactly at 1900, the Chinese forces began a continuous barrage combining 122mm artillery and 120mm mortar fire with machine-gun fire from their strongholds on Hills 44, 40, 35, and 33, exploding all along the 5th Marines' lines. At the same time, 5th Marine outposts Reno and Carson, each manned by a reinforced rifle platoon from C/1/5, came under attack from Chinese mortars and 76mm artillery.

Within a few minutes, my squad was called up to join a composite platoon as a "clutch unit" to go out and help reinforce the Marines fighting on Reno Block. This order was easier given than it was executed. The open ground in front of us was continuously being heaved skyward as artillery and heavy-mortar rounds slammed to earth. With no lull to the number of incoming rounds, there was little time to organize our movement. We understood the urgency of moving to help support Reno Block, but it was a matter of heroic individual effort to get there. Having returned from Reno only three days earlier, we knew the closer we got to reaching Reno Block the closer we would get to a minefield we had encountered during our return to the MLR. The enemy mines, hidden under snow, had been revealed after several days of torrential warm spring rain. The exposed antitank "box-mines" had been laid months earlier in the narrow avenues of approach and now presented a significant problem to anyone who dared to approach the area.

I had started to move off the MLR, with DeLuca, Fuller, Davis, and Augire right behind me, and Lopez, Fry, Sutton, and Signoski were in trace of them. But by the time we had moved less than three hundred yards, the number of incoming artillery rounds had increased, making progress virtually impossible. We could do little more than stay in the cold mud, hoping we would not fall victim to the continuous barrage.

By 2200 hours, my squad had been decimated from incoming artillery, mortar and small-arms fire. DeLuca was dead, killed by shrapnel, as were Augire, Signoski, and Davis. Sutton had been seriously wounded, along with Lopez. Miraculously, only Fry and myself had escaped being hit. Sometime close to 2300, Fry and I and a half dozen Marines of the platoon were joined by a squad of Marines from Item Company, 3/5, who had been in reserve and directed to shift from their positions on our right flank and come to the aid of those Marines still holding out on Reno Block. But despite our attempts to move up to the Block, we could get no closer than several hundred yards from it. We were caught in the middle of a no-man's-land crisscrossed with enemy machine-gun fire, able to stay alive only by killing the approaching Chinese soldiers silhouetted by the light of flares, and by not daring to move and expose ourselves. At that moment, a Marine's world was no greater than the five yards of the cold muddy ground around him. In the distance we could see that the Chinese had begun their assault on Reno and were using flamethrowers to push Marines back toward the top of the hill.

At the same time 5th Marines outposts Carson and Reno, each manned by a reinforced rifle platoon from C/1/5, came under attack from Chinese mortars and 76mm artillery. Approximately 1,200 mortar rounds struck COP Carson by 1920. As men of D/2/5, some of whom had been detailed to Carson earlier that night for an ambush, reported, "one round per second from Chinese 60mm and 82mm landed in or around our position during the first 20 minutes of the engagement. Thereafter, one round was received every 40 seconds until about 2200.[6]

Within ten minutes, Vegas, farthest east of the four OPs in 1/5 territory, became the object of serious enemy attention. Meanwhile, outposts Berlin and East Berlin, still farther east in the 3/5 sector proper, were also engaged by small-arms fire and mortars from Hills 15 (Detroit), and 13 (Frisco), and 98 to the northeast. As the coordinated fire attack raged throughout the 5th Marines regimental front, preparatory fire and diversionary probes hit the 1st Marines' sector. Outposts Hedy, Bunker, Esther, and Dagmar, in the center regimental area, were struck by small arms, mortars, and artillery shells a few minutes before 1900. Platoon- and squad-strength limited attacks were conducted against Dagmar, Hedy, and Esther, and enemy units were sighted moving in front of the KMC, farther west along the MLR.

At precisely 1910, a force of thirty-five hundred Chinese from the 358th Regiment, 120th Division, 46th CCF Army swarmed down from Ungok, Arrowhead, Hill 25A, and Hill 190, and launched a massive assault in regimental strength against the 5th Marine sector. (Map 6.) Elements of six companies from three battalions converged on the area from three directions. Two enemy platoons of the 1st Company, 1st Battalion from Ungok struck Carson while one infantry company each, initially, began direct assaults on Reno and Vegas. Units from 3d Company, 1st Battalion, from Arrowhead and Hill 29, crossed the Seoul road to hit Reno in a direct frontal assault. Elements of 7th Company, 3d Battalion moved down from Hill 190, a mile north, to encircle the left flank of Reno and strike from the rear of the Marine position. Other Chinese soldiers of 8th Company, 3d Battalion, supported by 9th Company, moved some five hundred yards south of their

6. Ibid., p. 280.

ridgeline positions on hills 25A and 155, immediately north of Vegas, to attack the outpost head-on.

As the enemy regiment advanced toward its objectives in a coordinated three-pronged attack, Marine artillery fired protective boxes and variable time (VT) on the outposts and routes of approach from the west, north, and east. Defending infantry also called down organic 60mm and 81mm mortar barrages. Actually, prior to the Chinese onslaught at 1900, 1/11, the direct support artillery battalion for the 5th Marines, began a registration and had laid its howitzer fires on the active area. The artillery regiment had also set up conference calls linking its four organic battalions and supporting U.S. Army units. The fire plan for the 11th Marines provided for its three light battalions to cover enemy approaches and assembly areas, deliver protective boxing and VT fires requested by the outposts, and furnish countermortar missions called in by forward observers. Medium artillery battalions were to reinforce defensive fires and destroy hostile mortars and artillery emplacements. Heavy 8-inch howitzer support would silence enemy counterbattery weapons. As it happened, on the night of the twenty-sixth Marine tanks were also registered before the time of the actual attack; eleven Company A tanks had earlier rumbled into firing position on the MLR to provide mechanized support for an infantry raid at dawn the next morning.

Despite this immediate Marine fire support, the Chinese invaders outnumbered the platoons holding the outposts by twenty to one. The sheer weight of numbers was the decisive factor. By 1935, the enemy had penetrated the lower trenches of Carson and Reno. At 2000, an hour after the onset of the attack, the Marines were throwing back Chinese forces with bayonets, knives, rifles, and bare fists in the close, heavy fighting at Carson. There, where fifty-four men had been on duty at the time of the initial attack, the outpost was successfully holding off the Communists. Four reinforcing squads quickly dispatched by battalion were designated to further strengthen the position. At 2000, just when D/1/5 and C/1/5 relief squads were leaving for the outpost, the Chinese unexpectedly began to release their grip on Carson in order to concentrate on Reno and Vegas, the two more isolated COPs that were farther from the MLR.

By 2000, developments at Reno and Vegas were more ominous. At Reno, two companies of CCF soldiers thrust into the position from a frontal and flank attack. Within a half hour they had made their way into the trench defenses. Although VT fires placed on the outpost and white phosphorous (WP) flare shells outlined the enemy for the gunners, Chinese in overpowering numbers continued to batter the Marine post. Due to the lack of fighting trenches and to limited fields of fire, Reno's defenders fell back on a cave defense within a half hour of the assault. (At both Reno and Vegas the Marines had moved into caves for protection from VT fire. This was the plan in event of an overwhelming enemy attack. In contrast, the detachment at Carson fought from covered fighting holes and employed the cave there only to get their wounded out of direct fire.)

At 2030, a message requesting more VT rounds and reinforcements indicated that the enemy had sealed all entrances to the cave and that the men were suffering from lack of air. Of the forty or so Company C Marines on the outpost at the time of attack an hour and a half earlier, only seven were reported still able to fight. To enable friendly machine guns and rockets to chop up the enemy, more illumination was furnished by artillery and by a flare plane that arrived on station at 2205. Two Marine tanks in position behind Reno were alerted and put their 90mm fires to good use on the enemy and his weapons emplacements.

Meanwhile, at Vegas, the situation was also deteriorating: By 1950, less than an hour after the enemy's first volley, more than a hundred Chinese had moved up under the perimeter of exploding shells and Marine defensive fires into the lower trenches. Ten minutes later, the Marines were forced to give way to overwhelming numbers of enemy soldiers who began to swarm over the outpost.

In addition to the sudden force and onslaught of the enemy, communications difficulties also plagued Marine detachments on the outposts, particularly at Vegas. Enemy mortar and artillery aimed at the main line command posts (CPs) had wrecked the ground lines. As early as 1940, communications between the 1st Battalion CP and Vegas went dead despite repeated attempts to reestablish contact. Carson and Reno also had wire troubles about this time, but reports and orders during the night and early morning hours were sent over company and battalion tactical radio nets. The intensity of the Chinese fire was not restricted just to forward positions; at one point, the 1/5 command post, a mile south of the MLR, received up to one hundred rounds of enemy incoming per minute!

While the Marines on the outposts were trying to drive off the enemy, reinforcements back at the MLR and in reserve ranks quickly saddled up. An F/2/5 advance platoon dispatched to Reno at 2015 by way of the Reno Block was ambushed near Hill 47 an hour later by two enemy squads that had moved south to cut off Marine reinforcements. After a fire exchange, the platoon made its way to the blocking position.

With the Reno and Vegas relief units pinned down at the Block, the situation at the outposts remained critical. Throughout the night, new waves of Communist soldiers poured from positions behind Hills 31 and 31D. At 2100, when a company of enemy troops was observed massing near Chogum-ni for a new assault, it was quickly disposed of by Marine artillery and Company A tankers. From Reno, where the immediate situation was the most grim, a message at 2145 reported the enemy still in the trenches, trying to dig down into the cave while Marines were attempting to work their way out by hand. About 2300, the final report from Reno was weak and could not be understood.

At Vegas, meanwhile, communications failure continued to complicate defensive measures. Because of that, on the order of Colonel Walt, the regimental commander, operational control had been transferred at 2119, from 1/5 to

3/5. Three minutes before midnight, all contact with Vegas was lost. As with Reno, reinforcements sent to buttress the Vegas detachment had been delayed by enemy action. When it became evident that the Company D platoon had been pinned down at the Block, a platoon from E/2/5 jumped off at 2323 for Vegas.

Shored up to reinforced company strength, the composite unit at the Block had prepared to move on for the ultimate relief of C/1/5 forces at Reno, but Chinese firepower and troops continued to lash the position. There seemed to be no limit to the number of reserve troops the enemy could throw into the attack. At 2157, two Chinese platoons hit the Block. Twenty minutes later, another two platoons struck. By 2300, the Marines had repulsed three attacks, numbering more than two hundred troops, amid a withering avalanche of bullets and shells. Shortly before midnight, a full enemy company had deployed south from Reno to the Block, but had been largely cut down by friendly 90mm tank fire and VT rounds from 1/11. Reinforced and reorganized, the Marines again prepared for a counterpunch on Reno.

By midnight on 26 March, after five blistering hours of battle—which became five days of intense conflict and continuing counterattacks—the early efforts of the enemy were partly successful. Two of the Nevada Hills outposts had fallen, and Marine attempts to strengthen them were being thwarted by Chinese troops who had overflowed the Block and moved southward toward the MLR. Carson was holding, but the enemy was in control of Reno and Vegas and was using the Reno position to mass troops and firepower to further brace his continuing assault on Vegas.

Initially, the 5th Marines had expected to launch an immediate counterattack to regain Reno. In the early hours of 27 March, however, it became apparent this plan would have to be revised. Reinforcing elements from the 5th Marines, composed largely of F/2/5, had been unable to mount out effectively from the Block for Reno. At 0144, the commanding officer of Company F, Capt. Ralph L. Walz, reported he had just one platoon left. Between then and 0220, his diminishing unit had rallied for attack three times. It had successively engaged the enemy in firefights, one of 30-minutes' duration, evacuated its wounded, regrouped, and then had come under heavy incoming again.

But as Marines built their defending platoon at the Block to company-plus size, the Chinese were throwing in unbroken mortar attacks and additional troops. At 0246, when another hostile company was seen spreading south from Reno toward the Block, the 1st Battalion directed artillery fires on the enemy and ordered its troops to disengage and return to the MLR. By 0300, early efforts to retake Reno were suspended. Relief forces from Companies F and C were on their way back to the battalion area, and ground action had ceased.

On the night of 26–27 March, during these early attempts to rescue Reno and its defenders, Marine elements had struggled for more than four hours to get to Reno, but the enemy had completely surrounded it. At Reno itself, the Marine in command of the outpost when the Chinese struck, 2d Lt. Rufus A. Seymour, machine-gun platoon commander of C/1/5, had been taken prisoner, along with several of his men. Of the Marines originally on duty there, all but five had been killed. Casualties of the units reinforcing Reno were later estimated by the regimental commander at "as high as 35 percent, with many dead."[7]

On the night of the twenty-sixth, navy Hospital Corpsman Francis C. Hammond was assigned to our relief platoon and it was because of him that a number of Marines had not died due to their wounds. During the four hours our platoon had moved, foot by foot, toward the Block, Doc Hammond had made his way from injured man to injured man and carried several Marines to a crater, which offered some degree of safety from enemy fire. Hammond had been hit by shrapnel in several places on the right leg, but his wounds did not stop him from repeatedly going back to help the wounded Marines in the area held by the leading squad of the platoon. Doc Hammond had man-

---

7. Meid and Yingling, Ch. 6, p. 287.

aged somehow to move about the area and helped to evacuate Marines for more than four hours before he was killed by the blast of a 120mm mortar round, which landed next to him. He was posthumously awarded the Medal of Honor for his bravery that night.

The units reinforcing Vegas in those dark early hours of 27 March, had come closer to their objective. Shortly after midnight, two platoons composed of elements from D/2/5 and C/1/5 had reached a point four hundred yards from the outpost, in the vicinity of the entrance to the communications trench. When the enemy threw in powerful new assault forces at Vegas, F/2/7, a company from the regimental reserve, came under operational control of 3/5 and moved out from the MLR to reinforce the position. Despite heavy and continuing Chinese barrages, by 0300 the first relief platoon got to within two hundred yards of the outpost. At that time, however, it was found the enemy was in control of Vegas as well as Reno. At 0417, on order, Marines from D/2/5, C/1/5, E/2/5, and F/2/7 relief forces began to pull back to the MLR. Initial attempts to regain control of the two outposts were temporarily halted, and instead, it was decided to launch a coordinated daylight attack.

At about the same time, 0430, the boundary between 1/5 and 3/5 was moved 250 yards westward to give 3/5 total responsibility for Vegas, although operational control had been transferred seven hours earlier the previous night.

Enemy casualties for the eight hours of action were heavy. An estimated six hundred Chinese had been wounded or killed. Marine losses were also heavy. In the action 1st Lt. Kenneth E. Taft, Jr., officer in charge at Vegas, was killed, and it was later learned, some of his H/3/5 defenders had been captured by the Chinese. By midnight, the two line battalions, 1/5 and 3/5, had reported a total of 150 casualties, and this figure did not include those wounded or killed among the relief platoons and companies being shuttled into action from 2/5, the reserve battalion. One platoon from E/2/5 had arrived at the Company C supply point about 0210 and, with a provisional unit from Headquarters and Service Company, 1/5, began to evacuate casualties in front of the MLR. By 0325, fifty-six wounded had passed through the C/1/5 aid station, and a cryptic entry in the G-3 journal noted "more who are able are going to assist in evacuation of casualties."[8]

With the first light of dawn, the Chinese had pulled back from the forward slopes of the hillsides they had occupied during the night, which allowed us the opportunity to locate our dead and wounded and move back to the MLR. As we made our way to the chewed-up, half-frozen ground that had been our platoon's position, we were stopped by LtCol. Robert J. Oddy, the commanding officer of 3/5. He surprised me by calling me "son" and explained to me, and to those Marines standing with me, that for the time being we would consider ourselves as members of 1/3/5, until the "confusion of our company's disposition and current strength had been sorted out." Meanwhile our immediate orders were to draw fresh ammunition and prepare for another try at reaching Reno Block. While we waited, we learned just how effective the enemy's uninterrupted artillery and mortar fire had been: Charlie Company had suffered more than 60 percent casualties. Among them were Sergeant McCarthy, our platoon guide, and 1st Lieutenant Workman, our company executive officer. As I sat next to the entrance to our bunker, I discovered just how close I had come to being a casualty during the night; a bullet had cut a deep crease across the top of my pack, missing my head by only a few inches.

With the 5th Marines reorganizing during the morning hours of the 27th for a new attack to recapture the lost outposts, General Pollock ordered mortars, tanks, artillery, including rockets, to neutralize the Reno and Vegas areas and enemy approaches.

From the time of the 1900 attack the preceding eve-

---

8. Ibid., p. 287.

ning until the temporary break in fighting eight hours later, at 0300, early estimates indicated 5,000 rounds of enemy mixed fire had been received in the "Wild" sector (code name for the 5th Marines, and appropriate it was for this late-March period). And this did not include the vast number of shells which had fallen on the three Nevada COPs. During the same period 1/11, in direct support of the 5th Marines, reported it had delivered some 4,209 rounds on the enemy. Throughout the early hours two battalions from the 11th Marines continued to pound away at Reno and Vegas with neutralizing fires to soften enemy positions, deter his resupply efforts, and silence those mortars and batteries which were troubling Marines.

Early on the 27th, at 0345 as the 5th Marines prepared for the counterattack, the division reserve, 2/7, was placed under operational control of the 5th Marines. A tentative H hour was set for 0900 with a dual jump-off for both Reno and Vegas. At 0930 the attacks still had not begun due to communications difficulties. While division Marines were waiting to get off the ground, 1st Marine Air Wing pilots were enjoying a busy morning. By 0930, six four-plane air strikes had been completed by VMF-115 and -311 plus sorties by Air Force Thunderjets. Tankers from Company A had also gotten in a few licks when two groups of Chinese were seen carrying logs for bunker support into Reno; one group was wiped out, the other got by. Shortly after 1100, friendly artillery batteries began delivering smoke on Hills 57A and 190, two enemy high points of observation. The fire plan was modified to eliminate an early 10-minute preparation on new objective areas. This time, the preparatory fires were to be on call, as was the 90mm fire support from the tankers. A further change was made when it was decided to limit the assault to Vegas and not retake Reno but neutralize it by fire.[9]

---

9. Ibid., pp. 290–291.

On the morning of the 27th those of us C Company Marines who had been absorbed into 3/5 were used as a base of fire to help defend the battalion's new western boundary. Later that morning, from our vantage point on the MLR, we watched as a company of Marines from D/2/5 moved out to retake Vegas. They had not gained more than two hundred yards of ground before they were taken under fire by enemy heavy mortars and artillery fire. Adding to the difficulty of their movement was a steadily increasing rain. Within minutes the ground, ripped open by the previous night's barrage, had become a quagmire, requiring Marines to crawl and claw their way forward.

In the afternoon, after we had received C rations and extra ammunition, a number of replacements, called "fill-ins," arrived to reinforce our portion of the line, and we were told our platoon was to move out toward the Reno Block area, once again under the cover of darkness, and hold positions in support of a new assault to regain Vegas by elements of the 7th Marines.

Within the first hour after leaving the battalion line, the Company F Marines nearly reached the advanced positions of 2/5, and Company D, which had been in the vanguard since 1100, returned to the regimental CP. During the next hour, however, heavy shelling slowed the Marine advance. At 1730, as F Company prepared to make its first major assault, a deluge of 60mm and 82mm mortar shell, 76mm and 122mm bursts, and machine-gun bullets rained on the troops. As the men crawled forward slowly, planes from VMA-323 which had arrived on scene two hours earlier, continued to smoke the enemy posts on Hills 190 and 139. A Company tanks also moved into their MLR positions to zero in their 90mm rifles on the CCF stronghold at the Vegas northern crest.

By 1800, Company F was continuing the Marine counterattack to regain Vegas and was approximately 400 yards from the outpost summit. Combining with

Company E Marines, for a total strength of three platoons in position, they were able to retake part of the objective. After an intense 90-minute firefight and hand-to-hand fighting in the lower trenches, E/2/7 advanced to the right finger of Vegas to within 50 yards of the peak, before being forced back by Chinese machine-gun fire and mortars lobbed from the Able (left) gate on Vegas. The enemy company occupying the outpost resisted the attacking Marines with mortars, grenades, and small-arms fire. In addition, the CCF employed firing positions at Reno for their machine guns, heavy mortars, and artillery supporting the Vegas defense and periodically reinforcing their troops from the newly captured Reno outpost.

Throughout the night the enemy counterattacked but was unsuccessful in driving the Marines off the outpost. Between 1830 and midnight, F/2/7 repulsed three enemy onslaughts and engaged in sporadic firefights. Although pushed back from the summit, Company F Marines set up a perimeter defense at the base of Vegas where the troops dug in for the rest of the night.

Gradually, heavy incoming on Vegas began to lift, and from midnight through the early hours of the following morning most of the enemy's artillery and mortar fires switched from Vegas to the Marine companies on the MLR. Intermittent small-arms fire still cracked and punctuated the night from enemy positions on Hills 57A, Detroit, and Frisco, to the northeast of Vegas.[10]

Having learned from the previous night's experience that command and control at the squad level was virtually impossible to maintain during an artillery and mortar barrage, I planned to keep my squad of new replacements close enough so they could respond to orders without hesitation. At 1900, we moved out again, as part of a composite platoon, and set up in a linear defense for the night, several hundred yards forward of the MLR.

---

10. Ibid., p. 294.

The initial Marine action on the 28th began at 0335 when 105mm and 155mm howitzers of the 1st, 2d, and 4th Battalion, 11th Marines, belched their streams of fire at the pocket of enemy troops on the northern slopes preparatory to the forthcoming Marine infantry assault. The 2,326-round pounding was aimed at Chinese assembly areas and weapons emplacements, with much of the preparation zeroed in on active enemy mortars.

Marines from F/2/7 assaulted Vegas at 0600 but were repulsed, having to pull back to a defilade position 375 south of Vegas to regroup. With air support from VMA-121, tanks, artillery, and mortars hitting the enemy in a renewed series of preparatory fires, beginning at 0920, F/2/7 jumped back into the attack. By 1015 they had made their way toward the hilltop and to within 15 yards of the trench line on the left side of Vegas. There they came under continuous small arms and grenade bursts from the crest and battled Chinese soldiers in an intense half-hour firefight.

Heavy air attacks were assisting the artillery in blasting out Communist defenses of the Vegas area. Between 0950 and 1300, seven four-plane strikes by pilots of MAG-12 had swept the outpost area and hill lairs of the enemy at 57A, the east slope of Reno, Hills 40D, and 90, and resupply points. Within one 23-minute period alone, 28 tons of bombs were laid squarely on the Vegas position. Supported by air, artillery, and mortars, Company E was 400 yards from the objective, and, by 1245, forward elements had moved up to within 150 yards of the crest. As Marine supporting fires lifted from Vegas to enemy assembly areas on Hills 150, 153, and 190, E/2/5 launched its final assault at 1301. Although small arms, bursts of mortar and enemy artillery fire traced their every move, the Marines' hard-hitting attack brought them to the top of Vegas where they literally dug the Chinese out of their defenses. At 1307, the Marines had secured their position and recaptured the Vegas outpost.

Two prisoners had been taken during the day's action, one by E/2/5 during its afternoon assault and the other by F/2/7 early in the day. The Chinese soldier seized by a fire team from Company E was a 21-year-old wounded litter bearer attached to the attacking force, 3rd Battalion, 358th Regiment. He told 5th Marine interrogators that for the preceding three months the mission of the 358th Regiment had been to prepare to occupy the Vegas and Reno outposts before the expected United Nations spring offensive could be launched. The two key installations overlooked CCF supply routes. Furthermore, occupation of these two hills, the Chinese believed, would serve as a valuable tactical example to the 46th Army, whose ranks at this time were composed of nearly 65 percent recruits. The POW also reported that prior to the CCF attack on Reno and Vegas, men of his regiment had practiced throwing hand grenades every day for the past two weeks. No political classes had been held during this period as practical proficiency, apparently, took priority over theoretical indoctrination.

The other Chinese prisoner, captured by Company F at 0610, was a grenadier with the 9th Company, 3d Battalion, 358th Regiment. Prior to the attack, his unit had occupied reverse slope positions on Hills 25A and 155 as reinforcements for the 8th Company. Each CCF battalion, he revealed, "held a front of approximately 1,000 meters, utilizing one company on line with two in support."[11]

For the next five hours, from 1440 to 1930, the Marines dug in on the crest and slopes of Vegas, buttressing their positions for the Chinese attack sure to come. A muster of the ragtag group left from the day's ten hours of fighting revealed a total strength of only five squads—fifty-eight effective riflemen from E/2/5 and eight from F/2/7.

11. Ibid., p. 297.

Altogether, during the night of 28–29 March, two battalions of Chinese troops made three separate, unsuccessful ventures to retake the Vegas crest, but were thrown back by Marine mortar, artillery, and tank fires. At 0130, following a heavy 37-minute artillery and mortar concentration, the enemy began to withdraw, but not before venting his displeasure with a resounding blast of small arms and bazooka fire from Reno hill. In their departure, the Chinese were given an assist by Company E, 7th Marines, which had broken through the enemy encirclement of Vegas in the early morning hours to join E/2/5 and F/2/5 defending forces and help drive the invaders off all but the northern tip of the hill. For the next two hours the 11th Marines battalions, together with the 1st 4.5-inch Rocket Battery, sealed off the outpost and blistered enemy fortifications at Reno with a total of 4,225 rounds. Air observers on station fired ten missions between midnight and 0430. Twenty minutes later, the artillerymen unleashed still another preparation to dislodge the unyielding CCF dug in at the Vegas topographical crest.[12]

From the two-man fighting holes we had prepared forward of the MLR, we watched as the Marines on Vegas fought to repulse two night attacks by the Chinese. As flares lit up the area, small groups of enemy soldiers tried to sprint from where they had been hiding near Reno Block to help their comrades attacking Vegas. Under the constant barrage from Marine artillery and mortars, we joined in the firefight and kept a steady stream of small-arms fire trained on the enemy movement less than one hundred yards forward of our positions. The hilltops of Carson, Reno, and Vegas remained silhouetted by the light of artillery and mortar illumination rounds, and as the automatic rifle fire diminished during the night, we began to feel the Chinese had finally lost their appetite for continuing their attack along our MLR.

---

12. Ibid., p. 302.

Although another enemy attack was quickly repulsed at 2045 in a brisk, savage fight, shortly before midnight the Chinese reappeared, moving up from behind the right finger of Hill 153. This was believed to be an attempt to recover their casualties, but Marine artillery, mortars, and rocket bursts sent them fleeing within ten minutes. Still the enemy obstinately refused to give up his goal of retaking the high ground at COP 21. In the early morning hours of the 30th, he again returned to hit the outpost in his second battalion-strength attack within six hours. Again he struck from Reno and Hill 153, and again he attempted to cut off the outpost Marines by encircling the position. Heavy pounding by artillery, mortar, and boxing fires snuffed out the enemy attack and by 0215 the Chinese had left the Vegas domain—this time, it was to prove, for good. Their casualties for this latest attempt had been 78 counted killed, 123 more estimated killed, and 174 estimated wounded.[13]

On the morning of 30 March, we returned to our original position on the MLR and watched as Marine close air support bombarded the trenches, bunkers, and those enemy soldiers who continued to occupy positions on Carson and Reno. The last direct confrontation with the enemy at Vegas had occurred that morning, about 1100 when five Chinese unconcernedly walked up to the outpost, apparently to surrender. Then, suddenly, they began throwing grenades and firing automatic weapons. The little delegation was promptly dispatched by two Marine fire teams. Three CCF soldiers were killed and two taken prisoner, one of whom later died.

No time was lost in trying to reorganize Company C, and as replacements began to arrive to fill in the massive gaps in what had once been a 150-man Marine rifle company, the work of recovering the dead also began. My squad—many of whose names I did not even know—was assigned, with two other composite squads, to spend the next several days searching the devastated area forward of the MLR to recover the bodies of Company C Marines.

Recapture and defense of the Vegas outposts was one of the intense, contained struggles which came to characterize the latter part of the Korean War. The action developed into a five-day siege involving over 4,000 ground and air Marines and was the most bloody action Marines on the western front had yet engaged in. Its cost can be seen, in part, by the casualties sustained by the 1st Marine Division. The infantry strength of two battalions was required to retake Outpost Vegas and defend it against successive Chinese counterattacks. A total of 520 Marine replacements were received during the operation. Marine casualties totaled 1,015: 116 killed, 441 wounded/evacuated, 360 wounded/not evacuated, and 98 missing, of which 19 were known to be prisoners. Losses for the critical five-day period represented 70 per cent of the division casualties for the entire month—1,488 killed, wounded, and missing (not including 128 in the Korean Marine Corps sector).

Enemy casualties were listed conservatively as 2,221. This represented 536 counted killed, 654 estimated killed, 174 counted wounded, 853 estimated wounded, and 4 prisoners. The Marines, moreover, in the five days of furious fighting had knocked out the 358th CCF Regiment, numbering between 3,000 and thirty-five hundred men, and destroyed its effectiveness as a unit.

During these five tense days the enemy deluged Marine positions with 45,000 rounds of artillery, mortar, and mixed fire. Indicative of the savage pounding the Vegas area took is the fact that incoming Chinese artillery for the full two-week period from 1–15 March totaled only 3,289 rounds. The artillery shelling was the hottest during a 24-hour period ending at 1600 on

29 March. During this time 35,809 rounds were fired (33,041 from the four Marine artillery battalions).

Battlefront tactics employed by the CCF in its assault of the Nevada cities outposts were largely consistent with their previous strategy. As in the past, the enemy launched simultaneous attacks against several Marine positions in an attempt to fragment defensive artillery firepower. Characteristically, the enemy preceded his thrust with heavy preassault concentrations of artillery and mortar fire. He also took advantage of the twin ploys of surprise and overwhelming strength, with wave after wave of Chinese rolling over the objective. Innovative techniques consisted of scaling ladders, fashioned from lightweight but sturdy bamboo, which were used to traverse Marine wire defenses, and of having an artillery liaison officer attached to infantry squads to better direct supporting fires during their attack. Analysis of Chinese firepower tactics indicated deliberate counterbattery efforts by the CCF, although this employment of artillery was secondary to its support of ground troops.[14]

Following the loss of Reno, a new outpost, Elko, was established on Hill 47, between what had been Reno Block and 765 yards forward of the MLR, to block the possibility of the Chinese using the position as an outpost of their own. To ensure that Vegas remained in Marine hands, the combat outpost was bolstered from platoon size to a reinforced detachment of 2 officers and 133 enlisted men.

With the end of March came a division order directing the 7th Marines to occupy the positions formerly held by the 5th Marines. We had spent sixty-eight days on the lines before moving out, first to Camp Rose, to become the division's reserve regiment.

When I think back to the many times at Hawaii, Quantico, and Camp Pendleton when I had asked my se-

---

14. Ibid., p. 309.

niors and superiors to help me in my pursuit of orders into combat, I am reminded of the adage, "Don't ask for something too many times; you may get it!"

CHAPTER 10

The End of the War and Armistice

Following the four days of heavy fighting for the Nevada cities outposts, C Company was reduced to 40 percent effectiveness, and we exchanged our positions with the 7th Marine Regiment, becoming part of the division's reserve unit. While United Nations representatives talked peace with the Communists at Panmunjom, our battalion was taken first to Camp Rose to rebuild, rest, train and to help complete the repairs along the secondary Kansas line, which needed work following several weeks of bad weather and neglect by Marines unable, because of battle, to dedicate their time to maintenance. At the same time, we began to receive replacements for the hundreds of Marine casualties lost during the past week's fighting. Of course, the majority of the replacements went to the division's 1st and 7th regiments, which were still serving on the line, but we did manage to replace some of the Marines lost in our own regiment.

During the first week of May, while we were still at Camp Rose, the 1st Marine Division began to be relieved from its positions along the Kansas line by the soldiers of the U.S. Army's 25th Infantry Division and sent to Camp Casey. A rear-area complex that became the temporary home to the 1st Marine Division, Casey consisted of three major camp areas to accommodate the regiments of the division. The center of the complex, Camp Casey, held the division headquarters element and the 5th Marine Regiment. To our north was Camp Indianhead, home to the 7th Marine Regiment, the 1st Korean Marine Corps (KMC) Regiment, the division's reconnaissance company, machine-gun and NCO Schools. To the south was Camp Britannia, where the three battalions of the 1st Marine Regiment, motor transport, engineer, and medical units were billeted.

As I recall, the artillerymen of the 11th Marine Regiment remained in their positions near the MLR to support the 25th Infantry Division as it moved in to assume its new positions. In addition, the division's 1st Tank Battalion also remained along the MLR and was temporarily under control of the 25th Infantry Division. Our battalion's relief was provided by soldiers of the 24th Infantry Regiment, and it was a very smooth transition, if only because we were in a reserve position. Now that the 1st Marine Division was in reserve for I Corps, the division's primary mission was that of a "counterattack" force, ready and able to be plugged into any of the four divisions' sectors of I Corps. The battalion's secondary mission was training, the improvement of existing facilities, and the rebuilding of our individual units. We were enjoying two hot meals each day, and relished the opportunity for a warm shower each day. Life for us grunts was improving.

On the morning of 10 May, our company was loaded onto trucks and taken to the Port of Inchon, where we boarded a navy LST for a landing exercise. Once aboard and settled in, we were briefed on the landing site and training objectives. We sailed on 12 May, heading south of Inchon for a placed called Yongjong-ni. Our exercise was conducted in preparation for Operation Plan 24-53, an amphibious landing of men, tanks, amtracks (amphibious tracked vehicles), and artillery onto Tokchok-do, which was several miles southwest of Inchon. Code-named MARLEX I, our landing was made difficult by unexpectedly shallow beach gradients, which hindered the off-loading of our vehicles. We were scheduled to participate in the landing portion of the exercise on the morning of the twelfth, but were delayed because of heavy fog, and actually landed on the thirteenth. When the exercise was completed we were taken back to Camp Casey by truck and resumed our duties, which then included providing security for the division command post.

At Camp Casey, our company, like all others, participated in an aggressive training program which called for four-phase progressive schooling from the individual level to battalion and regimental levels, conducted in all phases of offensive, defensive, and amphibious warfare. Weaponry familiarization, small-unit tactics, and combined-unit training, with tank-infantry deployment and integration of helicopters at company-level exercises, were emphasized, and culminated in a week-long field exercise. Because of this thorough training, the new men assigned to my squad quickly became proficient in the skills of the infantryman and were eager to go on the line when called. With the division schools located close by, I took advantage of the opportunity to send several of my men to mine-warfare school and one Marine to the scout-sniper school.

On the morning of 8 July, a truck convoy took us back to the MLR to reoccupy the defensive positions that had been held by the soldiers of the 25th Infantry Division. I remember that day because while we were crossing over Spoonbill Bridge, the skies parted, and a torrential rain began to fall. The slow movement back to our positions, burdened now with full combat packs, was under the same conditions as that day in March when we left the line—slipping and sliding in the ever-deepening mud. When we finally reached our new positions, we relieved the soldiers of the 3d Battalion, 35th Infantry, and they were certainly happy to see us arrive.

The 5th Marine Regiment took positions that had been occupied by the Marines of the 1st Marine Regiment before they were relieved by the U.S. Army. The 5th Marine

Regiment's 2d Battalion was on the left side of the sector; the 3d Battalion was on the right side, and our 1st Battalion was in regimental reserve behind the 3d Battalion's position.

Our relief of the army was conducted without incident, but I was shocked to learn from an army staff sergeant that the combat outposts of Carson, Vegas, and Elko, which we had fought so hard to keep, had all been lost by the U.S. Army during the past month and had fallen into the hands of Chinese Communist forces. As the thoughts of how many Marines had been killed or wounded trying to hold that ground, only to have it lost to the Chinese, began to sink in, I set about readying our positions and preparing ourselves to respond to any company or battalion that should need our help.

As I recall, it was on the nights of 24 through 26 July that the Red Chinese made their heaviest assaults along the MLR, trying to overrun our OPs, while attempting to punch holes in our regimental sector.

In a second-step operation, rather than striking simultaneously as was customary, the enemy at 2115 had jabbed at outposts Esther and Dagmar in the right battalion of the 5th Marines. The reinforced Chinese company from the 408th Regiment quickly began to concentrate its attention on Esther, outposted by Company H Marines. During the heavy fighting both Marines and Chinese reinforced. By early morning, the enemy had seized part of the front trench line, but the Marines controlled the rear trenches and reorganized the defense under rifle platoon leader, Second Lieutenant William H. Bates. The Chinese unsuccessfully attempted to isolate the position by heavy shelling and patrolled vigorously between Esther and the MLR.

Marines replied with flamethrowers and heavy supporting fires from the MLR, including machine guns, 81mm and 4.2-inch mortar fire. Three tanks—a section from the regimental antitank platoon and one from Company A—neutralized enemy targets with 153 rounds fired to assist the 3d and 2d Battalions. The 3/11 gunners supporting the 5th Marines also hurled 3,886 rounds against the Chinese in breaking up the attack. After several hours of strong resistance, the Chinese loosened their grip, and at 0640 on the 25th Esther was reported secured.

By this time an enemy battalion had been committed piecemeal at the position. The action had developed into the heaviest encounter of the month in the 5th Marines sector. During the night of 24–25 July, more than 4,000 artillery and mortar rounds fell in the outpost vicinity; total incoming for the regimental sector throughout July was recorded at 8,413 rounds. Twelve Marines lost their lives in the battle, with 35 wounded and evacuated, and 63 suffering minor injuries. A total of 85 CCF were counted dead, 110 more estimated killed, and an estimated 250 wounded.[1]

The same week we began to hear from the female Chinese Communist propagandist known as the Dragon Lady, whose amplified speeches where blasted at us each night from huge loudspeakers located on the enemy hills opposite our regimental sector. Her broadcasts seemed to be directed at our younger Marines, saying, "Marines, why do you want to die in this war when your girlfriend is going out with men at home? Tell your leaders you do not want to fight anymore. Come over to our side, and you will be treated well and with respect." Of course, no one responded to her invitation.

In the early morning of 27 July, we were informed of the signing of the armistice and that we were in a "cease-fire" status. After what we had endured during the preceding four days, those of us in defensive positions along the line had a difficult time believing the legitimacy of the claim. We had heard for several months that the likelihood of an armistice agreement was very real, but we had

---

1. Meid and Yingling, Ch. 9, p. 387.

quickly come to know that the Chinese were never to be trusted.

From the standpoint of casualties, the last month of the Korean War was a costly one, with 181 infantry Marines killed in action and total losses of 1,611 men: 86 missing, 862 wounded and evacuated, 474 wounded (not evacuated), and 10 non-battle deaths. This was the highest rate for any month during 1953. It was second only to the October 1952 outpost battles (during which time 186 were killed and 1,798 were listed as casualties), for any month during the year the 1st Marine Division defended the line in West Korea. The closing days of the war were much more costly to the Chinese. Eighth Army officials estimated that CCF casualties in July alone reached 72,000 men, with more than 25,000 of these dead. The enemy had lost the equivalent of *seven divisions of the five Chinese Communist armies* committed in attacks upon II and IX Corps sectors.

With the final resolution of hostilities at 1000, on the 27th of July, 1953, a flash message went out immediately to the 26,000 Marines of Major General Randolph McC. Pate's division directing that there be "no celebration firing related in any way to the advent of the armistice." Fraternization or communication with the enemy was expressly forbidden. Personnel were reminded that firing of all weapons was to be "restricted to the minimum justified by the tactical situation." No defensive firing was to take place after 2145 unless the Marines were actually attacked by enemy infantry. Each front line company was authorized to fire one white-star cluster at 2200, signalling the cease-fire.

The signing of the armistice agreement on 27 July ended 36 months of war for the Marines in Korea. On that date, the 1st Marine Division initiated plans for its withdrawal to defensive positions south of the Imjin River. One regiment, the 5th Marines, was left north of the river to man the general outpost line across the entire division front. A transition was made at this time from the customary wide-front linear defense to a defense in depth.

Briefly, the armistice agreement decreed that both UNC and Communists forces:

> Cease fire 12 hours (at 2200, 27 July) after signing of agreement;

> Withdraw all military forces, supplies, and equipment from the demilitarized zone (2,000 yards from line of contact) within 72 hours after effective time of cease-fire;

> Locate and list all fortification and minefields in the DMZ within 72 hours, to be dismantled during a subsequent salvage period;

> Replace combat personnel and supplies on a one-for-one basis, to prevent any build-up; and

> Begin repatriation of all POWs, with exchange to be completed within two months.[2]

Marines on the line that night warily scanned the darkness in front of their trenches. Slowly at first, then with increasing rapidity, the white-star cluster shells began to burst over positions all along the line. Thousands of flares illuminated the sky and craggy hills along the 155-mile front from the Yellow Sea to the Sea of Japan. The war in Korea was over. Of the men from one Marine division and air wing committed in Korea during the three-year conflict, 4,262 had been killed in battle. An additional 26,038 Marines were wounded. For outstanding valor, no fewer than forty-two Marines would receive the nation's highest combat decoration, the Medal of Honor—twenty-six of them posthumously.

On the morning of 28 July, ours was one of two platoons from our company assigned to dismantle COP Dagmar. We had only seventy-two hours to complete the job before returning to our positions. Once at the outpost, we collapsed the living caves, cut up and emptied all the sandbags, and hauled away all usable bunker material. We

---

2. Ibid., p. 395.

salvaged the timbers used to construct the bunkers and rolled up nearly all of the tactical barbed wire before we moved back to the rear. At the end of the seventy-two hours we had totally destroyed what had once been a defendable outpost and then returned without incident to our place on the MLR. By 30 July, we had moved away from the main line of resistance to the secondary Kansas line, and what we knew as the MLR became the southern boundary of what today is the DMZ. With the exception of work details sent onto the DMZ to dismantle positions, this area was now considered "out of bounds." And the work details were accompanied by special DMZ military police.

After all of the outpost positions on both sides were finally dismantled, a "no-pass" fence was constructed, which physically separated North Korea from South Korea. This fence consisted of a continuous double-strand of barbed wire that ran, east to west, across the entire breadth of Korea. Our regiment was responsible for constructing a huge section of it, and my platoon worked along with Marines from H/3/5 to help complete the job.

While we were working on the fence, the 1st Marine Regiment and the 7th Marine Regiment moved south of the Imjin River. Our regiment, 5th Marines, was to defend the entire general outpost line across what had been the entire frontal sector of the 1st Marine Division: 2/5 on the left flank, 1/5 in the center, and 3/5 holding down what had been the division's right flank. We were reinforced by Marines of the division's military police company.

Throughout the months of August and until 13 September, destruction of MLR positions and removal of materials took place concurrently with organization of defensive positions in the new sectors. After the initial three-day period and its top priority of physical withdrawal of troops from the DMZ, divisional tactical requirements called for completion of the MBP (main battle positions) as rapidly as possible. This now became the first priority. New company perimeter defense sites, battalion blocking positions, coordinated fire plans in event of attack, counterattack orders, and evacuation routes were mapped out. By 5 August, the new battalion camps had begun to take form and work on blocking positions was in progress.

Stockpiling, meanwhile, had been accomplished at company, battalion, and regimental dumps. All materials were stacked by size to facilitate reissue during constructions of new positions. As much as 90% of the materials salvaged were usable in the new fortifications. Although a certain amount of inter-battalion exchange took place, battalion stocks—with the exception of sandbags—were usually adequate to provide sufficient fortification materials for rebuilding. For 5th Marine units that had the least distance to relocate, timbers moved from the old MLR in the morning were sometimes employed in the new defensive positions by late afternoon.[3]

Division MLR supplies salvaged by the 5th Marines represented:

T/E material	12 tons
Signal equipment (wire)	2,000 miles
Engineer items	
barbed wire	2,850 rolls
concertina	340 rolls
pickets, 6-foot	11,000
pickets, 3-foot	8,000
sandbags	339,000
timbers 3×8 12×12	150,000 linear feet
Total tonnage	2,000 short tons

Responsibility for eliminating the old positions held by the division fell to our regimental commander, but the physical burden was placed on those Marines at the platoon and squad level. As the summer temperatures began

3. Meid and Yingling, Ch. 11, p. 455.

to rise, so did the stress level of the officers and noncommissioned officers who had to oversee a job of this magnitude. As Marines succumbed to heat exhaustion and, in some cases, heatstroke, company commanders issued orders for their men to take more frequent breaks. Occasionally, platoon leaders, seeing their Marines not working, would raise hell and counter orders to rest. We were learning quickly that Marines did not do well in a nonshooting, defensive environment. With the shooting stopped, platoons were rotated to the rear every two weeks, where hot chow, showers, and a change into clean uniforms awaited the men. Once this rotational plan was put into effect, problems with morale and personal hygiene began to disappear.

As the weeks of patrolling the DMZ grew into months, the dismantling of old camps continued, and construction of more permanent, defendable positions began. The cold winds from Manchuria began to push southward, and with the descending temperatures came the realization that I would soon be leaving Korea; my one-year tour was rapidly coming to a close. During the last week of November 1953, the Marines from our original draft battalion were notified that we were headed home. Although the size of our original draft battalion had been considerably diminished, those of us who had survived combat in Korea were brought to ASCOM City to begin administrative processing. After showers, shots, delousing, and deworming, we were marched to the supply area and reunited with our seabags, which had been in storage for a year. Two days after arriving at ASCOM City, we were trucked to the port of Inchon, where we boarded navy landing craft for transfer to the ships that would eventually take us back to the States.

I don't recall anyone looking back at the shoreline of Korea as we were ferried out to our waiting ship.

Many of the hard lessons of Korea—as well as some of its unique problems—resulted from the fact that this was America's first major experience in a modern, undeclared, and limited war. Accustomed to the tradition of hard-hitting, all-out war and decisive victory, both the fighting man at the front and the Nation tended to view the conflict as well as its ultimate accomplishments as inconclusive.

Most importantly, immediate collective security action by the UNC had prevented another small country from being subdued by direct, armed aggression. And the Communists had failed to attain their objective: the forced unification of Korea, not as a free nation but as a Russian satellite, as was North Korea.

Casualties for UNC forces numbered 996,937 killed, wounded, and missing. U.S. losses were 136,937, of which 33,629 represented battle deaths and 103,308 wounded in action. A measure of the role that ground forces played in Korea "may be judged from the fact that, of the total United States battle casualties for the entire conflict, the Army and Marines accounted for 97 percent." Casualties of other UNC countries exclusive of the U.S. and ROK, totaled approximately 17,000 although no other Allied nation lost as many as 1,000 dead. ROK casualties were listed as 850,000. Communists losses were estimated at 1,420,000 (CCF: 900,000 killed and wounded; NKPA: 520,000 killed and wounded).[4]

---

4. *U.S. Marine Operations in Korea*, 1950–1953, Vol. 5, Chapter XII, p. 532.

CHAPTER 11

Homeward Bound

Late on the afternoon of 10 December 1953, a navy Mike boat ferried us away from the busy port of Inchon and toward the distant silhouette of the ship that had been assigned to take us home. The ship was listing heavily to starboard in shallow water as we drew alongside, and I was surprised to see that our trip east would be aboard the USS *Brewster*, the very ship which had brought me to the shores of South Korea one year earlier.

Filled to near capacity with army soldiers, air force men, coastguardsmen, and several hundred United States Marines, the *Brewster* would be our home for the next thirteen days, and when I saw the number of passengers crammed onto every deck, I knew that her ability to answer to the needs of several thousand servicemen would be tested to the extreme.

The low-tide conditions at Inchon did not allow for the *Brewster* to sail until midnight, when a full tide flooded the channel and gave our ship the depth she needed to right herself and clear the harbor. Not long after we had gotten under way, the rolling, frigid, green waters and icy winds of the Sea of Japan had set the tempo for the beginning of our cruise. The constant rocking of the ship caused most of us to remain in our compartments, riding out the rough seas with little to do other than let our imaginations return home for Christmas.

An old buddy of mine named Fitch, who had just spent his year in Korea as an infantryman with the 7th Marines, was billeted in the same compartment as me, and since we were not feeling tired, we decided to go below to the open messdecks to find something to eat. The messdeck was one of the few places aboard the *Brewster* that was well ventilated and thus free of the acrid aroma of vomit which permeated most of the ship. It was on the near-empty messdeck that I found a copy of the ship's newspaper, *The Brewster Bugle*, which was published by the ship's administrative section, along with some help from the passengers. The *Bugle* contained a great deal of interesting material: a record of the ship's officers and our troop commanders, an explanation as to the significance of the ship's crossing through the international date line, and a chart that indicated the distance we traveled each day from Inchon and the distance remaining to San Francisco. That small piece of information, which affected all of us, and a series of daily cartoons about shipboard life made the *Bugle* a much sought after piece of reading material, as each day we plotted our progress east.

It was through reading copies of the *Bugle* that I learned more about the ship than I had known from the first time I had sailed on her. The USNS *Brewster* was a United States Military Transport ship, operated by the Military Sea Transportation Service Pacific, and was operated under the charge of the U.S. Navy. She was built in the Kaiser Shipyard, in Richmond, California and was commissioned by the navy in 1944 and assigned as a troop transport. The *Brewster* was a turbine-geared driven ship developing 9,500 horsepower, was 523 feet long, and had a displacement of 17,300 tons. She could carry us home at 17.5 knots. In June, 1946, the navy had released control of the *Brewster*, and she became an army transport. During the last war the *Brewster* had carried military personnel and had a capacity of approximately 3,000 troops. She had since been partially converted and now had a capacity of 2,200 troops, and more comfortable accommodations had been provided for women and children cabin passengers.

On the afternoon of our second day at sea, Fitch and I met out on deck near the ship's fantail. It was one of the few places not crowded by seasick soldiers, and it was close enough to our berthing compartment that we didn't have to travel far to return to the warmth of the ship. As we stood next to the ship's rail, something caught Fitch's immediate attention. "Jesus Christ, Jacques, look at that winch covering and tell me what you see."

At the base of one of the winches was a pair of uniformed legs exposed to the cold. The owner of the legs had obviously tried to hide himself between the winch and its protective canvas covering, and now we had discovered him. Thinking surely he was dead, we moved quickly to check. To our surprise, we unwrapped a shivering U.S. Army private who wore the Indianhead patch of the 2d Infantry Division on the shoulder of his field jacket. We carried him inside the ship, wrapped him in two wool blankets, and got him warm enough so he could tell us what had happened. He explained that while suffering greatly from seasickness, he had left his compartment the night before and stumbled through the ship's darkened passageways until he found himself out on deck. He could not remember how to get back to his bunk, let alone recall his compartment number, and wanting "only to die," he had tried to find relief from the freezing wind by hiding beneath the stiff canvas. He had been there for nearly eighteen hours before Fitch spotted him.

Still too sick to eat, he asked us to leave him with the two blankets so he could sleep among a stack of life jackets. We agreed. Later that day, he was still sleeping where we had left him. Not wanting him to worsen because of malnutrition, we brought him a few apples, several pocketsful of soda crackers and a bowl of hot broth from the messdecks. The next time we passed his sleeping spot, he was gone. Two days later, Fitch and I ran into the army private as we stood in line to eat. He hugged the both of us and thanked us repeatedly for having saved his life. What struck Fitch and me as odd was the fact that no one from the army had discovered this private to be missing for the better part of four days.

On our sixth day at sea, the front page of the *Brewster Bugle* reported our distance from Inchon was greater than to San Francisco and, once we'd passed the halfway point to home, a dramatic change in attitude swept over the ship. Suddenly, brown dress shoes, which had lain dormant for more than a year in the bottom of seabags, began to gleam from hours of spit shining; crisp, razor-sharp creases were ironed into starched uniforms; brass belt buckles shone like gold plates, and the black leather brims of our barracks covers took on mirrorlike qualities. The momentum of looking "squared away" was maintained for several more days as we continued eastward, and the crew of the *Brewster* added entertainment to the plan of the day, with bingo games and nightly talent shows conducted on the ship's covered main decks. Sailors, soldiers, and Marines sang hit songs, tap-danced, and played music in an effort to regain feelings lost to a year of combat and to separation from family, friends, and home. The prizes won at bingo games would be used as additional Christmas presents.

On the morning of our thirteenth day at sea, while still several miles west of the Golden Gate Bridge, I awoke to the deep-belly sound of foghorns announcing our arrival. The *Brewster* had come to a stop while waiting for a harbor pilot to come aboard and help guide her beneath the Golden Gate and on to her berthing spot within San Francisco Bay. Excited to be so close to U.S. soil, I went out on deck and listened to a local radio station as I watched automobile headlights light up the huge superstructure of the familiar bridge. As the *Brewster* finally came to rest alongside one of the many piers which jutted out into the bay, a feeling of subdued anxiety had crept over the ship. After more than forty years, it is still difficult for me to describe, but easy for those who had survived the ordeals associated with combat to understand; I had managed to come back to the country I had so many times thought I would never see again, and the chance to be reunited with my family, still two thousand eight hundred miles away in Lawrence, Massachusetts, was no less than a dream come true. It was the same for every combat veteran on board the *Brewster*. It seemed to take forever to get off our ship and onto solid ground so that each of us could begin our private journeys home.

Dozens of gray navy buses were lined up to take us to Treasure Island, where we would be processed for home. In less than two days, we would clear San Francisco and be on leave. The system making that possible had been refined over the last three years of the war in Korea, and those of us who were headed for points east benefited from those past lessons learned. After arriving at Treasure Island, Fitch and I and several hundred other Marines were taken first to a three-story building where we underwent the administrative "welcome home." Not wanting to keep any returning Marine waiting longer than necessary, the Corps saw that each of us received a small amount of cash known as a "flying fifty," which was considered enough money to keep us occupied during two days of liberty.

After stowing our gear in the NCO transient barracks, Fitch and I took a train from Oakland into San Francisco, and a cab brought us to the Marine's Memorial Club, located on the corner of Sutter and Mason Streets. For days abroad the *Brewster*, we had planned this trip. Asking the club's doorman, "Where's the beer?" we were directed toward the club's stag bar located on the third floor, where three Chinese bartenders took great pleasure in entertaining the patrons by juggling glasses and flipping whiskey bottles back and forth behind their backs as they made up mixed drinks. Once we were bored by the bartenders' routine, we made our way to the club's more formal bar located on the ninth floor, where we were suddenly joined by several women Marines who had undoubtedly made a habit of finding themselves at the Marine's Memorial Club not long after returning troop ships sailed into San

Francisco. Each one of those gals was bigger and looked meaner than any drill instructor I had seen on Parris Island. It must have been obvious to them that Fitch and I were "fresh off the boat," but, unfortunately, the last thing we wanted or needed was the unwanted company of a couple of freeloading WMs who wanted us to pick them up and their bar tab, too. After a couple of cold beers, I motioned to Fitch that it was time to make a head call. Once clear of the WMs we gave enough cash to our waiter to cover the cost of our drinks and left for the Fairbanks Club, located just a few blocks away on Mason Street.

The Fairbanks Club was packed with sailors, but the hostess invited us in, found us a booth and brought us each a cold beer. The Fairbanks Club also had a reputation as one of the better servicemen's clubs in San Francisco. While offering different types of finger sandwiches for the hungry, for those who cared to dance a large Wurlitzer jukebox blared out the latest hits, and every booth was equipped with a state-of-the-art telephone system that allowed record requests to be programmed directly into the jukebox. Two of the most popular songs of the time were "Jezebel," sung by Frankie Laine and "Music, Music, Music," sung by a young woman named Teresa Brewer. Fitch and I stayed at the Fairbanks until it closed at three A.M. and then spent the remainder of the night sobering up on black coffee and walking the cold city streets until the sun finally made its appearance in the eastern sky.

Following a cab ride back to the tar-paper transient barracks at Treasure Island, we enjoyed the luxury of a long hot shower before returning to the administrative unit to receive our travel orders and future assignments. Several long hours later, the process was complete. Fitch and I were pleased to have been paid, granted twenty days of leave, and transfer orders directing us to duty at Marine Corps Base, Camp Pendleton, California. With money and orders in hand, we headed for the closest ticket office, where Fitch bought a train ticket home to Seattle, Washington, and from where I would ride for four days by train back to Boston, and ultimately to my parents' home in Lawrence, Massachusetts. We departed Treasure Island 20 December 1953, and I hoped like hell the weather across the breadth of the country would allow me to arrive in time to surprise my parents before Christmas.

After saying good-bye to Fitch, reminding him I'd see him at Camp Pendleton in late January, I boarded the train and began the long trip home. I was filled with the spirit of Christmas, and the train could not travel fast enough to suit me. I had to struggle just to relax enough to enjoy the scenery as the train traveled through Sacramento and began a slow climb through the snow-covered, near-legendary Donner Pass. Our first stop was Reno, Nevada.

As the conductor announced our late-night arrival in Reno, I was jolted from sleep and into thinking about what had happened to me and to the Marines I had served with in combat during the past year. The words Reno, Carson City, and Vegas, had taken on an entirely different meaning, one which would remain with me forever. As America's "Biggest Little City" came into view, decorated in the traditional red, green, and white lights of the holiday season, I could only think back to the flashes of streaming red-and-green machine-gun tracers and the continuous glare of mortar and artillery illumination rounds that had lit up the sky for three terrible days, nine months earlier, around the hellish place known to us as Reno Block.

From Reno the train continued east, stopping at Salt Lake City and Omaha before finally arriving in Chicago, Illinois, late in the afternoon of 23 December. After we pulled into La Salle Station, I had to change from the Union Pacific Railroad Line to the New York Central Railroad, which passed through Gary, Indiana, and Toledo, Ohio, and the snowy Finger Lakes region of western New York State before stopping in Albany, New York. Several hours later the train entered western Massachusetts and passed through the farmlands, suburbs, and towns between Springfield and Worcester, before finally arriving at Bos-

ton's famous South Station. Carrying my seabag and one
small suitcase, I transferred over to North Station and purchased a one-way ticket for Lawrence, nearly thirty-five
miles north of Boston. At exactly 2200 on 24 December
1953 I got off the train, and lady luck must certainly have
been riding with me because I was able to hail the last
moving taxicab in downtown Lawrence.

As the cab approached my parents' house, I saw that
the lights were out, and after paying the cabdriver, I
walked up the front steps of the house and knocked on the
front door. Wearing only his long johns, my father appeared behind the front door and opened it to greet me.
The warmth of the house and the wonderful smell of a
freshly cut and decorated Christmas tree that had been
given a place of honor in the living room made my home-
coming so much better.

Within minutes the entire family was awake and had
joined my father and me in the living room. I was surrounded by them, answering their rapid-fire questions and
trying to ask many of my own. I was surprised to learn
that my brother Francis was away, serving in the 3d Marine Division as a member of the 3d Shore Party Battalion
and stationed at Camp McGill, Japan. My sister, Eleanor,
was attending St. Patrick's Parochial School, in the first
grade, and at seventeen, my youngest brother, Ted, had
just joined the Marine Corps and would leave for boot
camp at Parris Island, South Carolina, in February.

I moved into the kitchen where I saw my mother looking healthy and happy. She placed her warm hands on my
cold cheeks and looked into my eyes, seeing only her little boy safe at home for Christmas. Then she hugged me
deeply for what seemed to be the longest time, and I remember that although she had not spoken a word she was
smiling and crying.

Being able to walk into my parents' home on Christmas
Eve, and to hug the members of my family after having
spent a hellish year at war in Korea was very unsettling
to me. I wanted desperately to tell them what had happened, but I could not condense my experiences into con-

versation. All I could do was to sit at the kitchen table
and look at their smiling faces and be happy. That moment was the fulfillment of many days of hoping and
praying while I was in Korea. The tears I had tried so
hard to suppress during the most difficult times of the past
twelve months now flowed freely down my cheeks, and I
was not ashamed of it. We talked for several hours, until
I was emotionally and physically exhausted, and then I
climbed the thirteen stairs to the second floor and entered
my old bedroom, where I quickly fell asleep.

My rest was short-lived; I was awakened by my father
at seven A.M. and told to get up and be ready to attend
Christmas Mass. A sergeant of Marines and leader of men
I may have been, but my father was the king of his castle,
and his word was law. Wearing my uniform, I went to
church, where I gave thanks, once again, to the Almighty
and to my fellow Marines from C/1/5 for helping to bring
me home to my family for this Christmas.

CHAPTER 12

Camp Pendleton—1954–1955

I returned to Oceanside, California, on 27 January 1954, and since it was my second tour of duty at what was then the Marine Corps' largest base, I knew that a local bus would get me from the seaside town of Oceanside and to the base headquarters (24) area, where I would report in for my new duty assignment. At the base command post (CP), I presented my service record book (SRB) to a staff sergeant in the personnel section (S-1) who meticulously studied each page to determine, based upon my past duty stations and my qualifications, where I would be assigned. After only a few minutes of studying his list of options, and basing his decision on "the needs of the base," he told me that I had a choice between an assignment with the base military police or one as an instructor with the Training and Replacement Command (T&R) at Tent Camp #2 (Camp San Onofre). There was no hesitation on my part; I wanted nothing to do with becoming a military policeman so I told the staff sergeant that duty at T&R Command would be just fine. Although the shooting war in Korea was over, the Marine Corps was still training thousands of new replacements, just in case the North Koreans or Red Chinese should decide to renege on the signed armistice agreement.

Within an hour, transportation—a pickup truck—had

been arranged to take me the fifteen miles to the northern end of the base and deliver me to where I had spent my last months before going to Korea, T&R Command. All of the names and faces had changed, but the training requirements at Tent Camp #2 had not, and based on skills and combat experiences learned respectively at Quantico and in Korea, I was assigned as a noncommissioned officers in charge (NCOIC) of the demolitions instructor section.

After a brief "welcome aboard" by the T&R first sergeant, I was escorted by a clerk to the NCO barracks that was home to permanent personnel of the command. By late in the afternoon, I was settled in my Quonset hut and had visited the demolitions section to get acquainted with my new duties. I was surprised to learn that I would have no duties until I had attended what was then known as the Instructor Orientation Course (IOC) School. During the two weeks before my orders for IOC School arrived, I was able to study all of the demolition-class lesson plans and to observe all demolition classes taught in the field.

In my opinion, IOC School—at Pendleton's Camp Del Mar—was one of the best two-week schools the Marine Corps has ever designed. During the first week, each of the thirty students in the class, representing many different military occupational specialities (MOSs), was required to present an impromptu one-minute speech to the rest of the class as well as to learn how to prepare a written outline for a more lengthy, thirty-minute class.

Our one-minute speeches were to be about "household gadgets," so I chose the plastic soap-box as the subject of my sixty-second dissertation. When it was my turn to address the class, I took only a few steps onto the small classroom stage before performing a vaudevillian "slip and fall" onto the deck, as my "attention getter." Then, as quickly as I had fallen, I got back on my feet and presented my fellow students a safety lecture, stressing the fact that by using a plastic soap-box, falls like the one I had just taken could be prevented. The device—and the lecture—worked, and I was now on my way to feeling more comfortable in speaking to a large group and by learning how to prepare and give what the Marines call "periods of instruction" (POIs).

During the second week of IOC, we were taught how to prepare for a thirty-minute class followed by a question and answer period. For this presentation I chose a subject I was intimately familiar with, the M-1 service rifle, and I used no gimmicks to get the attention of the class. The ribbons that I wore above my left breast pocket, indicating that I had seen combat in Korea, were enough to indicate the seriousness of my thirty-minute speech.

Instructor Orientation Course had no class standing, it was either pass or fail, and I passed. But by having passed that course and by successfully doing the very thing that I had disliked so much in high school, I was better prepared for the classroom duties that awaited me when I returned to T&R Command, back at San Onofre.

The first class that I taught at T&R Command was on mines and booby traps, and I prepared as I had been taught at school—planned an outline and practiced my presentation before a group of critical fellow instructors who would help to fine-tune my presentation. I memorized the elements of a land mine, the elements of a booby trap, and how to react in combat to either one. I drew from my experiences at Quantico and from the many combat patrols I had experienced in Korea. Having credibility as a combat veteran with my students, I was very much at ease in teaching them and demonstrating the "practical application" portion of the class. The demolitions section at T&R Command did not always have daily classes, and when we had slack periods, we would lend a hand, either acting as members of the aggressor force during the five-day war, or by attending new classes and learning new tricks of the trade that professional infantrymen should know. Not only was I teaching, but I was learning, and for the first time since I had joined the Corps, I felt like a professional noncommissioned officer.

One day, during a morning formation in late March, the word was passed that all high-expert rifle shooters in the command would be required to go, with their rifles, to rifle range #214, and to meet there with a major and a warrant officer who represented the base rifle and pistol team. Those officers were Distinguished Shooters, and with the blessing of the commanding general, they were given the authority to select new members for the prestigious base rifle and pistol team from the "volunteers" who had previously demonstrated ability with either the M-1 service rifle or the .45 Colt automatic pistol.

Major Martin, the officer in charge of the rifle team, had each try-out fire twenty rounds from the standing ("offhand") position at an Able target, a circular 10-inch bull's-eye target, from the two-hundred-yard line. Then he moved all shooters back to the five-hundred-yard line, for twenty more rounds in the prone position, at a silhouetted, man-size Baker target. Once finished, we were told to return to our respective commands, when we would be notified as to whether we had shot well enough to be considered for additional training.

The following Monday, I was on my way to another base rifle range, this one known as Chappo Flats, for one week of shooting the National Match Rifle Course, four separate events, or "strings," of shooting:

(a) Slow fire—20 rounds, at 200 yards, "A" target, offhand position

(b) Rapid fire—10 rounds, at 200 yards, "A" target, sitting position

(c) Rapid fire—10 rounds, at 300 yards, "A" target, prone position

(d) Slow fire—20 rounds, at 600 yards, "B" target, prone position

The total possible point value was 300 points, and I had shot a 260, on my first attempt. Not great, but good enough for me to be joined to the base rifle team and temporarily transferred from T&R Command to the Camp Mathews rifle range, located on what is, today, the University of California, San Diego, campus, located just ten miles north of San Diego, there to compete in the Marine Corps' Western Division rifle matches.

The teams in the Western Division matches came from Marine Corps Base Camp Pendleton, the Marine Corps Recruit Depot at San Diego, the 1st Marine Division, in Korea, the 3d Marine Division, in Japan, the 1st Marine Air Wing, in Korea, the Marine Corps Air Station, at El Toro, California, and from all of the Marine barracks west of the Mississippi River.

The Eastern Division was comprised of teams from the 2d Marine Division, MCRD Parris Island, Marine Corps Base Quantico, Virginia, the 2d Marine Air Wing, and all Marine barracks, posts, and stations east of the Mississippi River.

Normally, the Western Division and Eastern Division held their respective matches at about the same time each year. Then, all medal winners met at the Marine Corps' Marksmanship Training Unit, located at Quantico, for the Marine Corps matches. The results of that rifle match provided the best shooters from the Corps to go to Camp Perry, Ohio, and shoot in the biggest event of the year: the National Matches.

All members of the Western Division team, which I had just joined, met at the Camp Mathews "Easy" range for three weeks of practice before the match. Reveille went at 0430 each morning, followed by chow, and then off to the range so that the first rounds fired downrange would "hit paper" just as the first rays of sunlight were rising in the eastern sky.

The two days prior to the event determined who would get to shoot first. Those who shot the highest two days' practice scores were selected for the first relays. I made the first relay, and began the final three days of shooting by firing well, but I ruined my chances of winning a bronze medal on the last day of firing. The last bronze medal awarded in 1954 went to a shooter with a score of 575 out of a possible 600; I had shot a 574. The Western Division matches ended in early April, and with the end of the shooting came orders returning me to my regular duties at

Camp Pendleton. I had added the experience of learning the strict discipline required of a competitive marksman. This experience would serve me well in later years.

When I returned to Camp Pendleton, I was more than ever determined to enhance my education. I had come to realize that I had made a big mistake when I quit high school, and as opportunity for me to learn presented itself, I jumped at the chance. It didn't require a genius to figure out that Marines who could not clearly express themselves would certainly be passed over by those who could, so I enrolled in numerous Marine Corps Institute (MCI) correspondence courses, and took a series of United States Armed Forces Institute (USAFI) tests, which gave me high school credit for my Marine Corps training and experiences. Weekend liberty was not a part of my life for several months, as I spent most of my spare time with my nose buried in books and training manuals, preparing myself for future advancement.

In May 1954, the United States Marine Corps changed its ideas on formalized training. "T&R Command" became the 2d Infantry Training Regiment, and we started to receive large numbers of recruits fresh from the parade deck at the recruit depot in San Diego. In the past, Marines had learned infantry skills in the first unit they joined after graduating from boot camp; the "thinkers" in the Corps had decided this was no longer a good idea and brought formal infantry training to Camp Pendleton and to what was to become the 1st Infantry Training Regiment at Camp Lejeune, North Carolina. In fact, Marines from Camp Pendleton's T&R Command were "temporarily" transferred to Camp Lejeune to help organize that new training regiment, but never returned to Camp Pendleton. The formal tactical training of newly graduated recruits at the 2d Infantry Training Regiment continued to produce young Marines who, upon graduation from our three-week school, were able to take positions as members of any Marine infantry rifle company.

While on liberty with a buddy in Oceanside, one day in late June, I happened to spot a very clean-looking 1947

Ford convertible on the used car lot of the Dixon Ford dealership. On further inspection and after asking a few questions of the manager, I learned that the price on the car was six hundred dollars and that the last forty dollars in my wallet would put the car on "hold" until I could return to Dixon's with the balance provided by the local base credit union. With the memory and scars from my past experience as a young car owner deeply etched in my mind and on my body, I treated this opportunity much differently. Drinking and driving were no longer a part of my life, and though I did use the Ford convertible on the weekends, I had become a much more responsible driver. Life in the Corps was good, and I took my position as a Marine sergeant seriously.

As training continued to improve on Camp Pendleton, and as the Cold War steadily intensified, new camps began to open aboard the base to support the shift in the use of the Marine Corps, making it a mobile force in readiness. And all Marines aboard the base were encouraged to visit these new camps. Camp Margarita, home to the 5th Marine Regiment, opened east of the Chappo Flats rifle range. Camp Pulgas replaced what was known as Tent Camp #1, and became the home of the 7th Marine Regiment. Camp Horno, west of Rifle Range #214, became the new home of the division's schools and a new antitank battalion. And camps named San Mateo and Christianitos were built in the northeastern corner of the base bordering on the town limits of San Clemente. These new camps were considered to be the ultimate in comfortable living for infantry Marines. The concrete buildings, each able to accommodate a forty-man platoon, were the invention of U.S. Navy Seabees and were called "tilt-up" barracks because the solid concrete slabs that made up their foundation, walls and roofs were simply tilted into position by construction cranes prior to the installation of wiring and plumbing fixtures.

In late July, I was told to report to our mess hall to take a written promotion test for the grade of staff sergeant. I was pleased to see that the first test presented to those of us being considered for promotion that morning was the GMST (general military speciality test). I had completed numerous MCI correspondence courses and had only recently taken out the Officer's Basic Extension Course, but the questions from the courses I had taken were the same ones that appeared on the GMST. We returned to the mess hall at 1300, and were faced with taking what was known as the TT (technical/tactical) test. This two-part test consisted first of a series of questions that would determine each Marine's knowledge of organic infantry weapons, including the M-1, BAR, M-1 carbine, .45 pistol, M-1919A4 machine gun, and the 75mm recoilless rifle. The second part of the examination tested each Marine's knowledge of platoon, company, and special-operations tactics. Questions about combat in built-up areas, offensive and defensive patrolling, attack on a fortified position, river crossings, and nuclear, biological, chemical contamination made this a difficult examination for Marines who failed to keep abreast of the changes in infantry tactics and training. When I had finished taking the test, I felt confident that I had scored well if for no other reason than I had spent so many hours attending, during my off-duty hours, every available class taught at 2d ITR. I was familiar with those subjects.

In August, a friend of mine named Skidmore, a sergeant assigned to Range Company, surprised me when he announced that he had decided to get out of the Corps and go to work with the Los Angeles police department. Skidmore regaled me with benefits of becoming an L.A. cop, told me that they were in the process of hiring, and asked me if I might be interested in doing the same thing. I told him that at the time I wasn't too interested, but if ever I decided to leave the Corps, I'd give the idea some serious thought.

For whatever reasons, the modest rainy season that southern California experiences each fall came earlier than normal in 1954, and with the rains came numerous closings of our live-fire and demolitions ranges. The last weeks of October and first week of November saw particularly bad weather, and as the streams on Camp Pendleton began to swell, roads were closed and all training aboard the base was canceled, as was all liberty, for five days. The first real break in the bad weather coincided with the 179th birthday of the Marine Corps, and it was the decision of our regimental commander, Col. J. H. Tinsley, to celebrate the event with the traditional cake-cutting ceremony held on the regimental parade field. As part of the ceremony, the colonel served the first piece of birthday cake to the oldest Marine present, a crusty old sergeant with a chestful of medals, known to those of us in the regiment as Pappy Breechblock. Pappy had seen combat as a corporal on Midway Island as a member of the island's defense battalion in December of 1941.

I remember driving down to San Diego, on the last weekend of November, to satisfy a longtime curiosity that began while I was on liberty in San Francisco after returning from Korea. There, a neon sign in the Fairbanks Club read: WHEN IN SAN DIEGO VISIT OUR CLUB 66 IN NATIONAL CITY. With a no-duty weekend at my disposal, I decided to find out what was so special about a club that would advertise for business nine hundred miles away.

Upon arriving, and much to my surprise, I could see that Club 66 was a navy hangout. Wearing my service uniform, I was the immediate subject of some friendly harassment and catcalls by the sailors occupying many of the club's booths and stools, but I kept my sense of humor, smiled politely, and found my way to an unoccupied seat at the far end of the bar. There was—and is—an unwritten rivalry between sailors and Marines, but those sailors meant no harm; they just wanted me to know that the Club 66 was their turf. Still, I kept a wary eye peeled for the resident seagoing tough guy who would want to impress his drinking buddies by challenging the Marine who had entered "his" club. And it didn't take too long for "him" to surface. I hadn't even finished my second bottle of beer when I began to hear progressively louder comments about "goddamned dumb jarheads" and "seagoing bellhops." Trouble was on its way in the shape of a big sailor, a first class boatswain's mate fueled by too many beers. He had been seated at the far end of the bar, but he suddenly got up from his stool and headed in my direction. By the look on his face, I could see that he wasn't coming my way just to talk.

Before he reached me, I was standing up and facing him, and when he stepped inside of my reach I threw two quick left jabs to see if he knew how to box. I sensed immediately that he wasn't a boxer, but he could still take a punch. Seeing that he outweighed me by twenty pounds, I set my feet and threw a straight right punch, using my legs and shoulders to add a little wallop, and I hit him so hard in the face that he backpedaled into a shuffleboard game, and as he fell, he hit his head on the leg of the machine before assuming the position of a cold mackerel.

When blood started to flow from his mouth, ears, and nose, I got a little concerned not only for his sake but for my own, too. In less than a minute, two members of the San Diego shore patrol (navy first class petty officers) entered Club 66 and walked up to me, demanding to know what had happened. I told the shore patrol my version of what had occurred, and much to my relief, the sailors in the bar backed up my story. They added that the unconscious sailor who was being carried out to the waiting ambulance was always looking for trouble, but that this time he'd found it. One of the shore patrol members wrote down my name and duty station, but he assured me that no follow-on report would be sent to Camp Pendleton because, in his opinion, the guy had gotten what was coming to him.

After the ambulance and shore patrol had left the club, a waitress came over and told me to sit down at the bar so that she could treat my injury. Her comment caught me by surprise, because until that moment I thought that I hadn't been hurt. "Take a look at your right hand, Sergeant." And that was when I noticed that I had a tooth embedded in the knuckle of my middle finger. The waitress gently wrapped my hand in a clean white, bar towel, then poured a shot of whiskey over the tooth before pulling it free. My curiosity satisfied, I drove back to Camp Pendleton and stopped by the regimental sick bay, where a corpsman gave me a tetanus shot and added a bandage to my swollen hand.

As was the custom at the time, half of the training command went on annual leave during the Christmas and New Year's holiday season. I was among those who remained in California for the beginning of 1955, but I spent the holidays with the family of an old friend; a navy first class petty officer named Martin, who I had known for a long time. When he told me that his ship would be at sea during the holidays, I decided to play Santa Claus to his wife and five young children. I rented a bright red Santa suit, complete with white beard and shiny black boots, and with a seabag full of toys draped over my shoulder, I went to their home in San Diego's Mission Beach and enjoyed one of my most memorable Christmas Days before returning to my duties at Camp Pendleton.

In March 1955, the 2d Infantry Training Regiment was again looking to field a shooting team for the annual Western Division matches. Once again I tried out and was accepted as a member of the base rifle team. The matches were held at Camp Pendleton's Chappo Flats Range, and all shooters were billeted in the 16 Area, making it much easier for me to get to the range in my Ford.

In 1954, we had made mistakes: The ammunition that we used was armor piercing, and when we fired it through brand-new M-1 rifles, the lands and grooves cut the metal jackets away from the bullets, and the only thing that reached the target was the tungsten core of the bullet. This time, however, we used match-quality ball ammunition for practice and while firing for record. I fired 573 out of the possible 600, but with competition being so keen that year, a score of 588 took the last bronze medal of the event. Once more I returned to 2d Infantry Training Regiment. Although I was welcomed back by the Marines of the training regiment, I knew that I could have done better.

Sometime in early April, the 1st Marine Division, understrength at ten thousand Marines, returned to Camp

Pendleton from Korea. The new camps that had just opened immediately became home to the thousands of returning men: The 1st Marine Regiment went to San Mateo, the 5th Marine Regiment went to Margarita, the 7th Marine Regiment went to Las Pulgas, and the 11th Marines went to the 16 Area. The division Headquarters and Headquarters Battalion went to the 15 Area, 1st Motor Transportation Battalion went to the 25 Area at Vado del Rio, 1st Shore Party Battalion went to Camp Del Mar, 1st Tank Battalion went to Las Pulgas (old Tent Camp #1), 1st Service Battalion went to the 12 Area, 1st Engineer Battalion went to Camp Telaga, and division Recon Company went to the 15 Area. The division's schools were at Camp Horno along with a new antitank battalion. And, with the return of the division, the graduates of 2d ITR quickly found their way into new infantry commands as the division began to come back up to strength.

On 23 June 1955, I received orders to ABCD (atomic, biological, chemical, and decontamination) School, located forty miles north of Camp Pendleton, at the Marine Corps Air Station, El Toro, California. I arrived at the school's NCO barracks during the weekend and was told to report to the school's administrative section at 0800 on Monday morning. After presenting my orders and service record book to the school's administrative chief, I was told that the officer in charge, a captain, wanted to see me; my academic past had returned to haunt me. The captain told me that he would have to terminate my orders because I had not finished high school and the course would not be easy for even the brightest students. But I told the captain that I wanted to complete the course and that his sending me back to Camp Pendleton would only discredit my unit, since they had seen fit to send me. I told him that if he would allow me to stay, I would seek necessary help to pass from the school's staff. My determination must have persuaded him; he said that if I was indeed that motivated to stay, then he would allow for it.

ABCD School was a four-week course designed to teach Marines about the dangers of atomic radiation and the use of tactical biological agents and chemical contaminants. Those who successfully completed the course would receive a secondary MOS of 5711, NBC technician. The first week of school was dedicated to learning about germ warfare, how and why bacteria were cultivated and the methods used to deliver them and to combat them. During the second week, we learned about chemical agents, how they could be identified, and how they were to be deactivated. The third week of ABCD School was dedicated to the study of nuclear weapons, and included the various types of weapons and bomb blasts, their effects on defensive positions, and the symptoms of radiation sickness. In the last week of school, we were shown how to use chemical and radiological detection equipment, how to decontaminate personnel and equipment, and how to compute the length of the radiation or chemical agents in a particular area.

The course relied a great deal on practical application: Using a spring-loaded styrette, each student was required to inject himself with atropine—a drug used against nerve agents; each of us had a single drop of mustard gas agent dropped onto his skin and watched as a large burning blister formed. We were required to physically decontaminate a jeep and an aircraft mock-up. Working with cobalt, we plotted radioactive "hot spots" to prevent personnel from entering a decontaminated area. We were introduced to several types of Geiger counters and were required to wear and to read a dosimeter, a clip-on device that indicated levels of radiation.

To successfully make it through the four weeks of ABCD School, as promised, I sought out the help of several tutors, NCOs on the school's staff, and together we spent long hours after each class going over the handouts and the many pages of notes.

I finished next to last in my class of thirty students, but I was nonetheless pleased with myself not only for having finished the most difficult school assignment I had ever undertaken but in knowing that the class goat, the student who had finished last in the class, was a guy who had two years of college under his belt before he had joined the Corps.

On 27 July 1955, the NCOIC of the school called out my name to come forward and receive my certificate and at that point the whole class and the school staff stood up and applauded my efforts. The four weeks of ABCD School might seem insignificant in a thirty-year career, but the event left an indelible mark on me. I had realized that education and hard work would always pay the greatest of dividends.

I returned to Camp Pendleton that same day and resumed my regular duties with the 2d Training Regiment. Not more than a week later, I decided to reconsider becoming a police officer with the Los Angeles police department. I can't honestly say what moved me to do that; it had been almost a year since Skidmore had told me about it, but with my enlistment nearly at an end, I reported in to the base separation center and was discharged from the Corps for the second time, on 12 August 1955.

It just so happened that a friend of mine, a sergeant named John Paradise, had asked me to be an usher in his wedding, which was scheduled to take place on August 17th, in Glendale, California. He also told me that he had a great surprise waiting for me there in his hometown. I told John that I would be honored to be a member of his wedding party, and left Camp Pendleton, heading for Glendale by way of Los Angeles to check in with the LAPD training department. But I was surprised to learn that the next class of police cadets would not convene for at least six months. I had missed the last class by just one week, and realized that I would have to do something to keep busy for six months, if I wanted to become a cop. I drove toward Glendale, wondering if I had made another big mistake.

John Paradise's wedding was to be a small family affair, but we were to wear tuxedos, and that meant I needed a fitting, which was scheduled to be done the day before the wedding. As it happened, a Marine Corps recruiting station was located next door to the tuxedo rental shop, and not wanting to miss an opportunity to talk to a couple of Marines, I went inside and told the Marine recruiters what I had done and what had happened to me. They said that if I wanted to reenlist, all I had to do was to take the oath of enlistment and, on the following day, report to the Armed Forces Induction Center in Los Angeles to complete a physical examination. I was to tell the doctor that my examination had been extended because I had attended a wedding reception and consumed a lot of alcohol. So, my future assured for the next six years, I reenlisted in the Marine Corps.

John's wedding was a wonderful event, and the reception that followed in the church meeting hall could not have been any better. At the reception, I learned that John's father worked as the technical director of demolitions for 20th Century Fox Studios, and as a surprise to me, John had asked his father to get me a job working as a demolitions man for 20th Century Fox. When Mr. Paradise told me that he had "locked on" a job for me, starting the following week, I was stunned. I could hardly bring myself to tell the two of them that I had just reenlisted for six years! I drank heavily to relieve the shock.

The following day, I returned the rented tuxedo, completed my physical examination, and went back to the Glendale recruiting station. I was told to go home and wait for my orders to arrive, but not wanting to return to Massachusetts, I gave the recruiters the address of my friends living in southern California, and went there to await the arrival of my orders and my future assignment. For twenty days, I baby-sat the five kids who belonged to Chief Petty Officer Martin, the sailor for whose family I had played Santa Claus the year before, in Mission Beach. On the twenty-first day came a letter directing that I go to the Marine Corps recruiting station in San Diego and sign for a new set of orders.

At the recruiting station, a gunnery sergeant handed me a large manila envelope, which I quickly opened. Inside were orders directing me to report to the 1st Marine Division, Camp Pendleton.

CHAPTER 13

New Cruise, New Duties— 1955–1958

On 7 September 1955, I checked into the 1st Marine Division personnel office and was quickly assigned to the ranks of the 1st Engineer Battalion, located at Camp Telega, the old Tent Camp #31/2. After checking into the battalion headquarters, I was assigned to Able Company as the 2d Platoon's right guide. My platoon leader was a first lieutenant named DeJong and our platoon sergeant was a "poster-type" marine staff sergeant named Richard Younghands.

The primary mission of an engineer battalion was to support a Marine infantry regiment with demolition capability, mine warfare, obstacle construction and destruction, and to support designated assault units.

Our battalion consisted of a Headquarters and Service Company, with a battalion supply section, a motor transportation section, and the battalion armory section. The battalion's Support Company consisted of a building section, a utilities section, and a heavy equipment section. Company's A, B, C, and D each consisted of a headquarters platoon, a heavy equipment platoon, a motor transportation platoon, and three platoons of engineers. With four squads of fifteen men per platoon, the following MOSs were represented: construction men, riggers, and demolitions men. The battalion's total strength was nearly 650 Marines.

At the time, a well-trained Marine demolitions man had to be proficient in the following areas:

1. Be able to prime all types of packaged explosives.
2. Be able to calculate explosive charges using correct tables and formulas.
3. Know the types of explosives and their detonating rates.
4. Be able to work with electric and nonelectric circuits.
5. Know how to construct improvised explosives, charges, and packages.
6. Know the ballistic theory of mines and their elements.
7. Be familiar with the various types of U.S.-made mines.
8. Know how to properly construct a minefield and be familiar with patterns.
9. Know how to arm and disarm mines and booby traps.
10. Know how to properly record the placing of a minefield.
11. Know how to install and disarm booby traps.
12. Know how to identify foreign-made mines.
13. Be familiar with how foreign-made mines function and how to disarm them.

Our quarters at Camp Telega consisted of Quonset huts. Each company had two rows of five huts, one Quonset hut per platoon and one hut converted into a head for use by all Marines in the company. One Quonset hut was used as the company office, and one hut was used exclusively as sergeants' quarters. The huts had double racks, and each was home to twenty to twenty-five men. The sergeants' Quonset hut was home to about twelve Marine NCOs. Our battalion mess hall was simply a larger Quonset hut. The largest section of the messdeck was used by corporals and below, one section was dedicated for sergeants, and one section each for the staff NCOs and officers. The quality of the food was consistently excellent.

Training was the mainstay of the battalion, and in 1955, our training was based on a fairly rigid schedule designed to keep proficiency at a peak. Typical training for a "letter" (company) in garrison began with reveille at 0500, followed by a brief cleanup of the barracks, and the racks being made up before we fell out for morning PT, which was run by the company's sergeants. After morning chow and a morning formation, normal training began at 0730, with the training for each MOS taking place in a classroom, in an outdoor class area, or as part of a practical lesson conducted in the field. Traditionally, one day each week was set aside for cross-training: demolition men were trained to handle the lengths of wire, cable, and rope commonly used by the riggers; construction men taught the rest of us how to properly tie knots and to make three-strand rope bridges or a more complicated suspension bridge.

The M-1 rifle was issued to all sergeants and below; each platoon sergeant and platoon leader was armed with a .45 Colt automatic. Each platoon had one light, .30-caliber, Browning air-cooled machine gun and one 3.5-inch rocket launcher. The equipment common to each platoon consisted of a demolition kit, one rigging kit, and one pioneer kit, which included saws, chain saws, and brush axes. Three mine-detector kits were also found in each platoon. The 782 gear we wore was identical to that carried by all Marine infantrymen.

On 20 September, our company boarded trucks and was taken to San Diego, where we boarded the USS *Teldaga*, along with the 3d Battalion, 1st Marine Division, to take part in an amphibious landing on Camp Pendleton's White Beach, the first amphibious landing conducted by a regimental landing team since the division had returned from Korea. The objective of the landing was to secure a beachhead and then move inland to neutralize several secondary objectives located on Basilone Road, the main thoroughfare that crossed Camp Pendleton. The regiment's 3d Battalion had received orders to land on White Beach and then move east for one mile before shifting direction to the south. Once it reached Stage Coach Road, it was to move parallel to the road as far as the northern end of the base airstrip. Able Company's primary mission would be to breach paths through minefields on White Beach and to breach roadblocks the battalion might encounter along Stage Coach Road.

After we had settled into the routine aboard the USS *Teldaga*, briefing sessions took up the majority of the day. D day was to be 26 September, H hour 0500, and a dress rehearsal was scheduled to take place two days earlier on a beach known as the Silver Strand on the Island of Coronado, just several miles south of San Diego. My section, two squads of engineers, was attached to the battalion's leading assault company, Item Company. After a successful rehearsal, we sailed north along the California coast and prepared for the actual event.

The amphibious landing went off like clockwork, and after simulated naval prep-fires were used to help neutralize the minefields, we spent the better part of D day creating paths for the infantry by using mine detectors to locate mines before neutralizing them. On the evening of D plus one, my section and the Marines of Item Company were taken out to sea aboard "Peter" boats, and using a Jacob's ladder, we transferred to a navy LST, which was loaded with LVT 3-Cs, amphibious tractors, protected by a steel cover and operated by a crew of three Marines. Each LVT-3C could ferry twenty Marines ashore. Affixed to their tracks were steel cups that just tore up any hard-surface roads they might cross.

The LST was a much smaller ship than an APA, and not being able to feed a reinforced company of Marines, the best the ship's crew could do was to provide us with hot coffee until we left the ship early the next morning. The Marines assigned to my demolitions section had been designated to ride ashore in the first tractor to disembark the LST. Our mission was to help breach obstacles ashore, and as we moved inland, our flanks would be protected by the infantrymen of Item Company.

The entire amphibious operation lasted for almost two

weeks, and by the time it had ended, Marines of the 3d Battalion had a much better understanding of our engineering capabilities, and the demolitions men of the 1st Engineer Battalion who had never participated in such an exercise now understood the team effort needed to make a success out of the most difficult of all joint military operations, the amphibious landing. Our demolitions section received a letter of commendation from the 1st Marine Regiment for our participation in that first landing exercise so it's clear that our men had successfully participated in the team effort.

On 10 November, we celebrated the Marine Corps' birthday in the mess hall because sergeants and below did not then have a birthday ball to attend as they do today. The celebration consisted of the traditional reading of the commandant's message, the reading of Gen. John C. Lejeune's inspirational message, and culminated with the cutting of the birthday cake, the first pieces going to the youngest and to the oldest Marines present. The oldest Marine present that day was Master Sergeant Criter, a veteran of the 2d Nicaraguan Campaign who had become a Distinguished Rifle Shooter in 1927. Top Criter worked in the 1st Engineer Battalion S-3 shop and was responsible for managing the battalion's annual rifle requalification training. He was regarded by many Marines as something of a legend, and in time, he would have a pronounced influence on my life as my shooting coach.

At 0730, on 27 November, the Marines of the 1st Engineers stood at attention during a battalion formation, and I could hardly believe my ears when my name was called out to join in a twenty-man detail and march forward, stopping "front and center" of our battalion commander. He moved almost mechanically down our line, stopping directly in front of each man, and when the colonel stopped in front of me, I listened as our battalion adjutant read my promotion warrant aloud, and I became a Marine staff sergeant (E-5).

My platoon sergeant, Richard Younghands, was also one of the group promoted, and as we walked back toward our company's area, I was about to assume Younghands's duties as platoon sergeant, while he became our new company gunnery sergeant. Tradition played a very large part in the lives of Marine noncommissioned officers, and with my promotion came not only the opportunity of becoming a member of the staff noncommissioned officers' club, but to participate in my first "wetting down" ceremony. The SNCO Club closest to Camp Telega was several miles away at Camp San Mateo, so my close friend, SSgt. Charles Jankowski, platoon sergeant of the company's 1st Platoon, took me to the club that afternoon. As we entered, dozens of SNCOs from the battalion had formed a welcoming line, shaking hands with those of us who had been promoted into their fraternal organization. Tradition called for us new SNCOs to pay the bartender the difference in one month's salary between our previous pay grade, E-4 ("buck" sergeant), and our new pay grade E-5 (Staff Sergeant), and that money was used to keep the beer flowing within the club. It was not until I had laid my money down on the bar and chugged several mugs of cold draft beer that I was considered by my peers to be a staff sergeant of Marines.

I took two weeks' leave for Christmas and New Year's that year, and again I spent the holidays playing host to Chief Martin's family at their home in Mission Beach. Upon my return to the battalion during the first week of January, I learned that my platoon had been designated to support the 1st Battalion, 7th Marines, in a ten-day live-fire exercise (DESFEX), which was to be conducted at the Marine Corps training area at Twenty-Nine Palms, California. We would fire all our organic weapons during the exercise and use live demolitions in support of the 7th Marine Regiment's plan of attack.

As a platoon sergeant, I was expected to attend all of the infantry battalion's planning sessions not only to learn the training objectives of the battalion but also to tell the grunts how we could best support their plans. At 0530 on 16 January, the Marines in my demolitions platoon packed their weapons, clothing, and equipment inside two trailers and boarded two six-by trucks that were to take us to the desert as part of a larger convoy. Our motorized march took us first through the Fallbrook Naval Weapons Station, a naval ammunition dump, and then through the sleepy little town of Fallbrook, before we headed north onto Route 395. Turning east, we continued along Route 60 and passed through the high desert town of Banning before making a pit stop. Outside Banning, we waited for the rest of the convoy to join us before driving through Morongo and Yucca valleys, past the town of Joshua Tree, to enter Twenty-nine Palms through the main gate.

My platoon was assigned to support the regiment's 1st Battalion, and as a supporting unit we became "attachments," dependent upon our "parent" organization for our needs. When we arrived at the battalion command post (CP), we pitched shelter halves along with Marines assigned to the battalion Headquarters and Service (H&S) Company, and learned we would eat our morning and evening meals at the battalion's field mess. While in the field, we would be served C rations for our noon meal.

The first six days of the exercise were spent in training to attack fortified positions, coordinating the use of both heavy and light machine guns, the 75mm recoilless rifle, the flamethrower, and using demolitions in the attack. The way we trained would be the way we would conduct the actual exercise. During each of the six days a different rifle company from the 1st and 2d Battalions of the regiment participated in that type of training. The 3d Battalion was designated as the aggressor force for the exercise and conducted its training in the "problem" area.

We viewed our training as serious business, and those of us who had learned how to eliminate an enemy bunker, whether during World War II or during the Korean War, knew that only a coordinated attack would bring the desired results. This was the textbook solution to taking a bunker:

1. On command, the long-range base of fire would commence with water-cooled heavy machine guns approx-

imately seventeen hundred yards from the bunker, to seal in the occupants and keep them away from the bunker's firing ports.

2. A green signal flare was used to signal to cease the long-range firing. A close-range base of fire would commence, to continue to keep the bunker occupants pinned down.

3. The assault element would move to a close flank range, approximately fifty to sixty yards.

4. Once in position, the assault element would fire a red signal flare, alerting the machine gunners to shift the base of fire away from the bunker.

5. Rifle grenades were then fired to help screen the assault force.

6. Flamethrower teams would then move to about twenty yards from the bunker and then shoot liquid fire into the apertures of the bunker.

7. The demolitions men would then advance toward the bunker carrying a pole charge of twenty-five pounds of TNT. They would then place the charge against the bunker, after having pulled the two fuse lighters on the charge. The twenty-five pounds of TNT, strategically placed, would destroy any bunker.

After each of the rifle companies had completed its week's training on assaulting fortified positions, a one-day break in training allowed for a field meet, which served as an additional training vehicle. Infantry weapons—light machine guns, M-1 rifles, and the 3.5-inch rocket launcher were used in timed disassembly and assembly relay races. With hot chow served in the field and a party atmosphere to help us unwind, we were ready to begin the actual firing exercise the following morning.

With the 1st Battalion assigned to lead the attack, my demolitions section was assigned to Able Company, the point element of the battalion. Our right flank was protected by two platoons from the company and our left flank was protected by one platoon. The main body, made up of H&S Company and C Company, was moving only several hundred yards forward of the 2d Battalion when the point element ran into a minefield on Baghdad Road (Figure 1). The momentum of the advance came to an immediate stop; at which time, my section and a platoon of infantrymen from A Company started to probe with bayonets and mine detectors to clear assault paths along the road. The simulated minefield did contain numerous practice mines equipped with training charges designated to detonate if the antipersonnel and antitank mines were not properly handled. And as we continued the painstaking task of clearing the mines, the aggressor force from the 3d Battalion wasted no time in taking us under fire, using blanks. It didn't require much imagination to understand how much more effective real bullets could have been.

While my section was still within the minefield, the Marines in the main element of the battalion had shifted to positions that allowed them to begin firing live ammunition at positions only recently vacated by the Marines of the aggressor force. The signal to commence firing was provided by designated umpires who fired four star clusters in the sky above the target area, indicating the area was clear and a free-fire zone. The battalion's 81mm mortars began to fire, and they were joined by the companies' 60mm mortars. When these fires were shifted, the assault on the fortified positions began, just as they were executed during the previous week's training portion of the exercise. As one bunker was taken out on the right flank, the next bunker was attacked on the left flank. After all four of the bunkers had been neutralized, the Marines of the demolitions section were called forward to blow up the bunkers for real.

The live-firing exercise was considered a great training success. New troops began to understand what was required of them in working as part of a combined effort on the battlefield. Given the obvious need for close supervision and safety, the exercise was made as realistic as possible, but a sense of realism was needed to make Marines think about what was happening and to alert them to the fact the battlefield was a constantly changing place.

When the exercise was over, 1st Lieutenant DeJong told us he was extremely pleased with how well things had gone and that we would be rewarded for our efforts. After we returned to Camp Pendleton, we spent several days cleaning our weapons and equipment before we passed the scrutiny of our company commander's inspection. But the lieutenant's pledge was made good; all members of the platoon where given ninety-six-hour passes.

In March 1956, our platoon was assigned to support my old battalion, 1st Battalion, 5th Marines, as part of a battalion raid. At a series of briefings I attended with my platoon commander at the 1st Battalion's command post at Camp Margarita, we learned this raid was to begin with an amphibious landing on White Beach, using LVT 3-Cs and LVTs to take us to our objective on Camp Pendleton's highest elevation, known as the Case Springs area. Following our actions within the objective area, we would retrograde back to White Beach and return to our ship. We also learned from the 1st Battalion's commanding officer, Lieutenant Colonel Mee, the exercise would be the last time LVTs would be used in an amphibious assault training exercise as the aging vehicles were to be replaced with the new LVT P-5 amphibious vehicle.

In the third week of March, we boarded trucks and were taken to Camp Del Mar, from where we were taken by Mike boats to board the LST *Jefferson County*, along with the Marines of B Company, 1/5, who had been designated as the assault company and the point element for the raid. One squad from our platoon had been attached to each of the three rifle companies in the battalion. Once we arrived at site of the objective, our company's primary mission was to destroy "an enemy rocket installation" in the area of Case Springs.

The amphibious landing went off according to plan, with no loss of time and no injuries. After coming ashore, our LVTs continued to move inland, moving up Allisio Canyon, crossing Basilone Road, and then climbing several thousand feet along Robalar Road into the Case Springs area. When we arrived at the objective area, I was surprised to see that, to lend some realism to the training exercise, a mock rocket had actually been built of six fifty-five-gallon drums welded together to form a fuse-lage, to which delta-type wings had been added to complete the picture. The rocket was mounted on a launching track, and from a distance, it looked quite impressive.

One of the indicators of a well-executed raid is timeliness, so we had been given only twenty minutes at the objective to rig multiple charges of C-3 (a plastic explosive) and to connect the charges with detonation cord, which had a double thirty-second fuse connected to a nonelectric blasting cap. When the area around the rocket was cleared of personnel and pronounced safe, the C-3 was detonated and the mock rocket flew for its one and only time.

The retrograde movement back toward White Beach also went smoothly. The rifle companies were able to move through one another (not an easy task) and, by doing so, provided "bounding" protection for one another as they moved toward the beach. The entire operation took only two days, but again, the experience was invaluable to all of us.

After returning to the engineer battalion, I was told by our company first sergeant that I had been selected as one of the Marines in the battalion to try out at Range 116 for the 1st Marine Division rifle and pistol team. I did as I was told, but I began to see the danger in having tried to become a competitive shooter when I was assigned to the base. My rifle shooting at Range 116 was good enough to make the team, and by doing so, I received orders to Chappo Flats to begin preparation for the division rifle matches.

The preliminary practice shoots were hampered by several days of heavy rains and exceedingly cold weather, and by the fourth day of shooting, I had managed to come down with a temperature of 103—good enough to be hospitalized at Camp Pendleton's naval hospital ward 32, the contagious ward, for a week's stay. The only "shooting" I experienced there were the well-aimed antibiotics fired into my ass by the ward's nurse. I was released after eight days and returned to division matches, but my shooting abilities were not up to par. At the conclusion of the matches, I returned to the battalion, again dejected at having worked so hard, but having so little to show for my efforts.

I returned to the battalion just in time to take part in the change of command ceremony welcoming LtCol F. X. Witt, Jr., as our new commanding officer. A veteran of World War II and Korea, Lieutenant Colonel Witt proved to be an outstanding officer who was respected by every Marine in the battalion.

In June, I left my duties as platoon sergeant and was assigned to work with Master Sergeant Criter to help run the battalion's rifle requalification details. Master Sergeant Criter was rapidly approaching his thirty-year retirement, and my apprenticeship would guarantee that much of his "corporate knowledge" would be passed along. I was also pleased to learn that my longtime friend, Staff Sergeant Jankowski, had also been assigned to the detail. While we were at the range, Jankowski brought his legendary, bolt-action '03 Springfield up to the firing line. I asked Ski if I could shoot the old service rifle, and liked it so much, I went on to shoot a score of 238 out of a possible 250 for my annual requalification score. Not to be outdone, Jankowski fired an identical score. He had purchased the rifle from a Marine armory for twenty-five dollars when Springfields became cheaply available as the M-1 Garand became the Corps' new service rifle. Unfortunately, the policy of being able to purchase an '03 for twenty-five dollars was brought to a halt several years later.

In December, I was asked to remain in the battalion's S-3 (training and operation) shop, to help set up an infantry training section for the engineer companies. The battalion's operations officer, Brytton, and his operation's chief, Master Sergeant Miller, gave me all of the support I asked for, and within two weeks, I had set up a course on infantry squad tactics starting at the fire-team level and progressing through the squad and platoon levels. At that time, several close friends assigned to the 2d Infantry

Training Regiment gave me lesson plans and student handouts and shared their ideas on how to construct the course. Each engineer company sent its Marines to us for three weeks, during which time they received classroom instruction, practical application, and a brief tactical exercise. This great assignment lasted until March of 1957, and it was not long after the last company of Marines had completed its infantry tactics training that I was presented with a Letter of Appreciation from Lieutenant Colonel Witt, for the fun I had teaching young Marines their trade.

With 1957 came many changes within the 1st Marine Division. The division was streamlined, becoming a light, mobile organization. Equipment long considered too big or too heavy was replaced with lighter, more efficient gear. The force structure of the Corps changed from what had been known as the "L-Series" to a more manageable "M-Series," and that, too, caused changes not only in how Marines would be assigned to battalions but also in how those battalions would be deployed. And at that time, the phonetic alphabet changed to its current form. Our battalion shed its utility section and most of its heavy equipment, and it was redesignated the 1st Pioneer Battalion. As part of the redesign of the battalion, I was transferred from what had become Alpha Company to Bravo Company, under the command of a Captain Cassidy, as the platoon sergeant of the 3d Platoon and, surprisingly, given guidance that we would begin to train at night, based on lessons learned from the Korean War.

With July came an incredible summer heat wave, and to find relief one night, I went to the 1st Marine's regimental swimming pool. While swimming there, I met a staff sergeant named Walter Webb, a Marine who would change my life forever. Webb had brought his scuba gear to the pool, and I asked if I could try it on. I was never afraid of the water and quickly decided that there wasn't anything Webb was doing that I could not do. He agreed to teach me about diving, beginning with a safety lecture, which immediately tested my resolve to learn how to dive. He explained and then demonstrated emergency procedures and how to buddy breathe. In 1957, sport scuba diving was a fledgling sport, but since the military had been using divers for more than twenty years, I felt confident that I was learning something that I could use during the rest of my military career. I was hooked, and that summer I spent every weekend possible diving around the kelp beds of nearby San Diego, Cardiff-by-the-sea, Oceanside, and Dana Point. Much to Webb's relief, I bought my own gear; a double-hose regulator, twin "38" tanks made from surplus oxygen bottles that had previously seen life aboard a C-119 Flying Boxcar, and a used wet suit, which had more patches on it than the law allowed.

In August I was called upon, once more, to help put together a demolitions school, this time at the division level. I was able to use the Marines in my platoon to help construct this one-week course, and with their physical help and their expertise, we put together a good training package. Utilizing one of the base's demolitions ranges as our classroom, we brought training aids, lesson plans, and provided handouts. We taught mostly corporals and sergeants, and sent back to the division Marines who were confident and competent in handling explosives. The frosting on that cake was the Letter of Appreciation from the division commanding general to each of the Marines in my platoon who helped to teach the course.

During November, I was assigned to help the base produce a thirty-minute training film called "Tank and Infantry Tactics with Air Observation," for which I provided all of the explosive demolitions and artillery simulation. With a seemingly inexhaustible supply of explosives made available to support the film, we helped to add a little realism to the show, and that, too, led to an early Christmas present—a Letter of Appreciation from the base commanding general to the Marines in my platoon.

With the end of 1957 in sight, I requested two weeks of annual leave and planned to visit the Martin family children, as Santa, once more.

CHAPTER 14

The Making of a Professional Marine—1958–1960

I returned to Camp Pendleton after the New Year and found myself having to assume the duties as platoon commander due to the unexpected departure of Lieutenant DeJong. I was directed by the company commander, Captain Cassidy, to start attending meetings at the headquarters of 3d Battalion, 5th Marines, in preparation for our supporting operation SNOW-FEX III, to be conducted at the Marine Corps Cold Weather Training Center at Bridgeport, California.

From the numerous briefings conducted by LtCol. S. S. Hughes, the commanding officer of 3/5, and his staff at Camp Margarita, we learned that his battalion was to be taken by 9th Motor Transportation Battalion truck convoy to the higher altitudes at Bridgeport. As part of this exercise, our objective was to support Lieutenant Colonel Hughes's infantry battalion under extreme cold-weather conditions. My platoon, which had been trimmed down in personnel to a very light pioneer platoon, was assigned to support the battalion, using only local materials and field expedient methods of engineering.

We had been given five tasks to be completed or mastered during the exercise:

1. Construct an obstacle crossing.
2. Destroy an obstacle using high explosives.
3. Remain light and mobile to support infantry attacks.
4. Demonstrate the clearing of mines and booby traps in mountainous terrain.
5. Be able to conduct all missions on foot.

Arriving in early February and still in time to experience the deep snow and extreme cold of the High Sierras, we were trucked up to the Pickle Meadows base camp, finding the snow so deep at the six thousand foot level that further travel by truck was impossible. Carrying our individual equipment on our backs and pulling all of our extra equipment on drag sleds called akios, we began the final march to the new base camp, located several miles away at Silver Creek. The effects of the high altitude, constant winds, and knee-deep snow made that one of the most difficult marches any of us had experienced.

The exercise was to last three weeks—the first dedicated to cold-weather training at the squad level and to staying out overnight in man-made snow caves; the second week was survival training at the platoon level, with reinforced platoons staying out in the snow overnight; the final week was for company-level training in preparation for Operation SNOW-FEX III, which was to last for three days.

The day before the operation was a Sunday, which Lieutentant Colonel Hughes had set aside for a battalion field meet. Using what we had learned during the preceding three weeks, the day's events included a three-mile snowshoe relay race, a five-mile cross-country ski race, a three-man akio race with two men in an akio pulled by a single Marine. The fourth event had the battalion's 81mm mortar teams displacing in the snow. The final event was a great tug-of-war pitting company against company. By the time the sun began to set over the mountains, every Marine in the battalion was tired and ready for a good night's sleep. But not too long after sunset, the weather changed, and snowflakes the size of quarters began to fall heavily. The next morning we awoke to find an additional foot of snow added to what had been left by earlier storms.

My platoon was attached to India Company, one squad of engineers attached to each of the company's three rifle platoons. I was moving with the company headquarters element at the start of the operation, and as we traveled throughout the day, we became extremely tired, trudging through the waist-high snow.

On the first night of the operation, the company gunnery sergeant and I had organized a few Marines from the headquarters element to help construct a snow cave large enough to protect a half-dozen men. We had begun digging out the cave at sunset, hollowing out places to store our weapons and packs, and using heat from candles to glaze the interior walls. Sometime close to midnight, after taking one last look around outside, the company commander, company gunnery sergeant, and I used our snowshoes to mark the location of our CP and moved into the cave to catch a few hours of much-needed sleep. We had laid out our sleeping bags and taken off most of our cold-weather clothing, when a faint voice from outside asked, "Where's the CP?" Suddenly the candles went out as a mountain of snow came crashing in on top of us. Once we had managed to work ourselves to the surface, I heard a very young Marine ask his incensed company commander, "Sir, I'm looking for the company CP."

"Son, goddamn it, you're *in* the company CP," the captain replied. "Now, what the hell do you want?"

After a moment of silence, surveying the total destruction of our snow cave, and sensing the futility of the situation, we began to laugh like men half-crazed.

On the final day of the operation, as each of the rifle companies began to return to the base camp, each commander was summoned to the battalion commander's tent for a short briefing. The colonel explained that four Marines from L Company were missing, having failed to return from a patrol they had gone out on the day before. The colonel's plan to find these lost men was simple: return to the field, and leaving no stone unturned, search for the men until they were found. My platoon of engineers, now assigned to Headquarters and Service Company, was given orders to move east of Lost Cannon Peak and to follow the Lost Cannon Creek toward the northeast, moving on a wide skirmish line.

It was the pilot of a Civil Air Patrol plane who first spotted the four lost men moving alongside the creek, and alerted us to their location by dropping a note tied to a rag as he passed over us. Our company commander passed the good news of their discovery to the battalion commander, and we were told to continue to move downstream toward the men until we made physical contact with them. Several hours later, when we finally linked up with them, the four Marines said that once they realized they were lost they did what they had been taught during their survival classes, moving toward lower ground, away from the snow line. Our mission completed, we chose the closest pickup point, along Highway 395, which required us to move across Mill Canyon Road before we could be met by the trucks that would take us back to Camp Pendleton. We crossed thirty miles of open countryside to get there on time.

In March 1958, seventeen "quotas" arrived for 1st Marine Division noncommissioned officers to attend the U.S. Army's Jungle Warfare Training Center at Fort Sherman, in the Panama Canal Zone, and I was selected to be one of the attendees. This was the first all-staff NCO Class selected to go to Fort Sherman, exclusively from the United States. The 2d Marine Division also received seventeen quotas, and the remainder of the class comprised soldiers from the 77th Special Forces, the 82d and 101st Airborne Divisions, the 2d and 10th Infantry Divisions, and an army ranger battalion. Our class of seventy-five students was organized like an army infantry company: four platoons of three squads with one machine-gun squad attached. Each training day all the leadership billets changed so each student would be given different responsibilities; I served as a squad leader, platoon sergeant, and as a weapons section leader.

The Jungle Warfare Training Center was created to teach well-trained units and individuals methods which the army considered best to conquer those difficulties encountered in a jungle environment, where the normal problems of visibility, movement, communications, tactics, and logistics are magnified. As difficult as these problems were made by the jungle, they could be minimized by applying sound battle-tested principles and doctrine. The principles and doctrine are not changed—only the technique of their application.

The Jungle Warfare Training Center occupied an irregular tract of land approximately seven miles wide and twelve miles long, which included the Fort Sherman military reservation plus certain contiguous areas on lease from the Canal Zone government. On the east was Limon Bay, which separated Fort Sherman from the cities of Colon, Republic of Panama, and Cristobal, Canal Zone. On the south was the Rio Pina, which was swollen and ran rapid during the rainy season. To the west and north was the Caribbean Sea. The area was overgrown with many types of tropical and semitropical growth, and it was broken only by three roads, several streams, and the Rio Chagres. The variety of jungle growth and the rugged terrain made it an excellent training area for all types of jungle warfare.

The course lasted for five weeks. The first week was an introduction to:

a. plants and edible foods
b. snakes and animals
c. living in the jungle
d. camouflage
e. obstacle crossing
f. land navigation
g. patrolling
h. escape and evasion
i. guerrilla warfare

Our second week was centered on squad tactics and on the elements of two-man escape-and-evasion techniques, lasting for two days. The third week was a study in platoon tactics, different types of patrolling, and culminated with a two-day raid patrol deep in the jungle. Week four was spent conducting company-size tactics and culminated in a company-size raid on an enemy POW camp. Our final week was spent firing a variety of organic infantry weapons; rifles, machine guns, and mortars, and in learning the techniques of calling for artillery fire in a double- and triple-canopy jungle environment.

Our training was always realistic, demanding, and to some degree hazardous. It was specialized and progressive from individual through company level; predicated on the premise that all participating individuals were well trained for normal military operations but had no particular experience in operations in the jungle. And it was because the U.S. Army was dedicated to developing and testing jungle warfare doctrine and techniques that the course was so valuable. The staff at the school was constantly on the alert for new ideas, and many had been generated by students attending the school. Items of equipment that were tested by the training center included lightweight poplin jungle uniforms, a new combat pack, an all-purpose stretch sock, a new general purpose tent, a new C ration, a carrying strap to replace the old wooden packboard, and a camouflage dye for web equipment.

The course was of great benefit to me in my later assignments as a platoon sergeant and platoon leader in the jungles of Vietnam, and I would say the lessons I learned there helped to save my life in combat later on.

Among the students I met some truly professional men, among them an army master sergeant from the 82d Airborne who had participated in four combat jumps during World War II and Marine Gunnery Sergeant I. V. Long, whom I would later serve with in combat.

I returned to the engineer battalion at Camp Pendleton a much better Marine SNCO.

In October 1958 I was given an interesting assignment

dealing with the demolitions portion of my duties as an engineer. The 1st Tank Battalion wanted to know exactly what a modern antitank mine would do to a tank, and I was given the job of preparing a demonstration that would answer that question. Using two antitank mines, the Marines in my platoon destroyed a perfectly good Sherman tank, which had previously belonged to the 3d Marine Division. We placed two types of mine—the M-15 antitank mine, consisting of twenty-one pounds of composition-B explosive, and the M-19 plastic antitank mine, consisting of twenty-two pounds of composition-B—at critical spots on the tank. Each mine was detonated separately, using a pull-type, booby-trap fuse, which had been tied to a long section of communications wire. After each detonation, the Marines of the tank battalion examined the damage. After the second explosion had reduced the Sherman to a smoking steel hulk, many of those "invincible" tankers were heard commenting that they were immediately ready to transfer into the closest infantry battalion.

During August 1959 our battalion received two quotas for students to attend the Mountain Leadership School, located at the Marine Corps Cold Weather Training Center at Bridgeport, California. I was selected to fill one of the two assignments. We were taken from Camp Pendleton by a KC-130 aircraft to a U.S. Navy Airfield at Fallon, Nevada, where we were transported by truck to the training center for four weeks of training.

Our first week began with a course known as "mountain walking," which was a series of walks at increasingly difficult angles of climb. We learned how to lock our knees after each step in elevation and became familiar with terms like scree and talus, which were used to describe terrain. The week ended with balanced climbing techniques being demonstrated to our class of thirty students, followed by hours of practice.

Second and third weeks began at a camp known as Levett's Lodge, also home to the famous outcropping known as Demonstration Rock, a granite monolith that had put many an inexperienced climber into the hospital.

On Demonstration Rock we honed our climbing skills. We began with rappelling and belaying techniques and progressed into the more difficult aspects of party climbing and free climbing, as well as learning medical evacuation techniques. During our fourth week, we were taken to a remote area known as Twin Lakes, where we received more advanced training under the instruction of 1st Lt. J. K. Reilly, the officer in charge of the Mountain Leadership School (later to become a colonel and the commanding officer of 1st Reconnaissance Battalion). From Twin Lakes, we began a morning climb that took us to the peak of a mountain just above the twelve thousand foot level, arriving there late in the afternoon, and affording the most spectacular view I had ever seen. Nearby was a deep blue lake with a glacierlike 2,000 acres of snow, on which we camped for a week, to learn the techniques of ice climbing, self-arrest, and crevasse rescue. To complete the crevasse rescue portion of the course, each of us was required to tie a climbing line around his waist, jump into a crevasse, then climb out using the rope.

Our last day on the mountain, and the last event of the course, was spent on a "graduation climb." The cliff we had to scale was 350 feet high and was covered with cracks, ledges, and loose rock, and had to be scaled using a three-party climb. My climbing party was led by a Gunnery Sergeant Young, myself in second position, and SSgt. Lonnie "Moose" Henderson, bringing up the rear. Young and Henderson enjoyed fine reputations as combat veterans and highly skilled mountaineering instructors, Moose Henderson being the easier of the two to identify at six feet five inches tall.

Our graduation climb took all morning to complete, and any feeling of apprehension on my part disappeared as I watched the climbing party on our right flank easily make its way to the top. One of three members of that climbing party was Sergeant Major Connelly, a forty-three-year-old veteran and the senior enlisted Marine stationed at the Cold Weather Training Center. I reasoned if he could make it to the top then so could I. And I did.

I had been back at Camp Pendleton less than a month when I was handed orders returning me to Bridgeport, this time to attend the evasion, escape and survival course, commonly known as E&E school. As with my earlier trip to Bridgeport, I flew to Fallon, Nevada, then was bussed to the Cold Weather Training Center. But this time I was surprised to see my old scuba instructor, SSgt. Walter Webb, seated on the C-130 that was taking us toward Northern California's Sierra Nevadas. Our two-hour flight and follow-on bus trip to Bridgeport was a pleasant experience as Webb and I caught up on old news. When our bus stopped outside a series of Quonset huts at the training center, a Marine hopped aboard, told us to place our seabags on a rack outside and to get back on board the bus, which would take us to an orientation class.

Our bus came to a slow stop in front of an outdoor amphitheater, and our group of thirty students was quickly seated. Wearing a fur-lined parka with the hood pulled up over his head, an instructor got up on stage then suddenly bent down behind the podium. When he stood and stripped off his parka he was wearing a Russian Army officer's uniform. He looked out over our surprised class and announced, "You are now prisoners of war of the Peoples Army." We began to stand up, but we noticed our class was completely surrounded by armed troops dressed in Soviet uniforms. Hands placed on the shoulders of the man in front of us, our heads down between our arms, we were marched away from the outdoor classroom.

Within several minutes, we arrived at a POW compound and were ordered inside and pushed down onto the cold ground. As we waited in silence, our guards would enter the compound and take away one "prisoner" at a time for interrogation. At the conclusion of the interrogation, with the exception of only a few students, each prisoner was stripped of his clothing. Each of us was given a number, and during the night our numbers were called out over a loudspeaker system. When a prisoner's number was called, he would have to present himself in front of the compound gate until one of the guards appeared and escorted him to another round of interrogation. After questioning, we were each placed in "the box," a wooden coffinlike contraption. Time in the box usually lasted up to half an hour, and it was particularly effective on prisoners who suffered from claustrophobia. Interrogators would ask questions, pound on the outside of the box, and try their best to trick us into making mistakes while answering their questions. This session in the compound lasted for at least thirty hours, during which time we received no food, water, or any offer by our Soviet captors to relieve ourselves. Realism was the name of the game, and that shock treatment made believers out of us all. We would avoid capture at all costs.

The last ten days of E&E School were an exercise in the survival and evasion phase of our training. As if we had parachuted into enemy-held territory, each student was dressed in cold-weather clothing, and wearing his 782 gear. We were each issued a section of nylon parachute canopy and several lengths of parachute suspension line before being inserted (by truck) as four-man teams into the most remote areas of the training center. Given absolutely nothing to eat, we were told to remain in the area, avoid discovery by roving patrols of "enemy soldiers," and to survive "off the land," using the techniques we had learned, until a "partisan soldier" appeared within a week to help guide us.

My three teammates consisted of two Marine first lieutenants—a fighter pilot and a helicopter pilot—and a corporal who was a C-130 aircrewman. I knew the exercise was not designed to be easy, but having three "wingwipers," who looked to me as their salvation, was certainly not upping our odds of survival.

For the first two days we found shelter from the cold but nothing to eat. On the third day, with the two lieutenants standing guard while huddled together for warmth in our makeshift shelter, the corporal and I went out on a food procurement patrol. We had spent the better part of the day searching for anything edible when the corporal spotted a huge porcupine sitting in the crotch of a tree.

Taking the initiative, the hungry corporal grabbed a limb, climbed the tree and knocked the animal from its perch. As soon as it hit the ground, I administered the necessary coup de grace, and we headed back to our shelter with dinner in hand.

Realizing I would not get much help from the two pilots—other than in the *eating* portion of what needed to be done—I built a small fire and began to prepare the evening meal. After burning off the quills, I gutted and skinned the porcupine, then cut him into small pieces. After melting enough snow to provide the necessary boiling water, we added the chunks of pink meat and waited. Oddly, the smoke and steam which rose from our little campfire appeared to be green, but that was not to deter four hungry Marines from their first taste of food in three days. After an hour, we felt sufficient time had passed to tenderize a tough ol' porcupine, and we doled out equal portions of meat. But the taste lay somewhere between boiled pine board and rubberized boot. What we'd taken was enough to stop our hunger pangs, but no one asked for seconds.

On our fifth day in the field a "friendly" partisan appeared (Marine Capt. Stan Waziniak) in dirty sheepherder's clothing. Speaking only Polish, he gave us a map and explained with hand signals that we were to move to a checkpoint marked on the map. After we arrived at the checkpoint, nearly six miles away, another friendly partisan directed us to another checkpoint. This process continued for three more days until we arrived at the training center base camp on the morning of our ninth day. When all the teams had been accounted for, we were marched to the camp's mess hall, where the cooks had prepared a breakfast of steak and eggs. The hot coffee, scrambled eggs, steak, and toast smelled great, but our stomachs had shrunk so much that we couldn't really dig in without becoming ill. I returned to Camp Pendleton ten pounds lighter than when I had left.

In December 1959 I was promoted to the rank of staff sergeant (E-6). It was at that time the rank structure in the armed forces changed, adding two grades, lance corporal (E-3) and staff sergeant (E-6), to the pay grade system. The year 1959 had been a very busy one for me, and the Christmas present of my promotion was the finishing touch, but with my promotion and the New Year would come a change in my current assignment. I didn't have long to wait.

In January 1960, along with several other SNCOs I was assigned to prepare a division demolitions and land-mine warfare school at Camp Christianitos. The project was extremely time-consuming but totally enjoyable. After the initial class was successful, the course began to grow in scope and in the number of attendees. A First Lieutenant Hunter was assigned as the school director, and with his guidance, we began to teach classes of SNCOs and NCOs so that they could return to their parent organizations and teach their Marines what they had learned from us. Our course of instruction was presented in four weeks organized like this:

Week One. Introduction to demolitions
Week Two. Introduction to land mines
Week Three. Installing and removing minefields
Week Four. Booby traps and introduction to foreign mines

That July I was ordered to report to a screening board that was selecting candidates for the Drill Instructor School at the Marine Corps Recruit Depot in San Diego. The screening board was headed by a captain who, with a gunnery sergeant, screened each candidate's service record book before any interview was conducted. Evidently, my record was considered worthy enough to take me to the final step, the all-important interview. The captain asked me a series of questions concerning my views on leadership, training, and recruit training. The gunnery sergeant asked me if I had my seabag packed. At the conclusion of the interview, I was told I would soon be receiving orders to attend the prestigious school, and if I completed it, I would then be assigned as a junior drill instructor at the largest of the Corps' two recruit depots: MCRD, San Diego, California.

CHAPTER 15

From the Drill Field at MCRD San Diego—Okinawa 1960–1964

In September 1960 I received orders to attend Drill Instructor School. Considered by its enlisted men one of the most prestigious schools of the Corps, the two-month course was also known to be one of the most demanding. To become a school-trained DI, every drill instructor had to graduate from one of the two drill instructor schools, either in San Diego or at Parris Island, South Carolina. For me, graduation from DI School was followed by a two-year assignment at the San Diego Recruit Depot. Drill Instructor School was designed to teach Marine NCOs the techniques of turning a young civilian into a United States Marine, one able to understand and obey orders and ready to train and fight as basic members of a Marine infantry platoon. The *Basic Recruit Training Instructions* (BRTI) was the bible used to train recruits, and served as the guidebook for students attending DI School.

Close-order drill (COD) for students at DI School and all non–Fleet Marine Force units during the 1960s was based on the eight-man squad. This type of drill was the "old drill," begun in the days of the Horse Marines and used during World War I and for years later. Each member of the squad had to execute different steps and every drill instructor had to memorize those steps to become proficient as a teacher. Seventy-eight hours of COD instruction helped guarantee we would be up to the task.

Inspections for us students were conducted each day and consisted of personal, clothing, rifle, billeting, and drill inspections. Our instructors, staff noncommissioned officers, treated us no differently than recruits were treated, and the unyielding pressure was designed to serve as the proper example for us to emulate when we became DIs. Physical training began each morning at 0530 with calisthenics and a three-mile run led by a new student whose leadership of the class was an evaluated and graded event. Strengthening our upper bodies while increasing our endurance through successively longer distance runs was the preferred method of exercise.

Drill Instructor School was located beside the commanding general's headquarters building (#31), so the school's buildings and grounds and our living spaces had to be kept shipshape and spotless at all times. Sea School, also located at the MCRD Recruit Depot, was viewed as our professional competition, making the chore of maintaining a noteworthy appearance a daily event. Each of our racks was made up so tightly that a quarter flipped onto any student's bed would bounce back into the air. The brass in the heads shone like gold, and the black linoleum decks, stripped and buffed each night, reflected a mirror image of any passerby.

Each student was required to become proficient as a "platform speaker" and part of the course known as "technique of military instruction" (TMI) demanded we be able to present a thirty-minute impromptu period of instruction. Because of the amount of platform time I had experienced while assigned to the infantry training regiment, I considered this to be my ace in the hole. And as luck would have it, I was assigned to present a thirty-minute lecture on the M-1 service rifle. My presentation went well and helped secure a good grade.

The first four weeks at Drill Instructor School was not a pleasant experience; it wasn't supposed to be. We were treated like recruits, cursed at, browbeaten, and required to do punitive physical exercise on command by the staff for the slightest infraction of any rule or regulation real or perceived. This was done to separate the wheat from the chaff; anyone who could not take the mental and physical abuse meted out was given the opportunity to immediately withdraw from the course.

On Friday of the fourth week, we were told that on the following Monday we would be taken to Camp Mathews, located on what today is the University of San Diego campus, and begin two weeks of primary marksmanship instruction (PMI), under the direction of CWO D. F. Fiori, a longtime Marine team shooter who had won numerous distinguished-shooting awards with rifle and pistol. We were taught how to use the training aids that would help us teach recruits the intricacies of military marksmanship. During our last week, we went to F Range and requalified with rifle and pistols before returning to the depot. Considered second in importance after close-order drill, sixty-eight hours of the course were dedicated to marksmanship training.

On 10 November 1960, the 184th anniversary of the Corps' birthday, I graduated from Drill Instructor School, receiving my diploma and campaign ("Smoky Bear") cover as evidence of my new status in the Corps. Immediately following the graduation ceremony, we learned our future assignments. I had been assigned to duty with the 2d Recruit Training Battalion, and was to join E Company the very same day.

After walking over to 2d Battalion, I joined all of the new drill instructors in a conference room where we met our battalion commander, LtCol. L. L. Graham. After shaking each man's hand, the colonel asked us to be seated before imparting his words of wisdom to the new members of his command. He began by telling us that our assignment, molding soon-to-be Marines, was one of the most important endeavors we could ever undertake. He concluded by saying, "During the twelve-week schedule of recruit training, new enlistees are carefully indoctrinated in the manner of performance of duty of a Marine.

To the young recruit facing his initial weeks of training, the singularly most important man in his life is his drill instructor, *you*—a specially selected noncommissioned officer, chosen for exceptional leadership abilities and military experience. It is through the DI that the raw recruit will begin his transformation into a Marine. Your responsibility to the young recruit, to this battalion, and to our Corps marks you as Marines who will stand apart from all others. The challenge to be the best drill instructors possible may, at first, seem overwhelming, but I am certain each of you is up to the task. If you accept this challenge, you will earn my respect and have my every confidence."

Five of us, all new drill instructors assigned to E Company, left the battalion commander's conference room and walked over to our new company headquarters building, a Quonset hut, where we were introduced to our company commander, Capt. R. Lloyd, Jr., who welcomed us aboard and told us we would only be allowed to bird-dog the recruits currently in training to familiarize ourselves with the daily routine and observe how recruit training was conducted by each platoon. Then, receiving directions to our respective duty huts, we headed off to join with our platoons, mine being Platoon 280, which was commanded by a Staff Sergeant Buckley. For Buckley, Platoon 208 was his last opportunity at turning out America's finest product as he was about to finish his tour on the drill field and rejoin the ranks of the 1st Marine Division. Fortunately, Buckley was every bit the professional who took numerous opportunities, during the next several weeks, to share his knowledge on the best ways to train recruits and how to survive my two-year tour of duty. I took notes and paid strict attention to what he said, hoping his advice would pay great dividends. It did. On 10 December 1960, I was told to go over to the receiving barracks and pick up my first platoon, which was then in the process of forming. That moment was one that I, like every other drill instructor, still look back on with mixed feelings of apprehension and intrepidity.

My first platoon was designated Platoon 2011, and I

would be ably assisted as the platoon commander by two junior drill instructors (JDIs), SSgt. W. G. Gouthro, a highly decorated veteran of the Korean War, who had already completed one year on the drill field, and Sergeant R. L. Demers, also a veteran of the Korean War, who was on his second tour of duty at the depot.

Platoon 2011 was unique in that half of the sixty privates who initially made up the platoon came from Illinois and Indiana, while the second half came from Louisiana and Texas. My job would be to take these two "teams" of young American citizens, defined only by their perceived geographical boundaries, and get them to act as one.

During the platoon's initial processing and indoctrination period an unusual situation began to develop. After we returned from Building 10, where all recruits had received their final physical examination before training, I was informed by a navy doctor, by letter, that one of my privates, a farm boy, had been found to have a deformed spine and would be recommended for immediate discharge. The private had been born with several of his spinal discs fused together, and though he had participated in high-school sports, the medical officers at the depot said that the private could be paralyzed if he were allowed to participate in the physical training required of every recruit. Complying with additional orders, I was to assign the private to limited duty as the platoon messenger and tell him that under no circumstances was he to run on the double time as he moved about.

I sent word that I wanted to speak with the private. Within minutes he was standing outside my office. Three loud raps on the outside of my office hatch were followed by the private's sounding off.

"Enter, Private, and take a seat. The reason I sent for you was to inform you that you will be dropped from training and you will be returned home to Texas." The look on the boy's face was one of confusion and immediate shock and before he could speak, I tried to explain the situation.

"The navy doctors told me about your back. They say

that despite your playing baseball and football back home, you could become crippled during training here or during any future service in the Corps."

I could see my explanation was falling on deaf ears, and despite his efforts to suppress a steady flow of tears, the private persisted.

"Sir, the private requests permission to speak to the drill instructor."

"Go ahead, Private, speak."

"Sir, all I have ever wanted was to be a Marine. My father was a Marine. He was killed in Korea in 1952, serving with the 5th Marines. I want to serve, to contribute, and I'll do anything to stay in, sir. I know I can hack it. All I'm asking for is the chance to prove it."

The next day, I walked over to Building #10 to talk with the navy doctor who had destroyed the private's dream of becoming a Marine. After sending for the recruit's health record, the doctor asked me to follow him into one of the empty examination rooms. He flipped on a switch that illuminated a glass panel and then shoved the private's X rays up on the panel wall.

"I appreciate your coming over here to talk about the boy, Staff Sergeant Jacques, but I think his X rays tell the story better than I can. He is lucky to have made it this far. He may have played sports in high school, but fortunately for him, he was never hit too hard. If he takes a hard blow to the spine, it could paralyze him from the waist down or it could kill him. You know the demands of combat, Jacques. You know from personal experience how heavy a combat pack can be. Would you want this man to be assigned to your platoon and then become a liability?"

It was a long walk back to the E Company duty hut, and I did not look forward to my next discussion with the private. He had watched me leave, earlier, hoping I would return with a decision reversed by the doctor. But it was not to be.

(Thirty-five years later, I still remember that brokenhearted young recruit. From time to time, I have wished like hell that we could have more young men like him in the ranks of the Marine Corps. And when I think of those cowardly bastards who throughout the decades have avoided any form of military service to this country, I think of men like that private and smile, knowing he is the sort of courageous individual who makes our country the place it is.)

That unfortunate incident was one of several unusual occurrences during the training of my first platoon. On the same day our training began we received written orders from Headquarters Marine Corps instructing us to discontinue the eight-man squad drill effective 1 January 1961. To complicate training, we were told that we would use the *Landing Party Manual* (LPM) as the new "bible" for close-order drill, but that we could not begin that instruction until 1 January 1961. The only place that I could use to drill my platoon using the LPM without being discovered, until the New Year, was the depot's football field.

I am proud to say that this platoon managed to distinguish itself as an honor platoon, accomplishing a 94 percent rifle qualification rate and winning the close-order drill competition within the battalion. I was, of course, extremely proud of those young Marines, and as they left the depot on 1 March 1961, and headed off to join the 2d Infantry Training Regiment at Camp Pendleton, I felt I would be proud to serve with any one of them in combat.

In May 1961, I was assigned as a junior DI for my second pickup. Our platoon was commanded by GySgt. H. C. Beebe, who had seen combat during numerous island landings in the Pacific before landing on Iwo Jima. Assisting Beebe and me was Gunnery Sergeant M. J. Evans, another outstanding drill instructor, who would not only be a competitor of mine on the drill field but would later be my company commander as CO of E Company 2d Battalion, 9th Marines.

One other Marine who was very much an influence on my life as a Marine was my series commander, and later my company commander, 1st Lt. A. W. Stremic. An all-American football player during his years at the U.S. Naval Academy, Stremic led the MCRD football team. First

Lieutenant Stremic helped get me into the best physical shape I had ever been in.

My next platoon, 231, began training on 23 May and graduated as a regimental honor platoon on 2 August 1961, achieving a 98 percent rifle qualification rate. Helping to train that platoon of sixty-four men was a wonderful experience for me because I learned leadership techniques from men who I believe were the best noncommissioned officers in the Corps. Gunnery Sergeant Beebe knew how to motivate young men to do things that they believed were impossible, and by watching his style, I began to develop one of my own. By constantly challenging young recruits, while leading by example, I felt we were turning out the best recruits possible.

With no break between pickup and graduation, I was assigned to my next platoon. Capt. W. W. Damewood was the E Company commander, assisted by 1st Lt. J. D. Haro as the series commander. Gunnery Sergeant Beebe and I were joined by an old friend of mine, SSgt. H. H. Henningfield, whom I had served with during my instructor days at the division's Demolitions and Land Mine Warfare School. Now, as a junior DI, Henningfield, who had seen duty in China and served during the Korean War, would bring additional expertise to our platoon.

Comprising recruits representing nearly every state west of the Mississippi River, Platoon 254 began its training cycle on 15 August. We began with eighty-nine privates and lost only two due to illness. With Gunnery Sergeant L. C. Palmore assigned as the series gunnery sergeant, and working closely with Beebe and Henningfield, we produced a platoon better than our last efffort. Platoon 254 graduated on 25 October 1961, earning honors as a regimental honor platoon and scoring an impressive 98 percent qualification on the rifle range.

The next challenge was Platoon 288, which began training during the last week of November 1961, with a new team of drill instructors. Our platoon commander was Gunnery Sergeant C. E. Edwards, a combat veteran of the Korean War and newly joined to the depot from the 7th

Marines at Camp Pendleton. He was assisted by me and a junior DI, Staff Sergeant Ames, a veteran of Korea and an "amtracker" (amphibious tractor driver) by trade.

Platoon 288 graduated in February 1962, also as an honor platoon, with a rifle qualification rate of 95 percent. But what made Platoon 288 unique was the fact that this was the last platoon to graduate from the depot that had used the M-1 Garand rifle for qualification. The M-14 rifle had come to Marine Corps, replacing the time-honored M-1 service rifle, and not only did the M-14 bring many changes to the challenge of marksmanship, but its design required close-order drill to be changed as well. Unlike the M-1, the M-14 had no stacking swivel, and we had to invent a new way to stack arms. Because the new rifle was magazine fed, a new way to execute inspection arms also had to be designed. From the powers above came word that every drill instructor at the depot was to return to Drill Instructor School and attend a five-day session to learn about the new service rifle. After learning all I could about this new weapon, I came to appreciate its design and function. In combat several years later, I would really come to value the rifle's accuracy and reliability. I felt prepared when the time came to pick up Platoon 221, this time assigned as the platoon commander and assisted by Sgts. D. M. Tennant and M. J. Evans.

With four platoons under my belt, and working with two outstanding junior drill instructors, we were ready to turn out one of the best platoons ever to have graduated from recruit training. By the time we had reached our third week of training, we had won the close-order drill evaluation and had bested every other platoon in the series during our third week inspection. When we went to the rifle range at Camp Mathews, we were fortunate to have a sergeant named Vance assigned to our platoon as an instructor and shooting coach. Due, in part, to his efforts we completed our rifle qualification phase of training, having only one private fail to qualify. When it was discovered that the private had been sick with a fever and had refused to go to sick call on Friday, the final day of shooting, it was noted he had fired expert scores on the previous Wednesday and Thursday. We left the range, winning honors as the best-shooting platoon in the series, and returned to the depot to prepare for the battalion commander's final inspection. Extra hours spent studying Marine Corps subjects, practicing close-order drill, and hours of additional PT, paid off handsomely. On 6 June 1962, Platoon 221 won its title as regimental honor platoon; attaining the highest scores for training in the regiment.

It is difficult to explain the sense of pride a Marine drill instructor has on graduation day, after all the hard work is over. But as each platoon departed San Diego, it took with it a part of each drill instructor who molded those young men into Marines. The dedication we drill instructors had for the task of training those men was never discussed but was nonetheless sincere and genuine.

The summer of 1962 saw the largest influx of recruits since the Korean War, and with the increase came the requirement to "double up" on training platoons. Before we graduated Platoon 221, we picked up our next one, Platoon 246.

While I was training Platoon 221, I had been working out with weights at the Special Training Unit (STU). One day, by chance, I ran into 1st Lieutenant Stremic, who asked me what type of physical workout I was going to do. After I described my weight-lifting program, he invited me to join him, promising that after following his workout, I'd never lift weights again. The lieutenant's program guaranteed long-term results. A typical workout began with a run of from five to fifteen miles. Our runs usually ended at the obstacle course, where we would choose to run the confidence course, the conditioning course, or the endurance course. Some days we would run all three of them, on other days 1st Lieutenant Stremic would show up with two packs, which he would fill with sand before we ran the obstacle course. The lieutenant's PT program began in June 1961, and by July 1962, I was in exceptionally good physical condition. When I picked up Platoon 246, I demonstrated to the recruits of the platoon what could be expected from a good conditioning program. As part of the endurance run, there was a rope-climbing station, which consisted of six lines suspended from a forty-foot frame. None of the six ropes had knots in them. 1st Lieutenant Stremic and I took one rope in each hand and, without using our feet, we climbed to the top of the ropes, going hand over hand, then lowered ourselves to the ground using the same technique.

Platoon 246 was the last of four platoons in our training series, which began with Platoon 243. For some unexplainable reason I knew this was going to be one hell of a fine series, because the platoons were staffed by some of the best drill instructors who would ever serve at the San Diego Recruit Depot.

We began training on 17 July 1962, and my pickup team consisted of Sgt. D. M. Tennant, who had worked with me previously; Sgt. J. G. Clampitt, an outstanding drill instructor; and Sgt. L. M. Shields, who had been sent over to bird-dog my platoon. Other Marines in this series consisted of Gunnery Sergeant M. C Rose; the series gunnery sergeant, and 1st Lt. H. E. West, who would later distinguish himself in Vietnam as a rifle company commander.

We knew we had our work cut out for us because of the caliber of competition we faced, but since 246 would be my last training platoon, I wanted to give my best effort to the training of these young men. The platoon finished the third week of training in good shape. We had received the highest physical fitness scores in the entire series and tied with Platoon 245 in our close-order drill evaluation. We received the grade of "noteworthy" during our personnel inspection, and departed the depot for the rifle range feeling ready for the next phase of training.

Our series was taken by bus to Clairmont Mesa Boulevard, where we offloaded and then marched by way of San Clemente Canyon to Camp Mathews, where I again got Sergeant Vance as my platoon's primary marksmanship instructor. The first two weeks on the rifle range went well. Snapping-in and familiarization firing of the M-14 allowed us to begin our third week of firing with a 100 percent prequalification grade. The truth of our training would not be evident until Friday, after the final round had gone downrange, and this was when we discovered that one recruit had failed to qualify—my "house mouse" (our platoon's runner) felt terrible about what he had done. He had fired well during the week, but I can only imagine the pressure to shoot well had caused him not to qualify.

With the range behind us, we returned to the depot and prepared for our final evaluations of physical fitness, close-order drill, and military subjects tests. Because we had made the recruits run, even while they were at the rifle range, their stamina and physical condition had remained constant. By graduation time, we had compiled some of the highest scores ever recorded at the Recruit Training Regiment. It was because these recruits did so well in training, I can still recall two of the best. Pvt. H. L. Ellis, was my platoon honor man, our series honor man, and was recommended for the American Spirit of Honor Medal. He called Texas home, had completed two years of college before enlisting in the Corps, and later became a commissioned officer and fighter pilot. Pvt. David H. Ames broke his wrist in the third week of training and had to have his arm placed in a cast. Ames begged me not to drop him from training and proved to all of us he could still fire his rifle, even while wearing his cast. He completed all of the PT tests, which every other recruit had to do, including pull-ups. Two days before graduation, his wrist was X-rayed, showing a clear separation of his fracture. He finished training because he had the guts to do so.

I wish, now, I could write about all of those recruits in Platoon 246. I was extremely proud of each of them. I believed the Marine Corps was getting the very best of what the country had to offer. Many of the Marines of that platoon later saw combat in Vietnam, not as a platoon, but representing many different MOSs.

Platoon 246 was my last training platoon at MCRD, San Diego, but while I waited for orders overseas, I worked with some of my fellow drill instructors, helping them with their platoons. For my two years of working on the drill field, one of the most rewarding experiences of my life, I received a Meritorious Mast from the depot's commanding general, and a set of orders directing me to join the ranks of the 3d Marine Division on the island of Okinawa.

Okinawa

In January 1963, I received orders to join the 3d Marine Division located on Okinawa. I flew from San Diego to San Francisco and was billeted at Treasure Island while awaiting transportation which would take me to Travis Air Force Base for a MATS flight to Okinawa. This was the first time I was to fly overseas, and unlike today's flight, which can get a person to Japan in less than half a day, the DC-4 took 48 hours to travel from California to Okinawa.

When I arrived at Kadena Air Base, I was met at the aircraft by a Marine gunnery sergeant, assigned as the liaison SNCO, who carried with him all of the assignments for all arriving Marine SNCOs. When he finally read off my name, I learned I had been assigned to an outfit called "Sub Unit #1" and would be going to Camp Hague, home of the division's headquarters.

It was very late at night when I arrived at Camp Hague, but after being shown to the staff quarters, I asked those few Marines who were still awake and moving around if they knew anything about the outfit with the exotic name of Sub Unit #1.

The next morning, I was rudely awakened by a gigantic, smiling master gunnery sergeant who was taking great pleasure kicking my rack. "Wake up, Jacques. My name is Big Lou Lucero, and I'm your new boss." Big Lou was a very colorful character who was to become not only a close friend but one of my mentors as well.

After breakfast, we took a ride to Camp Kinser, and it was there where Big Lou began to explain my new duties. I thought this was a little strange, because Camp Kinser was a navy Seabee camp. Master Gunnery Sergeant Lucero explained that I had been selected as a candidate for the Fleet Assistance Program (FAP) and he wanted to get me away from Camp Hague to prevent me from protesting to the division sergeant major. Those Marines who were assigned to duty at other camps outside of the division, referred to as "being fapped-out," were usually unhappy with the assignment. I was no different. My duties at Camp Kinser would be as an instructor for what was known as block training classes (designed to teach Marines from Camp Butler and Seabees from MCB #9); and along with Master Gunnery Sergeant Lucero, I would be responsible for teaching all infantry tactics and weapons classes, to include the new M-60 machine gun. We were also responsible for the conduct of all physical training, which included the running of the obstacle course.

Each class lasted for three weeks and was divided into three phases:

Week One: tactics—fire team, squad, and platoon.
Week Two: weapons—M-14, M-60, and all snapping-in classes.
Week Three: firing for score—requalification with the M-14 at Camp Hansen.

I accepted my fate and tried to make the most of it. My vision of duty with an infantry battalion in the 3d Marine Division remained just that—a vision. But after I had helped to conduct a few weeks of block training classes, I felt much better about the assignment. One of the better aspects of the training program was that the assignment allowed me enough time to learn more about scuba diving. I soon joined the Camp McTureous diving club known as the Depth Divers. Every weekend, I could be found diving off the shores of beautiful Okinawa. There was no doubt Okinawa offered the best diving in the Pacific: Warm, crystal-clear water and a great variety of tropical fish made each dive a new experience. The club was organized so that a minimum of three qualified divers accompanied each diving group. Safety was paramount; no instructor, no diving.

During April 1963, I was given the opportunity to attend the 3d Marine Division's Scuba Instructor School, which was conducted on the northeastern side of the island, at Camp Schwab, by the division's dive master, SSgt. Pete Hanson. The school lasted three weeks and covered all phases of diving, to include diving equipment, hazards of the sea, and the learning of diving tables used to compute allowable time underwater at various depths. Each student left the class certified as a Red Cross water survival instructor.

With all of the diving and PT I was doing, I kept myself in great shape and thought I would explore the possibilities of volunteering for a tour with a Force Reconnaissance Company when I returned to the States. I discussed my plans with Master Gunnery Sergeant Lucero, and he thought I should pursue that goal. In fact, he told me he would do whatever he could to help me get into Force Recon.

One day, Lou told me to go over to Camp Butler and meet with a Master Sergeant Echols who had just arrived on Okinawa from 1st Force Recon Company at Camp Pendleton. I explained to Master Sergeant Echols that I was about to rotate back to the States, and he gave me a good deal of information which he thought would help me to prepare myself for duty with 1st Force.

In January 1964, I received orders sending me to duty with the 1st Marine Division. I was able to take several weeks of leave, referred to in my orders as a "delay en route." On the advice of Master Sergeant Echols, I went to where 1st Force Reconnaissance Company was located and requested to take the physical fitness test required of all Marines who volunteered for duty with the company. I passed the test before checking into the division so the company could alert the division sergeant major to my request and know I was fit for duty with a Force Reconnaissance Company. Master Sergeant Echols's advice paid off; my orders were changed, directing me to join the ranks of 1st Force Reconnaissance Company.

My life as a Marine was about to change. Dramatically.

CHAPTER 16

1st Force Recon Company, Stateside—1964–1965

I was still on leave the day I visited 1st Force Recon to see if I could pass the tests, which would guarantee me a place in the company. I was directed to the company's S-3 shop where I was introduced to 1st Lt. David Whittingham, the assistant training officer (S-3A). The lieutenant invited me to sit down next to his desk and asked me to answer a series of questions, testing my knowledge of infantry skills. When he was satisfied, he directed me to report to the company's supply section, where I was handed a set of khaki-colored shorts, called brownies, and one pair of sneakers, in preparation for a test designed to immediately eliminate volunteers who could not meet the basic physical requirements of the company. Once dressed, I was met by a sergeant named Short who, carrying only a score sheet, clipboard, and pencil, asked me to follow him outside. The first event of the test was pull-ups. After Sergeant Short demonstrated how he wanted me to perform the exercise, I jumped up on the pull-up bar and did twenty-eight dead-hang pull-ups. The next exercise was "maximum sit-ups," and I did 186 before I could do no more. Push-ups were next, and I did 175 before I stopped. Squat-thrusts, an exercise that began in a standing position, required me to squat down, thrust my legs out behind me, and return to a standing position. I managed to do fifty-six before a serious case of dry heaves set in. Sergeant Short, betraying no emotion despite my pain, merely suggested I run in place to help "straighten myself out." Following these exercises, the unflagging Sergeant Short accompanied me on a five-mile run around the perimeter of Camp Del Mar, before ending at the beach. Next came the ocean swim. In late January, the water temperature of the Pacific Ocean off the California coast averages sixty degrees, but to help me in the event of any trouble, Sergeant Short had arranged for an IBS (inflatable boat, small) to be positioned one mile offshore, serving as a marker and a safety device. After adjusting to the shock of the cold water, I felt better, and began the two-mile swim, which took me through the surf line, around the rubber boat, and finally back to shore, exhausted.

Patiently waiting for my return, Sergeant Short walked me back to the company CP, where I took a shower and changed back into my uniform. I was told to report to the office of the company executive officer, Captain Turley, who had been given the results of my physical fitness test. Captain Turley then asked me about my motivation for volunteering for duty with the company. Apparently satisfied with my answers, Captain Turley said something like, "Staff Sergeant Jacques, you are well qualified to be a member of this company. I will call over to the division reception center and request you be transferred to 1st Force. Since you are on leave, I would like to know when you plan to check into the division. You know, we have a junior jump school class starting next Monday, and you might consider coming aboard early." I thanked the captain for selecting me and told him I would check in the next day to be ready for junior-jump ("JJ" or prejump) school training. Captain Turley merely smiled.

There were two good reasons for conducting a prejump school. The first was a "gut check," to confirm an individual's motivation, and the second was to insure that no quota to the army's jump school presented to the company would be wasted on a Marine who was only halfhearted about going. Orders for Marines to attend the U.S. Army's jump school were scarce and were used to reward for a job well done those Marines in the company who were not jump qualified. With JJ behind him, any Marine fortunate enough to be selected would arrive at Fort Benning knowing what was expected of him, familiar with all of the equipment used, and know the correct terminology.

As promised, on Monday morning, I began JJ, commencing with a personnel inspection followed by a six-mile run. Immediately following the run, we were taught the fundamentals of parachute landing falls (PLFs), demonstrated from atop a six-foot-high platform. Jumps forward, sideward, and backward were done over and over again by each student until our instructors were satisfied, then we piled into the rear of a six-by truck, and at ten miles per hour we practiced PLFs on the Del Mar beach. With the exception of the 34-foot and 250-foot towers, every piece of equipment that we would use at Fort Benning was available at Camp Del Mar. Using the swing-landing trainer—a mock airplane door and a suspended parachute harness—we prepared ourselves for the demands of parachute training. Anyone caught slacking off was immediately required to stop training and knock out a minimum of ten push-ups. More often than not, the entire class was held accountable, and hundreds of push-ups daily, performed by the entire JJ class, became a part of the course.

Our training began each day with a personnel inspection conducted by Gunnery Sergeant Burke, the NCOIC of the class, and ended each afternoon at 1730. By the end of each training day, we smelled terribly, but my harassment as a student continued long after school ended because I lived at the 21 Area SNCO club and was hounded by Gunnery Sergeant Burke and the other SNCOs of the company. I was thankful for the fact that the majority of the company's SNCOs were away on an operation on Okinawa.

At the end of ten days' training, I graduated from JJ and was ready for jump school at Fort Benning, Georgia. On 5 May 1964, I arrived in Columbus, Georgia and boarded an army truck that took me to the base, where I was assigned to the 46th Training Company and told training would begin on Monday morning.

Ground week was the title given to our first week of training, and after being marched to a large parade field on that first Monday morning, nine hundred students waited to begin training. The first words spoken to our class were in the form of a statement, notifying all students that if anyone wanted to drop out, they were to fall in next to a cable laid out on the ground. At least one hundred students with second thoughts took advantage of the offer, and, in fact, each day after that our class strength decreased by at least ten students who chose to stand beside the "quitter's cable." Push-ups and hundreds of PLFs were also performed as a part of ground week, as was the ritual morning run, conducted at a speed known as the "Airborne shuffle." Since I was a staff sergeant, I was assigned as a training-platoon sergeant and held accountable for the conduct of the men assigned to my cadre.

The second week of training, tower week, began with a greatly reduced number of students. Tower week was dedicated to learning the jump commands and to performing individual "tap outs," practice jumps performed in a parachute harness suspended from a platform thirty-four feet above the ground. Those allowed each student to experience having to "stand in the door" before undergoing the gut-wrenching shock of a canopy deployment. The thirty-four-foot tower was also used in preparation for "mass exit jumps" of more than a dozen student jumpers, simulating a static-line jump. But the real attention-getter of tower week was the 250-foot tower. Each student, suited up in a parachute harness, was then hauled up to one of four arms, and with our ground instructors talking to us by way of bullhorns, we were released 250 feet above Georgia and descended down and away from the tower. The prior two weeks' training had been in preparation for that one event, but no training on the ground could simulate the feeling of trepidation while being helplessly suspended 250 feet in the air. Surviving the 250-foot tower was each student's ticket to jump week.

On the morning of the first day of jump week, we marched to the airstrip, where each student donned a T-10 parachute, its harness adjusted so tightly we looked like groups of stooped-over old men as we shuffled into the C-119s (Flying Boxcars), which took us to the drop zone for our first tap-out jump. That first jump was a hell of an experience for me and many other men, and I suddenly began to wonder what in hell's name I was doing, jumping out of perfectly good airplanes. The next day we executed our first "stick" jump; fifteen parachutists per stick making a static-line jump. Wednesday called for two jumps to be made with larger numbers of jumpers in each stick, and Thursday brought our fifth and final jump, using multiple aircraft and with each student outfitted in full combat equipment.

On Friday morning, 28 May 1964, our class fell out for graduation formation wearing the uniform of the day, which for Marines was our "tropical" uniform with garrison covers. I was called out of ranks and presented with a letter of appreciation and recognized as an outstanding SNCO graduate of the Airborne course. Not a part of the army's graduation ceremony, but a ritual for Force Recon Marines, was the pinning on of "blood wings." Rather than having the army's parachutist insignia just pinned on our uniforms, all Force Recon Marines had their jump wings pounded into their bare chests above the heart. Asinine or not, it was a tradition, and I, and every other Marine jumper, had my wings nailed on my chest before I departed Fort Benning and returned to Camp Pendleton. Nonetheless, I was impressed with the way the U.S. Army ran its Airborne school. I returned to Camp Del Mar quite proud of having completed the course.

Upon returning to sunny California, I found that the Marines who had been in Okinawa when I first joined the company had since returned, and with them was the company commander, Maj. R. R. Dickey, III. The major assigned me to be the platoon sergeant of the 4th Platoon, which was ably led by 1st Lt. Barry L. Rupp.

All company platoon sergeants were required to be qualified as jumpmasters. I was given a proficiency checklist and was told I would soon be qualified in the following areas of military parachuting:

1. Reserve parachute static line
2. Jump weapons bag
3. Jump general-purpose bag
4. Jump rucksack
5. Self-determination exit
6. Drop zone commander
7. Conducting the jump briefing
8. Water jumps
9. Second checks of parachutes

I remember my first jump with 1st Force Recon Company as though it happened yesterday. Our jumpmaster was Gunnery Sergeant Burke, who had brought to the jump briefing an emblem of a large red cherry the size of an orange, which he pasted on the front of my helmet. The dubious distinction of being a "cherry jumper" belonged solely to me, and after all of the company's jump-qualified SNCOs had a great laugh at my expense, we boarded a C-47 and took to the sky. The C-47 was rigged differently than the C-119s I had jumped from at Fort Benning. In the C-47, the anchor cable, to which we attached our static lines, ran from the plane's bulkhead, which separated the pilot from the cabin, and was anchored to the deck next to the rear exit door. Our stick of jumpers numbered eight men, and we exited the aircraft on directions from Gunnery Sergeant Burke, landing without incident. But it was not until I had completed ten jumps from a number of different types of aircraft that I could shed the U.S. Army's gray jump wings of a basic parachutist and be classified as an advanced parachutist, authorized to wear the coveted gold wings of a recon Marine.

My next formal training within the company was prescuba school. Prescuba school was to scuba diving as JJ was to parachuting. The course lasted for three weeks, during which time we students were introduced to the two-hundred-foot diving chamber at the navy's amphibious base on the island of Coronado, just south of San Diego. Having to take a carbon-dioxide tolerance test and a physical examination before beginning training, I was found to be in excellent condition and ready for the physical demands placed on student divers.

Our introduction to scuba diving began at the pool, where we divided into pairs known as buddy teams, to practice face-mask clearing, buddy breathing, and emergency procedures. One such procedure was called ditching and donning, where we jettisoned our diving equipment on the bottom of the pool, swam to the surface for a breath of fresh air, and then returned to the bottom of the pool and our scuba gear. In the ocean, we were required to negotiate an underwater compass course, during the day and at night, and to experience the worst in underwater visibility we were required to dive in the muddy waters of the Del Mar boat basin; the final resting place of amphibious tracked vehicles, anchors, and assorted rusting trash.

The most difficult part of the prescuba course was a harassment dive formally known as the "spontaneous emergency procedure." Prior to entering the water, one of our instructors, Staff Sergeant Phebus, had removed the air-hose clamps from each student's breathing regulator. The purpose of the dive was to see which buddy team would be the last to leave the water. It was our diving instructor's job to harass each team, trying to make them surface out of fear. Any team that quit was dropped from prescuba school. It wasn't too long before all of the students had their equipment stripped away with the exception of one set of tanks and one regulator left between each pair of students. When the regulators were yanked away, students had to place their mouths over their twin-tank's manifold to get any air. When there were only two teams left in the pool, Phebus swam down to where my buddy and I were seated at the bottom of the pool, and he took away our tanks and regulator. He handed back the tanks, and I struggled to get just the right mixture of air and water to allow myself to breath underwater. At that moment I was not concerned about my buddy because it was all I could do to stay with my tanks. I was the last man to surface, but I received a critical grade for not sharing my air with my partner.

With prescuba school completed, I received orders to the U.S. Navy's 2d Class Diver's School, located at the 32d Street Naval Station in San Diego. Reporting in on a Sunday, I was told to check in at Pier #6 on Monday morning. Following Monday morning's check-in and welcome-aboard lecture, our class of thirty students was marched over to the school's gear locker. We were introduced to two sets of hard-hat diving equipment, and following a class on the use of this gear, our class was broken down into two-man teams; one diver and one tender.

The reason for the speed with which our first hard-hat dive was conducted was simply to weed out quickly any student who suffered from claustrophobia. The diver's procedure was simple: After putting on the canvas diving suit, a large breastplate was placed over his head and bolted onto the chest of the suit. Next came the massive brass diving helmet, which was placed over the diver's head and then locked into position with the face window left open. Finally, the diver's tender helped to place the weighted diving shoes on his partner's feet. Once completely dressed, the diver sampled his air and practiced hitting the helmet's purge valve with his chin. After a final equipment check, the faceplate was bolted closed, and the incoming air supply was shut off. The diver would walk over to the descending ladder and then climb down into the cool waters of San Diego's harbor. On the way down to the bottom, the diver would adjust his air and, once safely on the bottom, notify the people at the surface that he was on the bottom and safe. This test produced the desired results; three navy students could not descend into the water wearing a hard-hat diving suit and were immediately dropped from training. The remainder of the week was spent learning about diving tables and computing repetitive dives, bottom and surface times.

During the second week of school, I received a surprise telephone call from the 1st Force Recon Company office. I was told I would have to return to Camp Pendleton, because the navy Bureau of Medicine (BuMed) had disapproved my waiver to dive because I was now over thirty years old. After returning to Camp Del Mar, I was told to report to the company commander, and after talking to him, he said I should not worry because he would write a letter to BuMed and I would get my waiver and finish the school I had worked so hard to complete. Within a week, an approval did come in, allowing men to the age of forty years old to participate in navy diving operations.

I was asked which school I would like to attend, the diving school in San Diego, or the Underwater Swimmers School at Key West, Florida. There was no hesitation when I said that Florida would probably be more to my liking.

In late August 1964, I received orders to the U.S. Naval Underwater Swimmers School, located at Key West, Florida, with classes beginning on 3 September. This school was very different from the diver's school in San Diego, being geared more as a combat scuba diver's school. All long-distance swims required the use of a compass and were timed events, demanding that all swimmers/divers arrive at an exact spot, on time.

Our first week of school began with classes at the pool on how to repair regulators and how to conduct emergency procedures. Next came underwater swims in the pool, without scuba gear, designed to see how long students could remain underwater. The school also had an escape trunk designed to simulate the kind used on submarines. We were required to free dive to the trunk, enter it, and then complete a buoyant ascent back to the surface.

All of our underwater swims were done in the ocean

and classified as combat swims. We were taken by Papa
boats out to sea and dropped off at regular intervals, and
each day the ocean swims got longer. One diver would
have a compass mounted on a board called an attack
board, and the other member of the two-man team carried
a depth gauge and was tasked to maintain them at a certain depth in deeper waters. Frequent night swims and
nighttime dives were an important part of the course and
were in preparation for bottom searches and timed work
projects done in the ocean under conditions of reduced
visibility. As an example, each pair of student divers was
given a large section of pipe connected by bolted flanges.
We were required to carry the two sections of pipe to the
bottom, remove the connecting bolts, leaving the two sections on the seafloor, and return to the surface, where instructors would count the bolts. We then returned to the
bottom and rebolted the pipe sections, all as part of a
timed event.

The final two events of the course consisted of a
135-foot dive, with a ten-minute bottom time, with
a timed ascent for decompression at specific intervals. The
last event was a free dive to a suspended steel diving bell,
thirty-five feet below the surface. Once inside the first
bell, we were required to exit the bell and swim to a second bell suspended at sixty-five feet beneath the surface.
At that depth, our instructors guided us out of the diving
bell, and once assured all of the air was expelled from our
lungs, we were released to the surface. I graduated from
the U.S. Naval School, Underwater Swimmers, on the
second day of October 1964, as a qualified U.S. Navy
scuba diver.

After returning to the company as a qualified diver, I
was ready to participate in submarine operations, which
were periodically conducted along the southern California
coast. My first operation was on board the USS *Redfish*
(AGSS 395), where I paired up with Staff Sergeant
Phebus and was taught how to operate the submarine's escape trunk located in the boat's forward torpedo room.

The objective area for the first submarine operation I

participated in was off the coast of San Clemente Island. Our group of divers consisted of eight four-man teams, given the mission of practicing ascents to the surface and descending back down to the submerged submarine. In chronological order, the exact procedures for insertion and recovery of a four-man team worked like this:

Insertion	Recovery
1. Four swimmers enter the escape trunk	1. Swimmers spot submarine
2. They close and dog the bottom hatch	2. Two swimmers deploy fifty-foot line
3. They undog the trunk's side hatch	3. Submarine hits center of line
4. They request permission to flood trunk	4. Swimmers move to periscope
5. Turn on the flood valve	5. TL checks scuba gear
6. Flood the trunk with water	6. TL and #2 swimmer descend
7. Turn off the flood valve	7. Both swimmers reach deck
8. Request permission to pressurize	8. TL moves into trunk
9. Turn on the pressure valve	9. TL moves to #2 swimmer
10. Open the side hatch	10. Both inflate life jackets
11. Turn off the pressure	11. Scuba tanks ascend
12. Request to vent the trunk	12. #3 and #4 swimmers descend
13. Turn on the vent	13. Swimmers reach deck
14. Turn off the vent	14. Swimmers secure tanks
15. Request permission to leave the trunk	15. #3 and #4 enter trunk
16. #1 and #2 swimmers leave the trunk	16. Swimmers dog side hatch
17. #1 and #2 swimmers "blow and go"	17. Request to vent trunk

18. #3 and #4 swimmers leave the trunk	18. Turn on vent
19. #4 swimmer closes side hatch	19. Request to purge trunk
20. #3 and #4 swimmers "blow and go"	20. Turn on pressure
21. Swimmers rendezvous at surface	21. Flood trunk
22. Team leader shoots a compass azimuth	22. Request to depressurize
23. Recon Team swims to shore	23. Turn on the vent
	24. Turn off vent and open bottom hatch

After two "dry runs" learning how to operate the escape trunk, Staff Sergeant Phebus passed the word that we were ready for a "wet run" at team insertion and recovery. When it came to my turn in the trunk, I experienced no initial problems, other than leaving the venting valve on for too long, which nearly caused my team to lose its air bubble. After my partner and I exited the trunk, we made our forty-foot ascent to the ocean's surface, where we rested for several minutes before beginning our return trip. But while we were pulling ourselves along the descending cable, the submarine lost its trim, forcing the captain to regain his forward speed from two to five knots. The sudden surge of power caused my diving partner and me to have our face masks ripped away from our faces. We held onto the descending cable, fearing for our lives, for if either of us released our grasp of the cable, we would have been crushed against the submarine's sail (conning tower). The submarine restored its trim in a matter of seconds, and we made our way back to the safety of the escape trunk, but I suddenly realized why, during prescuba school, we had been forced to endure the "spontaneous emergency procedure." I also realized it did require a particular type of Marine to volunteer for this type of hazardous duty with a Force Reconnaissance Company. There was little margin for error and even less for panic, especially at forty feet underwater.

Similar to the company's requirements for jumpmaster, all operational platoon sergeants were required to become certified as diving supervisors and were required to:

1. Operate a submarine escape trunk.
2. Conduct a submarine operation of "lock-ins" and "lock-outs."
3. Conduct a submarine operational briefing.
4. Conduct a scuba-diving briefing.
5. Conduct day and nighttime surface swims.

By January 1964, I had been on enough submarine exercises to pass the tests required as a diving supervisor. The U.S. Navy's diesel boats, USS *Redfish*, USS *Perch*, USS *Grayback* (LPSS 574), USS *Bashaw* and USS *Sabalo* were the boats we most commonly sailed on, and the submarine crewmen were, without any doubt, the best in the navy.

It was on 20 November 1964, that I was handed a set of orders directing me to attend the Counterguerrilla Warfare Indoctrination School for Marine officers and SNCOs, which was conducted at the 1st Marine Division Schools Command at Camp Horno. The course began with an overview of the history of guerrilla warfare and then focused on the then-current situation in Southeast Asia. Many of the school's instructors had been advisers who had recently returned from Vietnam. The second week of the course was dedicated to countering the tactics used by the guerrilla forces known as the Viet Cong (VC), and the training was based on operations which had been conducted by the British in Malaya, by the Dutch in Indonesia, and by South Vietnamese forces within their own country.

The final two weeks of the course were used for the practical application of what we had studied in the classroom. We began with an attack on a small village near Camp Horno. It was an extremely detailed copy of the genuine article, including thatched-roofed bamboo huts, VC look-alikes, and a realistic sampling of livestock to include chickens, pigs, sheep, goats, ducks, and geese. Those native animals were important because in Vietnam they sounded the alarm of possible trespassers as quickly as any village dog, and we had to prepare for that possibility. Even though we viewed the training as serious business, the class members of the first assault team provided those of us observing with howls of laughter as startled chickens flew into the air, covering the aggressors with chickenshit.

The final phase of the course took place in DeLuz Canyon; a search-and-destroy operation, covering a dozen miles of day and nighttime cross-country patrolling. By week's end we had a much greater understanding of the difficulty of a military adviser's role and how elusive the indigenous peoples could be. Nonetheless, the four-week class helped prepare each of us for what was to come in Vietnam, and on 18 December, I graduated a much wiser Marine.

When I returned to the company, I learned that the tempo of our training, particularly night training, had increased. Parachute operations were included as normal methods of reconnaissance team insertions, and with each new training exercise I got closer to finalizing my checklist for qualification as one of the company's jumpmasters.

Our operational platoons were given a great deal of leeway in creating the concept of training. With the exception of training required by the commanding officer, platoon leaders and platoon sergeants were held responsible for the conduct and content of platoon training. Specific, isolated training areas aboard Camp Pendleton and the methods of team insertions and extractions were chosen by platoon leaders. On occasion, platoons combined their training, one platoon acting as an aggressor force for another. We trained as though it were "the real thing," and that added realism. Of course, the intelligent use of imagination always made the training experience that much better.

An example of imaginative training is easy to describe. It was based on following routine elements of a reconnaissance patrol for guidance:

1. Insertion
2. Movement to the objective
3. Action at the objective
4. Movement to the extraction point
5. The extraction

Our training exercise took place in the mountainous terrain forty miles east of San Diego. The team was inserted by parachute drop and extracted by truck. Insertion began at 0200 with a jump from a U.S. Navy prop-driven aircraft known as the C 1-A. The drop zone, a small cow pasture bordering Lake Cuyamaca, would serve as a team rallying point after each team member landed safely. The movement to the objective phase had two purposes: the first, to move, undetected, past the Camp Barret Honor Camp prison facility; the second, to conduct a team reconnaissance of Barret Dam, which required our climbing from an initial level of two-thousand feet up to thirty-three hundred feet of very rugged terrain, with local deputies and members of the California Highway Patrol searching for us.

At our objective area we were to sketch, in detail, the layout of the prison camp and describe the construction of the dam. Our mission at the dam required our having to climb all around it while taking measurements and photographs. Movement to the extraction point meant that the team would be extracted from a place, Sky Valley Ranch, at an elevation higher than the dam. For the "extraction," we used a truck to simulate an aircraft landing in a nearby field: We met the truck at the downwind side of the field and, once we were picked up, drove down the field as if taking off in an airplane. That type of realistic, imaginative, and innovative training made our time in the field so valuable.

On 1 February 1965, I was ordered to report, in the

uniform of the day, to the office of the 1st Force Recon commanding officer. I had no idea why I had been summoned, but as soon as I had centered myself in front of Major Dickey's desk, First Sergeant Whisler began to read from a warrant he held in his hands. "To all who shall see these presents, greetings: Know Ye that reposing special trust and confidence in the fidelity and abilities of Maurice J. Jacques, 1073618, I do appoint him a Gunnery Sergeant in the United States Marine Corps . . ." It was signed, Wallace M. Greene, Jr., Commandant of the Marine Corps. I didn't let my amazement stop me from enjoying a wetting down celebration with the Marines in the company at the 21 Area SNCO Club.

On 15 February I received orders directing me to report to the U.S. Army's Infantry School at Fort Benning, Georgia, to attend their pathfinder course, as a member of Class 6-65, for five weeks. The class comprised fifty officers and SNCOs, the majority of whom were soldiers from Australia, Thailand, Canada, Korea, and Saudi Arabia. I was the only Marine student in the class. The majority of NCOs in the class came from the 82d and 101st Airborne Division, and the forerunner of the 1st Cav., a unit called the 11th Air Assault Division from Fort Benning.

The first week of training consisted of classes in land navigation, basic communications, the rigging of army aircraft for parachute operations, and the rigging, for air drops, of pathfinder equipment used by the U.S. Army. The second week of training covered setting up drop zones (DZs) for personnel and equipment, and the preparation of landing zones (LZs) for helicopters and fixed-wing aircraft. In week number three, we were organized as a pathfinder company, with three pathfinder platoons. All of the leadership billets were filled by students. We went to the field with combat packs and armed with M-14s, M-60 machine guns, 3.5-inch rocket launchers, and grenade launchers. We carried PRC-25 and PRC-6 radios. Our long-range communications required the use of the ANGRC-9 radio.

The last three days of the third week began with our parachuting into a DZ known as Lee Field, where we set up a DZ for a company from the 11th Air Assault Division, which made one day and one night jump into the zone.

During the fourth week of the course, we made six night jumps into drop zones in Reniat, Alabama. The LZs for helicopters and fixed-wing aircraft required us to jump in at Friar DZ and set up an expedient landing field, so that four aircraft could practice their touch-and-gos. Our last week was also spent away from Fort Benning; we were loaded into H-34 helicopters and flown to Fort McClellan, Alabama, to finish pathfinder training under simulated CBR (chemical, bacteriological and radiological) field conditions.

We returned to Fort Benning for class graduation on 22 March. I was greatly impressed by that school as it was professionally run and administered. The subjects taught, although refresher courses to many of the students, would come up again—for real—for many of the students in the months ahead.

When I returned to Camp Pendleton, I found a Major MacDonald assigned as the new commanding officer. The major welcomed me back and told me I would be putting to use what I had just learned, as the company had received orders to support helicopter squadron HMH 467 with pathfinder operations at Yuma, Arizona, during the month of May.

In February 1965, two truly outstanding Marines came to 1st Force Recon Company, having been transferred from Camp Lejeune's 2d Force Recon Company. SSgt. Ken Hall and I soon began a great friendship, and I was truly amazed at his knowledge of reconnaissance tactics and the experiences he recounted from his time spent in the Mediterranean. A week after Staff Sergeant Hall joined the company, my longtime friend from our days together at Jungle Warfare School, Gunnery Sergeant I. V. Long, came to 1st Force and replaced Gunnery Sergeant Burke as the company gunnery sergeant. Assigned as an

SERGEANT MAJOR, U.S. MARINES

PVT. M. J. JACQUES, PLATOON 127, 4TH BATTALION, PARRIS ISLAND, SOUTH CAROLINA, 1948. WITH A SCORE OF 324, JUST 2 POINTS SHORT OF RECRUIT OF THE YEAR.

GOLDEN GLOVES CHAMPIONSHIP IN HAWAII, 1949. JACQUES WON!

Colonel Lewis B. "Chesty" Puller, commanding officer, Marine Barracks, Hawaii, cutting the cake at the 174th USMC birthday in 1949.

Drill instructor at MCRD, San Diego, 1962.

ABOARD THE USS VALLEY FORGE IN 1965 ON THE WAY TO OKINAWA. LEFT TO RIGHT: SERGEANTS SCHMIDT, CRAIG, BLANTON, AKIOKA, AND BAKER.

HELICOPTER DESTROYED BY VC SAPPERS IN ATTACK AT MARBLE MOUNTAIN, 1965.

CAPTAIN PAT J. RYAN AND GUNNERY SERGEANT JOHN ECHOLS OF 1ST FORCE RECON. U.S. MARINE CORPS PHOTOGRAPH.

PERFORMING A RIGGER'S CHECK ON A RESERVE PARACHUTE .

First combat jump in USMC history, 14 June 1966. Kneeling (left to right): Haferkamp, Speese, Paull, Jacques, Griggs, Clay, Martin. Standing: unknown, unknown, Cobb, Bacta, unknown, Hernandez.

HM3 Doc Norton of 1st Force Recon.

ECHO COMPANY, 1ST RECON BATTALION, AT CAMP REASONER, DA NANG, VIETNAM, 18 NOVEMBER 1968. STANDING (LEFT TO RIGHT): GYSGT. GILES, SSGT. HARMONS. SEATED: LT. WARE, 1ST SGT. JACQUES, CAPT. WHITE, LT. BADGER.

HILL 146, ECHO COMPANY'S OUTPOST, 1968.

Sergeant Major Billy Lyday of 1st Recon Battalion, 1968.

1st Sgt. Jacques holding an M-14 with grenade launcher, 1968.

UNDER FIRE FROM A HOT LZ, VIETNAM, 1970.

COL. ED SNELLING, REGIMENTAL COMMANDER, 1ST MARINES, 1975. OFFICIAL U.S. MARINE CORPS PHOTOGRAPH.

enlisted platoon leader, Burke departed California for a one-year tour on Okinawa.

In early May, assigned to a detachment of recon Marines, we loaded a C-130 with the gear necessary to conduct terminal guidance in support of HMH 467, which was a unit of H-37 helicopters; at the time, the H-37 was the largest helicopter in the Marine Corps aviation inventory. All of our training inserts would be accomplished by parachuting into the objective area, during the day and at night, but what made our training at Yuma so much different from that at Camp Pendleton was the uncertain winds. In Yuma, the ground winds could easily gust to thirty-five knots before a jump was canceled; at Camp Pendleton jumps were canceled when winds exceeded fifteen knots. We had considered the desert as one giant drop zone and reasoned that a Marine had plenty of time to "pop his Capewells" and disengage himself from the parachute canopy should he be dragged across the desert floor.

During our time at Yuma, we jumped in to the U.S. Army Parachute Test Center. The drop zone at the test center was strewn with sections of petrified wood, i.e. stone. One of the Marines in our group was unlucky enough to be dragged into a chunk of it resulting in a cracked helmet and a brief period of unconsciousness.

During the second week of training, 1st Lieutenant Suttle, the OIC, received a telephone call from our commanding officer, directing us to return to Camp Pendleton as quickly as possible. We returned on a Sunday morning and were met at the airfield by Major MacDonald, who had a list of almost forty names on a slip of paper. Those of us whose names he read aloud were instructed to report to the company's conference room. My name was called.

Once our group had assembled, the major spoke. "You men are not going to remain in the States much longer. I cannot tell you where you are headed, but I can tell you your chances of getting shot at will be high."

I knew Marines from the 3d Marine Division had been in Vietnam, so it didn't take a rocket scientist to figure out where we were going. We were broken down into two platoons—I was the platoon sergeant for one platoon, GySgt. I. V. Long was the other platoon leader. We were given seven days to take care of our personal business and told that we should plan on conducting any last-minute training as quickly as possible. During those seven days, I completed my final check ride and was qualified as a jumpmaster. The last training we did was to zero in our M3A1 submachine guns, "grease guns," as they were commonly called, and then familiarize ourselves with the M-79 40mm grenade launcher and a new antiarmor rocket, called a LAAW (light antiarmor weapon).

On 27 May 1965, we loaded our gear onto trucks, then boarded buses for Long Beach, California. We stopped at Camp Las Pulgas and were joined by Marines of the 3d Battalion, 7th Marine Regiment, before boarding the navy's aircraft carrier, USS *Valley Forge*. From Long Beach we sailed south to San Diego, where we picked up the aircraft that would fill the hangar deck and cover the ship's flight deck. Sailing from southern California, we set a course that would have us arriving at Yokosuka, Japan, more than a week later. The navy's fixed-wing aircraft flew off the ship near Yokosuka, and we weighed anchor and departed Japan, heading south for the island of Okinawa.

Off the coast of Okinawa we waited as artillery units from the 11th Marine Regiment were flown ashore, then we were taken by helicopter to Camp Schwab, on the northeastern side of the island. From Camp Schwab, our two platoons of Force Reconnaissance Marines were taken by truck south to Camp Hansen and billeted with the Marines of C Company, 1st Reconnaissance Battalion. After only one day at Camp Hansen, we received word that Gunnery Sergeant Long's platoon would be going back aboard the USS *Valley Forge*, but the Marines in my platoon would be sent to a training area known as Red Beach to help teach tactics at the division's Raid School.

While we were at Raid School, the officer in charge, a Captain Richards, spoke with our platoon leader, 1st Lieutenant Lenker, and asked if the Marines in our platoon could put on a demonstration of free jumping into the surf from a helicopter. The demonstration would require the men in the platoon to exit from the rear of a helicopter flying parallel to the surf line of the beach at a height of twenty-five feet and at a speed of twenty-five knots. This dog and pony show was performed for visiting members of Japan's Self-defense Force, and when we had completed the jump and had returned to the beach, the visiting dignitaries came down to the water and shook hands with all of the Marines who had participated in the demonstration.

From Raid School, we received the word to move to a place called White Beach, where we boarded the submarine USS *Perch* to conduct reconnaissance operations from a submarine. To a man, we thought we would be leaving for a classified mission, but after several days of practicing lock ins and lock outs we returned to White Beach, only to be taken by truck to the Marine Corps Air Facility (MCAF) about twenty miles away at Camp Futima.

After several days of waiting at Futima, 1st Lieutenant Lenker received word that we would be flown to the naval facility at Subic Bay, in the Philippines, go aboard the USS *Diachenko* (APD 123), and be attached to Task Force 77 to conduct beach reconnaissance along the coast of Vietnam with Underwater Demolition Team 12 (UDT). After arriving at Subic Bay, we located the USS *Diachenko* and loaded thirty-two parachutes, eight sets of scuba gear, and three rubber boats, known as IBSs (inflatable boat, small), with motors, and the remainder of our individual equipment.

Aboard the ship we were soon joined by a detachment of UDT-12 members, led by a Commander Stevens and a Chief Reynolds. The rapport between Marines and sailors was totally professional, and we settled in to preparing for the mission. While waiting for the ship to get her boilers refitted, we trained. High-speed drop-offs and recovery operations required a few days to achieve perfection, and the remainder of our training time was spent performing requalification dives, parachute jumps, and numerous long-distance endurance runs. When the USS *Diachenko* was found ready, so were we, and early in the morning hours of 14 June 1965, we quietly slipped away from our berthing spot at the Subic Bay pier and headed toward combat in Vietnam.

CHAPTER 17

1st Force Recon in Vietnam— 1965–1966

By midmorning the USS *Diachenko* had passed from the calm coastal waters of the Philippines and moved into the rougher waters of the South China Sea. With the Marines of my platoon comfortably billeted in the troop quarters on the starboard side of the ship, the sailors of UDT-12 occupied the ship's port side. Hosting a complement of two hundred crew members, the *Diachenko* was not a very big ship. With a displacement of 1020 tons, she was 314 feet long, had a beam of 31 feet and a draft of only 9 feet, making her ideal for work close to shore. Her twin screws could move her at a respectable twenty-five knots. Commissioned on 8 December 1944, as DE-690, she saw service in World War II as a destroyer escort vessel before being converted to an APD (attack personnel destroyer). During the Korean War, the *Diachenko* was a high-speed transport ship used by UDT and Marine reconnaissance platoons. The ship had since been equipped with two Papa boats and had storage space for three fully inflated IBSs (inflatable boat, small). To inflate our rubber boats and charge our scuba tanks, the ship had a compressor in its diving locker.

Diachenko's armament consisted of one five-inch gun mounted forward, two quad-40mm guns on each side of the ship, and two 40mm AA guns. Several machine-gun mounts were located on the ship's upper deck, and the ship's armory held M-1s, BARs, Thompson submachine guns, and numerous rifle-grenade launchers. Before we departed Subic Bay, the navy had assigned a doctor to serve aboard the USS *Diachenko* in the event we should incur casualties. We learned later that the USS *Cook*, the APD whose mission we were assuming, had lost the first Force Recon Marine killed in action. A member of a seven-man recon team led by Sgt. Herman P. Vialpando, Cpl. Lowell H. Merrell, had been doing the same type of reconnaissance work that our platoon was about to begin. While operating from the USS *Cook*, near Chu Lai, and in conjunction with UDT-12, Merrell's team had been given a one thousand-meter stretch of beach to recon. Taken under fire during their insertion, they managed to break contact with a small group of Viet Cong. Just two days later, Merrell's team was being inserted into a new area by LCVP when the recon team again came under fire, this time by a larger group of dug-in enemy soldiers. Merrell, wounded in cross fire, was pulled away from the line of fire by Cpl. Dennis Taylor, but as Taylor was dragging Merrell toward the beach and the waiting LCVP, the wounded Marine was struck again by rifle fire. Sergeant Vialpando covered the exit of his team by throwing hand grenades at the approaching Viet Cong forces.[1] While the bow-mounted .30-caliber machine gun of the USS *Cook*'s gig provided covering fire, the LCVP moved to shore and picked up the trapped team. Merrell, wounded in the chest, shoulder, and leg, was given first aid by the UDT corpsman, but succumbed to his wounds during a medevac flight that had been called in to take him to a military hospital in Da Nang.

I was extremely happy the navy had decided to include a doctor with the crew.

As we steamed on toward the objective area, we conducted training every day. Classes in map reading, com-

---

1. See attached Citation for Bronze Star Medal with Combat "V" signed by Lt. Gen. Victor H. Krulak.

munication procedures, and first aid were routine. While we shared the fantail of the ship with our UDT counterparts, we also learned from the ship's gunners mates how to fire the 40mm guns and the ship's machine guns. I was extremely proud of the spirit displayed by the Marines in my platoon. To a man, they enjoyed what they were doing aboard ship, and they didn't have to be told twice to do what was asked of them. I was convinced they were well trained and ready for combat. They had that exceptional "something extra" which was the trademark of a Force Reconnaissance Marine. These were the men of our four-team platoon.

Platoon Headquarters:
   1st Lieutenant J. C. Lenker (Platoon leader)
   Gunnery Sergeant M. J. Jacques (Platoon sergeant)
   Lance Corporal Celick (Platoon radio operator)
   Lance Corporal Care (Parachute rigger)
   Team 2-1
   Sergeant H. Akioka (Team leader)
   Corporal R. S. Joy (Assistant team leader)
   Lance Corporal Stranko (Radio operator)
   Lance Corporal M. Brown (Rifleman)
   Team 2-2
   Sergeant W. Baker (Team leader)
   Corporal E. Young (Assistant team leader)
   Lance Corporal Constance (Radio operator)
   Lance Corporal Moore (Rifleman)
   Team 2-3
   Sergeant Blanton (Team leader)
   Lance Corporal Pullas (Assistant Team leader)
   Lance Corporal Trammel (Radio operator)
   Lance Corporal D. M. Woo (Rifleman)

It became readily apparent we would have to maintain a daily regimen of physical training while aboard the *Diachenko* because the quality and quantity of chow was exceptional. Eating regularly and not working off the calories could quickly reduce the effectiveness of the platoon, particularly under the demands that would be made on each man going into combat. Adding to the demands made on physical conditioning was the increase in temperature and humidity, so I made PT for the entire platoon a twice-daily event. When rain squalls appeared, the entire platoon assembled on the fantail, broke out Ivory soap, and showered in the rain, helping to conserve the ship's limited freshwater.

One morning, I accompanied Lieutenant Lenker to the ship's wardroom, where we were met by the leaders of the UDT group for a briefing on the first objective area in Vietnam, a stretch of beach east of Saigon called Vung Tau. The men of the UDT group would perform the hydrographic survey of the beach while we went inland to conduct a reconnaissance of the beach, pinpointing access and exit routes.

On the day of the landing, our platoon went ashore using a Papa boat for insertion and landed on a spit of beach several hundred yards north of the actual objective area. From the insertion point, we traveled inland several hundred yards and then moved effortlessly over and around a series of sand dunes until we came to an elevated mound that offered us an excellent view of the objective area. I broke out my 7×50 binoculars to take a better look to the south, and there, much to my surprise, were dozens of Vietnamese people on towels along the beach and swimming in the surf. At least half of them were young women wearing bikinis. With Lieutenant Lenker kneeling by my side, I said, "Sir, is this supposed to be a war? Take a look down the beach." I handed him my binoculars, and he studied the area for several minutes, before handing the binos back to me. He looked at me, shook his head and said, "Gunny, I don't know about you, but I feel like a fool wearing all of this combat gear and armed to the teeth. Let's make notes then get the hell out of here."

We were to find out later that the stretch of beach was actually an R & R center for the Vietnamese, French, and Military Advisory Command Vietnam (MACV) personnel. It was also rumored that the place was used by the

Viet Cong (VC) as well, and that was why *they* usually left the place alone.

After we had completed that dangerous and demanding mission, we returned to the ship and spent the remainder of the day feeling rather useless. Of course a lot of the sailors from UDT and the ship's crew immediately volunteered to go ashore with us on our next beach recon.

With the hydrographic survey completed, the USS *Diachenko* headed back out to sea, and not long after we had gotten under way, Lieutenant Lenker and I were back in the ship's wardroom to attend a briefing on the next objective area, north of the first and close to a place named Phan Rang. After landing there, we moved inland, and following the completion of our reconnaissance and while making our way back toward the beach, a sniper opened up on us, firing several rounds overhead from a distance of several hundred yards. The rules of engagement under which we operated forbade us to open fire first. We were allowed to fire, only when fired upon. Several of us did return fire, but with the effective accurate range of our short-barreled M3A1 submachine guns being less than one hundred yards, that was a futile gesture. We never came close to hitting him. We called for our Papa boat and returned to the ship without further incident.

Moving north, several days later, we reconned Phan Rang, where the open, rolling terrain was very different from the dry scrub we had first encountered. Since terrain dictates everything we could do, we carried M-1 Garands and several BARs. That particular beach reconnaissance also went without incident, and we returned to the *Diachenko* later the same day and headed back out to sea.

Our next objective area was one day's travel to the north, and in later years would become the largest seaport in South Vietnam—Cam Ranh Bay. It took four days to complete the reconnaissance and hydrographic survey of the entire bay area, and our platoon assisted the UDT group in completing that survey.

Following the completion of that survey, USS *Diachenko* was ordered by Task Force 77 to proceed to

Hong Kong for scheduled R & R. But it didn't take very long for all my team leaders to approach me and ask permission to remain ashore in Vietnam. One of them summed it up best, saying, "Gunny Jacques, we came here to fight, not go on a vacation in Hong Kong with a bunch of squids." Those Marines were very serious about their desires to remain in Vietnam, but I told them I thought it would be better to go to Hong Kong and enjoy a few days of rest because we might not get another chance for a long, long time.

During the second week of July, we dropped anchor in Hong Kong Bay to begin our unexpected five-day R & R. All the Marines in the platoon were dressed in neatly pressed tropical uniforms. Wearing our jump-wing insignias above the left breast pocket, we went ashore to enjoy all that Hong Kong had to offer.

On the next to last day of liberty, we decided to host a small party and invite our UDT counterparts. We went to the Hilton Hotel and checked into two adjoining rooms, filled the bathtub in one room with ice to chill half a dozen cases of beer, and used the second room exclusively for mixed drinks. Three of my Marines and three UDT sailors had been assigned to set up the party, with a navy Petty Officer First Class Cunningham having been placed in charge of the group. Cunningham's party was a great success; there was plenty of food and more than enough to drink, and I tried to make it a point to thank him but I could not find him in either room. When I started to ask if anyone had seen him, one of my Marines began to laugh out loud, then motioned to me to follow him toward the queen-size bed in the corner of the room. Covered by a single bedsheet, Cunningham was lying motionless on the center of the bed. Ol' Cunningham had sampled several drinks too many before he passed out. As he was unable to move, several Marines placed him on the bed and arranged his body with a single white lily held between his hands.

We (including Cunningham) returned to the waters of Vietnam several days later and resumed our ritual of daily wardroom briefings before we entered our objective areas. The next mission was to conduct a beach reconnaissance at Qui Nhon. The mission was identical to the one we had done at Cam Ranh Bay, with the navy doing the hydrographic work and with us Marines surveying the beaches. When we had finished our mission at Qui Nhon, we again headed out to sea.

On 18 August 1965, the *Diachenko* received orders to proceed at top speed to a point off the coast of Chu Lai, there to support the Marine Corps forces committed to Operation STARLIGHT. This operation began when a Viet Cong regiment was caught in its jump-off position in final preparation to attack the newly constructed air base at Chu Lai. Operation STARLIGHT was the first large operation Marines were to participate in against the Viet Cong after their landing in March 1965. It ended with the 1st VC Regiment getting badly mauled. Although we were situated not too far offshore, there were no requests for our assistance, but our inactivity changed only several days later.

During the last week of August, we were scheduled to land at 0730, south of Quang Ngai. With the USS *Diachenko* anchored less than a half mile offshore, our platoon was loaded into one of the ship's Papa boats and taken to the beach south of the objective area. Two teams moved to the south, while the third team headed north, leaving the platoon's headquarters element to move inland through a series of rolling sand dunes that offered us excellent concealment. As we patrolled inland from the beach, I saw that we were headed toward a thick tree line that ran perpendicular to our route. For some reason, perhaps nothing more than intuition, I began to have second thoughts about that tree line. The hair on the back of my neck began to bristle, and I was just about to warn Lieutenant Lenker, when the sand around us began to kick up, and the distinct *pop* of impacting bullets filled the air. The four of us immediately hit the deck and began to return fire with our M-1s in the direction of the tree line. Taking a good look around at our position, I knew we couldn't move back in the direction we had come because of the strong likelihood of us getting hit.

We had no way of knowing the recon team to our right had not been brought under enemy fire and that they were in a good defilade position. Sergeant Akioka was experienced enough to move his team farther north and away from where we were, before opening up on the tree line with several M-1s and a BAR and maintaining a heavy volume of fire. This gave us enough time to move to a better position. The VC must have thought they were being flanked by another unit because they immediately stopped firing at us and could be seen running from the safety of the tree-line position. Not knowing the size of their force, we contacted the remaining three teams and began to move back toward the beach while radioing to the *Diachenko* for the return of the landing craft. We got back to the ship without having anyone wounded.

At our wardroom debriefing, it was decided that we would return to the same area several days later, but this time we would link up with a Vietnamese Army Ranger company and use them as a security force to protect us during the remainder of our patrol. When we went ashore the second time, we felt much more comfortable with the Ranger company nearby. This was our first encounter with South Vietnamese forces. The reconnaissance mission went off smoothly, and when we returned to the *Diachenko*, we received orders to conduct a hydrographic survey within the confines of a large inlet near Chu Lai that was later to be known as the "sand ramp," where U.S. Navy LSTs would unload the ever-increasing amount of supplies needed to conduct the war in I Corps, the northernmost of Vietnam's four corps tactical zones (CTZ), the one bordering North Vietnam.

The operation near Chu Lai would be the last one we performed as a joint mission with the navy, but it was not without incident. As we tried to make our way toward the objective, we came under enemy fire from a small island located near the inlet. As soon as we were fired upon, an infantry platoon, which was located on the same island, took the VC snipers under fire, and within a few minutes all shooting had stopped. We continued on to shore and completed the reconnaissance mission.

When we returned to the USS *Diachenko*, we received word we were going to Da Nang and that we would be leaving the ship to rejoin our reconnaissance company, which had relocated from Camp Pendleton to the South Vietnamese coastal city. After the ship anchored in Da Nang harbor, all the Marines in the platoon and all of our equipment were transported by one of our company's trucks to the new company area.

Built on the beach about one mile south of the Marble Mountain Air Facility, the new company area was named Camp Merrell, in honor of Corporal Merrell who on 23 April 1965, had the unfortunate distinction of being the first Marine from 1st Force Reconnaissance Company to be killed in Vietnam.

We found the company headquarters had been there for only a few days before our arrival. It had been joined by the remainder of the Marines in the company, who had flown in from different parts of Vietnam. The high quality of life aboard ship had just given way to the reality of life in Vietnam. We would live in GP (general purpose) tents pitched in the sand, and our chow would be canned C rations for every meal. Welcome to Vietnam.

It was good for me to see that so many of the Marines I had come to know back in the States were still within the company. To be in the presence of Marines I knew well and could rely on was like a great breath of fresh air. GySgt. I. V. Long, had only recently returned to the company from a deployment with 3d Battalion, 7th Marine Regiment, and SSgt. K. Hall had just returned from Chu Lai, where his recon platoon had seen action during Operation STARLIGHT. A new gunnery sergeant, Ado Mobley, had taken Gunnery Sergeant Burke's platoon after Burke was wounded and medevacked back to the States. Fortunately, Mobley had a great deal of past reconnaissance experience from his days in 2d Force Recon Company, and originally had landed in Vietnam to provide reconnaissance expertise to the 9th Marine Amphibious Brigade (MAB).

In September 1965, Camp Merrell was not a well-protected camp. A single strand of tactical wire surrounded it, and fighting holes were scattered around the area to cover the most likely avenues of approach by the enemy. To correct that problem, all the Marines within the operational platoons worked during the day to improve the defensive positions. The company had not arrived in country intact: Our company "rear" (Marines in the administrative and supply sections) had remained on Okinawa, along with our executive officer, Captain Shaver. The sixth platoon was operating in the southern delta region of Vietnam, participating in Operation JACKSTAY under the control of Gunnery Sergeant B. M. Donaldson.

Messing arrangements for the Marines in the company had been made by our company commander, Major Gaffen, and we were allowed to eat morning chow at the MAG-16 (Marine Air Group) chow hall. The availability of hot chow was a good deal as long as it lasted, but as soon as the MAG was brought up to T/O troop strength, we were told to find messing facilities elsewhere. Fortunately, the commanding officer of the nearby 1st Battalion, 9th Marines, took pity on us and allowed us to join their mess. In the meantime, living conditions for the Marines in the company were actually not too bad.

It was not long before we received word to begin patrolling around the Da Nang area, and my first patrol caused a significant change in our policy on making contact with the enemy. Prior to coming to Vietnam, we had been trained to avoid *all* possible contact with the enemy. If we made contact, our orders were to scatter and to meet up at a given rally point, usually determined by the patrol leader.

That policy changed when the patrol on which my six-man reconnaissance team was inserted by Swift boat about two miles away from a small island on the northern side of the Da Nang Bay. Our mission seemed fairly simple—we would swim to the island, keeping our radios and equipment dry, and then move to a ridgeline suspected of being the home of a small group of Viet Cong snipers who had been taking shots at passing merchant vessels. We were given three days to pinpoint the location of the snipers for the infantry to deal with later. Then we were to move to the northern end of the island to wait until nightfall, so we could swim away from the island to a rendezvous point for the team's recovery by Swift boat.

The swim to the island was tedious but uneventful. Our movement ashore was made difficult, however, because there was virtually no sandy shoreline on the side of the island where we had come ashore, and making matters worse, the island's dense vegetation prevented our moving ashore quickly. At best, the jungle growth restricted our progress to no more than several yards per hour. By morning, I made the disturbing discovery that four of the hand grenades I had attached to the sides of my magazine pouches had come unscrewed from their fuses and had fallen away, lost forever to the jungle. By the afternoon of the second day, we had managed to work our way to a position near the top of the targeted ridgeline. I signaled three of my men to cross to the opposite side of the ridgeline, and as they did, chaos suddenly erupted. From the sound of the AK-47 fire, at least four VC had either seen or heard us, and as the last of my leading three Marines crested the ridgeline, they had come under their fire. Luckily, none of them was hit, but the firing had temporarily divided the team. As they stayed put, hoping to prevent the VC from hitting our flanks, I rigged several booby traps, using the remainder of the grenades I had stowed in my pack. Following orders, we did not return fire, but waited until nightfall before joining up with the rest of the team. Then we made our way safely to the far end of the island and waited there until the third night before slipping into the water to begin the swim to the prearranged pickup point.

But, again, luck was not with us. We swam out to the preplanned point and arrived there on time, but saw no sign of the promised Swift boat. By first morning light, my six-man team had been taken away from land by the current, and we found ourselves halfway across Da Nang Bay, bobbing up and down in the middle of the busiest shipping lanes in Southeast Asia. The local fishing boats avoided us, and soon we were floating in front of a rapidly approaching oil tanker. Trying desperately to signal the oncoming ship, we managed to alert them to our presence, but not to our predicament, and instead of slowing to help us, they poured on the steam and sailed away. But not before they had alerting a navy patrol boat to our position.

As the patrol boat came speeding toward us, my men and I watched in horror as one of the sailors on board moved forward to the bow-mounted .50-caliber machine gun, and loaded the weapon, and took aim at us. My Marines and I began to wave frantically at the patrol boat, while praying that the navy could tell the difference between recon Marines and VC swimmers. The sailor resisted the temptation to shoot, and we were pulled aboard the patrol boat for a slow ride back to Da Nang.

The debriefing of that patrol was conducted the following day at the MAF (Marine Amphibious Force) headquarters in Da Nang. A Marine major, Paul Xavier Kelly, (later to become the twenty-sixth commandant of the Marine Corps) was the only officer present to conduct the debriefing, and I wanted him to know a few things about that patrol. Feeling professionally embarrassed, I stood up and explained to him that I felt we had been ordered to run with our tails between our legs when we received the word to break contact from the four VC sharpshooters. "Major Kelly," I said, "what's the purpose of sending us over here to find and kill the VC when we're told to break contact and run away after every firefight? I know what my Marines are capable of doing, and we can beat four gooks in any firefight. If you came here to do something with the information we're giving you, Major, then I hope you'll get a change made to the rules of engagement that seem to keep us from doing our job." Evidently,

Major Kelly agreed with what I had said. The following day, the word was passed to the team leaders and the team members in the 1st Force Company area: From that day on we would not break contact with the enemy, but would fight it out when necessary. Morale soared.

A dramatic increase in the number of patrols began in the fall of 1965. Normally, our patrols lasted for four days, followed by two or three days within the company area while we worked to improve camp security. At the same time, a navy construction battalion (Seabee) detachment came to our compound and began building "strongback" tents for us to live in. More important, the Seabees began work on a much-needed mess hall, making us independent of other units' dining facilities.

In retrospect, 1965 was a strange time for the Marines of 1st Force Recon Company. Team members would come in from several days of patrolling, often having engaged the enemy in numerous firefights, change out of their dirty uniforms, clean up their gear and themselves, and then take a truck ride into the city of Da Nang for several hours of well-earned liberty spent eating, drinking, and sightseeing, before returning to Camp Merrell to prepare for the next patrol.

The increase in reconnaissance patrols using Huey helicopters as our primary means of insertion had soon become a smooth and very professional operation. Following a briefing session with our pilots prior to the insertion flight, we would fly to the selected LZ, usually with two A-4 Skyhawk jets providing cover for us and for the helicopters. The Huey helicopter could easily carry a fully armed recon team, and as we became more acquainted with our pilots, we began to have them perform "false inserts," hoping to confuse the enemy as to the actual insertion point. As our tactics improved, so did our confidence in our helicopter support, which was superb.

On the night of 27 October 1965, after my team had just returned from a six-day patrol and was sleeping soundly, the stillness of the night was shattered by gunfire and a series of explosions. Awakened by the sounds of battle, we grabbed for clothing, helmets, and weapons, and manned our defensive positions on the camp's perimeter. As enemy machine-gun fire began to reach out from the darkness for our camp, it pinned down the majority of the Marines in the company. The coordinated attack on the MAG-16 airfield was well planned. As the VC tried to hold in check those of us who would come to the aid of the airfield, their sappers, armed with grenades and satchel charges, raced across the airfield and began the systematic destruction of Marine helicopters and fixed-wing aircraft. In no more than twenty minutes, the VC destroyed nearly a dozen helicopters parked in neat rows at the airfield. Several Marine Huey helicopter crew chiefs were killed that night when the VC threw satchel charges and grenades inside the birds in which they were sleeping. At least fifteen VC were killed by rifle fire as they continued their attack between our camp and the airfield. By morning's light we helped the airfield security force collect the dead VC, throwing their bodies into the back of a dump truck before they were unceremoniously taken away to be buried.

With November came the rainy season, and with the monsoon rains came the reduced visibility that made the helicopter insertion of recon teams unreliable at best. It was also during the beginning of the monsoon season when we began to conduct reconnaissance patrols in a place called Elephant Valley, which was located northwest of Da Nang. Since the floor of the valley was consistently socked in by early-morning and late-afternoon fog, we relied on trucks to take us to a river crossing known as the Nam-O Bridge, where we waited until dark before crossing a series of rice paddies and moving past a huge hill mass as we patrolled to our objective areas. In some instances it took us two days to reach our reconnaissance zones.

That November, on one such patrol to locate a fortified VC company area, while we were moving west along a streambed, my point man signaled a freeze and reported back to me that he had found a parachute canopy lying beside the stream. The first thoughts I had were to radio back to our COC (company operations center) and ask if any aircraft had been recently downed in the area. As we waited for more information, I deployed the team to search for signs of a downed pilot. That was when we discovered an aircraft that had obviously been hidden in the jungle.

We had discovered a plane painted black, and looking very much like a Russian MiG-15. In actuality, we had stumbled upon a top secret U.S. Air Force drone aircraft that had been discovered by the VC and covered with limbs and brush to prevent it from being spotted from the air. Knowing that if the VC had already discovered it, we were in serious trouble, I radioed in a sitrep (situation report) and began to examine the aircraft. There was no cockpit on the drone, but I did locate a small door on the side of its fuselage and decided to open the door in order to remove any important instrumentation inside. I studied that door from every angle for several minutes, looking for the slightest hint that the drone had been booby-trapped by the VC, but making an educated guess that I would be the first to open the drone, I did so. On the inside of the drone, I found a plate with the words "Mfg. Rohr Aircraft, San Diego, Calif." stamped across it.

Within a few minutes a radio call from the COC instructed me to take up security positions around the drone and to wait until a helicopter was made available to carry it away. Less than an hour later, a Marine H-37 helicopter came in and lowered a cable for us to hook up to the drone. Unfortunately, the helicopter did not have the lift power necessary to take the drone up and away. Not wanting to remain in the area unprotected, the H-37 bid us farewell and disappeared.

The next word from our COC was that I list the types of explosives I would need to completely destroy the drone in place. While we waited for the explosives to arrive, we maintained security positions, but removed electrical panels and equipment modules from within the drone. Once finished, I radioed back to the COC what we had done. I was then told that the instrumentation and my recon team would be extracted from the site by another helicopter using a device known as a jungle penetrator, a steel cable attached to a winch on the helicopter that had the lift capacity to raise injured men and equipment from areas where landings were not possible.

As soon as the helicopter arrived overhead, I signaled to our first man, Lance Corporal Pullas, to hook himself into the jungle penetrator first so that he could assist the rest of us with the equipment and the instruments from the drone as we came aboard. Lance Corporal Pullas did as he was instructed, but when he was forty feet above the ground, the cable snapped, and Pullas fell, still outfitted with his rifle and a sixty-pound pack. Pullas suffered multiple fractures to both legs, internal injuries, and a fractured skull.

Unable to complete its mission, the second helicopter also disappeared.

Doc Haston, my team corpsman, immediately scrambled to where Pullas had landed and began working on him. While he performed his lifesaving magic, I called for an emergency medevac helicopter. This time a Marine SAR (search and rescue) bird came in and took Lance Corporal Pullas back to Da Nang. Ultimately he was evacuated to the States for a full recovery. The next radio transmission that I received from the COC directed me to carry all of the electronic equipment we had removed from the drone to the Nam-O Bridge for pickup. Needless to say, I was not overly happy with those instructions since every VC unit within miles would know of our exact location as soon as I set off the explosive charges to destroy the drone.

As darkness fell, I set the fuses to the explosives I had placed in and around the drone, and we began to walk back toward the Nam-O Bridge. Expecting to be ambushed at any moment, we moved quietly all night long. For once luck was on our side. By morning, we had come out of the jungle, had skirted the stinking rice paddies, and moved toward open ground, where an H-34 Choctaw helicopter came in and picked us up.

When we landed at the LZ next to Camp Merrell, we were met by two air force officers who were most anxious to get their hands on the drone's instrumentation. The following day we received word from the COC that the air force was most grateful for our work.

After that patrol, while I was sitting outside my tent, I was surprised to hear a loud boom and see a cloud of smoke rising from the direction of our newly constructed paraloft. Not knowing what to expect, I moved at a dog-trot in the direction of the explosion, then I saw the smoke was actually coming from within the paraloft. I also noticed that a group of Marines from within the company was standing and looking down at the ground outside of the nearby mess hall. As I approached them I saw that Captain Whittingham was one of the Marines standing in the group. "Gunny Jacques, you're just the man we're looking for. What you are looking at is an unexploded LAAW rocket. I'd like for you to blow this thing in place, Gunny, but not blow up our new mess hall while you're at it."

Apparently one of the company's parachute riggers had been fooling around with the LAAW when he accidentally fired it. The rocket had not traveled far enough to arm itself. Unfortunately, where it was made it impossible to move without blowing it and whoever moved it into countless little pieces. I was given two pounds of C-4 plastic explosive, which I then molded around the nose of the rocket without disturbing it. I stacked thirty sandbags over the rocket before detonating the charge. A great explosion was followed by a great cloud of red dust and a crater several feet deep, but the rocket was gone, and the mess hall survived without a scratch. It seemed a fitting end to a very long day.

CHAPTER 18

Life and Death at a Place Called Ba To

Early on the morning of 26 November 1965, our recon platoon was summoned to the company mess hall to meet with the commanding general of III MAF, MGen. Lewis W. Walt. The general was sending us to U.S. Army Special Forces camp A-106, near the village of Ba To, forty-two kilometers south-southwest of Chu Lai, to locate elements of the 325B PAVN (People's Army of Vietnam) Division, thought to be rebuilding itself after a recent and costly clash with the 7th Marine Regiment. We would operate from Camp A-106, but the general had also planned for a second platoon to go to Special Forces camp A-107, near the village of Tra Bong, twenty-seven kilometers southwest of Chu Lai, to "test the feasibility of deep reconnaissance patrols, on a mission code-named BIRD-WATCHER."

General Walt, who looked like a rugged football player, was also one of the Corps' most decorated officers, having won two Navy Crosses and the Silver Star during World War II and Korea. In my opinion, the general was one of the few officers who realized that reconnaissance units, when properly utilized, were well equipped to locate an enemy who had already established a reputation for blending into his surroundings—a phantom army that was seldom seen armed and concentrated. Even when enemy concentrations were sighted, they were usually on the move and presented just fleeting targets. Regular Marine ground forces, General Walt believed, were too clumsy for this mission; the VC they found generally wanted to be found. General Walt had decided that since reconnaissance patrols could find the VC, then our patrols should be provided with the means to destroy the enemy. Accordingly, he allowed our recon teams to call in air and artillery strikes directly. Sluggish clearance procedures had hindered this application in the Da Nang TAOR (tactical area of responsibility), but the system was very successful at Chu Lai. The concept was being refined, but by 1966 would be adopted as a standard recon tactic known as a Stingray mission.

General Walt spent several hours discussing the significance of the mission, and even took some time to speak about the new weapon systems and specialized equipment that were coming into the Marine Corps' supply system. The general had done his homework on us, too. As he sat across from my men, he ended his briefing by making me feel distinguished when he told my platoon, "This is not the first time that some of us have served together in combat. Gunnery Sergeant Jacques and I go back a few years, men. I was his regimental commander in the 5th Marines during the Korean War. It's good to be with you again, Gunny."

On the morning of 27 November, my platoon, loaded down with combat equipment and weapons, boarded a truck and was taken to the Special Forces C-camp airstrip where we boarded a DeHavilland Caribou (CV-2) aircraft for the twenty-minute flight to Ba To. The villages of Ba To and Tra Bong were in the center of Quang Ngai Province, an area crisscrossed with jungle trails, rice paddies, and shallow streams. As we flew over it, surrounded by mountains which for years had been home to Viet Cong and North Vietnamese regulars who had infiltrated the area, the ground below gave me the impression of a huge punch bowl.

As we made our final approach into Ba To, I saw the

small airstrip that had been cut out of the jungle next to the camp, and within seconds our pilot had dropped the nose of the Caribou and delivered us onto the strip, then reversed his props to help slow his landing. Turning the aircraft in a quick 180-degree spin, he came to a stop at the camp's main entrance, and we quickly departed the plane. We were welcomed aboard by a Captain Patton, the officer in charge.

Carved out of the jungle, Special Forces Camp A-106 was situated on a gently sloping finger. It was laid out as two concentric circles; the outermost circle was the perimeter. It was defended by local South Vietnamese forces known as CIDGs (civilian irregular defense group), while the inner circle and its eight small buildings belonged exclusively to the Special Forces soldiers. Those buildings housed a COC bunker, the LLDB (Vietnamese Special Forces) team house, a small sick bay, a weapons bunker, an ordnance bunker, a supply shack, and two billeting huts. The two compounds were connected by a series of waist-deep trenches and two-man fighting positions, with single and double strands of razor-sharp concertina wire used to protect the camp's outer perimeter and channeled avenues of approach. A series of .30-caliber machine-gun emplacements was set up to cover those avenues of approach, and while the camp had no artillery, it did boast two 4.2-inch mortars and one 81mm mortar in the inner compound and two 60mm mortars in the outer compound.

Inside the camp's weapons bunker was one of the best stocked armories I had ever seen. There was no doubt in my mind the army was spending a great deal of money keeping their Special Forces teams well supplied. M-1 carbines, M-2 carbines, AR-15 rifles, and AK-47 automatic rifles were stacked next to numerous shotguns and light and medium machine guns manufactured by a host of foreign countries. The Special Forces soldiers suggested we stack our M-3 grease guns and help ourselves to any particular weapon we wanted to carry on patrol. I opted to carry a lightweight M-2 automatic carbine.

Immediately following a tour of the camp, we were

shown to our quarters, which were located in different sections of the compound. The camp commander's idea of not wanting to place all of his eggs in the same basket was understandable. To help us to blend in with our surroundings, each of us was issued several sets of tiger-stripe utilities and black pajamas—the traditional uniform of the Viet Cong. Backpacks known as IP packs (indigenous pack) were also made available to anyone who wanted one. To add to the defensive capabilities within the camp, we were assigned to two-man fighting holes, paired up with a Special Forces soldier and given specific fields of fire along the camp's perimeter. Each of us got inside our fighting holes to study our areas of responsibility before we were taken to the camp's COC bunker for a briefing on the local situation.

We had come to find the enemy, and after only a few days to settle in, we were paid another visit by General Walt. His III MAF intelligence section (G-2) had told him they suspected the local Viet Cong and the NVA were regrouping after a series of firefights with the 7th Marines. The general said our mission was to find the access and egress routes that the enemy might use to regain its lost initiative. Additionally, we were to find and monitor a large enemy staging area, an underground hospital, and several high-speed trails, which we were told were in the area.

We began to plan our first platoon-size patrol. Included in the patrol with my reconnaissance Marines was a Special Forces staff sergeant named West, a professional soldier who was extremely familiar with the surrounding area, a Vietnamese interpreter named Truong, and a platoon of CIDG forces. The area that particularly interested us was four clicks (kilometers) northeast of Goi Loa village, where the headquarters element of a VC company was reported to be located. Observation posts (OPs) and listening posts (LPs) were said to be positioned all around the village. The patrol's chain of command and order of march had Lieutenant Lenker as the patrol leader and myself as assistant patrol leader. The CIDG platoon would walk as the platoon's leading element.

On the morning of our first patrol, we gathered at 0430 and made final radio checks with the camp's COC before moving away from the camp, paralleling a stream which was covered on both sides by thick vegetation. Oddly, as we left Ba To, a Buddhist monk began to ring his prayer bell. We had heard the ringing of the monk's bell when we had first arrived at Ba To, and were told what it meant, but we were soon to learn the tolling of the bell carried a signal of far greater significance than a monk's call to prayer—the bell also alerted the enemy to our presence.

After several hours of moving toward Goi Loa, we stopped to rest just several hundred yards from the village, and that was when the VC opened up on us with 60mm mortars and automatic weapons, pinning us in place. Staff Sergeant West wasted no time in calling back to the Ba To COC with an urgent fire mission for the "four-deuce" mortars. The army's response time was impressive, and Staff Sergeant West adjusted fire quickly and accurately. During the VC's initial firing, the skies opened up, and we were caught in a downpour, which just added to the confusion caused by incoming enemy fire and our countermortar and outgoing rifle fire. The caustic smell of cordite filled our noses, and soon the screams of our wounded began to fill the air. My platoon corpsman, Doc Haston, was treating the two CIDG casualties, and we protected his movement with calls for additional mortar fire on the enemy's known positions. Once our wounded were stabilized and made ready for travel, we continued to call in mortar fire to protect our movement all the way back to Ba To.

During the next two weeks, we ran a series of reconnaissance patrols from Ba To, trying new techniques with each one, but virtually every patrol made contact with enemy forces not long after leaving the Ba To area. Making matters worse was the fact that with the monsoon season came the reduced likelihood of any close air support being available in the event of a serious firefight. In the meantime, we were learning a great deal about the enemy we were pitted against, and with each returning patrol came a debriefing session followed by a complete report of the team's activities, which was radioed to III MAF for study.

In assessing the enemy's location, we reasoned that the most likely place the PAVN soldiers would be found in significant numbers was in an area called Vuc Liem. At the time, it was thought that our contacts had only been with the VC, and we had not found any indication of North Vietnamese regulars operating in the area. We changed our plans and decided to take a CIDG company from Ba To to set up a combat outpost within range of Vuc Liem; from that outpost, we intended to send out reconnaissance patrols to fix the position of the enemy company. With Lieutenant Lenker remaining in the rear at Ba To, I was to radio back the recon team's information to him, and he would relay our message traffic back to Da Nang.

On the morning of 14 December 1965, at approximately 0530, a company of sixty-one CIDG soldiers led by a South Vietnamese Army lieutenant, sixteen Marines from my platoon—comprising three recon teams, Staff Sergeant West from the Special Forces team, and my South Vietnamese interpreter Truong—departed Ba To and moved onto a hilltop approximately eight kilometers away, where we would have a commanding view of the Vuc Liem area. We arrived at our objective at 1400 that same day, and after setting up our platoon patrol base, I sent out Teams 2-1, 2-2, and 2-3, to take a look around the area. I wanted the teams to concentrate on using stealth as they moved through unfamiliar territory at night, and it paid off in remarkable dividends. Shortly after sunrise, the teams began reporting information, which I was relaying back to Lieutenant Lenker.

Our teams reported the discovery of several large hootches, recent cooking fires, and the locations of enemy observation and listening posts, all of which was considered as significant. Large groups of uniformed North Vietnamese soldiers carrying AK-47 and SKS (semiautomatic) rifles, the locations of express trails, way stations, and the eating and sleeping locations used by the PAVN unit, caused quite a stir at the III MAF headquarters.

It was planned that our three reconnaissance teams would return to the hilltop patrol base by midday on 16 December, but it was very late in the afternoon when the last team returned. Because of that, the South Vietnamese lieutenant in command of the patrol base insisted that it would be "too dangerous" to move a force the size of ours during the night; he decided to "wait until the first light of morning" before we would move to a new location. I tried to get him to change his mind, but he refused to listen to my reasons for wanting to move.

The platoon patrol base had been set up on what can only be described as a kidney-shaped piece of ground with a shallow stream running beneath the face of the hill. The back side of our encampment was approachable from a gradual slope covered in knee-deep elephant grass. At each end of the crescent-shaped hill, two long fingers extended to the low ground, where two-man listening posts had been established for security. The Vietnamese lieutenant's command post was positioned on the left side of the hill. Our recon teams occupied the hill's right side.

As the darkness of evening began to cover the hilltop, squads of well-camouflaged North Vietnamese soldiers began to silently slither through the elephant grass and onto the two fingers, intent on killing all of the defenders on the tiny hill above them.

At 1900 hours that night two well-aimed 60mm mortar rounds impacted on the northwestern side of our hill, signaling the commencement of a major assault against our position. The dubious honor of being the first casualty went, posthumously, to the young Vietnamese lieutenant who had insisted on remaining at the hill for three days. Hot chunks of shrapnel had ripped open his back and shredded his lungs, allowing him to die slowly as he gulped in the cool night air and exhaled his life's blood through his twisted nose and mouth. Of far greater loss to me was the lieutenant's primary radio, which was shattered by the incoming mortar rounds. Along with the impacting mortar rounds came ribbons of green machine-gun tracers and automatic-rifle fire from enemy positions in the grass and in the jungle. Within minutes our Special Forces liaison Staff Sergeant West also lay dying, his radio smashed, and leaving us without communications.

From 1900 to 2100, the enemy dropped an estimated one hundred 60mm mortar rounds on the small pinnacle that had defined our defensive perimeter. As the group of 150 to 200 attacking North Vietnamese soldiers continued its advance, our CIDG defense was broken into small sections. The assaulting soldiers raked the open ground with a steady volume of heavy, automatic-weapons fire from Chinese RPD machine guns, and dozens of hand grenades were hurled at pockets of resistance. As we returned fire, the possibility of us getting into firefights with our own men became a reality; fire discipline, the trademark of U.S. Marines, was not practiced by the South Vietnamese soldiers. The jungle terrain, difficult enough for us to move in during the day let alone at night, the dense surrounding vegetation allowing men to remain hidden, the incessant monsoon rain, and the reduced visibility at night, were all elements the enemy used to his advantage.

When the enemy's assault firing began, the CIDG soldiers scattered in all directions. By hitting us at night, the NVA were able to split us up and then attack our smaller groups with superior numbers. My interpreter, Truong, kept telling me that the voices around us were shouting in a distinct North Vietnamese dialect, directing fire and calling for replacements to continue the assault. Their initial attack was just too well planned. I believe a number of the soldiers in the CIDG unit were VC sympathizers who had probably led the attacking forces past the listening posts.

I tried frantically to set up a hasty defense with my Marines and those few men from the CIDG group I could grab and hold in place, but my attention was quickly being divided between trying to put up a defense and taking care of the increasing number of wounded.

Sergeant Akioka and Corporals Woo and Lynch, along with Lance Corporals Brown and Session had started to take automatic-weapons fire from an adjacent hillside. We had to knock out that firing with our mortars, but our defensive group had not begun to return any mortar fire. Impatient with their failure to return fire, one of my lance corporals, William P. Moore, left the safety of his covered position to look for the Vietnamese who were supposed to be firing countermortar fire. But he discovered they had all run away. He found one of them hiding in the grass near the mortar pit. Moore pulled him by his ears, screaming and kicking, back to the firing pit. Lance Corporal Moore was pissed, but not being able to speak Vietnamese, he could do little to persuade the bastard to help him fire the unmanned mortar. When Moore turned away to unwrap some high-explosive rounds, the little Vietnamese soldier jumped up and ran off into the night. I saw Moore standing there, alone in the mortar pit, and ran over to help him fire the 60mm mortar. But when the gooks saw we were getting ready to fire, they dropped half a dozen rounds in on top of us. Moore was seriously wounded by flying shrapnel, but he could still move and was able to talk. I yelled for Doc Haston, but he, too, was badly wounded by the incoming mortar fire. I ran over to where Doc Haston was lying and tried to stop his bleeding. He had a hole so big in his chest that even in the diminished light I could see exposed bone. I wanted to give him an injection of morphine, but I knew if I doped him up too much he would not be able to walk, and I'd end up having to carry him. I bandaged his wounds as best I could and carried him to where our group had gathered.

Just when I thought I had a handle on what was happening to us, Corporal Joy was wounded in the head. Joy and Doc Haston were the closest of friends, and when Haston saw his best friend get hit, he went crazy. He crawled to where Joy lay, and despite his own wounds, tried to stop Joy's bleeding and bandage his head wound.

But there was nothing anyone could have done; Corporal Joy was dying in the arms of his best friend.

I knew if we remained where we were, we would all be dead within a few minutes. The gooks had bracketed our position with mortars and were trying to shift machine-gun fire to rake us with a more accurate volume of fire. I yelled to Truong to join us because it was becoming impossible to tell one gook from another. They were all wearing black pajama tops, and I didn't want our only interpreter to get killed in the darkness simply because he looked like the enemy. I decided our only hope was to move and get my wounded men down from the hilltop and into a defilade position that might allow us to escape from the oncoming North Vietnamese soldiers who, using well-rehearsed tactics, were trying to roll up our flanks. I called for the Marines in the platoon to join up with our group so we could cover our movement with protective fire. The only Marines able to respond were Sergeant Akioka, who had been wounded, Sergeant Blanton, and Corporal Lynch. As we began to move over the steep side of the hill, one of the CIDG soldiers who had been hiding in the dense grass, unarmed, jumped on my back. He must have thought I would get him out of the mess we were in, but disgusted by his cowardice, I grabbed him by the throat and threw him into some bushes as I waited for Sergeant Blanton to crawl over to join me.

Sergeant Blanton and I covered the withdrawal of the rest of the men as they moved over the crest of the hill and headed down toward the safety of a banana grove. With Blanton and myself being the last two men left on the hill, we began to move in trace of our own men, and that was when I felt a sudden blow to my upper chest which knocked me backwards, followed by a burning pain radiating from my neck. Because it was dark and raining heavily, I could not tell how badly I was bleeding. I swept warm liquid away from my throat to see if it was blood, but the rain immediately washed my hands clean and I could not tell. I tried to keep moving, but the sickening-sweet smell and salty taste of blood filled my mouth. I knew I had been hit in the throat and the wound was serious. I began to choke, but managed to keep breathing by swallowing my blood. Using the fingers of my left hand to keep my tiger-stripe shirt pressed against the wound, I grabbed my M-2 carbine in my right hand and crawled off in the direction of the banana grove. I had only one magazine left for my rifle.

At the first opportunity to take care of myself, I discovered how lucky I had been. As I tried to open the first-aid pouch, which I kept fastened on my suspender-strap harness, I noticed the bullet had hit my first-aid pouch before ricocheting into my neck. If I had taken the AK-47 round directly, there is little doubt I would have been killed.

As my throat swelled, I was having difficulty speaking, but knew if I couldn't give orders Sergeant Blanton would be able to help me. When we joined up with the rest of the group, we knew we couldn't move down into the stream below us because we had seen the muzzle flashes of several enemy machine guns near the water's edge. The North Vietnamese had now gained control of the CIDG side of the hill and had begun a systematic search for escaping and wounded soldiers. Their green tracer rounds flicked out like little tongues of death, and anyone caught moving was fired upon by several machine guns.

Luckily, the NVA had to physically shift their machine guns to get at us, and that gave us a little time to find deeper cover in the grove. It was while searching for cover that Sergeant Baker and Corporal Young became separated from our group. Using banana leaves to cover up the wounded and to hide ourselves, we set up a very hasty defense, waiting and thinking it would only be a matter of time before the NVA search teams found our trail and came looking for us. And as we hid there, we heard two NVA soldiers shouting to one another as they came upon the wounded body of Lance Corporal Brown. They pulled his fighting harness from his body and had begun to strip away his uniform when they heard Corporal Joy moaning in pain just a short distance away from where they stood. They stopped working on Brown and ran over to where Joy lay dying and shot him to death.

They returned to Brown and forced him to his feet, motioning to him to begin walking in a single file with his arm on the shoulder of the man in front of him, and they began to lead Brown away from the hilltop. Realizing that immediate escape would be his only chance of survival, Brown waited until the moving column of men had reached a narrow portion of the trail before he dove, headfirst, over the trail's edge and scrambled away into the dense vegetation. Several of the surprised NVA fired in the direction of his escape, but managed only to cut down some branches and banana leaves with their automatic fire. Amazingly, Brown had managed to roll away from the NVA and ended up just behind where we lay hidden in the grove. We grabbed the very surprised Brown, pulled him in with our group, and had just started to move downhill again, when the sky was suddenly lit up by an NVA searchlight mounted on a tripod, complete with handlebars. This searchlight had obviously been brought along for the attack, and when the NVA had gained the advantage of occupying the hilltop, they turned on their light and began to scan the surrounding area to locate those men who had been wounded but had not made it off the hill. As quickly as they could shine the light on a wounded South Vietnamese soldier or Marine they would shoot to kill. All we could do was remain motionless in the banana grove and pray that aerial spotter planes would find us and be able to coordinate an emergency extraction plan by early morning.

With the first light of morning came the realization there would be no emergency extraction. A thick blanket of fog covered the ground and made aerial observation impossible. We managed to crawl farther west, in hope of moving onto a nearby ridgeline, but our first attempt was met by a hail of enemy gunfire. As I directed my men to another route, the NVA started firing again. We froze in place, only to discover the enemy fire was not directed at us but at CIDG survivors who were trying to get away from the hill. With the enemy still occupying the hilltop above us, we moved to another section of the ridgeline and away from the hill.

We had moved about three thousand yards away from our hiding place before I thought it would be safe to rest. I had put our team in a tight 360-degree defensive position when I heard the sound of brush breaking nearby. I thought to myself, This is it. I've done everything I can think of to get my men away from the NVA, but they don't give up. I had one magazine left, but I wasn't about to let those bastards take us alive. I pulled my last magazine of .30-caliber rounds from its pouch and stuck it into my carbine and took up the slack in the trigger. One of the CIDG soldiers who was traveling in our group, placed the fingers of one hand over his mouth, gesturing for me to be quiet, and then placed his other hand over the barrel of my rifle, signaling for me not to shoot. Together we sat, waiting and watching for the approaching sound to take form.

The noise turned out to be two more CIDG soldiers who happened across our trail. After the three soldiers congratulated themselves on having survived the night, we rejoined the team and moved out from our resting place.

We came across another high-speed trail that was running in the same direction we wanted to travel, and although our tactics taught us never to use an enemy trail, I wanted to take advantage of what little time we had before the NVA continued their search for us. We had not moved down the trail more than several hundred yards before we heard movement behind us. On signal, we spread out into a hasty defense before we saw Sergeant Baker and Corporal Young were coming up the trail. To say I was happy to see them is an understatement since I had thought they had most certainly been killed after becoming separated from us during the night. And adding to my thrill was the fact that each of them was armed. To me, the addition of two Marine riflemen meant the difference between our team getting back alive and its not returning at all.

All I wanted to do was return to the safety of the Special Forces camp without running head-on into the North Vietnamese or having them hit us from behind. Knowing our chances of encountering enemy forces still in the area would be high, I decided we would take the same trail to get back to Ba To that we had used to get to Vuc Liem. But getting our wounded safely back to the Ba To aid station was more important than moving slowly through the jungle. I reasoned the smart way to do that was by putting out two of the CIDG soldiers with Sergeant Baker as my leading element. Since we were resorting to gook trails for our escape, I thought that if the NVA should see two Vietnamese approaching on their trail, it might just give us enough time to break through any ambush.

With Sergeant Baker carrying one of the wounded CIDG soldiers on his back, two of the CIDG soldiers as point men, and with several CIDG soldiers moving on our flanks, Sergeant Blanton then brought up the rear of our main group as we moved back to Ba To. And though at any other time we would have cursed the monsoon season for the terrible weather and loss of close air support, this time the heavy winds of winter served us well by masking our noisy movement from the enemy as we moved toward the Special Forces camp. All morning long as we moved to Ba To, the dense fog clung low to the ground, and by noon another cold front was passing through the area.

It wasn't until the two CIDG point men signaled a freeze and pointed down at the trail, that we realized the trail had become a well-used road with unmanned fighting holes alongside it. We were walking through the assembly area which the North Vietnamese had used to stage their men before their attack.

It was 1400 on 17 December, when the nine of us finally walked through the Ba To perimeter wire. By then I had lost my voice due to the swelling from the bullet wound in my neck, but in the distance I could see Maj. Mal Gaffen waiting for us. He seemed more than a little happy to see we had made it back alive. We were taken directly to the Special Forces aid station where initial treatment for the wounded began. Our blood-soaked uniforms were removed, and we were given black pajamas to wear. Within an hour an emergency medevac helicopter came in and took Doc Haston, Sergeant Akioka, and me to a U.S. Navy medical battalion at Chu Lai.

Upon our arrival at B Company, 3d Medical Battalion, we were taken into a triage unit. In one of the operating rooms, a navy commander, a doctor named McHale, started to clean and bandage my neck wound. He cut away the flesh ripped open by the bullet, placed a wad of gauze pads in the hole, and then applied a large bandage to the wound. After taking a few minutes to admire his work, he stepped back and said, "Well, Gunny Jacques, it looks to me like we will have you back to your unit in a few minutes." My eyes must have bulged to the size of golf balls in disbelief because he patted me on the shoulder and said he was only joking, adding I would be staying on at the hospital for several days. He said I was a very lucky Marine. "That bullet passed through a small portion of your trachea which has no bones near it. A fraction of an inch either way, Gunny Jacques, and you would probably have drowned in your own blood. After the swelling goes down, and if there's no infection, you'll be fine and can return to your unit."

I remember a number of navy corpsmen and a few curious Marines were looking in and pointing at us. I heard Sergeant Akioka ask one of the corpsmen what all the excitement was about. The doc told Akioka that because we were dressed in black pajamas they thought we were prisoners of war who had managed to escape from the NVA.

The next day, several corpsmen came to the tent ward where Doc Haston, Sergeant Akioka, and I were resting, and began to prepare Haston for a medevac flight to the naval hospital in Yokosuka, Japan. Haston had lost the use of his right arm and had a large piece of shrapnel embedded in his shoulder. He needed to have the nerves in his arm and chest repaired, and Yokosuka was the closest place to have that type of delicate surgery performed. Sergeant Akioka was medevacked to the Naval Support Activity hospital in Da Nang for additional treatment of his wounds.

On my third day in the field hospital at Chu Lai, I was asked to go to the operating room to talk to a "Vietnamese soldier who had been on the hill with us." To my surprise, the "Vietnamese soldier" turned out to be Marine Corporal Woo, who had been mistaken for a wounded Vietnamese soldier. Overcome with joy at seeing he was alive, I hugged Woo, for I had been convinced he had never made it off the hilltop.

Undoubtedly, the most remarkable story of individual survival by any Marine at Ba To was that of Cpl. Donald M. Woo. Corporal Woo, a Chinese-American from San Francisco, had become separated from his team and subsequently wounded during the initial minutes of the first mortar barrage. As the NVA assault forces swarmed over the hill, they discovered Woo's motionless body, and, believing him to be mortally wounded, stripped him of his equipment, weapon, and uniform, and left him to bleed to death from multiple bullet and shrapnel wounds he had suffered to his legs and groin. After the NVA search teams had moved away, Corporal Woo recovered enough of his strength to crawl away from the hilltop, administer first aid to his own wounds, and to search the ground for something to cover himself against the rain. All he could find was one discarded K-bar knife and one large green waterproof equipment bag, commonly referred to as a willie-peter bag. Corporal Woo cut holes in the bottom and sides of the rubberized bag, inverted it, stuck his head and arms through it, and wore it to keep dry. Not long after he regained consciousness, two CIDG soldiers returned to the scene of the assault and discovered Corporal Woo and carried him away from the hill. Corporal Woo was carried into Ba To between the two CIDG soldiers, with his arms around their necks. As soon as the Special Forces soldiers saw Corporal Woo and his two companions, they took charge of the situation and called for an emergency medevac helicopter.

Corporal Woo's arrival and admission to the naval field

hospital caused some confusion with the hospital staff, Navy personnel who were new to Vietnam. When Corporal Woo kept asking to speak to "any Marine" in the hospital, the corpsmen initially believed he was a Vietnamese soldier who happened to speak good English. When General Walt learned of what had happened to Corporal Woo, he sent two of his senior intelligence officers to visit with the corporal, hoping to gain important information about his experience and his successful method of escape from the NVA.

The pace at 3d Medical Battalion picked up quickly during the time I was hospitalized. Operation HARVEST MOON/LIEN KET was under way, and on 18 December Lieutenant Colonel Utter's 2d Battalion, 7th Marines, was marching out toward Tam Ky when they were ambushed by the 80th Viet Cong Battalion. The combined USMC-ARVN operation against the VC resulted in 45 Marines killed and 218 wounded. As a result of the significant increase in Marine patients, I saw Corporal Woo for the last time on my fifth day in the hospital—he was medevacked that same day to the naval hospital at Yokosuka, Japan. I never saw or heard from him again.

On 21 December, a combat patrol from Ba To recovered the bodies at the scene of the battle: Marines Joy, Constance, Sessions, and Moore; Special Forces Staff Sergeant West; the Vietnamese lieutenant patrol leader, and ten CIDG soldiers. The bodies of the dead where brought to the hospital for positive identification. Each Marine had been deliberately mutilated by the NVA, and they had died badly. The same day that the bodies were brought in to the hospital, a major showed up and asked me— *ordered* me, really—to sign a statement attesting to the fact that no mutilations had occurred. He said that by signing that paper I would be protecting the dead, and I did sign the prepared statement.

During morning sick call on 24 December, I asked Commander McHale if I could return to 1st Force Recon Company, explaining that we had very capable corpsmen in the company and any bandage changes could be handled by them. The good doctor had his reservations but allowed me to go. I caught the C-47 medevac flight out of Chu Lai and flew back to Da Nang. Spotting a jeep with MAG-16 markings on the side, I asked the captain in it for a ride back to the company area. I spent Christmas Day with my Marines at Camp Merrell and was able to attend Christmas services, where I gave thanks to God for allowing me and some of my Marines to live through the ordeal at Ba To.

On New Year's Day I was handed a copy of the Pacific *Stars and Stripes* newspaper. A front page article written by Wallace Beene, the S & S Vietnam bureau chief, captured my attention. It read:

REDS SLAY, MUTILATE 3 MARINES

Saigon—The murder and mutilation of three U.S. Marines and eight Vietnamese soldiers was reported here Thursday.

The men were shot in the face at close range after an estimated 300 North Vietnamese regulars overran a 75-man patrol 25 miles south of Quang Ngai in the central highlands.

The victims were found in shallow graves. Three of the Vietnamese had their hands tied behind their backs, and one Marine had been hit in the face with a machete.

The Marines were members of a 3d Marine Division Amphibious Force based at Da Nang. They were part of a special patrol sent out in an attempt to determine if the North Vietnamese 18th Regt. was in the area, as reported.

The patrol, made up of 13 Marines and one Special Forces sergeant, plus some 62 Vietnamese troops, was hit shortly after dusk Dec. 16 and overrun about an hour later. One Marine managed to escape, despite a severe leg wound. Fourteen men were killed, including the Special Forces sergeant. Three of the men were believed to have died from battle wounds. Nine Vietnamese were still missing.

As a direct result of the Ba To experience, a long-standing Force Reconnaissance operational procedure was suspended. Previous training practices had dictated that when a Force Reconnaissance patrol was discovered it was to split up, each member evading the enemy on his own. After Ba To, Force patrols went in together, stayed together, and came out together.

As 1965 ended, 1st Force Recon Company was, in my opinion, much improved tactically. Coordination and the understanding of reconaissance Marines had been changed forever as a result of Ba To.

CHAPTER 19

Getting to Know My Enemy—1966

Not unlike an inexperienced rider who takes a bad spill from a horse or a driver who miraculously walks away from his burning wreck, I knew that if I didn't return to the bush as quickly as possible after Ba To, I would lose my nerve. I can make this statement today, and without reservation, that after experiencing the confusion of having been overrun at night by a battalion-size force, and having come very close to having my throat shot away, I was more than a little apprehensive about going back to the bush—I was scared as hell. But once I returned to the field with my men, I was able to control my fear because I knew that as a Marine Force Recon team we were better equipped and better trained than our enemy.

My next reconnaissance patrol was in early January in an area only thirty-five miles northwest of Da Nang—a place suspected as a training area for the NVA. After four days in the bush with numerous sightings of enemy movement, I was finally relaxed and in control and knew that I was functioning normally. Nonetheless, I was still grateful when the UH-34 helicopters came in on time and extracted us at the end of that first mission in 1966.

After cleaning my rifle and equipment, I walked over to the company aid station to get the bandage on my neck changed. Doc Cox, our senior corpsman, was in the aid station and he offered to clean up my recent wound. He unwrapped the dirty green battle dressing I had been wearing for five days and studied the wound before saying, "Oh shit, Jacques. It looks to me like you've got an infection. What in the hell are you doing out in the bush, when you're still draining?" After giving me a ten-minute lecture on how stupid I had been, he changed my dressing, handed me an envelope of penicillin tablets, and informed the company commander of my condition, which kept me from going out on patrol until my wound had completely healed.

Within several days, our company received an operational order (op order) to have four platoons and a headquarters element inserted by helicopter at Ba To in support of Operation DOUBLE EAGLE I, to search for elements of the 325A PAVN Division, which was known to be operating in the geographical area that separated I and II Corps. The company headquarters element was led by Capt. William C. Shaver, formerly our operations officer, who had replaced Major Gaffen on the latter's promotion to lieutenant colonel. The four platoons from 1st Force Recon Company were a large portion of the reconnaissance force, which also had two platoons from Company B, 3d Reconnaissance Battalion, and several U.S. Army Special Forces units. To our relief, we also learned a section of Marine artillery from H Battery, 12th Marine Regiment, comprising four 105mm howitzers, would be flown into Ba To the day we arrived by six U.S. Air Force Sikorsky CH-3C helicopters for use in direct support of our reconnaissance efforts.

My first mission after returning to Ba To was a five-man patrol with Sergeant Akioka as my assistant patrol leader. Our patrol's objective area was, again, Vuc Liem, and we would return to the very same hilltop where we had been overrun little more than a month earlier. Because of the number of killed and wounded we had taken, our platoon was so small it could only field two teams. Lieutenant Lenker would lead one recon team; I led the second.

At 0400 hours on 23 January, we began a walk into our team's assigned objective area. Using every technique to move as quietly as possible, it took my team two days to reach our area—the exact same hill where we had been so badly mauled by the NVA on 16 December. This time we arrived undetected and were so well camouflaged in our OP site that we were able to spend the entire day observing groups of enemy soldiers as they moved in and out of a small village located to our south. And we were able to call in several artillery fire missions. The strong smell of rotting bodies left over from the battle on 16 December served as a ready reminder of the enemy's presence. Despite the heavy enemy presence, we were able to spend four days in that reconnaissance zone, and by moving at night, we were able to set up different OPs each day without detection. At the end of the fourth day, we withdrew back to Ba To—this time, without incident.

After returning from that mission, the officer in charge of the H Battery's forward observers (FOs), conducted an advanced school for us on methods for calling in artillery, naval gunfire, and close-air strikes. This class helped me and my Marines during the remainder of the time we spent in Vietnam. And because of classes such as those, Force Recon Marines earned a reputation for proficiency at calling in artillery and close-air support.

I went out on four missions while we were at Ba To, all in support of Operation DOUBLE EAGLE, and during that time we reported many enemy sightings. That operation lasted until 16 February, during which time our four platoons conducted a total of thirty-five team-size and five platoon-size patrols, thirty-one of those patrols making contact with the VC/NVA. During this period, we suffered one Marine killed in action, one wounded, and one captured by the enemy: LCpl. D. S. Dowling was with Lieutenant Lenker's recon team when he climbed into a tree to observe an enemy trail. For whatever reason, Dowling began to move around in the tree, and his noise or movement caught the attention of an approaching NVA patrol, which shot and killed Dowling and wounded his teammate Cpl. G. P. Solovskoy, hitting him in the legs with rifle fire. However, the most somber incident to occur within the company during that period was the capture of LCpl. Edwin R. Grissett, by the NVA. Lance Corporal Grissett had been walking as point man on a patrol led by 1st Lt. R. F. Parker. During a rest period he had distanced himself ahead of his team. When the recon patrol was assaulted by an NVA unit, Grissett was captured and led away. Years later, I was to learn Grissett had been forced to walk from the place of his capture all the way to Hanoi. He was held there as a prisoner of war until 1968, when he died of malnutrition at the hands of his NVA prison guards.

On 16 February, we departed Ba To in H-34 helicopters and returned to the company compound in Da Nang. During March, we began to receive replacements for Marines who had been wounded or killed. The majority of those new Force Recon Marines came to Vietnam from 2d Force Recon Company, Camp Lejeune, North Carolina. They were well trained in patrolling techniques but needed some time to become acclimated to the humidity and heat of Vietnam.

During this time, our company began to reorganize. We received a new company commander, Maj. D. A. Colby, and I became the company gunnery sergeant, relieving Gunnery Sergeant Reynolds, who took over my position as platoon leader. Lieutenant Lenker was moved to the company's operations and training office (S-3), and the two of us were tasked with getting our new Marines in shape and trained up to our standards. In part, our exercise program consisted of daily runs along the beach toward Monkey Mountain. Our introduction to patrolling included actual patrols around the Monkey Mountain area.

On 21 February, Brigadier General English, the assistant division commander of the 3d Marine Division, came to the company area and formally dedicated our camp to the memory of Cpl. L. H. Merrell. Following the dedication, the general also presented personal awards to four members of 1st Force Recon Company.

During the entire operation, our teams conducted more than forty patrols, sighted nearly one thousand enemy soldiers, called for more than twenty artillery and naval gunfire missions resulting in nineteen known enemy deaths. Battery H, 12th Marines at Ba To, fired more than one thousand, nine hundred rounds in support of our teams alone.

As the Vietnam War was new to us in 1966, so was the recognition of deeds done. At the end of February, Lt. J. C. Lenker received the Navy Commendation Medal for his work in the destruction of the air force drone, and Lt. R. F. Parker, who had led the recon patrol on which Corporal Grissett was captured, also received a Navy Commendation Medal. Cpl. G. P. Solovskoy, wounded twice in the leg during the firefight in which Lance Corporal Dowling was killed, and I, for my earlier wounding at Ba To, received Purple Hearts.

Teams from 1st Force participated in Operation DOUBLE EAGLE II, near the village of Tam Ky, for seven days in mid-March, and upon the completion of the operation, the company sent a forward unit of four platoons north to Phu Bai, to patrol outside Hue, the summer capital, and in the A Shau Valley. My platoon had suffered enough casualties to make it virtually ineffective, and I remained at Da Nang to work in the operations section and help train Marines new to the company. Fortunately, this assignment lasted for little more than a month. On 24 April, I received a telephone call on the Lima-Lima (landline) from our company commander, telling me to pack my gear, leave the S-3 shop, and come up to Phu Bai to take over duties as the platoon leader of the company's fourth platoon. This message was not the best of news because my best friend in the company, SSgt. K. R. Hall, had been the platoon leader until he was killed on patrol outside Phu Bai. It would be his platoon which I would now lead. The following day I was driven to MAG-16 where I caught a UH-34 ride heading north. I felt terrible about the death of Staff Sergeant Hall. He and I had spent many hours talking about the war and what we would do if, and when, we returned home. We were both Yankees—Hall calling the state of New Hampshire home—and we had both requested and had been granted extensions to stay in Vietnam as long as possible. We had gone so far as to make plans to drive Hall's car across the country after we returned home so that we could travel around the New England states for several weeks visiting friends.

The incredible extremes taken to recover Staff Sergeant Hall's body served well to remind every Marine in the company of the efforts that would be made to bring back the body of any dead Marine. Staff Sergeant Hall's team had been ambushed at dusk just as it was about to enter a harbor site to sleep. During the ensuing firefight, Staff Sergeant Hall was killed—hit in the head by enemy fire. Thanks mainly to the efforts of Sgt. Johann Haferkamp, who had rejoined our company following a highly classified six-month tour as a MACV/SOG team leader, the team survived the enemy ambush. The following day, Sergeant Haferkamp called for a UH-34 helicopter to perform an emergency extract of the team. A wire-mesh stretcher was lowered on a jungle penetrator to recover the staff sergeant's body from jungle terrain, which prevented the helicopter's landing. But as the Marine's body was being lifted skyward, the helicopter's exterior cable snapped, and his body fell to earth. Three days later, a second patrol was inserted into the area and searched the floor of the jungle until Staff Sergeant Hall's body was found again. Using the same technique as had been tried several days earlier, the recovery of the dead Marine's body was completed and his body eventually sent home.

I had only been at the company area in Phu Bai for several days before we were flown to Chu Lai, where we would fall under the operational control (op con) of the 1st Marine Division's 1st Reconnaissance Battalion, for Operation WASHINGTON. But after we'd been at Chu Lai for only three days, the word filtered down that the operation would be delayed for at least a month. As the company prepared to return to Phu Bai, 1st Reconnaissance Battalion requested two platoons be assigned for long-range reconnaissance patrols, and it was decided the fourth and fifth platoons would work for the requesting battalion.

After the company's two remaining platoons had returned to Phu Bai, 1st Lt. Jerome Paull, who had also joined the company from a six-month tour with MACV/ SOG, and I were summoned to the reconnaissance battalion's S-3 shop to meet with the commanding officer, Lt. Col. Arthur J. Sullivan. He gave us his welcome-aboard brief and said we would be well supported.

On 5 May, my platoon was inserted by UH-34 helicopter into a recon zone northwest of Quang Ngai and approximately thirty-five miles from Chu Lai as recon support for Operation MONTGOMERY, to take place on 9 May. MONTGOMERY was to support a regimental landing by the division's 7th Marines. Our platoon was to be inserted four days before the landing to locate positions that might be occupied by the VC/NVA and to remain in place as a blocking force in the event the regiment's landing flushed the enemy from his positions.

After landing in our LZ without coming under fire, sometime close to 1730, we headed off in a westerly direction and into the heavy vegetation, which would provide us with a good place for our evening harbor site. We then set up in a very tight 360-degree defense and went on a 70 percent alert for the remainder of the night. With Sergeant Haferkamp as my assistant platoon sergeant, I felt extremely comfortable that we would be able to handle any problem we might encounter.

Our patrol was made up of seven Marines armed with new M-14 rifles, with the exception of Lance Corporal Rossi, my team's grenadier, who was armed with the M-79 grenade launcher, capable of accurately firing 40mm high-explosive rounds out to a distance of three hundred yards. Rossi carried with him thirty high-explosive (HE) rounds and one lightweight antiarmor rocket known as an LAAW. Our basic load of rifle ammunition was approximately 240 7.62mm rounds per man in twelve, twenty-round magazines. Each man carried six M-26 or M-33 hand grenades.

Just before first light, we moved out of the harbor site and slipped into an OP site that offered us a commanding view toward the west and south-southeast. Before long, we were reporting cooking fires in the valley nearly half a mile to our west, and could see NVA soldiers getting water and washing pots and pans in a streambed. This sighting was considered so significant that we quickly received word the enemy's position would become the target of an Arc Light carpet-bombing strike by 1200 that same day. We remained at our position, and at approximately 1203, though we never saw or heard any aircraft, the ground beneath our feet began to shake, rattle, and roll. The constant thundering roar from exploding five-hundred-pound bombs delivered on target by air force B-52 bombers became so bad one of my new men, a private first class, became so frightened at the sight and sound of the bombing that he fouled his trousers. He began to talk out loud, saying we would all be killed, but before he could give away our position, Sergeant Haferkamp jumped him and slapped his hands over the man's mouth until he calmed down and returned to his senses.

During the next several days, we had to watch the new man's every move. By giving our position away, he could be as dangerous as the enemy. Believing we would have more trouble with him, we called back to the COC and requested he be extracted. The word came back that a helicopter would be sent in to pick up our team, take us to a new OP, and deliver the new man to the closest medical battalion for observation. While waiting for our extraction bird, we watched a Marine rifle company helolifted into an area about two clicks away from us to the southeast. To effectively put an entire Marine rifle company into a landing zone, numerous helicopters were required, and we had not frequently seen so many in one place since we had arrived in Vietnam. More impressive was watching those Marine infantrymen scramble out of the UH-34 helicopters and move toward a tree line in front of them. Before they could reach the trees, their own mortar sections had covered the area with smoke rounds to obscure their movement. I mentioned to Sergeant Haferkamp that I had never witnessed 60mm mortars fire so fast or so accurately. The vision remained with me as an idea to be used later.

Finally the word came over the radio that our helicopter was inbound, so we started to move in the direction of our planned LZ. Two UH-34 helicopters came in for the pickup and had us in the air within a matter of seconds. I briefed our pilot as to where we wanted to go, and was told by radio that we were to look for enemy movement in the north and northwest of our new recon zone. As we were dropped off, we immediately saw that the only available cover was in some elephant grass, which was about four feet tall. We had just begun to move toward an area of high ground when my point man, Lance Corporal Whitfield, turned and looked at me, saying, "Gunny, there's a booby trap right under my foot." I told Whitfield to freeze and crawled up to him. I saw a length of catgut laying over the arch of his left foot. After tracing out the catgut, I found it attached to a Soviet-made stake mine. I took a section of guide wire, which I carried in my pack, and tied it to the mine with the trailing end of the wire tied to the stake that anchored the mine. I moved the team away from the mine and then pulled up the enemy mine, disarmed it and placed it in my pack, planning to pass the device on to our recon battalion's intelligence section when we returned.

After taking care of the booby trap, we moved to a new location on a nearby hill to begin our observation of the area to the north. With only elephant grass on our OP site and virtually no overhead cover, we stayed in place and began a duel with the blazing sun. By noontime, the temperature had reached 114 degrees, and we were down to our last few mouthfuls of hot canteen water. I passed the word to my team members to redistribute their water so each man would have at least one quarter of a canteen of water to help him through the afternoon. As we watched and sweated, observations of squad-size NVA patrols increased and we called in artillery fire on them. From our vantage point, I could communicate with the rifle company commander who was moving toward a village and warn him of NVA positions in his way.

It was on this patrol that our corpsman started to act in an unusual manner. He had been on as many patrols as any Marine in the company, and had been involved in just as many firefights, but now his complexion was pale and he began crying and talking in an unintelligible way. Sergeant Haferkamp and I became concerned about his going off the deep end so we decided to call in a medevac bird to get him out of the bush. We moved away from the OP site, and within half an hour, a Huey gunship came in and took away the corpsman. We returned to OP and spent one more day watching the enemy before we were extracted. As quickly as we returned to the company area I checked on the status of the new private first class and the corpsman. The private first class was gone, medevacked to the States, but our corpsman had been hospitalized nearby at the 1st Medical Battalion, so I got a jeep and went over to find out how he was getting along. I wasn't able to see the doc, but I was able to talk to the doctor who was treating him. He told me we had been lucky, and if we hadn't gotten the man out of the field when we did, he might not have made it. The corpsman would not see anymore of what Vietnam had to offer—he, too, was homeward bound, but, unlike the private first class, he at least, would make it back with his body and mind intact.

Only one day after returning from Operation MONTGOMERY, I was summoned to the battalion's S-3 shop to talk with Lieutenant Colonel Sullivan. When I walked in, he was standing beside a large tactical map of I Corps and was pointing to the western part of the Que Son Mountains. He said he wanted me to go into the Que Sons for three days to locate enemy movement in the area for a possible operation in the near future. On the morning of 17 May, a six-man recon team walked up to the battalion's helicopter LZ and loaded into two UH-34 helicopters for a long ride to the objective area. Our LZ was a tricky one—a steep hill with a rocky top only thirty meters in diameter—requiring us to jump out of the hovering birds.

The insert went surprisingly well except for one Marine, who lost his footing and started to roll off the pinnacle after he had made his jump. But we caught the back of his pack just as he was about to go over the edge. After he recovered from the close call, we moved from the hilltop and began a trek east along the ridgeline, but the rocky terrain made our movement slow and difficult. Within the three days, we covered about eight grid squares on our map and reported numerous high-speed trails, freshly dug trench lines, and even some recently used fire pits. Late in the afternoon of our third day in the bush, our extract helicopters came in, on time, and lifted us safely back to Chu Lai.

Upon our arrival, I knew my platoon was due for a big change. The majority of my men were due to rotate back to the States, and no well-trained replacements were scheduled to take the places of experienced men, so the battalion decided to merge the members of the fourth and fifth platoons.

Late on the afternoon of 24 May, our platoon was inserted into what had formerly been the tactical area for Operation STARLIGHT, to support the 1st Battalion, 7th Marine Regiment, in what was now Operation MOBILE. The change in our chain of command allowed for Lieutenant Paull to be the platoon leader with myself as the assistant platoon leader. We used my platoon's radio call sign of Hateful. The objective for this mission was a hill mass just forty-seven meters high, which had a small saddle between the two small hills that made it up. Our LZ was less than several hundred yards from the two hills. Inserted by two H-34 helicopters, we landed in a rice paddy big enough for only one bird at a time. As soon as the second helicopter had lifted out of the rice paddy, we began to take sniper fire from a nearby village, which had a dense hedgerow growing around it.

After moving quickly away from the LZ, we moved off toward the military crest of the hill mass and waited until nightfall before we planned our final move to the higher of the two hills. At the time, we were still receiving sporadic enemy sniper fire, with the gooks hoping our return fire would pinpoint our location. As soon as our point man reached the saddle between the two hills, he walked into the tail end of an NVA ambush. He reacted instinctively, firing one round from his rifle into the enemy soldier in front of him, killing the man instantly.

The sound of rifle firing caused the NVA to panic, and the quiet of the night was shattered by the sounds of AK-47s firing and hand grenades exploding. For nearly five minutes there was one hell of a one-sided firefight, with all fires directed into the empty kill zone. Once the enemy's firing died down, we moved back to our original position and set up in a very tight 360-degree defense.

We began to receive fire from all directions and believed we would soon be assaulted by a far superior force, and that was when Lieutenant Paull called for illumination rounds from an 8-inch howitzer battery, which was firing in direct support of the platoon. Once the illumination rounds were centered directly over the saddle, we decided to change our tactics. The NVA, no doubt, wanted us to give away our position, but our fire discipline was exceptional. It was decided by the CO of the 1st Battalion, 7th Marines, that our platoon should be "boxed in" by the 8-inch howitzers that were protecting us. From the data the battery had received from our calls for illumination, the battery began to fire high-explosive shells at a rate of one round per minute—from 2000 until first light—expending an estimated six hundred rounds of high explosive shells throughout the night. While the noise was almost deafening, the ground around our position was turned inside out. But the accuracy and volume of the 8-inch guns broke the NVA's advance on our position. It was decided that after first light our team would be extracted and the battalion would move through the area in a coordinated sweep for the enemy. Within an hour, two UH-34 helicopters came in and picked us up, with three A-4 jets flying providing close-air support for the team's extraction. We were lifted out without incident, but we had been lucky to have avoided being hit by our own supporting fire.

Two days later, I was with a gunnery sergeant whose cousin was assigned to the 8-inch battery that had boxed us in. We went over to the battery, and I met the battery commander and told him that I was a member of the recon patrol his men had saved. He asked me if I would like to talk to his Marines and tell them how well they had done. I jumped at the chance; without question, they had saved our lives.

During the first week of June, Lieutenant Paull and I met with Lieutenant Colonel Sullivan to be briefed on a new mission in support of Operation WASHINGTON. Surprisingly, the colonel wanted us to parachute into our objective, at night, at an altitude of eight-hundred feet, and he assigned a specific area for our follow-on reconnaissance patrol. The colonel said we had six days to prepare for the jump.

The thirteen-man team consisted of the following Marines: 1st Lt. Jerome Paull, Sergeants Johann Haferkamp and Griggs, Corporals Tommy Clay, Martin, Cobb, Bacta, Hernandez, four other Marines, and myself.

As an aside, I'd like to note that this military jump was, in fact, the first *combat jump* conducted in Marine Corps history. While there were hundreds of practice jumps made by Marine parachute battalions during World War II, no *combat jumps* were ever made. Nor were combat jumps conducted by Marines during the Korean War. It should be noted that some Marine paratroopers assigned to duty in the Office of Strategic Services—OSS, the forerunner of the Central Intelligence Agency—did make several World War II team and individual jumps. And though several Marine Corps air delivery platoon members did make jumps in Vietnam prior to 14 June 1966, none of those jumps were planned *combat jumps*, nor where they in support of any infantry or reconnaissance operations. I can only wait for "armchair military historians" to argue this claim, but I'll defend it, just the same.

We were told that we could choose the aircraft for the jump and that aircraft would be at our disposal, day and night. We selected the U.S. Army's CV-2 Caribou as our choice of aircraft, reasoning that since this particular prop-driven aircraft was visually known to the enemy in the targeted area, they would think less of its daily appearance. We selected a drop zone west of Special Forces Camp A-107, near the village of Tra Bong. We dispatched the company parachute rigger to Da Nang with instructions to return to Chu Lai with forty parachutes. After the return of our rigger, we made our first practice jump on 10 June 1966, trying to perfect an extremely tight stick of jumpers. To successfully carry off the night jump, the entire team had to exit the aircraft as quickly as possible, assemble in the air, and land in the same tight formation. On the first practice jump, our group of thirteen experienced jumpers performed a mass exit in less than five seconds—good, but it would have to be better. A second practice jump was scheduled for the morning of 11 June, and this one was performed in less time than our first attempt. We reported to Lieutenant Colonel Sullivan that we had our technique down pat and were ready to go.

That same afternoon, we conducted a visual reconnaissance of the objective DZ (drop zone) then reported that we would be prepared for a night jump scheduled at 0200, but when we returned to 1st Recon Battalion, Lieutenant Colonel Sullivan told us that Operation WASHINGTON had been placed on hold. We were thinking that our parachute capabilities wouldn't be needed so we were surprised when the Colonel suddenly pointed to his map and announced, "We have decided that we can use your recon team in support of Operation KANSAS. You'll still get to jump, and we'll have four teams in the bush. Your drop zone is close to a suspected NVA divisional headquarters."

During the day of 12 June, we made a visual reconnaissance of the new objective area, Hill 555, south of the village of Hiep Duc, and tried to locate a drop zone close enough to make the jump worthwhile. Lady luck must certainly have been riding with us because we spotted a small hill that was not too distant from the objective. The hill, however, sat next to the Tranh River, at a ninety-degree bend, making the drop zone easy to spot. The river was not very deep and had white sandy shores on both of its banks, but it was a place we certainly had to avoid.

On 13 June, at approximately 0100, we climbed aboard the CV-2 with our parachutes, packs, and weapons, and carefully rehearsed the jump. I constructed a strip map indicating all the checkpoints from Chu Lai to our drop zone, and we returned to Chu Lai without incident. All that remained was for Lieutenant Paull and me to go to the battalion's S-2 shop and get the latest intelligence information on the objective area. As we already had been told, a North Vietnamese divisional headquarters was suspected to be located in the objective area, and numerous NVA and VC units were known to be operating there. In addition to that good news, a small village was located on the down-leg portion of our flight to the DZ. That meant we would have to exit the aircraft faster than we had ever done so we would not find ourselves in the river or having to land in the village.

At 2400 on 14 June, our team was loaded onto a six-by-six truck, with all of our equipment, and we took one last trip to the Chu Lai airstrip to await the arrival of our CV-2. Before the plane arrived, we suited up and began to check parachute harnesses and equipment rigs. Corporal Hernandez, our rigger, waited for me to complete my initial inspection as the team jumpmaster, before he performed his final checks on each member of the team. At 0100, we heard the familiar sound of the approaching CV-2, and waited impatiently for the pilot to taxi over to our assembly area and shut down his engines. Corporal

Hernandez and I climbed aboard and rigged the Caribou for the static-line jump. We loaded ourselves in inverse order with three observers climbing in first, and Sergeant Haferkamp as the first jumper to enter, tasked with pushing the stick out of the aircraft. The last Marine to climb in was Lieutenant Paull, who would be the first man to exit the plane.

We flew up the coast of South Vietnam for approximately thirty-five miles, then banked to the left and headed west. As we flew in trace of the Chang River, an eastern tributary of the Tranh River, I marked off the checkpoints on the map and talked directly to our pilot until I had only one checkpoint left unmarked. At that point, the pilot told me he had our DZ in view. He then banked the plane sharply to the right and once more to the left to align himself on course straight for our drop zone.

I instructed the team to hook up and gave the command to "stand by."

The pilot flipped on the green go light, the instant the nose of his Caribou crossed over the Thanh River. At that moment I shouted, "Go," at the top of my lungs, and Sergeant Haferkamp shoved twelve men out into the darkness in less than four seconds. As the last man cleared the exit, I jumped from the Caribou's side door to join the men of my team.

After feeling one hell of an opening jolt, I looked up at my canopy, and seeing I had a good opening, I immediately began to break the ties that fastened my rifle to my pack. As I came closer to the ground, I was startled by the sound of some large bird screaming at my approach, but in seconds I was on the ground. I shrugged off my parachute harness and buried it along with my nylon canopy. Within less than twenty minutes, the entire team had assembled. The only injury to any team member was a sprained ankle suffered by Corporal Martin. Lieutenant Paull contacted the COC and informed the folks in the rear that we were headed for our objective.

Before the first rays of the sun had crept into the eastern sky, we were set up in our OP, on a hill that overlooked the DZ and gave us a commanding view down the length of the river.

I was quite surprised at the size of the village of Hiep Duc, which we were carefully observing on the far side of the river. Within half an hour after sunrise, we began to see large numbers of uniformed soldiers moving in and out of the village, carrying a variety of weapons—AK-47s, SKSs, DP machine guns, RPG-40s and RPD machine guns. The majority of enemy soldiers wore green and gray uniforms and green pith helmets.

Early in the afternoon, we watched two unarmed men wearing gray shirts and dark green pants walk up a trail that ran past our drop zone. A dog walked beside them. As soon as they got close to the DZ, their dog began to bark, and they moved to a bush where one of the men had tried to stash his parachute. The dog's barking brought the two soldiers to the bush where they discovered the parachute. We watched as the three of them ran like hell for the village. Less than an hour later, approximately seventy-five NVA soldiers emerged from the river's edge, about three kilometers distant and began to move on our position. We called in this sighting to the COC, and within half an hour we received a radio message from Lieutenant Colonel Sullivan saying we would be extracted and that we should start moving for a likely LZ. A quick check of the map showed us we had several choices of landing zone, and once Lieutenant Paull made his selection, we notified the COC and began to move out. The location of our LZ put some distance between us and our former OP site and it would take at least thirty minutes for us to reach the LZ and be extracted.

By the time we reached the LZ, the sun was getting low in the sky, but two UH-34 helicopters sat down at the same time as four A-4 jets swept in over us and began to orbit. One of the two helicopters had landed in elephant grass so deep it was impossible to see. Incredibly, the pilot from the closest helicopter motioned for all of us to climb aboard his bird. In our haste to scramble into the one UH-34, which was designed to hold ten men at most, there was confusion as to who was in and who was not. When our bird began to throttle-up and climb, it shook like hell as it headed toward the river. That was when we began to take hits from enemy ground fire. Within seconds there was the sound of a tremendous "crack" in the tail section and we thought we were going to go down, but our pilot recovered control of his shuddering bird and began to climb slowly back into the sky before heading in the direction of Tam Ky. Pleased with the results of our combat jump and knowing we had made history, we returned to Chu Lai.

Several days later I happened to be sitting in our mess hall during evening chow when I was joined by a staff sergeant and a sergeant from F Company, 2d Battalion, 7th Marine Regiment, who were assigned to provide security for a bomb dump that was located on the opposite side of a hill near the company compound. The staff sergeant's name was Pete Connors, and he came from South Boston, Massachusetts. During our meal, he mentioned that he had participated in Operation MONTGOMERY, and it was then I realized it was Connors's company I had observed assaulting the tree line near the village. I told him I had watched their progress that day and was impressed with how rapidly they had been able to put their 60mm WP (white phosphorus) rounds into the tree line. Staff Sergeant Connors laughed and said that what I had witnessed was not 60mm mortar fire, but rifle grenades used in a unique manner. Connors told me he assigned one M-14 grenade launcher to each squad. Since new men had a problem telling where enemy firing was coming from, he gave the rifle grenade launcher to his most experienced men. The M-14 required the spindle valve be turned to the off position to fire the rifle grenade. Connors said he required his grenadier to have one WP grenade attached to the rifle and a crimped cartridge in the rifle's chamber. The grenadier also had a full magazine of 7.62mm rounds locked in his rifle's magazine well. As soon as he fired the WP grenade, the rifleman/grenadier immediately turned the spindle valve to the on position, pulled back on the operating rod, and loaded a live round into the chamber. He followed the burst of his WP grenade with a stream of nineteen rounds of accurate rifle fire. Knowing where the enemy was located, the rest of the rifle squad could key in on the bursting white phosphorous grenade and deliver more accurate fire.

The next day, I assembled my platoon down on the beach, where we test-fired our M-14 grenade launchers and practiced Pete Connors's idea until we had it down pat. On several later reconnaissance patrols, we were able to break contact with the NVA and live to fight again because of Connors's innovation. Later in my extended tour with 1st Force Recon, I learned that SSgt. Pete Connors, Fox Company, 2/7, was killed in action trying to save one of his men who lay wounded in a rice paddy.

The remainder of June and July found us busy on long-range patrols, even participating in the long-postponed Operation WASHINGTON during 6–14 July. While we were working out of Chu Lai, I gained even more respect for my enemy, having learned that in order to survive we had to be extremely aggressive and ready at all times to fight.

In mid-July, after returning from a patrol, I was sitting in the mess hall when a mess sergeant came up to me and said, "Hey, Gunny Jacques, your brother was here, asking about you." I told the sergeant that he must be mistaken, I had no brother serving in Vietnam. He said, "Well, you have now. Your brother is in the Seabees, and he was here helping to build a new helicopter landing pad. He said he was living at the sand ramp with MCB-3." SSgt. Bill Armor was sitting with me during this exchange and he offered me the use of his jeep and driver to get me to where my brother was stationed.

After checking with a few of the Seabee companies, I found my brother Francis, whom I had not seen in more than twelve years, the last time being when I was hospitalized at the naval hospital at Quantico, following the automobile accident. Francis looked fit and happy. We shook hands, hugged one another, and stared at each other for a long time before I suggested we return to 1st Recon Battalion, where he would be a welcome guest in our battalion's little club. There we could sit down and try to catch up on the years since we had last seen each other. At the club, I introduced Francis to all of the company's staff NCOs. And the cold beer flowed. Although my brother Francis hardly ever drank, he made an exception for that night.

Francis told me that after he had served in the Marine Corps for eight years, he had decided to get out and went to work as a heavy equipment operator. When the war in Vietnam began to heat up, the navy began to search for heavy equipment operators, promising an enlistment that began at the grade of third class petty officer (E-4). We spent the night drinking and telling stories about our days growing up in Lawrence to anyone who would listen. Before he left, we cautioned each other to be careful and promised each other we would not wait so long between visits.

During the time I was in Vietnam, I never had the opportunity to see my brother Francis again. I wish I had. Only several days later, I was a member of an awards ceremony held by 1st Reconnaissance Battalion at Chu Lai, and wished Francis had been there to observe the events of the day; I was one of several Marines called to the front and center of the formation and awarded the Bronze Star for my participation in the events which occurred on the night of 16 December, eight kilometers away from Ba To.

An important part of that battalion awards ceremony was the recognition given to the members of the eighteen-man recon team led by a fellow SNCO team leader, SSgt. Jimmie L. Howard, from 1st Reconnaissance Battalion. After an insertion on 13 June, Staff Sergeant Howard's team found a fifteen-hundred-foot hill to be an excellent observation position, and for two days they remained in place and reported important enemy activity in the area. Supported by a South Vietnamese Army 105mm artillery battery located at the Tien Phuoc Special Forces camp, seven miles south of Nui Vu, the recon Marines called artillery missions in on targets of opportunity.

Although Howard had taken the precaution to call fire missions only when an American spotter plane or helicopter was in the area, by the fifteenth the enemy had become aware of the patrol's presence in the area. Late that night, a patrol from the Special Forces camp reported an enemy battalion moving toward Nui Vu from the southeast. Between 2130 and 2330, Howard called for artillery support as the Marines heard North Vietnamese troops massing at the bottom of the hill. Shortly after midnight, the Communists probed the Marine defenses and then followed with a three-sided, all-out attack. According to the navy corpsman with the Marines, the enemy forces, ". . . were within twenty feet of us. Suddenly there were grenades all over. Then people started hollering. It seemed everybody got hit at the same time." Despite the intensity of the enemy assault, which was supported by heavy machine-gun fire, the Marine perimeter held. But Howard radioed LtCol. A. J. Sullivan, the battalion commander, "You've gotta get us out of here . . . There are too many of them for my people." Sullivan attempted to reassure the patrol leader and told him that assistance would be on the way.

About 0200, supporting air arrived overhead, including Marine and air force flare planes, helicopters, and attack aircraft. Marine jets and Huey gunships attacked the enemy forces massing at the bottom of the hill. At times, VMO-6 gunships strafed to within twenty meters of the patrol's perimeter, and fixed-wing aircraft dropped bombs and napalm as close as one hundred meters. At 0300, enemy ground fire drove off a flight of MAG-36 helicopters that was trying to pick up the patrol. Lieutenant Colonel Sullivan told Howard that the patrol could not expect any reinforcements that night and to hold on as best he could.

The action on and around the hill was reduced to small, scattered, individual firefights. Wary of the U.S. aircraft orbiting overhead, the Communist forces decided against another mass assault, but continued to fire at the Marines throughout the night. Running short of ammunition, Howard and his men fired single shots, even throwing rocks at suspected enemy positions, hoping the NVA would mistake the rocks for grenades. The fighting was exacting a heavy toll on the reconnaissance patrol—each man had been wounded at least once, and six were dead. Sergeant Howard was struck in the back by a ricochet, temporarily paralyzing his legs. Unable to use his lower limbs, Howard pulled himself from hole to hole, encouraging his men and directing fire.

At dawn on 16 June, MAG-36 UH-34s, escorted by Huey gunships, safely landed Company C, 1st Battalion, 5th Marines, near the base of Nui Vu. One of the gunships, piloted by Maj. William J. Goodsell, the commanding officer of VMO-6, was hit by enemy fire and crash-landed. Major Goodsell and his copilot were evacuated, but Goodsell later died of his wounds.

The Marine company on the ground met some resistance as it advanced up Nui Vu to relieve Howard's patrol. When the relief force finally reached the top of the hill, Howard greeted them with the warning, "Get down . . . There are snipers right in front of us." 1st Lt. Marshall B. Darling, the Company C commander, remembered that he found Howard's men mostly armed with AK-47s taken from dead North Vietnamese. The North Vietnamese, later identified as a battalion from the 3d NVA Regiment, continued to battle the Marines for control of the hill until noon, and then disengaged. They left behind forty-two dead and nineteen weapons. Company C suffered two dead and two wounded.

For this action, fifteen men of Staff Sergeant Howard's platoon were awarded the Silver Star and two more the Navy Cross. Staff Sergeant Howard was awarded the Medal of Honor.[1]

On 20 July, we received orders to leave Chu Lai and fly north to Dong Ha, where several of our platoons were

---

1. Jack Shulimson, *U.S. Marines in Vietnam, an Expanding War,* Chapter 8, pp. 113–135.

engaged in support of Operation HASTINGS. This operation was a big one. It had started on 15 July, with teams from 1st Force supporting the 4th Marines and battalions from the 3d Marine Division, and both the 9th and the 1st Marine Regiments. The North Vietnamese Army had sent the 324 B Division across the DMZ in their attempt to take over Quang Tri Province.

Once we had arrived at Dong Ha, my platoon was brought up to strength, and each platoon was able to field two or three patrols with the platoon leader, platoon sergeant, and the senior team leader each heading up a patrol. The size of the patrols varied from five to seven men, armed with M-14 rifles, with one M-79 grenade launcher, and three LAAWs per team. Taking a lesson from the late Pete Connors, I still had my team carrying one rifle grenade launcher and five WP rounds to the field. In all of our operational orders, specific reference was made to each team's being tasked with capturing NVA prisoners.

There were so many NVA regulars operating in our TAOR, that the majority of our LZs were covered by enemy fire. It was the standard tactic of the NVA to try to surround a reconnaissance team and then wait for the opportunity to shoot down any helicopter that might try to land and extract it. There is, of course, no doubt in my mind that we had the very best helicopter pilots available to us. Words fail to describe the everyday heroic efforts of our helicopter pilots. They never abandoned a recon team in trouble and often placed themselves and their helicopters between the NVA and the recon teams.

After conducting three more patrols out of Dong Ha, my platoon was assigned to the Rock Pile to relieve the 2d Platoon, which had been there for nearly one week. The Rock Pile was a jungle-covered pinnacle, seven hundred feet high, four feet wide, and not more than seven feet long, which served as a commanding OP site first used by recon teams from 1st Force Recon in the spring of 1966.

We were transported out to the Rock Pile by three UH-34 helicopters, but the hilltop LZ allowed for only one helicopter at a time to get into position for a landing. In fact, it required each helicopter pilot to have the skill to position the front two wheels of his helicopter on a small wooden platform constructed by the Marines of the 2d Platoon, and to hover in place, while men and supplies left and entered the waiting helicopter. On one piece of rock outcropping, three field jackets had been placed over the jagged edge of the rocks to prevent helicopters having their skin punctured or hydraulic lines damaged by the sharp rocks.

Once on the ground, I immediately assigned fighting positions and fields of fire to the team members. We were pleased to find that 2d Platoon had left two M-60 machine guns on the hill, which gave us much greater confidence in our ability to defend the hilltop. We had also brought along two M-79 grenade launchers with seventy-five rounds of ammunition, and sixteen LAAWs. I placed four of the antitank rockets in holes that surrounded the hill and saved my best surprise for last. I had brought along two cases of C-4 plastic explosive, more than eighty pounds of the stuff. Using sandbags, I made enough satchel charges to supply four to each of my fighting positions. Each charge had nearly five pounds of C-4.

There were friendly forces to our south and southeast, but the most likely avenue of enemy approach was from a high rocky area off to our west, known as the razorback. And it was from the direction of the razorback that we began to draw our first sporadic sniper fire. We answered the enemy's fire with the M-60 machine guns or the M-79 grenade launchers. We suffered no casualties during the initial period when we occupied the Rock Pile, and we began to settle into a routine. By August, we realized the valley beneath us was void of friendly troops.

A funny thing happened not long after the friendlies had departed. Sergeant Haferkamp, my platoon sergeant, asked me if I was sure the sandbag satchel charges I had made would work. He suggested we test one, and it didn't take long to find out why Sergeant Haferkamp was so anxious to set off one of the charges. A troop of dozens of black-and-white monkeys had occupied a ledge on one of the rocky outcroppings near our position, and they became the target of the experimental satchel charge. One of the satchel charges was thrown over the side of our position and landed on top of the monkeys' ledge. At first the monkeys scattered when the satchel landed nearby, but within a few seconds their curiosity got the better of them, and they moved in for a closer look at the smoking fuses, which were wrapped around the sandbag charge. The explosion caused by five pounds of C-4 was very powerful, and when the smoke cleared and the last of the flying rocks had come back to earth, not a single monkey was in sight.

After fourteen days on the Rock Pile, we were relieved by another platoon. Operation PRAIRIE was getting under way, and when we returned to the company area, we learned that another reorganization effort was under way. I was transferred to the company's fifth platoon and said good-bye to Lieutenant Paull and Sergeant Haferkamp as they met their rotation dates and returned to the States. SSgt. Gary Marte, known within the company as Buddha, became my new platoon sergeant. We split the platoon into two teams, with Marte leading one team and myself leading the other.

As enemy activity began to pick up again, our pace followed suit. On our next patrol we were inserted late in the afternoon into an LZ where the surrounding elephant grass was only three feet high and offered little concealment. I could see a small island of trees not too distant from the LZ so we headed off to find concealment among them. Once we arrived, we set up in a 360-degree defense and waited for darkness so that we could move out to a better location.

It was near dusk when one of my new men leaned over and whispered, "Gunny, there are lights down at the LZ." I whispered back that the lights were probably fireflies and that he shouldn't worry about it. My answer seemed to settle him; he moved off a few feet and sat there watching. Several minutes later he came back to where I was sitting and whispered, "Gunny, them fireflies of yours are now beating the grass, looking for us." I took a look with my binoculars, and sure enough the new kid was right—the NVA had come calling—this time they came carrying flashlights. The NVA had found the signs of crushed grass in our landing zone and were trying to pick up our trail. But we also knew from past interrogation of enemy prisoners that the NVA, when unfamiliar with the area, were terrified of the possibility of running into snakes and would use their flashlights to illuminate their way. As we watched their progress from several hundred yards away, they began to come toward us, moving single file. There were about thirty-five of them, and they carried AK-47s and RDG machine guns. Our only hope was to sit tight and hope they would pass by. For nearly fifteen minutes we remained absolutely motionless, hoping and praying that their column would continue on and that they had not spotted anything suspicious enough to cause them to double back and check out our little island in the grass. After their tail-end Charlie had passed by, and waiting for half an hour, we started to follow the NVA platoon, walking cautiously in trace of them. Finally, we could no longer see their lights or their trail, and we moved into a harbor site for the rest of the evening.

On the fourth day of that patrol, we moved to our extraction point and waited for the birds. On our way out of the LZ, our UH-34 took several hits from ground fire, probably from the same NVA force we had encountered earlier in the week. After we returned to the company compound and went to the S-2 shop for the patrol debriefing, the new debriefing officer, who had little, if any, time in the field, demanded to know why I hadn't called in Puff, a close-support aircraft with Vulcan cannon capability of firing two thousand rounds per minute, to take the NVA platoon under fire. My answer, that "The NVA were only fifteen feet away from us, sir," seemed to satisfy his curiosity.

During this time, the use of B-52 Arc Light bombing strikes was a familiar tactic, and it was during our next patrol that we received word, a day ahead of time, to move to our LZ for an early extraction. Since the area we had been patrolling was full of NVA, we thought they wanted to pull us out to protect us from five-hundred-pound bombs dropped from an altitude of thirty-five thousand feet. We started for the planned LZ, and on four occasions we nearly made point-to-point contact with NVA patrols. When we finally arrived near our LZ, I contacted the COC and told them we were ready for pickup. When the two birds came in, I headed for the second one and handed my rifle to the crew chief and started to pull myself into the helicopter. I grabbed for the right wheel strut when the helicopter suddenly lunged forward and up, and I ended up hanging onto the right wheel strut for dear life. We were nearly one hundred feet in the air before the pilot learned of my position outside his aircraft. He quickly set down on a small hill, and my radio operator and the crew chief pulled me back inside. After landing at Dong Ha, we made it back to the company compound and were met by one of the SNCOs assigned to the S-3 shop. He told me we had been extracted a day early because my team and I were supposed to be interviewed by a writer from *Life* magazine. I could have shot the idiot who thought up the idea of pulling our team out early, jeopardizing the lives of seven men.

I was introduced to a Mr. Sherrod, who photographed us and then asked us a number of questions about our feelings toward civilians and students who were demonstrating against the war in Vietnam back in the States. His announcement was news to me. I hadn't seen a copy of a *Star and Stripes* newspaper in a long time and couldn't imagine what he was talking about. But he certainly got me thinking about what he claimed was going on back home.

After my first night back from the bush, I came down with a severe fever. The following day, I did go out on a visual reconnaissance flight in preparation for our next patrol, but as soon as I returned from the airstrip, I visited the sick bay for a checkup. The doc took my temperature and told me I had a fever of 103 degrees. The following morning I was medevacked to the Naval Support Activity (NSA) hospital, Da Nang, where I was admitted and diagnosed as having a "fever of undetermined origin."

CHAPTER 20

The Kindness of Strangers—1967

I arrived at Da Nang on an air force C-123 medevac flight from Chu Lai and was taken by a navy bus directly to the Naval Support Activity hospital, where I was admitted to the malaria ward. Treatment was started immediately, and within a few days my fever had broken, and I was feeling much better. I remained a patient at NSA for only eight days before being discharged to full duty and allowed to return to Camp Merrell. Back at Camp Merrell, I met up with GySgt. "Art" Torizzo, who was waiting to take his platoon aboard ship as the reconnaissance element for the SLF (special landing force). Gunnery Sergeant Torizzo and I had become well acquainted at Dong Ha after he had joined our company upon reassignment from 2d Force Recon Company at Camp Lejeune, North Carolina. He was one hell of a fine Marine. While I was renewing my friendship with Torizzo and preparing for my return to Dong Ha, I received a phone call on the landline from our company commander, Major Colby, instructing me to get rid of all the land mines that were stored in our company's ammunition bunkers. A very large minefield had been laid between MAG-16 and Camp Merrell during January 1966, and when the Marine air group decided to expand its cantonment area, the land mines were removed and became the property of 1st Force Recon Company. Now having an opportunity to rid himself of these explosive devices, Major Colby told me to load the mines onto a truck and take them for proper disposal to the nearest dump in Da Nang.

With the help of a few Marines from Gunnery Sergeant Torizzo's platoon, and an aged truck from the company's motor pool, the land mines were removed from their bunker and placed on the bed of the truck, which was also due to be turned in for disposal. With Torizzo and myself riding in the cab, we headed off toward the local ammunition dump. Arriving at the dump, we met the Marine warrant officer in charge, and he told us directly that he did not want to take custody of land mines that had already spent time in the ground. After explaining that our company had to get rid of the mines, "lest they fall into enemy hands," the warrant officer reconsidered. But when we unloaded the first crate of mines, we were astonished to find the explosive fuses still in them and that no safety pins had been put in place to prevent an accidental explosion. The majority of the devices were M-16 "bouncing-Betty" antipersonnel mines, and to convince the warrant officer to accept our dangerous cargo, Torizzo and I had to remove all the fuses and deactivate all of the mines. Only then did the warrant officer finally accept the mines and provide us with an area to off-load them. Once finished with that job, we drove our obsolete truck to a vehicle turn-in point and hitchhiked back to Camp Merrell. After calling to Dong Ha to let the major know that all of the mines had been turned in, I was told to remain at Camp Merrell because the company was returning to Da Nang and my platoon was about to be "chopped" op con and ad con (transferred operationally and administratively) to the 1st Marine Division's 1st Reconnaissance Battalion.

The headquarters of the 3d Marine Division had moved north, to Phu Bai, and with the growing TAOR of 1st Marine Division ranging from Chu Lai to Da Nang, the need for additional reconnaissance assets would be greater than ever before. Additionally, I learned from our new company executive officer, Captain Ceretta, that Camp Merrell was to be deactivated and our equipment moved to Camp Reasoner[1] as MAG-16 expanded to meet the requirements for additional helicopters.

With the closure of Camp Merrell in November, we moved to Camp Reasoner, and for the first time in nineteen months, I recovered my seabag and opened it to check on the condition of my extra clothing and equipment. Virtually all of my military clothing was dry-rotted, but paperwork submitted to the company first sergeant would allow me to obtain a replacement issue at no expense to myself. With our move to Camp Reasoner, I met a number of Marines who had recently joined the company; one of them being GySgt. Walter Webb, the Marine who had taught me to scuba dive at Camp Pendleton in 1957. When we first moved to Camp Reasoner, we also had a change of command in the company; Maj. B. G. Lowery relieved Major Colby.

For me, a day of particular import was 18 December when I met SSgt. J. L. Dunning, who had joined our company in November, coming from the 2d Battalion, 4th Marines, at Dong Ha. Staff Sergeant Dunning and I became traveling companions, departing the Republic of Vietnam for our long-awaited trip back home. My final destination was Lawrence, Massachusetts, but Dunning was headed for home in Michigan. Our flight to freedom was on a Marine Corps C-130, which took us to Okinawa, five hours away, where we would stay at Camp Hansen before being processed back to the States.

At Camp Hansen, I received a partial issue of my clothing allowance, enough to get me home in a new set of greens, but before I could wear the uniform, I first had to purchase a set of gunnery sergeant chevrons and the appropriate number of hash marks to designate the number of years I had spent overseas. With Staff Sergeant Dunning in tow, I went outside the camp's main gate to a tailor shop called Sang Woo's. After we left Mr. Woo's

---

1. Camp Reasoner was named in honor of 1st Lieutenant Frank Reasoner, who was awarded the Medal of Honor.

establishment, we headed for the Topper Club, located south of Camp Hansen in the town of Zukeran. The Topper Club was the first halfway decent club either of us had seen in a very long time. We spent hours drinking ice-cold beer, telling stories to anyone who would listen, and dancing the night away with the bar girls. The next morning, we came roaring back to Camp Hansen by cab, and headed straight to the transient office to learn about the possibility of leaving Okinawa. To our surprise, we saw that our names had been added to a flight manifest indicating that we would fly that same afternoon. It was nothing short of devastating for the both of us to tell one of the transient NCOs that we would not be able to make the flight because our uniforms would not be ready for at least one more day. After telling our story to the Marine gunnery sergeant in charge of the transient flight section, he told us our scheduled flight was, in fact, the last flight scheduled to leave Okinawa for the States until after the New Year. He told us that because we could not fly by jet, the only way back to California, was on a prop-driven C-130 cargo plane—island-hopping our way across the Pacific—a flight which required forty-eight hours of flying time. We accepted our fate.

After we had retrieved our uniforms from Mr. Woo's tailor shop, we checked out of Camp Hansen and headed for the Marine Corps air station at Futema, to check in for our C-130 flight home. It was then we discovered our plane would not leave the island until 0400 on 21 December. With spare time on our hands, I asked Staff Sergeant Dunning to join me at the Topper Club to eat a steak dinner and celebrate our going home after having spent nineteen of the most difficult months of my life in Vietnam. The hostess at the Topper Club treated us well, and I remember drinking toasts to all the Marines who were still in combat and to those Marines who would not be going home. And by the time we left the Topper Club and headed by cab for Futema, Dunning and I were pleasantly drunk.

As our small group of thirty passengers milled around

the C-130, we were addressed by our pilots who said that they, too, had just finished tours in Vietnam and wanted to be safely home by Christmas. Our plane was carrying a significant amount of cargo, and as we went aboard, we were told by the crew chief that we could change into utilities to make the flight a little more enjoyable. It didn't take long before we were airborne. With the help of the residual effect of alcohol, Dunning and I fell quickly asleep in our bucket-style seats. When I awoke, my eyes slowly focused on a set of lieutenant colonel's silver oak leaves attached to a blue wool coat, which was covering me. I remember thinking, Oh shit, what in the hell did I do last night? As I lifted my head, the man in the seat next to mine noticed that my bloodshot eyes were open. He leaned over and said, "I saw that you were freezing, Gunny, so I covered you up with my overcoat." The gentleman who had helped me was a navy chaplain, a commander, whose presence on our C-130 made me feel just a little more comfortable about our chances for a safe flight across the Pacific.

Our first stop, early in the morning, was at Wake Island, and we were bussed to the Pan-American mess hall for breakfast. By the time we returned to the flight line, our plane was refueled and ready to continue east. The next event of the day was an announcement by our pilot that we had crossed the international date line and had returned in time to the original date of our departure from Okinawa. What seemed like days later, we finally landed at Hawaii's Hickam Air Force Base. After we had finished taxiing, the pilots gathered us together and told us that flight regulations required that they sleep for eight hours before beginning the final leg of our flight. They warned us that if we were not ready to go when they were, there would be no waiting for anyone regardless of rank. They suggested that we enlisted men check into the BEQ, and the officers in our group check in at the BOQ. We all would get a wake-up call when our pilots were ready to depart.

After a long hot shower, Dunning and I headed for the

staff NCO club to have breakfast, and remembering the price we paid for our foolishness at the Topper Club, didn't consider touching even a single drop of beer. We returned to the BEQ, and only four hours later got a wake-up call telling us to get our tails back down to the flight line. No questions were asked about the eight-hour layover rule as our eager pilots had completed their pre-flight inspection by the time we arrived.

After what seemed like an eternity, our pilot's voice came over the C-130's intercom system, and we were told to look to either side of the aircraft and we'd see the California islands of Catalina and San Clemente. Within ten minutes, we were landing at Marine Corps Air Station, El Toro, California, and a bus came out to the plane and took us and our baggage to the processing center. Since they had only thirty passengers to process, in no time we were dressed in our greens and headed for the closest ticket office and connecting flights home. It was suggested at the processing center that we purchase Space-A (space available) tickets for civilian flights to points east, and surprisingly, we were not given any written orders for our next duty assignment. We received only a single page of paper, granting each of us thirty days of leave, and explaining we would receive orders to our next command while on leave.

We boarded a navy bus and were taken north to Los Angeles International Airport. I had purchased a ticket for a United Airlines flight to Boston, Massachusetts, and I said good-bye to Staff Sergeant Dunning. Upon our arrival at the United terminal, I was surprised to see a penned area exclusively for servicemen who held space available tickets. And the pen was packed with dozens of navy recruits, also headed home for Christmas. I realized I had made a great mistake in electing to buy a Space-A ticket. A first-class ticket would have saved time waiting, and I had a considerable amount of money in my wallet after saving nineteen months of regular, combat, and jump pay.

As I sat on a bench for an hour, watching and waiting

for any sign of progress, I noticed that only the navy recruits were being selected to fill those seats not taken by
regular passengers. I walked over to a United ticket
counter and explained to an agent that I wanted to up-
grade my ticket, adding that I had not been home in
twelve years, and wanted very much to get home before
Christmas. I did not tell him that I had just returned from
Vietnam, but can only guess that it was written all over
my face. The agent was kind enough to make a call on
my behalf, and within a minute, he issued me a ticket for
a flight leaving for Chicago, with a transfer to Boston. In
less than twenty minutes, I was in the air, on my way
home, and suffering from a stomach full of butterflies.
The change of planes at O'Hare International was uneventful, and in less than half an hour, I was airborne
again, headed for Boston's Logan Airport.

When I landed in Boston, it was snowing nickle-size
flakes, and the temperature had dropped to a cold twenty
degrees. I hailed a taxi and told the driver to take me to
Boston's North Station as quickly as possible. I pulled my
seabag and suitcase from the trunk of his cab and found
a bench to wait on, shielding myself from the snowstorm.
About an hour later, a Boston City cop came walking up
to where I sat, and in the thickest Irish brogue, asked,
"Me boy, what in heaven's name are ya' doin' sittin'
here?" I told the officer I was waiting to purchase a ticket
on the B&M railroad for my home in Lawrence. The cop
began to suppress his laughter, and said, "Me boy, there
hasn't been a train out of this railroad station in more than
five years." Realizing he was dealing with someone who
had been away from Boston for a very long time, the policeman asked if I had come "from that place over there"
meaning Vietnam. I told him that I had just arrived in
Boston after nineteen months of being "over there."
About fifteen minutes later, the cop returned with a friend,
a cabdriver who offered to take me to Lawrence for
twenty dollars. I agreed, and as we started for Lawrence,
he began asking me a number of questions about the war
in Vietnam. His first question was, "What in the hell are

we doing over there?" I told him that I believed we were trying to stop the spread of Communism there and in other countries, and believed that if we didn't stop the spread of it, we could end up trying to stop it in our own cities.

By the time we reached Lawrence the cabbie said he had a better understanding of what was happening in Vietnam and he thanked me for answering so many of his questions. I gave him directions to my father's house, and after I had unloaded my gear from his cab, he stepped out from behind the wheel, came smartly to the position of attention, and saluted me. He said there would be no charge. He added that he, too, was a veteran. His war had been World War II. Then he welcomed me home, and he thanked me for a job well done with a handshake.

I guess the sound of the taxi's door had alerted my father—he was standing at the door when I walked up onto the porch. My father was very happy to see me, and said he had thought that I would make it home for Christmas. He stood there looking at me for what seemed to be a long time, then hugged me and invited me into the warmth of his house. The smell of home came flooding back and instantly erased the void of senses which the past twelve years had created. My mother came out from her bedroom with a great warming smile on her face. She hugged me very tightly for a long, long time and kissed me, thanking me for coming home to be with her and to celebrate Christmas as a family.

My mother had aged during the twelve years I had been gone, and having two of her sons in Vietnam had added more than a few gray hairs to her head, but she looked wonderful to me. My parents were the only two people now living in the house—all of us kids had moved out, and the house's being so quiet did seem strange. I learned that my sister Eleanor was married, and she and her husband were the proud parents of a little girl named Cheryl, who was the spitting image of her mother when she was a little girl. Eleanor and her husband lived less than a mile away. My brother Ted and his wife Phyllis were married while Ted was still in the Marine Corps at Camp Lejeune, North Carolina. They now lived nearby on Adams Street, across from the first house we had lived in when I was a child.

I talked with my mother and father for a very long time, and told them all about meeting up with my brother Francis at Chu Lai. When I could no longer keep my eyes open, I asked to be excused, and went upstairs to get some sleep. When I awakened the next morning, I was feeling ill, having chills and a low-grade fever, but I tried not to let my illness bother me, as my sister and brother Ted were coming to the house to welcome me home. Just to be in the presence of my family, especially at Christmas, was the fulfillment of many prayers I had uttered during the past several years.

One day, not long after Christmas, my father and I drove to the local barbershop, which happened to belong to one of my uncles. We hadn't been in the shop for more than a few seconds before my uncle asked me for my autograph. He laughed, and said it wasn't too often that a "real celebrity" came into his little shop. Then he produced a copy of *Life* magazine and showed me a picture of me and my Marines after we had been prematurely extracted from the bush while patrolling outside of Dong Ha. I had no idea that any of the pictures the photographer from *Life* had taken would be published, but after we were finished at the barbershop, my father stopped by the drugstore and bought several issues of that copy of *Life* magazine to take home to the family.

Patriotic affection—the acceptance, recognition, and appreciation for the American veteran returning home from war—was a legitimate feeling I had known, particularly after I had returned home from Korea. But things were decidedly different now. The feelings for soldiers that used to be expressed by the people of the country, particularly those in the New England states, seemed gone forever. It was a disturbing and saddening experience for me, and one which has unfortunately lasted over the years. One particular event may explain it best.

My sister Eleanor and her husband, my brother Ted and his wife, and an uncle and aunt, had asked me to join them for dinner at a local nightspot called Bob White's Dine and Dance Club, located outside Lawrence near the township of North Andover. My relatives had asked me to wear my uniform, and I agreed to their request. After taking time to press out my uniform, complete with its several rows of ribbons and my jump wings, I put it on. That undeniable sense of Marine pride, which I had known when I had first come home following my recruit training at Parris Island and again after I had returned home from Korea, was still there when I walked through the door at Bob White's. But Bob's happened to be full of New England college students, who also happened to be home for the holidays.

As the evening progressed, I was challenged to fight at least four times (incidents my brother and brother-in-law took care of a short time later). I was called a baby killer and a warmonger, and when several of my young tormentors saw that I was wearing a Purple Heart, some suggested I should have been killed in Vietnam rather than just wounded in a war which no "real American supports." With my naive feelings shattered and in disbelief at what had occurred, we left Bob White's and went home. To this day, my feelings of disgust, contempt, and pity for the so-called peace-loving "flower children" of the 1960s has never, and will never, change.

On my twentieth day of leave, when I had still not received orders for my next duty station, I went to the office of the local Marine Corps recruiter in downtown Lawrence, and met First Sergeant Sheehan, a Korean War veteran who had been running that recruiting station for the past two years. After I introduced myself to him, he remembered my name and told me he was damned happy to see that I had made it home in one piece for, one year earlier, he had been the Marine who delivered the Corps' telegram to my parents stating that I had been wounded at Ba To and hospitalized at Chu Lai. I told First Sergeant Sheehan the reason for my visit, and he immediately picked up the telephone and made a call. After he hung up, he told me that my orders to join the 5th Marine Division, forming at Camp Pendleton, California, were in the mail. First Sergeant Sheehan, who had been wounded during the Korean War, had not yet been to Vietnam; he asked me to stay a while and tell him about duty there. As I left the recruiting station, I remember First Sergeant Sheehan's final words to me, saying, "Gunny Jacques, I've got to get my ass over there and see what's going on." First Sergeant Sheehan got his wish. In 1968, he was killed in action against the North Vietnamese, operating in an area close to the Rock Pile. He left behind a grieving wife and seven children, and I was proud to have known him.

When my leave was up, I said good-bye to my parents and extended family, and returned to Camp Pendleton in late January 1967. After reporting in to the division reception center, I was assigned to the division's 5th Reconnaissance Battalion, located at Camp Horno. At the battalion, I was assigned to the S-3 (training and operations) shop as the ops and training chief for the fundamentals of reconnaissance patrolling. My boss was a 1st Lieutenant Cassidy, an outstanding young officer who had just returned from a tour of duty as a platoon leader with 3d Reconnaissance Battalion, where he had won the Silver Star for conspicuous gallantry.

The 5th Marine Division had been reactivated for duty in Vietnam in early 1966, and had one regiment—the 26th Marines—in combat by the middle of the year. It was the 26th Marines who had distinguished themselves during World War II on the island of Iwo Jima. To complement the 26th Marines, the 27th and 28th Marines, as well as the 13th Marine Artillery Regiment were also formed at Camp Pendleton. To support the 5th Marine Division, the 5th Reconnaissance Battalion had already placed its A Company in the field in Vietnam, while B Company was formed and Marines for C Company were arriving at Camp Pendleton daily.

After serving in the S-3 shop for nearly three months,

I was called to the battalion sergeant major's office and told to take a seat. The sergeant major unfolded a list of Marine gunnery sergeants who had been selected for promotion to the rank of master sergeant and first sergeant. The sergeant major read my name from his list and then congratulated me on having been selected for the rank of first sergeant. He told me that my MOS would immediately be changed to an "unrestricted MOS" of 9999, and that I had been selected as the first sergeant of C Company, 5th Reconnaissance Battalion.

It was close to June 1967 when C Company began to form and Capt. Bill Warren, my new company commander came aboard. The captain had come to the company by way of the division's G-3 training section. As we got more men into the company, we saw that the majority of our company NCOs were, fortunately, Vietnam returnees, but the majority of non-NCOs were just youngsters fresh from ITR who would have plenty to learn from our veteran NCOs. Captain Warren knew that I had recently returned from Vietnam and asked that I get involved in the training of the Marines in the company; we both knew they would see action soon enough. Captain Warren knew I had just recently been promoted to first sergeant. He promised that if I worked with him to prepare a solid training program, he would make sure that I would fill a quota for First Sergeant's School, so that I could learn the administrative skills required of Marine first sergeants.

It seemed as though the 5th Reconnaissance Battalion was becoming a staging battalion for Marines returning to WestPac, as new orders arrived every day, and Marines departed the company for their first or second tours. Finally, Captain Warren received his orders for a second tour. When he left the battalion, I assumed his duties as the battalion diving officer, finding myself having to conduct prescuba courses and submarine operations. With everyone else leaving for Vietnam, I too submitted an AA (administrative assistance) form requesting orders back to Vietnam.

As had been promised by Captain Warren, I received

orders to First Sergeant's School, located at Parris Island, South Carolina, and before I left Camp Pendleton to attend the school, I was promoted to the grade of first sergeant in August 1967. I arrived at Parris Island wearing my new chevrons. At First Sergeant's School, I put a great deal of effort into learning the complexities of administration, and managed to keep in shape by working out each evening in the gym and by taking short runs around the depot. I enjoyed the course, but honestly, I had more on my mind than wanting to become a desk-flying administrative whiz, particularly when there was a war on in Vietnam. I graduated from First Sergeant's School on 22 September 1967, and was handed two pieces of paper; a diploma for successfully completing the course, and orders transferring me from 5th Reconnaissance Battalion to WestPac Ground Forces.

Upon my return to 5th Recon Battalion, I finally saw a copy of my orders and much to my surprise they read that I was to be sent to FLC (Force Logistics Command), an organization made up of logistical types who enjoy counting beans and making bread—necessary jobs, but certainly not very appealing to me. I asked to see our battalion commander, LtCol. Larry P. Charron, and asked if he could help me get my orders changed so that I could join up with a FMF (Fleet Marine Force) unit. Lieutenant Colonel Charron came through, as I had hoped, and the orders which could have made me a combat doughnut-maker were changed.

My orders to Vietnam required that I be sent to Staging Battalion at Marine Corps Base, Camp Pendleton, and after checking into that organization, I was told that because of the lack of officers, I would be the acting training company commander until a captain came in to take over. We began the training cycle at Camp Las Pulgas, where all of the 150 Marines in the company learned or relearned basic infantry training skills and fired a new course of rifle fire known as "quick kill," designed to teach young Marines how to properly respond to sudden rifle fire or ambush. The course of training was much better than I had received in preparation for Korea, and I could see that lessons learned in Vietnam were now being applied to those Marines, both young and old, who would soon find themselves in combat on foreign soil.

Our training began on 6 November 1967 and was completed by 23 November. We departed Marine Corps Air Station, El Toro, California, as a training company, on 25 November, on a chartered civilian jet airliner and arrived on Okinawa one day later. Our individual orders were rewritten to reflect the needs of the Marine Corps, and my orders now directed me to join the 1st Marine Division, headquartered in Vietnam. On my second day on Okinawa, I boarded another chartered Flying Tiger airliner and headed west for Vietnam, arriving at Da Nang at 1000 that morning. And as we were about to land, I looked out the small window over my left shoulder and saw dozens of columns of black smoke rising into the air around the airport, none caused by incoming mortar or artillery rounds. As I walked through the forward hatch of our plane and descended the steps of the ladder, I was immediately reunited with the familiar and inescapable, pungent odor of burning diesel fuel used to reduce the vast amounts of human waste that were burned away each day.

Welcome back to Vietnam.

CHAPTER 21

Echo Company, 1st Reconnaissance Battalion—1967–1969

It was late in the afternoon when a jeep driver finally came into the III MAF transit facility to pick up me and two other first sergeants and take us to the office of the 1st Marine Division sergeant major for further assignments. I was the last man called into the sergeant major's office, and as I walked in he held out his hand, welcoming me aboard, and said, "First Sergeant Jacques, seeing that this is your second tour, I'm sending you to be the first sergeant at 1st Medical Battalion."

His statement took me by surprise. I said, "Sergeant Major, what in the hell are you doing to me? I worked my ass off to get over here, and I sure didn't have duty with 1st Medical Battalion in mind. I'd rather go to an infantry company or to a recon company if that's possible."

The sergeant major could see I was serious and said, "Well, if that's what you want, Jacques, then I'll send you over to 1st Recon Battalion." Thank God, I thought, for obliging sergeants major.

It was late in the day by the time I'd carried my gear down from the division command post and crossed the road, entering the compound known as Camp Reasoner, the home of 1st Reconnaissance Battalion. I found my way to Sgt. Maj. Bill Lyday's office, and following a brief discussion with him, I learned that I would probably be heading over to 1st Force Recon Company to relieve a First Sergeant Olsen, who was due to return to the States. But all plans for my assignment were contingent on the desires of the battalion commander, and I would have to wait until morning before meeting with him. I spent my first night back in Vietnam with 1st Reconnaissance Battalion.

Following an early breakfast with the sergeant major, I went with him to meet Lt. Col. Craig R. Steinmetz, the commanding officer of the battalion. After being introduced to the colonel, I handed him my service record book, sat down, and waited patiently as he went over my record, page by page, before he began asking me questions. I told the colonel about my last tour in Vietnam and mentioned that I had come from 5th Force Recon Battalion, where I had helped form a new company prior to coming back to Vietnam. The colonel became interested in the training that we had done in 5th Force and before I knew it, he said, "First Sergeant Jacques, I think that I have changed my mind on sending you over to 1st Force Recon Company. Instead, I would like you to be the first sergeant of a new company called E Company, and it will be a large company with four operating platoons." When he asked what I thought of his offer, I told him that the opportunity would be a great challenge for me, and that I was honored to take the assignment, promising to do the best job I was capable of doing. My orders were endorsed, and I was taken by jeep to Hill 134, where E Company was being formed.

I went into the company office to meet with the new company commander, Capt. J. P. Cahill, and was joined by the company's executive officer, 1st Lt. Andy Finlayson. Both of these officers had extensive reconnaissance backgrounds. The CO and XO wasted little time in telling me as much as they could about our new company and their plans for its activation. All of the Marines in the company in the grades of lance corporal and below had graduated from the reconnaissance school, which was being conducted at Camp Pendleton's Infantry Training Regiment (ITR), and been given the military occupational specialty (MOS) of 8651, Basic Reconnaissance Marine. These new men were highly motivated. All of the non-commissioned officers, (corporals and sergeants), had come to the company from the infantry regiments of the 1st Marine Division which had recon MOSs. The majority of them had combat experience, and nearly all of them had volunteered for this hazardous duty. The staff non-commissioned officers in E Company had also come to us from the infantry regiments, many having served in reconnaissance companies back in the States. Some of the best SNCOs from the reconnaissance battalion, those who were short-timers, came to the company to be instructors before returning to the States. With the exception of three newly joined second lieutenants who had come to us directly from the basic school at Quantico, Virginia, all of our officers had considerable combat experience. But what those three young lieutenants lacked in combat experience, they made up for with their devotion and enthusiasm to learn the special skills that would keep them and their men alive.

Captain Cahill told me that we had an exceptional administrative chief, and he wanted me to get personally involved in the company's training schedule, saying that I was not to be too concerned over the administrative needs of the company. To him, and to me, training was more significant than mundane paperwork. All in all, I was joined to the ranks of a company of experienced men and eager volunteers, young men from all walks of life and from every part of the country. I was pleased that we had the makings of a remarkable organization. But combat waited for no man; I went to work, ready to contribute to the needs of the company.

Echo Company was organized into five platoons: one headquarters platoon, consisting of an administrative section, a supply section, and a communications section; four operational platoons of three squads each with nine men per squad. We had seven officers and one hundred and thirty-three enlisted men, including five navy hospital corpsmen. Initially, we had been told that our company was going to be used in a Stingray-type role, but that concept was changed due to the heavy requirement for reconnaissance teams in the field. We would operate as a regular reconnaissance company, and it would not be long before we had more recon teams in the field than any company in the battalion, including 1st Force Recon Company, which was still colocated with 1st Recon Battalion. As Christmas approached, we initiated our first phase of training, training designed to separate the wheat from the chaff. As the first sergeant, I ran the company's physical training program, which was conducted twice each day, rain or shine. After a half-hour period of rigorous calisthenics, each PT session ended with a five-mile run, every man running in combat boots and wearing utility trousers. Classes on reconnaissance subjects were conducted daily. We were allowed to train at a nearby ARVN training camp. Our other training area was at the Namo Bridge, where IBS (inflatable boat, small) drills and team swimming skills were mastered. The second phase of our company training, lasting for a period of eight weeks, was to take place on Okinawa. That was scheduled to begin immediately after the New Year.

During that first week of January 1968, the company was taken by three C-130 flights to Okinawa then brought to Camp Schwab for a period of intensive training in reconnaissance patrolling, live-fire exercises, and more physical endurance training. Traveling on the last of the C-130 flights, along with the headquarters platoon and Captain Cahill, I arrived at Camp Schwab around 1900 that night and was met by the platoon sergeant from the company's 3d Platoon, SSgt. Bill Rash. Rash said that my presence was requested in the camp's SNCO club, because the SNCOs of the 9th MAF (Marine Amphibious Force), stationed at Camp Schwarb, had invited the staff NCOs of E Company to join them in a unique ritual, a formal dinner known as a Mess Night. Making things that much easier, we were allowed to wear our jungle utilities in their SNCO club. The MAF's Mess Night proved to be a great event. The chow was great, and the wine flowed freely. Noting that those of us in E Company had come from a combat zone, the Marines of the 9th MAF honored us with a toast, and we in turn proposed toasts to all Marine Corps units in combat. By the end of the evening, we had a little trouble finding our way back to the barracks, and those with lesser constitutions had to be helped into their racks. But when the sun rose the following morning, every Marine in the company was present for a ten-mile endurance run. All of my SNCOs were getting well that morning—the hard way.

Our training kicked off in high gear as we had only a short time to prepare for Vietnam and to be ready for the bush. The "motivation factor" of actually preparing for combat enhanced this process by keeping everyone focused on why we were there. Our first two weeks of training were dedicated to the basics: squad and team reconnaissance and combat patrolling, with SNCO instructors accompanying each patrol and acting as "lane graders" for each exercise. In addition to the patrolling package, we concentrated on live-firing exercises on the rifle range and along the jungle trails, which had been built specifically at the island's Northern Training Area. In my opinion, the time we spent on those quick-fire/quick-kill ranges would later prove valuable to our recon team's ability to counter the ambush threat of the NVA. To prepare for what was to come, we adjusted our training schedule to ensure that 70 percent of all training was conducted at night. By "training the way we would fight," the nights in Vietnam would no longer belong to the enemy. The months of January and February are traditionally wet in Vietnam, but they were much colder on Okinawa. As training transitioned to the platoon level, special emphasis was placed on platoon-size patrolling, ambush techniques, and raids. Practicing raids on POW camp mock-ups and POW recovery operations worked wonders for the morale of the company.

While we were in our final phase of training—training as a company—the word came that we were to immediately return to Vietnam. Coinciding with the celebration of the lunar New Year, known as Tet, the NVA had launched the largest offensive of the war. We quickly found ourselves aboard several air force C-130s, headed straight back to Da Nang. When we returned to Camp Reasoner, we moved into living spaces formerly occupied by 1st Force Recon Company, which had moved north to patrol in the Hue/Phu Bai area. By the second day back in country, we had eight recon teams working in the field. During those first eight patrols E Company began to enjoy a fine reputation within the battalion, as six of our eight patrols made contact with superior enemy forces and, using supporting arms, kicked the hell out of the NVA. Our training on Okinawa had begun to pay off with great returns.

When we first returned to Vietnam, the operational control for our battalion's four combat outposts began to be rotated amongst the five companies, giving them specific dual missions: calling in artillery fire and close-air support on observed enemy concentrations and acting as radio-relays for reconnaissance teams patrolling at the extreme edge of radio communication capabilities.

Each of these OPs required from a squad to a platoon-size team. One outpost, Dong Din, was located on a large hilltop twenty miles north-northwest of Da Nang, and was usually shrouded by low-lying clouds. Duty at Dong Din was considered unofficial R & R. Our second outpost was Hill 427, about thirty miles southwest of Da Nang. Hill 427 would usually get probed by the NVA weekly. Hill 427 was located along one of the primary NVA infiltration routes, and our OP was a very good place for calling in artillery fire from the Marine artillery unit located at nearby An Hoa. Hill 427 had three well-constructed bunkers, which housed M-60 machine guns. The third outpost, called Ben Na, was actually the ruins of an old French hotel. Duty at Ben Na was also considered to be easy but defended by less than twenty men, any one of those outposts could become a very easy target for the NVA. The fourth, and the most dangerous of the company's outposts, was Hill 200, northwest of An Hoa and close to an infamous area known as the Arizona Territory, which for years had belonged to the Viet Cong and was now shared by the infiltrating soldiers of the North Vietnamese Army. It was at Hill 200 where, during the months ahead, we would suffer our heaviest casualties.

Not long after we returned to Vietnam, we lost our company commander, Captain Cahill, to rotation to the States. He was temporarily replaced by our company operations and training officer, First Lieutenant Badger. We felt fortunate that Lieutenant Badger was given the opportunity to command the company, even though it was not for long, because he not only had spent a great deal of time in the bush, but he had also extended his tour of duty to stay with the company for as long as possible. In May Capt. William "Doc" White came to E Company and assumed duties as the commanding officer. Captain White also enjoyed a fine reputation, and I truly enjoyed serving as his company first sergeant as I was not tied to a desk and spent as much time in the field as possible. To be more specific, I went out on reconnaissance patrols with each of the four platoons. I did not go out as a patrol leader, but as an additional rifleman. In that way, I was able to watch and learn and see who were the better patrol leaders and who needed additional help. I also went to each of the four company outposts so that I would have a better understanding of how the defense was set up on each, what was needed to enhance the fortifications, and to learn how those positions were being protected by the patrolling that was done "outside the wire."

Once, while I was on Hill 427, a North Vietnamese force was discovered in a jump-off position prior to launching an attack on the outpost. We caught them just below a cliff and were able to call in an air force C-47 Spooky gunship. The accurate close-air support provided by the Gatling gun system aboard Spooky covered the NVA assembly area with a cyclic rate of more than two thousand rounds per minute, resulting in seventy-five dead NVA before they could mount their attack and do us any harm. Uncharacteristically, the NVA let the bodies of their comrades remain where they had died, and Hill 427 became known as OP Stink Hill.

During the last week of May, we suffered the first casualty in E Company, when Cpl. Raymond A. Tibbetts was injured when he fell and slid down a muddy slope and was deeply impaled on a punji stake which penetrated his rectum. He was medevacked to the navy hospital at NSA Da Nang, where emergency surgery was performed to remove the stake, saving his life. He returned to the States, where today he owns and operates a sporting goods store in Springfield, Massachusetts, that caters to the needs of backpackers.

In June, when enemy activity had increased significantly, Captain White organized and trained within the company a reaction force that could go to the immediate aid of any recon team that found itself in serious trouble. We began training teams as they returned from patrols and each platoon was brought on line in this manner. Within a few weeks all of E Company was ready to assume duty as a reaction force. It wasn't long before we had to try out our new mission for real.

In July, a team of nineteen men on OP Hill 200 was attacked after midnight by a large force, approximately two hundred NVA regulars. Those of us within the company compound were summoned to the COC (combat operations center), and within minutes we had assembled the reaction force, drawn required ammunition, and moved to the battalion's LZ for a briefing prior to flying to Hill 200. We were airborne close to 0400. Approximately two clicks from Hill 200, we could look down from our helicopter and see that a hell of a firefight was still going on all around the OP, which prevented us from landing until first light.

After we had managed to get down, we radioed our position and the direction of our movement to the Marines on the OP. They told us that the NVA had broken off their attack and had moved off toward the east, and we wasted no time in moving up to the perimeter wire of the Hill 200. The scene that greeted us inside the wire was incredible. Every defensive bunker had been destroyed by explosive charges or direct hits from well-aimed RPGs. Five of our Marines were dead, and everyone else had been wounded. Leaving some of the Marines in the reaction force and several corpsmen on the hill, we moved out in trace of the NVA force, finding more than twenty of their dead hidden in the nearby brush. I found one NVA soldier still alive, and called for one of our corpsmen to examine the soldier before moving him. I carried him over my shoulder to the top of the OP, but he had taken a round in the head and died several minutes later.

A helicopter landed on the LZ, and we immediately loaded all of our wounded and dead aboard the bird for a fast trip back to 1st Med Battalion. As soon as that bird was airborne, Captain White decided that the first task was to clear the hilltop of all unexploded ordnance. During the initial stages of their attack, the NVA had managed to hit the OP's ammunition bunker with an RPG-40 round, and the resulting explosion had scattered ammunition and satchel charges, theirs and ours, all around the OP.

During the attack, one of our E Company Marines had distinguished himself with courage and the grim determination to protect his fellow Marines from the attacking NVA force. LCpl. Kenneth Jones was inside one of the destroyed bunkers, and was standing up with his M-79 grenade launcher, firing into the ranks of the NVA. He had fired so many rounds from the 40mm grenade launcher that he had worn down the lands and grooves from the weapon before he was killed by the attacking enemy soldiers. For his heroic action that night, Lance Corporal Jones was recommended by Captain White for the nation's second highest award for bravery, the Navy Cross. I was to learn that Jones's recommendation for the Navy Cross was downgraded and that he was awarded, posthumously, the Silver Star. We lost five outstanding Marines during that night, but the team leader had done his best to save his men, and they had, in turn, killed many of the NVA.

Another first for E Company was our use of the *Chieu Hoi* (open arms) program. The *Chieu Hoi* program was an attempt, through a promise of amnesty and cash rewards, to induce Viet Cong and the North Vietnamese rank and file to leave their units. Defectors who came over to our side were reeducated at government-run centers, and from those came *Chieu Hois* who volunteered to take up arms against their former comrades. E Company was the first reconnaissance company to accept two of these characters. The Marine infantry regiments had realized a fair amount of success in using *Chieu Hois* to educate our men into the ways of the enemy, and using them on patrol. Of the two *Chieu Hois* who had volunteered to come to work for E Company, one was a former NVA corporal, and the other was a former Viet Cong sapper. And although the majority of the Marines in the company found those two to be something of a curiosity, with the exception of SSgt. William Rash, virtually no one wanted to trust them. It was Bill Rash and his recon team who went out to OP Hill 200 to see how well the two *Chieu Hois* would perform. Staff Sergeant Rash reported that they did exceptionally well, willingly patrolling around the OP, identifying trail markings, and pointing out possible ambush sites that might be used by the NVA but were used instead by Rash and his men.

Ironically, while Staff Sergeant Rash was again on Hill 200, the outpost was attacked by a large force of sappers. The ensuing firefight lasted for several hours, but the enemy was never able to penetrate the perimeter. Unfortunately, Staff Sergeant Rash was killed in this action against the NVA, just after he had learned that he had become the father of a baby girl named Kim. SSgt. Bill Rash was one of the bravest Marines I have known, and his ability to train and to take care of his men was evident from his team's ability to repel the attack by a vastly superior enemy force.

During August, the decision was made at the battalion level for each company to man its own OP. Since there were only four OPs, and five companies, it was also decided that we of E Company would find and construct our own outpost. Our OP was located twelve clicks west of An Hoa, just three clicks north of the Vu Gia River, on what was called Hill 146. The same hilltop had been used as an OP in early 1967, but the recon team occupying the position had been overrun and only two Marines had survived the night attack. This time things would be different.

To help things get started, a thousand-pound bomb was dropped on Hill 146. The resulting explosion left a huge crater more than twenty feet deep and leveled everything within thirty meters. Captain White decided that we would use the bomb crater for cover while we called in the helicopter lifts that would bring in the supplies we required to fortify our position. It did not take the NVA long to figure out that something new was happening in what had been their neck of the woods.

The Marine Corps did not want to use the new CH-53 helicopter to ferry in our supplies, reasoning that if one CH-53 were shot down, it would be too costly in lives and in the cost of the newest model helicopter in the Corps' inventory, so the CH-46 helicopter was used instead, carrying internal and external loads. The supplies consisted of tactical wire, barbed-wire stakes, bunker material, sandbags, ammunition, high explosives, chow, and water. With less than a dozen lifts, the job was accomplished in one morning.

On the first day that we went in to build our outpost, we landed with two combat-loaded platoons. With one platoon providing security for the other, we began installing the tactical barbed wire, tanglefoot, and a double apron of concertina wire, complete with primary and alternate routes through the protective wire. At the same time, we used shaped charges to blast holes in the ground, then lowered cratering charges into those holes and exploded them to create a base for our primary bunker position. Captain White and I had made up a hootch using crates of unexploded shaped and cratering charges. The Marines in the platoons thought this was a little unorthodox, but the

Captain dismissed their concerns, explaining that if anything should happen to us and we got hit, we would never know about it because we would both be "vaporized" by the sympathetic explosion.

After one week's time we had made a great deal of progress—bunkers, fighting holes, connected trenches, and an LZ at the center of the hill. Each day we would send out patrols to look for enemy activity and to set up night ambushes.

I was able to use the knowledge I had gained from my time in the defense during the Korean War and the engineer skills I had learned years later to ensure that we had built the most defendable position possible. I was particularly proud of the work that went into the construction of the single-bird landing zone (LZ). To assist our pilots, particularly during periods of reduced visibility, we used ammunition cans filled with sand and buried them around the perimeter of the LZ. We poured diesel fuel over the sand, and when needed, the ammo cans would be lighted to provide incoming helicopter pilots with a clear outline of the intended landing zone.

Only a few days after we had settled in on the hill, we began sighting enemy troop movement in the valley to our northwest. It did not take long for our request for artillery fire support to be answered from the guns located at An Hoa, but as soon as the artillery units had finished firing, the NVA would be on the move again. Our success at calling in fire missions became so good that for the next five months, OP Hill 146 led the division for fire missions called in on enemy troop concentrations.

If the NVA hadn't already realized we were on the hill, it certainly didn't take them very long to figure it out. Within several days, Hill 146 became the center of attention for sniper fire and nighttime probes. Each time, we were ready for them. Our first line of defense—our early warning system—was provided by the acute hearing of a scout dog that had been brought out to the OP. The dog and his handler, from the division's scout dog platoon, were a valuable asset. Each time the dog responded to the sound or scent of an approaching enemy soldier, the Marines on the perimeter would throw white-phosphorous grenades into the wire. (Fragmentation grenades were not the weapons of choice, as they destroyed the wire.) The gooks feared WP more than any other weapon, and we capitalized on that fear.

To help as a further deterrent, I had requested supplies to manufacture my own surprise for the NVA. With gasoline, napalm mix, and a series of containers for mixing, I would pour the napalm mixture into a machine-gun ammunition can, which had a seven-sixteenth-inch hole drilled into the back side of the can. Inserting a fuse from a WP grenade through the hole, I screwed the grenade onto the fuse from inside the ammunition can. Once the can was filled with napalm, and with the lid locked tight, the contents became an airtight bomb. All that needed to be done was to hold the safety lever down, pull the pin on the grenade, and then heave the can in the direction of any noise in the perimeter wire. The resulting explosion sprayed the immediate area, and hopefully the approaching enemy, with burning napalm. Once the fortifications on Hill 146 were near completion, the OP was manned by the Marines of just one platoon, but the work to improve the OP was continuous. The company commander, the XO, or I, would flip-flop out to the hill to make sure that work was on schedule. During the day, 50 percent of the Marines at the OP would provide security and work, while the other half would sleep. Then they would change places. During the dark, the platoon would be on 70 percent alert, until contact was made, which happened almost every night. There was no doubt that the NVA wanted to silence our OP as we had become a very large thorn in their side.

Two major events which affected the company took place in August 1968. The first was a change of command when Lieutenant Colonel Charron, who had been my former battalion commander in 5th Reconnaissance Battalion, relieved Lieutenant Colonel Steinmetz as our new battalion commander. Colonel Steinmetz was headed back to the States. At the same time, we received a new operations officer, when Maj. Dave Whittingham, former company commander of 1st Force Reconnaissance Company, reported aboard. Major Whittingham streamlined the battalion's COC (combat operations center) and oversaw the construction of its underground bunker, which was built beneath the battalion's S-2 (intelligence section) hootch. The S-2 hootch was used as a briefing room for the helicopter pilots who flew insertions and extractions of our teams. At the time, the briefing room was considered "state of the art" with large TAOR maps, overlays, outpost and recon-team position maps provided for all of I and II Corps. With enemy situation maps and friendly-force positions updated each hour, the current situation for 1st Reconnaissance Battalion was always available for us and for our pilots.

During the month of August, the North Vietnamese launched their summer offensive and penetrated the Da Nang TAOR, capturing the Cam Lee Bridge and half of the Ca Do Bridge. Savage fighting for the Ca Do Bridge and the village of Phong Bac, south of the perimeter of the Da Nang airfield, took place involving the 1st Tank Battalion and the division's military police battalion. As the 27th Marines took back the Cam Lee Bridge, recon teams from 1st Recon Battalion went to the aid of the tankers and MPs at the Ca Do Bridge. The NVA offensive ended when its attacking regiment was virtually annihilated south of Highway 1 as they were cordoned off by the 27th Marines and reduced with artillery and close-air support.

During the first week of September, I was reunited with an old friend from my days spent at Camp Del Mar, at Camp Pendleton. GySgt. Jim Giles reported in to Echo Company as our new company gunnery sergeant. Jim Giles, a decorated veteran of the Korean War, had served with the division's recon company in 1952. Now he brought that experience, and much more, to Echo Company. As a black belt judo champion, he was a valuable instructor in self-defense but, more importantly, he made my job much easier, serving as an outstanding example for the younger Marines of the company to emulate.

During the first week of September, 1st Reconnaissance Battalion suffered a number of casualties, and of course, with the loss of experienced men came a loss of morale. One incident, however did much to boost the spirit of the company. 1st Lt. Pete R. Badger, our company's executive officer, was leading a ten-man recon patrol nearly twenty miles southwest of Da Nang on a four-day mission to locate enemy infiltration routes, storage areas, fortifications, and routes of egress. They were to call in artillery and air strikes on any targets of opportunity.

On their first day out, the team's assistant patrol leader, Sgt. William E. Smallwood, was searching a bunker complex, when he smelled burning Vietnamese cigarettes. He had just passed this information to Lieutenant Badger, when the team's point man, Pfc. D. L. Pack, who was checking out a streambed about two hundred meters to the east of the team, heard voices approaching. Pack and the team's assistant patrol leader, Cpl. O. C. Carter, rushed back and signaled the rest of the patrol to freeze, hoping to have enough time for Lieutenant Badger to call for an artillery mission. But, as they waited, the approaching NVA walked right up on top of them. When the two NVA point men came up the trail, Pack and Carter reacted. They jumped them, subdued them quickly, and radioed back their success. Less than fifteen minutes later, another unsuspecting NVA soldier came walking up the same trail, and Pack jumped and subdued that soldier, too. As quickly as Pack could tie up the third POW, a forth NVA soldier appeared and saw what was happening. He pulled his AK-47 off his shoulder and began to aim in on Pack. Pack shot him, and he fell backward over a cliff. As Pack moved to see where he had fallen, he had peered over the edge of the cliff and was surprised to see the dead NVA soldier being carried off by a squad of NVA.

Lieutenant Badger quickly moved his team about two hundred yards away from the center of this activity and requested an emergency extraction for his team and their three North Vietnamese guests. The call for the team's extraction was answered quickly, and within a short period of time, a Marine helicopter picked up the team.

Lieutenant Colonel Charron decided to boost the morale in the battalion and received permission from the division to have the extraction helicopter land, with the three POWs, at our battalion LZ. Within minutes the hill on the side of the landing zone was covered with curious Marines. When the helicopter landed, you would have thought that these were the first prisoners ever captured by the battalion. Cheers and shouts of "Well done!" were called at the returning team, and they and their prisoners were led away for debriefing and follow-on interrogation. Morale within the battalion was given quite a boost that day.

On 12 September, I went back out to OP Hill 146 for a fourteen-day visit, which gave me enough time to construct a few more fougasse napalm canisters and to observe how the OP was operating. The rainy season was just beginning, and I knew from past experience that most Marines didn't enjoy moving around in the mud— particularly those sitting in defensive positions. Patrolling would be adversely affected, and out on that isolated post, we could not afford to let our guard down for a moment. To enhance our chances for survival, I brought three new items out to the OP. The first was a two-man scout-sniper team. Armed with the M40 Remington, a 7.62mm, bolt-action rifle, topped with a Redfield 3×–9× variable telescope, the sniper team recorded a number of thousand-yard kills from OP Hill 146, which added a standoff factor the NVA obviously respected.

The second new item brought to Hill 146 was a 60mm mortar, which we used primarily for illumination. Many times in the past, our requests for immediate illumination were not answered by our closest artillery battery as quickly as we would have liked, and twenty minutes without illumination on an OP can seem like a lifetime. That little mortar proved to be worth its weight in gold on several occasions. The third innovation was the arrival of a

.50-caliber, heavy machine gun, which, coupled with an M-49 scope, allowed the Marines on the OP to make one-round kills in the valley below the OP.

Just after I returned from my two weeks out on Hill 146, I began to feel ill. My joints began to ache, and I couldn't hold down any food. On 26 September I was medevacked to the U.S. Navy's hospital ship, USS *Sanctuary* (AH-17), where I was diagnosed with malaria (*Plasmodium falciparum* malaria, to be exact) for the second time. Abdominal cramping, fever of 104 degrees, and anorexia, kept me on board the *Sanctuary* for treatment until 10 October, when I was finally discharged and returned to Echo Company.

During the second week of October, an unfortunate accident occurred. Our company gunnery sergeant, Jim Giles, was out on patrol when his recon team needed to be extracted. Because of the difficult terrain, the only means of extraction available was the aluminum ladder, which was held in place from the tail of a CH-46 helicopter. With Gunnery Sergeant Giles on the lower rung of the extraction ladder, the ladder became entangled in the tree-tops and Giles fell off, landing on his back from a height of forty feet. Fortunate not to have been killed, Giles was badly injured and was eventually evacuated to the States. After a lengthy period of hospitalization, he was eventually released from active duty. (Nearly twenty-six years later, I ran into Jim Giles at a reunion for Marines of 1st Reconnaissance Battalion. I was pleased to see that Jim had not only survived the fall but had recovered to the degree that he was teaching judo to young kids.)

During the last week of October, I happened to be walking into our battalion mess hall for a cup of coffee when I heard the unmistakable sound of a large incoming rocket, as it passed overhead. The sound of the explosion, not far away, had me headed out of the mess hall, but not before a second rocket came right behind the first one. The explosion of that second rocket was next door, in the battalion's motor pool, and the mess hall was immediately ripped with pieces of flying shrapnel. As I looked around, two Marines were heading for the open mess hall door, and I was running right behind them when the sound of the approaching third rocket could be heard. My feet never touched the steps leading out of the mess hall. I landed on the ground, jumped up and dove again, this time going headfirst over two levels of terraces before making my way into the closest bunker. As I hit the entrance, a tire and wheel rim landed on the roof of the hootch next to my bunker. About an hour later, I learned that one of the rockets had slammed into four brand-new jeeps, which had been destined for service with 1st Force Recon Company. It became rather amusing during the next week to see the rear-echelon Marines wearing for the first time, their helmets and flak jackets. The experience of being on the receiving end of those three incoming B-120 rockets had suddenly made believers out of most of them.

It was the policy of the reconnaissance battalion that all qualified divers, regardless of rank, would be required to make bridge dives if they expected to continue to receive monthly dive pay. Bridge dives were extremely important as the many bridges surrounding Da Nang were routinely made the target of explosive charges placed on them by the Viet Cong or the NVA.

During the dry season, I had made a number of bridge dives using scuba gear as there was very little current, but during the notorious rainy season, the rivers swelled, and the currents were so severe that free diving was the only means possible of ensuring that the bridge was clear of obstacles. On one particular day, I was free diving with a recon team on the Cam Lee Bridge, using both arms to wrap myself around each of the pilings. What I didn't know was that the bridge pilings had been treated with a thick application of creosote. Not long after leaving the bridge, my arms and chest began to feel as though they were on fire. I was able to get myself to our company sick bay, where the corpsmen gave me a special salve to help ease the pain. Two days later, I was still peeling sheets of dead skin from my chest and arms.

During the first week of November, we had to respond to an emergency request with the company's reaction force. One of our recon teams, eight men led by Sgt. Skip Morris, was on patrol nearly twenty miles south of Da Nang. Morris had a reputation as an outstanding patrol leader, so a request for extraction by him was not considered the knee-jerk reaction of an inexperienced team leader to a minor problem. Sergeant Morris's team had been moving along a steep slope in a heavily vegetated area when it was ambushed by a large force of NVA regulars. One of Morris's team members, Pfc. Melvin W. Burkett, was hit by two bullets, one in the chest and one in his left side. He immediately slumped to the ground. Two of his closest teammates tried to rescue him, but were driven back by the heavy volume of automatic-weapons fire. Sergeant Morris had a very difficult decision to make—did he leave Burkett, believing him dead, and pull back his team, or did he risk the lives of his team to recover the body?

Sergeant Morris yelled to his radioman, Private First Class Compton, "Call the COC for everything you can get—artillery, gunships, and the reaction force." Five minutes later, an aerial observer was overhead. He came in low and raked the NVA with machine guns, then fired a white phosphorous rocket to mark the target for the helicopter gunships. Artillery fire and the machine guns and rockets of the gunships soon were ripping into the enemy ambush position.

Sergeant Morris's first reaction was to find a safe position from which he could adjust his calls for fire since the NVA were trying to surround his team. At that time, the COC wanted him to try to break contact and move to the closest LZ. Still not knowing if Burkett was dead or alive, Sergeant Morris radioed back his situation, saying that he wanted to stay and attempt to recover the body.

At that time, Captain White was called to the battalion COC. On his way, Captain White asked me to accompany him, and after a quick map study, we decided on a plan of action and passed the word to assemble the company's reaction force. In less than twenty minutes, we had a sizable force assembled, complete with special ordnance, weapons, and ammunition. The battalion operations officer had briefed the helicopter pilots, and within minutes, the reaction force, including Captain White and myself, was airborne, being flown out in two Marine CH-46 helicopters accompanied by three Cobra gunships.

Our pilots did a fantastic job of plotting the best LZ near Sergeant Morris's position. We were inserted less than 250 meters from the team, and as soon as we were on the deck, Sergeant Morris came up on the radio and helped guide us to his team. With Cobra gunships overhead, the NVA broke off their contact, and we reached Sergeant Morris just before darkness set in. A Pfc. William Goodwin, one of Morris's team members, knew where Burkett lay and volunteered to go out and bring him in.

Amazingly, and much to his own credit and training, Burkett was found still alive. After being hit, he had crawled into a bush where he couldn't be seen when the NVA passed by only a few feet away. When he heard the voices of the Marines coming toward him, he pulled himself into the open and had his M-16 rifle cradled in his lap when he was found.

"I knew you'd come out to get me" were his first words. He had bandaged himself as best as he could with a battle dressing. The team corpsman treated his wounds and applied fresh bandages, and four team members carried him down the trail in a poncho. A medevac helicopter arrived quickly, and Burkett was lifted aboard, using a Neilson stretcher attached to a cable and guided by one of our strobe lights. As soon as the medevac bird flew away, Captain White set the reaction force in a 360-degree defensive position, and for the rest of the night, we remained on full alert. To assist us, a C-130 flare ship dropped illumination flares all night long. There were no probes by the NVA, and at first light, our two CH-46 helicopters took us back to Da Nang. As we flew toward Da Nang, Captain White learned that Private First Class Burkett was hospitalized at NSA (Naval Support Activity) Hospital, and the captain's jeep was waiting to take us there.

On our way to the hospital, Captain White turned to me and said, "First Sergeant, our troops sure did perform in an exemplary manner yesterday. I am really proud of every one of them. Sergeant Morris showed that he has great courage and showed good leadership under fire. For a brand-new man, Pfc. Burkett did all the right things to stay alive."

We went into the hospital and were brought to the intensive care unit by a navy nurse. Private First Class Burkett was awake, and when he saw the captain and me, a great big smile grew on his face. He had tubes coming out of his nose and his arms, but still he managed to speak although in a very weak voice.

"Sir, I knew that you would come for me, just because I was in Echo Company. They always take care of their Marines. That's what kept me going. Thank you, sir." I looked down at that twenty-year-old Marine and saw a man with a lot of guts. I fought back tears just thinking about how much faith he had in us. Private First Class Burkett had been in Vietnam for fourteen days and in Echo Company for four of those days.

In reflecting on my second tour of duty in Vietnam, I know that I could not have been assigned to a better company of Marines. From the day when we formed and began training until the day I left country, my time with Echo Company, 1st Reconnaissance Battalion, will always remain as an extraordinary memory. I feel that I formed an uncommon bond with the Marines of that company. When the Marines of Echo Company bled, I bled; when one of them died, I died a little, too. I believe, too, that I owe a great deal to the experiences I had during my first tour in Vietnam and relied on those experiences to better myself and my company. I knew what the Marines in Echo Company would have to face, and I did everything possible to give them a winning advantage over our enemy.

On 10 January 1969, I picked up orders for transfer to

the States. I passed through the III MAF transit facility and began the age-old routine of administrative processing from one duty station to another. After several hours of paper stamping and waiting in lines, I was taken, along with several dozen other Marine staff noncommissioned officers, to the Da Nang Air Base, where we boarded a Continental airliner for a trip to Kadena Air Base, Okinawa, the first stop on our journey back home. As the wheels of our jet lifted from the Republic of South Vietnam, a great cheer of three "Hip-hip-hoorays" was shouted by everyone aboard. I had cheated death, again.

CHAPTER 22

An Indeterminate Year— 1968-1969

Shortly after our plane landed at Kadena Air Base, we were taken north by bus to Camp Hansen for further processing. My orders directed me to report to the 5th Marine Division at Camp Pendleton. During this time on Okinawa, I was able to complete an undertaking that I had begun in January 1968 when I had come to Okinawa as the first sergeant of E Company, 1st Reconnaissance Battalion. Back then I had asked Nobuko Takeshima to marry me. She accepted my proposal, but we had agreed to wait until I finished my second tour of duty in Vietnam before she would become my bride. As Nobuko was a foreign national, it was my responsibility to submit the required paperwork which would allow her to come to the States on a visa. To help me make the necessary arrangements, Colonel Charron had sent me from Vietnam to Okinawa as a courier, and on 27 December 1968, Nobuko and I were married at the American embassy.

Within days after we had married, the visa we had requested was granted, and we went to Camp Butler to arrange for transportation back home. I was granted permission to travel with my dependent, and rather than fly home on a military hop, we purchased tickets that allowed us the luxury of flying to California on a chartered civilian airline. In southern California, we leased an apartment and quickly set up housekeeping in the nearby town of Oceanside.

Reporting in for duty with the 5th Marine Division, I went to the office of the division's sergeant major, Sgt. Maj. Chuck, for assignment. After he reviewed my service record book, he assigned me to the 5th Reconnaissance Battalion once again, as the first sergeant of C Company.

The company commander of C Company was Capt. R. E. Fields, Jr., who had an outstanding reputation within the battalion. The company gunnery sergeant was SSgt. R. K. Liu, whom I had served with previously in 5th Recon Battalion and during my last tour in Vietnam when Liu was assigned to B Company, 5th Recon Battalion, when that company was attached to 1st Reconnaissance Battalion. The majority of the company's SNCOs and NCOs I knew from my past tours in Vietnam, and I was pleased to learn that the company was not lacking Marines with combat experience. The majority of the junior enlisted men were one-tour veterans of Vietnam.

The composition of the battalion was quite different from anything I had seen in the past. Company A was still in Vietnam, serving in direct support of the 26th Marines. Company B had returned from Vietnam, along with the 27th Marines, minus 1/27 and a reinforced platoon from B Company, and was stationed in Hawaii, at Kaneohe Bay as part of the 1st Marine Brigade. Company C was at full strength, with all the company's platoons located on Camp Pendleton at Camp Horno. Company D had been disbanded, and the battalion's Headquarters and Service Company had two new sections—the interrogator translator team, (ITT) and the counterintelligence translator team, (CITT).

Training for the company was centered on preparations for duty in Vietnam. Special emphasis was placed on nighttime patrolling, long-range patrolling, raids, and land navigation. In addition to an aggressive training schedule, instruction in the various types of insertions and extractions for reconnaissance teams was standard, to include all types of water work. Once again I was given a secondary responsibility as the battalion's diving officer and was told to start a prescuba class, and to write a new battalion operation order on submarine operations, to include lock-ins and lock-outs and "wet-deck" launch and recovery of the six-man rubber boats used by our reconnaissance teams.

In 1967, during my last tour of duty with 5th Reconnaissance Battalion, I had bought a new pickup truck and a small travel trailer. Before going back to Vietnam, I stored the two vehicles at my parents' home in Lawrence, Massachusetts. With plenty of annual leave time still on the books, I requested leave to fly back home and introduce my wife to my family. It was in late February and we landed in Boston just as a heavy snowstorm blanketed the northeast. In addition to difficulty caused by the weather, my father thought we'd be arriving on a flight from San Francisco instead of San Diego. When he didn't find us at the airport, he drove back home to Lawrence, and we had to take a cab to his home. At my parents' house, I was stunned to find that my mother was confined to a wheelchair, having suffered the amputation of her leg due to a loss of circulation caused by diabetes. Not wanting to create any additional concerns for me, my parents had decided they would not mention this to me in their letters while I was in Vietnam. On the brighter side, my sister Eleanor had given birth to a son, Bobby. After Nobuko and I had spent ten days with my parents, we planned our departure from New England just ahead of another large snowstorm, which was headed south from Canada. We managed to stay ahead of the foul weather, and spent a week crossing the country. We returned to southern California just in time for me to begin a prescuba school class.

This class was somewhat unique in its makeup—a captain from the battalion's communications platoon, the battalion surgeon, and two of his corpsmen. Twenty-two Marines from the recon battalion's letter companies made up the remainder of the class. Assisted by Staff Sergeant Liu and a half-dozen instructors, we prepared our students for scuba school. Our pool work was conducted at the

Camp Horno pool, and all of our ocean swims were performed at the Camp Del Mar boat basin using a navy Mike boat to take the students out for their longer swims and deeper dives. Our class lasted for three weeks, and we were able to graduate every student and send them off to the navy's scuba school in San Diego.

On 23 May 1969, all the qualified divers within the battalion were sent to the Camp Del Mar boat basin for transfer by Mike boat to the SS *Bream*, to conduct lock-in and lock-out exercises west of San Clemente Island, approximately thirty-five miles off the California coast. Our objective was to train the battalion's divers to operate the submarine's escape trunk, conduct underwater swims to San Clemente Island, then move to our objective at the island's airfield, where we would conduct a reconnaissance of the local facilities before swimming out to a rendezvous point to make contact with the submarine. On signal, we would be picked up by the submarine and brought back aboard using the escape trunk while the submarine was traveling fifty feet below the surface at a constant speed of two knots. This dangerous and complex training was repeated during the night. Upon completion of these submarine operations, all the battalion's divers were qualified to operate the escape trunk, and our officers and SNCOs became qualified to conduct submarine operations. When the Mike boat picked us up off the Del Mar beach, we refilled our scuba tanks, assembled ourselves in two-man teams, and then swam in to the Del Mar boat basin from the drop-off point, two miles offshore.

Late in the spring, reorganization again affected the battalion. Headquarters and Service Company, Company B, and the battalion headquarters were to be disbanded, along with the 27th Marines, minus its 1st Battalion in Hawaii. Our company was redesignated C Company, 5th Reconnaissance Battalion, 5th Marine Brigade.

During the latter part of July, I received a call from Sergeant Major Chuck, now assigned as the brigade sergeant major, who wanted me to go to 5th Force Reconnaissance Company to relieve 1st Sgt. Don "Woody" Hamblen, who had decided to retire after twenty years in the Corps. First Sergeant Hamblen was something of a legend, not only in the specialized world of the reconnaissance community, but as a "one of a kind" Marine staff noncommissioned officer.

Don Hamblen was raised as a Quaker on his family's farm near East Winthrop, Maine. He was dyslexic but didn't know it because in those days young farm kids didn't get to see the doctor very often. Don quit school after finishing the tenth grade, then enlisted in the Marine Corps at the age of seventeen. Don was wounded twice during the Korean War, the second time while he lay wounded from an earlier shrapnel wound. Hamblen stayed in the Corps, and in 1960 he joined 1st Force Reconnaissance Company, where he attended jump and scuba school. In September 1962, Don was getting ready for a one-year tour with his pathfinder platoon on Okinawa. In preparation, he and his men were conducting a parachute jump near Camp Las Flores when Don's parachute became entangled in a series of sixty-nine-thousand-volt high-tension lines. He was electrocuted, set on fire, and fell forty feet to the ground. And survived.

Don's left leg was amputated four days later at the Camp Pendleton Naval Hospital, and he was transferred to the Oak Knoll Naval Hospital two months later. Amazingly, Hamblen spent less than two months at Oak Knoll before he returned to Camp Pendleton to rejoin 1st Force Recon Company. He passed the physical readiness test, requalified as a parachutist, and scuba diver, and was found fit for full duty! Don even went to Washington, D.C., in 1964, as the guest of President Johnson.

In 1964, Don Hamblen volunteered for duty in Vietnam with MACV/SOG, in the Naval Advisory Detachment, a CIA-front organization in Da Nang. He led a thirty-seven-man SOG team into North Vietnam on more than forty cross-border missions during the thirty consecutive months that he was in country. A number of these missions were assassination assignments personally ordered by then-premier Nguyen Cao Ky. Don was wounded three more times while serving in Vietnam.

It was Don Hamblen who helped us get settled in Da Nang when the 1st Force Recon arrived in country. I remember one day when Don drove a dump truck into our company compound. He stopped in front of our little mess hall and then began to raise the bed of the truck, dumping a dozen cases of cold beer onto the sand. He drove off without so much as a word. That was the kind of Marine Don Hamblen was.

I checked in at 5th Force Reconnaissance Company, and familiar faces made it seem like old home week. The company commander was Maj. William C. Shaver, who had been my company commander in Vietnam in 1966. Our XO was Capt. H. H. Dupler, whom I had also met in Vietnam. The company's operations officer was 1st Lt. L. J. Bender, whom I served with during my second tour in Vietnam, and his assistant was 1st Lt. Larry H. Livingston, who had won the Navy Cross for conspicuous bravery while serving with 1st Force Reconnaissance Company in Vietnam. Our company gunnery sergeant was Gunnery Sergeant Solomon, whom I had attended the navy's diving school with, years before, in San Diego. The majority of our SNCOs and NCOs had themselves only recently returned from Vietnam, and our youngest Marines had come to the company directly from the Infantry Training Regiment. All things considered, we had a remarkable company. The only problem was that this company was not unlike any other company that was used as a replacement pool for Marines returning to Vietnam.

Don Hamblen and I, working as "port and starboard" first sergeants, made training interesting. We arranged for numerous parachute jumps, and diving was practically a daily event on the company's training schedule. We requested a high number of quotas for our Marines to attend the army's Airborne course at Fort Benning, Georgia, and those Marines who survived prescuba school and became scuba qualified went to the amphibious base on the island of Coronado to participate in the amphibious reconnaissance course that was taught there. That course was considered a notable experience, as it specialized in classes on beach reconnaissance, hydrographic surveys, and basic oceanography classes.

During the middle of September, our company received word that 5th Force Reconnaissance Company was to be disbanded and that certain personnel would be transferred to C Company, 5th Reconnaissance Battalion. On 15 October 1969, I returned to my old company, along with Lieutenant Bender, who had been assigned as the executive officer, and Lieutenant Livingston, who was assigned as the operations officer. The company was commanded by Captain Fields and consisted of a headquarters platoon and five reconnaissance platoons. Nearly all of the platoon commanders had also come over from 5th Force. The loss of morale suffered when 5th Force Recon Company was disbanded was short-lived, as our new company had an excellent scuba and parachuting capability, but along with so many changes in organization came an influx of unwanted personnel. The Vietnam War had created a large supply of deserters who, when returned to military authorities, had to be sent somewhere. During the history of the company, we never had any Marine desert our ranks, but we did receive a number of deserters who were "force-joined" following their time in the brig. We managed to make life difficult for these unwanted individuals, and most were gone within one day of joining the company.

On 5 November, those of us who were scuba qualified went from Camp Pendleton to San Diego's Ballast Point and boarded the SS *Caiman*, for submarine operations off San Clemente Island. This particular submarine operation turned out to be one of the high points in the year's training. We were able to conduct lock-ins and lock-outs and wet-deck rubber-boat launching and recovery operations for a period of five days. Upon our return to Camp Pendleton, we witnessed the return of the first Marine Corps unit to come home from Vietnam—the 3d Marines. Actually in a cadre status, all of the attached units to this regiment came, too. To complicate our organization one more time during the year, our company was again redesignated and we became A Company, 3d Reconnaissance Battalion, 5th Marine Expeditionary Brigade.

During this period of change, Lieutenants Bender and Livingston and Gunnery Sergeant Solomon received orders to Vietnam. Not wanting to remain at Camp Pendleton, I submitted a request to join them overseas. Much to my surprise, and less than nine days later, I received orders that read, "for WestPac Ground Forces."

Now that I was married, my responsibilities and priorities had changed. I could not go back to Vietnam and leave my wife in what was, to her, still a foreign country. I requested permission to relocate my dependent bride on Okinawa, her birthplace, while I served my third tour of duty in Vietnam. Before leaving California, I sold my 1965 Mustang and Ford F-100 pickup truck, and placed my little trailer in storage. With money from the sale of both vehicles, I would be able to fly my wife back to Okinawa and have enough left over to lease an apartment and purchase a car for her. While we waited for our flight date, we stayed with GySgt. Dick Dossche and his wife, and spent time at the local attractions of southern California, camping in the Sierra Nevadas near Bridgeport, and visiting the beach cities one last time.

On 14 December 1969, my wife and I flew from San Diego to Okinawa on a commercial flight. Being familiar with the island, it did not take long for us to find a suitably furnished apartment and for me to buy a car. While Nobuko set up housekeeping, I spent a few days investigating what was happening on the island. I learned that the 3d Marine Division was removed from the war in Vietnam and relocating on Okinawa. The division's headquarters was located at Camp Courtney, the 9th Marine Regiment was at Camp Schwab, the 4th Marine Regiment was moving into Camp Hansen, and the 12th Marine Artillery Regiment was located at Camp Hague. The remainder of the 3d Marine Division's supporting units were spread throughout the island's different camps, with 3d Reconnaissance Battalion being at Camp Schwab.

While helping my wife get settled into our apartment, I had reason to go to the island's main PX at Fort Buckner, and I happened to run into a number of Marines I had served with during the years. They thought that my orders would be changed and that I, too, would be a member of the 3d Marine Division. But the day of reckoning came when I checked in at the transit facility for my next assignment. The building was set up like a bank, with teller windows to accommodate all ranks. As I stood in line, with nearly a dozen senior staff noncommissioned officers ahead of me, I inched along noting that each Marine before me was given orders to join the 3d Marine Division.

When it was my turn to stand at the window, I handed my travel orders over to the clerk, who told me that he had an envelope addressed from Headquarters Marine Corps, to me. He walked over to a filing cabinet, withdrew a manila folder, and stamped it before handing it to me. I took a quick look inside and walked out of the transit facility with a great smile across my face. The orders I had requested from Headquarters Marine Corps, for assignment to Vietnam had, miraculously, come through. Now when I told my fellow first sergeants that I had orders "back to Vietnam with the 1st Marine Division," I was immediately asked in envy, "Who the hell do you know at Headquarters Marine Corps?"

Late in the following afternoon, I left Okinawa aboard a Marine KC-130 aircraft and settled in for the five-hour flight to Vietnam. As we approached the Da Nang airstrip, I could see illumination flares exploding all around the Da Nang TAOR. We landed without incident, and within a few minutes I was inside the flight terminal. A corporal walked up to me, and asked if I was First Sergeant Jacques. When I told him I was, he said that he had been sent to meet me and to take me to the office of the 1st Marine Division's sergeant major. As we drove away from the air base, I could see that little had changed during my year's absence. The Da Nang Air Base was still the busiest one in the world, and the sounds of jet aircraft continuously taking off and landing reinforced the fact. As my young corporal driver and I headed down the road toward the division's command post, I looked at him and wondered how many months he had been in Vietnam—three, maybe four? It was getting late, and I was anxious to begin my thirty-fourth month of combat in the Republic of Vietnam.

CHAPTER 23

My Third Tour—1969–1970

I arrived at the 1st Marine Division command post bunker, and was reminded of the number of times that I had been there since it was originally constructed as the command post for the 3d Marine Division in 1965. I looked at the division logo—a large wooden sign with the number 1 superimposed on a field of six white stars that depict the formation of the Southern Cross—and saw that the commanding general was MGen. Edwin B. Wheller and his sergeant major was Sgt. Maj. Hunter C. Murray. Being eminently familiar with the layout of the division's command post, I needed no assistance in finding my way to the office of the sergeant major.

Sergeant Major Murray's door was open, but out of respect for the senior enlisted Marine staff noncommissioned officer of the division, I gave his door frame three healthy raps. He looked up and said, "Come on in here, First Sergeant Jacques. I've been waiting for you." After I sat down in front of his desk, the sergeant major wasted no time in discussing my next assignment. He asked, "How'd you like to go to an artillery battery?" I told him that although I had a great deal of respect for artillerymen, if I had my choice I would rather go to an infantry battalion or a reconnaissance, if that was possible. The sergeant major picked up a large three-ring binder from his desk and opened it. It contained a listing of all the first sergeants and sergeants major in the division, and next to each man's name was his rotation date, the date he would actually leave Vietnam and return to the States. He ran his fingertip over several pages and then stopped. "I have a very special company for you in the 3d Battalion, 1st Marine Regiment. Mike Company is where I want you to go, but first you'll have to check in at the regiment, located on Hill 55. I know it's getting late, but I think that my driver has enough time to run you over there."

The sergeant major's driver brought me to the regimental command post just in time for me to enjoy the evening meal before introducing myself to Sergeant Major Planer, the regimental sergeant major of the 1st Marine Regiment. He offered his hand and welcomed me to his regiment. He had already received a call that I was headed in his direction, and he said, "So, you're going down to Mike Company to relieve First Sergeant Marquotte. He's headed home with the 26th Marines, but he's done a great job with that company. You'll have to spend the night here, First Sergeant. The company CP is over on Hill 37, and you'll have to drive through Indian country to get there. There's no night rides to Hill 37."

I tried to get a good sleep, but the night hours were punctuated by the continual sound of a nearby artillery battery firing harassment and interdiction (H & I) fires. I was eager to get on to my new assignment, and while I was eating breakfast, First Sergeant Marquotte came to the regimental mess hall and introduced himself. He wanted to accompany me to the Mike Company CP and meet the company commander. He explained that the company commander, Captain Williams, and the company gunnery sergeant, Gunnery Sergeant Morton, stayed on Hill 55 and ran the company operations from the regimental COC since the Marines of Mike Company were spread out by squads and platoons in different villages. Working with local South Vietnamese militia, they lived in these villages, providing protection from the Viet Cong and North Vietnamese regulars by their aggressive patrolling.

Our company command post was at Hill 37, but the only Marines who occupied positions on the hill were clerks, several radiomen, and those men leaving on or returning from R & R.

After I met with Captain Williams, he brought me up to date on the enemy situation and the location of every Marine in the company. It would take me more than two weeks to meet each of them, but as the company first sergeant, that was one of my responsibilities.

During my last tour in Vietnam I began to hear about the Combined Action Platoons (CAP) and Combined Action Groups (CAG) and the unique work they did. The basic concept was to bring peace to the villages by linking Marines with the Vietnamese Popular Forces (PFs) soldiers, matching local knowledge of the area with the skills and fire superiority of Marine infantry. Usually a squad of Marines and one hospital corpsman joined with a platoon of Vietnamese Popular Forces as the reaction force for a single village.

The CAP idea began in August 1965 when a Marine civil affairs officer from 3/4 introduced the program in the Hue/Phu Bai area. The program quickly spread, and by 1967, there were seventy-five CAPs operating under fourteen company headquarters. The pacification program involved the reinforcement of villagers' aspirations to be independent of control by the Viet Cong and the NVA. By late 1969, with the 3d Marine Division standing down—redeploying to Okinawa and Hawaii—it was decided to deactivate some of the CAP units and turn the war back over to the Vietnamese. This also caused the creation of the Combined Unit Pacification Program (CUPP), which used individual squads from Marine rifle companies to work with the PF platoons within the Marine area of operation (AO). Mike Company 3/1, was one of the first companies to be trained for that type of squad work, and once Mike Company proved that the program was still effective, each Marine regiment was required to send one rifle company for CUPP training and assignments to that duty within the regimental AO.

First Sergeant Marquotte and I spent most of that first day on Hill 55, visiting with as many of the Marines in the company as possible. Late in the afternoon, we loaded my gear in a jeep trailer and headed for Hill 37, the company command post. The secondary road to Hill 55 took us past the base of Charlie Ridge, an area notorious for snipers, and in preparation for any trouble we were locked and loaded as we passed by, but no enemy fire was aimed in our direction that day.

The next day, First Sergeant Marquotte took me to the battalion headquarters to meet the battalion commander, all the company commanders, and their first sergeants. By the end of the week, I was beginning to feel at home, said good-bye to First Sergeant Marquotte as he headed off to join the 26th Marines for their departure for Okinawa, and began to get to know the Marines of Mike Company.

Soon after I joined the company, my administrative chief briefed me on a little bit of its history. Before the company had been assigned to CAP duty, it had been based at a place they called the Sandbox, located on the coast, only two clicks below Marble Mountain. It seems that the company office took a direct hit from a B-140 rocket, and everything within the hootch was destroyed except for the steel embossing plates used to identify the individual records of each Marine in the company. First Sergeant Marquotte and his clerks had sifted through the sand until they recovered nearly every one of the plates. The monumental task of reconstructing each man's record fell to the company administrative section, but what records they were unable to find were requested from Headquarters Marine Corps. Thanks to their hard work, the unit diary—the administrative record of the company's activity—was maintained.

In March 1970, 3d Battalion, 1st Marines, moved out from Hill 37 and took over the area that had recently been occupied by the 3d Battalion, 26th Marines, near the Nam-O Bridge. It was 3d Battalion's good fortune to be rotating back to the States, but it was my luck to have to take four of the company's administrative clerks and occupy the battalion's former command post position while waiting for an ARVN rifle company to come into our area. The ARVN company failed to materialize, and during the next two nights, the five of us could hear the sounds of someone, or something, moving in and out of the unoccupied hootches. We spent the following two days in two fighting holes, hoping that we would not become engaged in any firefight larger than squad-level. Much to our relief, on the morning of the third day, the ARVN company finally drove into the camp's cantonment area.

As Marine ground units continued to depart Vietnam, the enemy continued its encroachment into a TAOR less well guarded than before. During the months of February and March, Mike Company led the division in casualties due, primarily, to wounding and death caused by numerous booby traps placed by the enemy. The NVA and VC had dramatically increased the use of booby traps to maim, causing us to expend a great deal of effort to evacuate the wounded, thereby increasing the possibility of inflicting additional casualties. During the last week of March, I received a message from the division sergeant major, requesting my presence. The following morning my driver and I traveled by jeep to the division command post. I reported in to the sergeant major, and after taking a seat in his office, he came quickly to the point. "First Sergeant, how would you like to go over to 1st Force Recon Company?" Surprised at his question, I answered him truthfully, saying that I was perfectly happy where I was and that if I had any choice, I would like to stay as the first sergeant of Mike Company. The sergeant major looked me squarely in the eyes and said, "First Sergeant, you don't have a choice in this matter, and I need you there because we have a very big problem in that company." I asked him to explain.

"The problem is that the company first sergeant and the company executive officer are involved in financial dealings, and they are both being relieved, awaiting courts-martial. That company will need leadership, and I believe that you are the man for the job. After you leave this office, I want you to go over to 1st Force and visit the company commander. After you see him, come back here, pick up First Sergeant Hoffsteadler at 1st Recon Battalion, and take him with you as your relief." I did as I was asked, and after only four days getting my replacement settled in, I left Mike Company on 30 March, reporting to 1st Force Reconnaissance Company for duty.

Upon my arrival, I had a long discussion with the CO, Maj. Bill Bond, while he reviewed my service record book. He told me that he, too, thought that I was the right man for the job, and asked that I work closely with the company's executive officer, Capt. Norman Centers, to help restore the low morale in the company. I knew that my job was cut out for me as the Marines in 1st Force Recon had lost all respect for the position of first sergeant, thanks primarily to the actions of the former first sergeant, whose policy it had been to wander around the company compound looking for any discrepancy that he deemed a "chargeable" offense. His list of such "crimes" ranged from finding empty beer cans in a hootch to judging weapons to be unclean. The first sergeant would then mete out a monetary fine against offending Marines but pocketed the money. The fines ranged from as little as a few dollars to much more sizable amounts. Marines in the company wanted only to maintain clean records and reasoned that it was easier to pay the first sergeant than argue with his logic and have a blemished record. The first sergeant's contemptible little scheme was exposed when several Marines brought charges against him. The resulting investigation also exposed the involvement of the company's executive officer, who was immediately relieved of his duties, too.

I knew that I had to gain the respect of the men in the company, not by pampering them but by setting the proper example. It was most fortunate that I had an extensive background in reconnaissance work, knowing firsthand not only what kind of men made up the company but having shared similar experiences. My solution to attacking the problem of low morale was to get to know the men on an individual basis and show them that I could be trusted.

I began by riding along on all of the insertion and extraction flights for every team in the company. I watched the way the teams worked and paid particular attention to the younger team members. I quickly got involved in the jump and diving operations that the company training officer had scheduled, and within a month I could see a dramatic change in the attitude of the Marines in the company toward me—for the better. And with the overall improvement in morale, I had to reflect on the obvious changes in attitude that were affecting all Marines. What caused these problems, new to those of us who had been in Vietnam since the war's beginning?

In 1969 came the beginning of the demoralization of the American ground forces serving in Vietnam. Historically, a military organization becomes demoralized either by a devastating defeat or by corrupt or incompetent leadership. But the demoralization of the American ground units in Vietnam could be attributed to none of the causes generally accepted as destructive of the spirit of a military force. American troops, particularly United States Marines, were never defeated; casualties (looked at historically) were light; the troops lived in conditions that in previous American wars would have been thought luxurious; most military leaders were competent professionals.

A combination of events and factors caused this breakdown of morale and discipline. President Nixon's policies struck a heavy blow at military morale. Vietnamization, troop withdrawals, and emphasis on peace with North Vietnam brought about through negotiations meant to the American servicemen and women in Vietnam that the United States in 1969 was openly engaged in a no-win war. More than that, these activities created false hope that the war would shortly be over or, at least, that the war would end soon for the individual because of our early withdrawal. Why fight, why get killed or wounded in a war that might soon be ended by withdrawal or peace?

Who wants to be the last man killed in this war, became an often-repeated phrase. And in a combat situation, when a Marine's will to fight falters, his morale soon follows. Dissent on the home front also sapped military morale in Vietnam. The men resented the lack of support at home for their efforts and sacrifices. The "grunts" held the college protesters and other antiwar dissenters in contempt and hatred, a loathing deepened by difference in values and class.

Some of the morale problems the servicemen brought with them to Vietnam. Racial tension strained an already bad state of morale, dividing and shredding unit cohesiveness. A growing sense of permissiveness, along with a lowering of respect for authority—both characteristics of the sixties—undermined discipline. There were men who brought with them to Vietnam the drug culture of the young, a vice made worse by the relative ease with which drugs could be obtained in Vietnam.

Conditions of service in Vietnam also helped to compound the problems of morale and discipline. For the ground-combat units, there were the demanding physical hardships and stresses of combat: heat, humidity, mud, leeches, biting insects, poisonous snakes, booby traps, mines, woundings, death, fatigue, fear, loss of close friends, irregular hours, poor food or no food. Over an extended period, these things drain a man physically and psychologically. In the rear areas, conditions were less dangerous and debilitating, but in many cases, not much better.

The tactical situation in Vietnam in April 1970 was, in my opinion, completely different from the tempo of offensive operations conducted by Marines from 1965 to 1969. Those Marines who were actually fighting in Vietnam knew little of the change from a "win" to a "no-win" political policy. In those earlier years, 1965–1967, we certainly believed that we would win the war against Communist aggression. We had never lost an engagement with the VC or the NVA, and in fact, had usually managed to kick the hell out of them whenever they decided to stand and fight. And we certainly did not believe the stories of defeat and failure that were being portrayed by the American news media. But now, in 1970, with the war in Vietnam winding down, it took the very best in personal leadership on the part of officers and staff noncommissioned officers to operate in a combat environment that in itself contributed its own influence to lower morale. The enemy refused most contact and evaded aggressive patrolling. Frustration set in as units redoubled their efforts to get at the elusive enemy. Casualties mounted, produced mostly by the ubiquitous booby trap. The decrease in the intensity of combat produced inaction, boredom, and lethargy in many army units. Boredom and inaction are breeding grounds for lowered morale and discipline, and with lowered morale came increased problems with alcohol, drugs, and discipline. Fortunately, 1st Force Reconnaissance Company had the leadership to challenge all those difficult problems.

In April, 1st Force Recon Company was located in Da Nang, at Camp Adenir, and sharing part of the camp with a Seabee unit and an army motor transportation company. The company commander, Maj. Bill Bond, Jr., was an Annapolis graduate on his second tour in Vietnam. His first tour was as a captain assigned as an adviser to the South Vietnamese Marines. Our company executive officer was Capt. Norman B. Centers, a prior enlisted man, veteran of the Korean War, and former drill instructor at Parris Island. Centers, too, was on his second tour in Vietnam. Our operations officer was 1st Lt. J. J. Holly, an Annapolis graduate serving out an extension from his first tour with 1st Reconnaissance Battalion. Having participated in dozens of long-range reconnaissance patrols, he was extremely well qualified for the job. He was assisted by SSgt. C. B. Lynch, the company's operations chief, whom I had served with during my first tour in Vietnam. The S-2 (intelligence) section was run by a Captain Houle, and Gunnery Sergeant Hemphling was the company gunnery sergeant. He was trying to fill the recent void created when the former company gunnery sergeant,

Vincent R. Thornburg, was killed. Gunnery Sergeant Thornburg was operating with Team Motor, on 3 February, when they made a point-to-point contact. As the team tried to withdraw from the area, the gunnery sergeant fell from a 150-foot cliff and died from internal injuries.

Our company's administrative chief was Staff Sergeant Vanner, whose extensive knowledge of administrative procedures allowed me to spend my time where I thought I was needed most—with the tactical teaching and operational running of the company. Serving with Staff Sergeant Vanner was Sgt. Don Scanlon. Sergeant Scanlon's first tour in Vietnam had been as an infantryman with G/2/9. He was wounded during his first tour and returned to the States and later attended one of the Corps' administrative schools. Following his graduation from admin school, he volunteered for duty with 5th Force Recon Company before joining 1st Force in October 1969.

The officers assigned to lead the company's operational platoons were outstanding men with extensive combat experience. 1st Lieutenants Sans Robnick, Steve Corbett, Louis "Stump" Stamm, and Z. Johnson, had earned the admiration of the Marines of the company, leading numerous reconnaissance patrols. Assisting those lieutenants were their platoon sergeants, Staff Sergeants Martin, Arthur A. Brown, and Seagriff, all on their second tours in Vietnam.

The company's hospital corpsmen were the very best available. Our senior corpsman was HM-1 Lloyd Palmer, who ran the company aid station, taught many of the first-aid classes, and insured that the chances of his Marines' contracting malaria were kept to a minimum. Hospitalman-2 Harrison and Hospitalman-3 Doyle were well known for the number of "contact" patrols that they participated in, too.

Around the same time that I came to 1st Force Recon Company, more than a dozen recon Marines from 3d Force Recon Company were joined to our rolls. Third Force had been placed in a cadre status, and those Marines had either extended their tours or had only recently joined Third Force. They brought a tremendous amount of experience with them, as they had spent months patrolling along the DMZ and more recently in the notorious A Shau Valley. But the high casualties the company's recon teams had suffered in the A Shau, along the Laotian border, led to the company's termination. Among those new arrivals to our company was Doc Norton. Doc had spent nine months with 3d Force Recon Company and had joined us after attending scuba school and jump school. During his time with 3d Force, he had participated in more than twenty long-range reconnaissance patrols north of the DMZ and in the A Shau Valley, and had held every position in his recon team from tail-end Charley to point man, and was a highly qualified team leader. What made this remarkable was that Norton was a navy hospital corpsman third class. I chose him as my scuba diving partner.

As part of my duties as company first sergeant, I was the company diving supervisor, and I was one of the few jumpmasters for all parachute operations for the company. I was first required to run a check ride with the company commander to demonstrate that I was fully qualified in all aspects of parachute operations. My first check ride as jumpmaster was a static-line jump from a Marine CH-46 helicopter at a drop zone known as Red Beach, located on the coast south of Da Nang. Thirty-five jump-qualified Marines and two jump-qualified corpsmen made up my manifest of jumpers. I began with the formal jump brief, then conducted "first checks" before putting the sticks of jumpers out over the drop zone. Over the years, I had jumped onto Red Beach many times, and this jump was conducted without any problems. With my position as jumpmaster confirmed, I joined Staff Sergeant Lynch and Major Bond as the third qualified jumpmaster in the company. To certify my qualifications as a dive master, a diving operation was planned in Da Nang harbor. Having been familiar with the harbor from past hours spent beneath its surface, I suggested that we dive on a sunken survey ship lying in about sixty feet of water. With twelve divers out for the dive, we experienced no difficulties with the dive, and I was then qualified to conduct future diving operations.

When I joined the company, we were without a communications chief, a position that needed filling as quickly as possible. In late April, Captain Centers notified me that we had a staff noncommissioned officer, a communications chief with past reconnaissance experience, coming into the company, and asked if I knew a gunnery sergeant named Bud Fowler. I told him yes, and that he and I went back a long way. I had served with Bud in the States and during my first tour in Vietnam. He had an extensive background in reconnaissance operations, was jump and scuba qualified, and had firsthand combat experience. Bud also possessed a great sense of humor. But where extensive knowledge of radio communications has been the cornerstone to timely and accurate reconnaissance work, GySgt. Bud Fowler and his ability to teach its use to the Marines of the company, served as a valuable asset.

In early 1969 SSgt. Richard White, a parachute rigger from 1st Force Recon Company, devised an ingenious nylon-strap system designed to pick up the members of recon teams in areas where the landing of a helicopter was impractical if not impossible. The prototype was made from cargo straps normally used to rig large and heavy equipment for air-delivery parachute drops. Six nylon straps, held together by steel keepers, were rigged to the floor of a CH-46 helicopter and then lowered through the helicopter's center hatch, the hellhole. The 200-foot-long nylon strap had a twenty-five-pound barbell weight attached to its free end, and at twenty-foot intervals two large steel D-rings were sewn into it for the team members to attach themselves. Whitey's device enabled the helicopter to quickly lift ten team members up from the hostile terrain. The name given to this device was the Special Purpose Insertion/Extraction rig or SPIE rig. In 1970, the SPIE rig was used by 1st Force and by the Marines of 1st Reconnaissance Battalion. As a refinement of the SPIE rig, each member of a recon team carried at least one nylon harness as individual equipment, thus enabling all team members, and any prisoners, to be plucked from firefights that turned into difficult situations. For improving the company's unique capabilities, Staff Sergeant White was awarded the Navy Commendation Medal.

Based upon lessons learned, we tried to prepare for every probability in training the Marines in our company, but one particularly terrible event confirmed that we simply could not plan for every situation.

Early in the morning of 5 May, the team members of Rock Mat went through final equipment inspection before the arrival of the truck that would take them to the MAG 16 airstrip in Da Nang. The team, led by Sgt. Robert Crain Phleger, consisted of seven men, including a Kit Carson Scout named Bong Dinh. Their mission was to conduct a five-day reconnaissance patrol in the Phu Loc area twenty miles northwest of Da Nang. After Rock Mat had been inserted near a place known as Razorback Ridge, the men began a steady climb to gain the high ground for better observation and communications. There was not much room for the maneuver as the terrain that made up the ridgeline was extremely narrow. By 1800 on their first night in the bush, they had completed the day's climb. After finishing the evening meal, they made a final move to a harbor site, only to discover that the narrow and rocky ledge of the Razorback would not allow them an area large enough to gather into their normal 360-degree defense. Instead, the men positioned themselves for the night, lying down in a single file, with Sergeant Phleger having placed himself as the last man at the end of the column. To further complicate things, the team was experiencing communications problems so severe that the Marines in the rear who were assigned to monitor the recon team's radio traffic suspected that, because of the lack of communication, whoever had been assigned to radio-watch duty might have fallen asleep.

At 2000, those members of the team not yet asleep heard a sudden disturbance in the dense brush, followed by several short muffled screams from Sergeant Phleger.

Then, only silence and darkness. The primary radio operator immediately radioed back to the rear and reported that it sounded as though Phleger was fighting someone in the bushes.

1st Lieutenant Holly, Gunnery Sergeant Fowler, and I were in the company's command and control (COC) bunker, in Da Nang, when the team's radio call came in. An immediate radio call went out to the team, then led by Cpl. Jerry Brown, urging the men to stay calm and alert. Not knowing what could possibly be wrong, and unable to help, we reasoned that perhaps Sergeant Phleger had experienced a nightmare and, upon wakening, was disoriented and had run off into the jungle. In total darkness and confused by the silence, the team could do little but search the immediate area, feeling the ground nearby for signs of Sergeant Phleger, and stay on full alert throughout the night.

Weapons at the ready, the team remained in place on the ridgeline until the first light of dawn revealed Phleger's sleeping position. There lay his rifle, pack, and gas mask as he had placed them before going to sleep. Leading away from his area, the team found his bush cover and poncho liner, both streaked with blood. They radioed back that information and then said that they had also discovered what appeared to be drag marks leading away from the harbor site and down the slope of the ridgeline into patches of thicker brush growing alongside the hill. They were instructed to follow the drag marks.

The first sight of Sergeant Phleger's body was of a combat boot sticking out from beside a large bush. On seeing the motionless boot, Corporal Smith radioed back that they had found the missing sergeant's body. While Smith was passing that information over the radio handset, the entire team was astonished by the great roar of a Bengal tiger, which stood less than fifteen feet away, having returned to claim its kill. Several team members fired at the animal, but the tiger bolted from the scene. Returning their attention to the dead sergeant's body, the team members were horrified to discover that the tiger had eaten most of the sergeant from the waist up.

Believing that the earlier firing of their weapons had scared the tiger into leaving the area, the team members prepared for extraction. Suddenly, hearing another tremendous roar, the team members looked up to see the tiger had returned. It now stood directly between them and the body of Sergeant Phleger. They scrambled to fire at the huge cat. One Marine threw a fragmentation grenade in the direction of the animal. Not certain that anyone had even managed to hit the tiger, they radioed back that the animal had returned to claim its unfinished meal, but they had now driven him away.

That morning, when the emergency helicopter extraction finally removed the recon team from the lower portion of Razorback Ridge, the remains of Sergeant Phleger, wrapped in a poncho, were taken to the graves registration section of 1st Medical Battalion in Da Nang, and the team returned to the company compound. Taking Sergeant Phleger's records with me, I went to 1st Med Battalion to make a positive identification of his body. It was one of the more difficult things I have ever had to do. Autopsy determined that Sergeant Phleger had been asleep with his poncho liner pulled over his head when the tiger attacked and killed him by breaking his neck. The members of team Rock Mat were so devastated by the traumatic death of their team leader that none of them ever returned to the bush.

On 9 May, it became apparent that the nine-man team operating on a ridgeline between hills 510 and 487 in the Thuong Duc River valley was being followed. The patrol leader, Sgt. James R. Christopher, moved his team three hundred meters away toward a hilltop. As the team continued to move, the point man, LCpl. Samuel Bayles, encountered a second group of NVA soldiers. Bayles opened fire and killed two of the enemy, but the remainder scattered for cover in the dense jungle and began to deliver automatic-weapons fire at the team's position. Reacting to this new threat, Sergeant Christopher directed his M-79 grenadier forward to provide fire support to the front, and ordered the team to fall back and away from the enemy force. As the team began to move, they were engaged by a machine gun from the flank and by an estimated fifteen NVA to the rear of the team. Though his team was badly outnumbered and engaged on three sides, Sergeant Christopher demonstrated extreme calm under fire and joined the firefight with his rifle and hand grenades, while redeploying his M-79 man and several riflemen to the rear, and brought two radiomen to his side to exchange radios. During the ensuing firefight, Corporal Bayles assumed control of the fighting in his sector, to suppress the machine-gun fire. While the team was engaged in a forty-five minute firefight, Sergeant Christopher directed Marine helicopter gunships, and fixed-wing aircraft, which delivered small arms, 40mm automatic fire, 250-pound bombs, and napalm on the surrounding enemy force. The team was subsequently extracted under heavy fire without sustaining a single friendly casualty, while accounting for at least six enemy soldiers killed.

In early June I learned that my mother was hospitalized due to complications caused by her diabetes. Poor circulation had caused a gangrenous infection to set in and her right leg was amputated. With my father, brother, and sister at her side, I knew that she would have the best of care. I thought that I would be of little help if I returned home on a brief emergency leave, but I wrote dozens of letters home, encouraging her, and letting her know how much I loved her.

On 4 June 1970, 1st Force Reconnaissance Company witnessed a change of command when Maj. Dale D. Dorman relieved Major Bond, who had commanded 1st Force since 4 October 1969. The new company commander was coming from the 2d Battalion, 1st Marine Regiment, where he had served as the operations officer. Major Dorman was coming to 1st Force as the tempo of operations was picking up, and our teams were operating west of An Hoa and occupying a combat outpost on Hill 510, along the Laotian border in the Thuong Duc River corridor. While the recon teams conducted deep reconnaissance, they were able to provide an extremely valuable intelligence asset to the Force commander, particularly in the western region of the Thuong Duc area. In the face of numerically superior enemy forces who were employing aggressive, well-trained counterreconnaissance forces, our recon teams repeatedly reentered enemy sanctuaries and provided information vital to fixing and destroying untold numbers of enemy forces. A major enemy supply route was located some forty miles outside the main allied defensive perimeter and well beyond the range of supporting arms. It was determined that the "Yellow Brick Road" (Route 614), which had been believed to be the NVA's main supply route, was, in fact, not being used. After further extensive patrolling to within several miles of the Laotian border, our recon teams confirmed that the new supply artery was Route 610.

During the siege of the Thuong Duc Special Forces Camp (1 May–30 June 1970), 1st Force Recon Company fixed and located enemy rocket-firing sites used in support of the ground assaults; with this information, succeeding in silencing the majority of the NVA positions. Further patrolling in the area of the rocket launches disclosed the location of an enemy base camp. The NVA realized their difficulties were caused by Recon and they wanted to exact a price for the destruction of their equipment and men, and turned their attention to the combat outpost on Hill 510, manned by the Marines of the company. Their first probing attack on Hill 510 occurred during the last week of June, during which time HM-3 Doc Norton was wounded and brought by helicopter to the NSA hospital in Da Nang. Along with Captain Centers and Norton's platoon leader Lieutenant Corbett, we were able to pay him a visit before he was medevacked to the naval hospital in Yokosuka, Japan. It would be another five years before I would see my diving partner again.

During the first week of July, the company commander was scheduled to begin parachute training. Major Dorman asked me to provide some personal instruction before he began a crash course in parachute operations. The CO was joined by Staff Sergeant Martin, Hospitalman-1 Palmer, and six other Marines whose platoon leaders thought they could handle the rigors of a two-week junior-jump course. As soon as they had demonstrated that they had mastered the fundamentals of parachute training, we would depart Da Nang and fly to Subic Bay in the Philippines, where I would assist as jumpmaster, while the navy's paramedic rescue team would allow our men several days in which to make five static-line jumps from a navy VH-16 aircraft.

But on 15 July, during the second week of junior-jump school, I was called to the company's COC to be briefed on a special mission. On the night of 14 July, one of the 101st AirCav's Cobra gunships belonging to C Battery, 4th Battalion, 77th Artillery, had gone down in the water east of Camp Eagle. Along with Lieutenant Holly, I was joined by Staff Sergeant Lynch and Gunnery Sergeant Fowler to fly to the location of the downed bird and hook up a sling to lift the Cobra from the water.

At the site, we were met by a group of soldiers and helicopter technicians who warned us the Cobra was heavily armed and that we were to exercise extreme caution in touching the helicopter's instruments or its minigun. With Gunnery Sergeant Fowler as my new diving partner, we were schooled in the proper manner of rigging the helicopter, and then swam out to its location. The Cobra lay on its side in fifteen feet of water, one of its skids buried in the mud. After working for about an hour, we were able to rig the Cobra so that an army CH-47 Chinook could lift the Cobra out of the water and salvage the bird. The army was kind enough to send letters of appreciation to the four of us.

On 23 July, with their five static-line jumps completed, Major Dorman, Staff Sergeant Martin, Hospitalman-1 Palmer, and the other Marines who had accompanied us became qualified as basic parachutists. Not wanting to ignore tradition, Major Dorman insisted that I punch his jump wings into his chest. I did, but the two holes that resulted from his being impaled by his new set of "blood wings" caused him to bleed so badly that he had to throw away his utility shirt.

We returned in time to observe the last combat action in Vietnam by Marines of 1st Force Recon Company, Team Hansworth's battle against the NVA for control of Hill 510. On 1 August six teams were inserted by Marine CH-46 helicopter in the Thuong Duc River valley. To support that effort, Team Hansworth, eighteen Marines, had been given the mission of setting up a radio-relay site and monitoring the radio traffic from the other five teams as they patrolled below in the valley. After the teams were inserted onto Hill 510, they moved off into their respective recon zones, leaving Team Hansworth in place to defend the small relay site. With Lieutenant Prinz, and taking half the men to the top of the hill, Cpl. Jim Holzmann and seven other team members spread out to occupy and defend the LZ. After setting up booby traps and preparing fields of fire, Corporal Holzmann's team continued to dig in, preparing for the possibility of a night attack. They didn't have long to wait.

Early in the morning of 4 August, at approximately 0135, the team's defensive positions were assaulted by a numerically superior NVA force, hurling satchel charges and Chicom grenades and firing automatic weapons. The first round the NVA fired was an RPG (rocket propelled grenade), which struck Lance Corporal Clark in the chest, killing him instantly. As the NVA continued to crawl toward their objective, they fired several more RPGs onto the hilltop, hitting Lieutenant Prinz in the neck with a chunk of shrapnel and also wounding Lance Corporal Bradshaw. As the lieutenant went into shock, Corporal Holzmann and Cpl. Michael A. Lorens rallied the team members and repulsed the NVA attack. Despite the fact that more than fifteen satchel charges were used by the NVA, the Marines defended their positions and used close-air support throughout the night. When help finally arrived at dawn the next morning, drag marks were found around the fighting positions. Wounded Marines were taken to NSA Da Nang, while the remaining team members were brought back to the company area.

During the second week of August, the four of us who had made up the diving teams that assisted with the salvaging of the army Cobra gunship, were asked to fly to Okinawa to test a new underwater communication device. After we landed on Okinawa, we boarded SS *Sabalo*, a submarine, which took us off the island's White Beach area, where we conducted lock-ins and lock-outs while we tested the new communications equipment. The device, a mouthpiece that was to allow us to communicate with the submarine's crew, worked pretty well but only one way— the submarine could hear us, but we could not receive messages from the submarine. Nonetheless, the tests were considered a success. We returned to Da Nang several days later.

When we returned to Da Nang, we learned that the company had received instructions to "stand down." Some Marines in the company were to be transferred to other units, and the rest of the company was to prepare for its return to the States. From 1965 until 1970, the Marines of 1st Force Recon Company had conducted more than two thousand reconnaissance patrols in Vietnam. I felt fortunate that I had been with the company when it first arrived in Vietnam and was there when we finally cased our colors. Two days before the company was scheduled to depart, several of us were transferred to 1st Reconnaissance Battalion. Major Dorman was assigned as the battalion's new executive officer, and Lieutenant Robnick and Staff Sergeant Martin were assigned as the platoon leader and platoon sergeant, respectively, of Sub Unit #1, First Force Recon Company, attached to 1st Reconnaissance Battalion. I was assigned as the first sergeant of B Company, 1st Recon Battalion, and discovered that I was about to join an outstanding company with a superb combat record. I looked forward to this new assignment.

On 24 August 1970, the Marines of 1st Force Recon Company boarded the USS *St. Louis* and set sail from Da

Nang. Only nineteen Marines remained in the organization when it arrived in Long Beach, California, on 11 September 1970.

CHAPTER 24

1st Reconnaissance Battalion, late 1970–1971

At the beginning of 1970, III MAF reconnaissance forces consisted of the 1st Reconnaissance Battalion and 1st and 3d Force Reconnaissance Companies. The two Force Reconnaissance companies were controlled by III MAF, while 1st Reconnaissance Battalion was under its parent 1st Marine Division.

The 1st and 3d Force Reconnaissance Companies, directed by the III MAF Surveillance and Reconnaissance Center, conducted patrols deep in enemy base areas, usually beyond the 1st Marine Division TAOR. Based at Phu Bai, the 3d Force Reconnaissance Company concentrated its efforts on the A Shau Valley, a major Communist infiltration route and assembly area in western Thua Thien. Patrols from this company, usually inserted and extracted by helicopters from the U.S. Army's 2d Squadron, 17th U.S. Cavalry, ventured far into the mountains to locate and destroy enemy units, camps, and storage sites. They spotted targets for artillery fire and B-52 strikes and fought small Communist units. During January 1970, the company observed or encountered 159 enemy and killed 26 in eight separate engagements with losses of only 1 Marine killed and 14 wounded. The company also directed 38 artillery fire missions.

The 1st Force Reconnaissance Company, working from Da Nang, conducted long-range patrols in Quang Nam and Quang Tin provinces. During January, this company saw much less action than 3d Force. The company completed only 13 patrols, sighted 12 enemy, and killed 1, with no casualties.[1]

At the beginning of 1970, the 1st Reconnaissance Battalion was over strength—it had five letter companies instead of the usual four. Company A, 5th Reconnaissance Battalion was attached, but it redeployed during Operation KEYSTONE BLUEJAY. The battalion performed a variety of missions. It furnished teams to support infantry search and destroy operations, secure firebases, and locate targets for artillery strikes. Scuba divers from the battalion checked bridges in the 1st Marine Division TAOR for underwater demolitions, and searched streams for submerged cave entrances and weapons caches. Detachments from the battalion also protected four of the IOD (integrated observation device) observation posts.

Patrolling the western fringes of the division TAOR was the reconnaissance battalion's principle function. In those generally mountainous areas, the enemy could move less cautiously because of the cover provided by the jungle canopy. Six-man reconnaissance teams monitored movement over the network of trails which linked the rugged base areas to the fertile lowlands surrounding Da Nang. Each team included an officer or NCO patrol leader, a radioman, three specially trained riflemen, and a navy corpsman. During most of 1970, the battalion had forty-eight such teams available for duty. Normally, about half the teams were in the field, scattered from Elephant Valley to the far reaches of Base Area 112. Teams not patrolling or on other assignments protected the battalion

---

1. Graham A. Cosmas and Lieutenant Colonel Terrence P. Murray, USMC, *U.S. Marines in Vietnam,* Vietnamization and redeployment, 1970–1971, p. 307.

cantonment near Division Ridge, underwent refresher training, and prepared for their next mission.

In the first months of 1970, many contacts resulted from an aggressive counterreconnaissance effort begun at the orders of General Binh, the Front 4 commander. At Binh's direction, North Vietnamese regulars and main force Viet Cong formed fifteen- to twenty-five-man teams to protect their base areas. Some of these teams carried captured M-16s and wore American clothing and camouflage paint to confuse the Marines during firefights. The counterreconnaissance units watched for helicopters inserting Marine teams and signaled the Marines' arrival with rifle shots, then tried to close in and attack the Marines before they could leave the landing zone.

The Marines responded to these enemy tactics by making false insertions, often complete with helicopter gunship and fixed-wing landing zone preparation, before actually putting in a team. To avoid forewarning the enemy, some insertions were made without LZ preparation fires. As a result of these varied measures, most reconnaissance teams were able to move out of their landing zones before the enemy arrived. The Communists then tried to track Marines across country. These deadly games of hide-and-seek frequently culminated in firefights and emergency extractions. Due to Marine small-arms proficiency and the availability of lavish air and artillery support for recon teams in contact, the enemy invariably suffered many more casualties in these engagements than they ever inflicted.

When I joined Bravo Company, 1st Recon Battalion, the company was commanded by a First Lieutenant Allard, a Silver Star winner and a man who had spent plenty of time in the bush. The company's platoon leaders were professionals who had excellent reputations. First Lieutenants Murphy, Green, and Harvey and a staff sergeant with the odd nickname of Locker Box Jones each led one of the four platoons.

Much to my surprise, an old friend was the first sergeant of Charlie Company, First Sergeant Burke, whom I had not seen since my first tour with 1st Force in 1964. He was able to tell me much about what the battalion had been doing while I was with 1st Force, but I would not be seeing him for long as the battalion's C and D Companies were being sent back to the States. Only two companies, A and B Companies, would remain in country with H&S. With the size of the battalion's TAOR not having changed in more than two years, there was ample ground for our recon teams to cover.

At the time, our battalion commander was Col. William C. Leftwich, who had come to the battalion in September from command of 2d Battalion, 1st Marine Regiment. In my opinion, he was one of the better officers I had known, and he had a knack for being a good listener. As we had joined the battalion at the same time, I knew that he was spending a good deal of time getting to know the Marines in his battalion. After I had been in the battalion for nearly two months, I went to talk with Lieutenant Colonel Leftwich concerning what I considered to be a leadership problem.

One of my administrative clerks had become extremely depressed when he learned that his father, a man he adored, had been diagnosed as having terminal cancer. The young Marine didn't know how to cope with the news and had not talked about the situation with anyone. Overcome with distress, he went to his hootch and tried to commit suicide by cutting his wrists. Fortunately, less than twenty minutes later, he was discovered by one of my corpsmen who lived in the same hootch. The doc stopped the man's bleeding, and we were able to get him medevacked to 1st Medical Battalion for treatment. I visited with him and tried to learn what had caused him to try to take his own life. He told me that he loved his father, and without him, he did not want to live either. He talked to me for a long time, explaining his situation at home, and I listened to every word, understanding that his family problems were very much like my own. When he was finished, I talked to him about his own need to live because soon he would be depended upon to take care of his mother. That young Marine finally told me that he had indeed been foolish and realized that he had made a terrible mistake. He said that after he finished his tour, he would go home a different man. I believed him.

Unfortunately, my views were not shared by our battalion adjutant. In fact, the adjutant, a young and inexperienced officer, said, "First Sergeant, as soon as that Marine of yours, the one who tried to kill himself, gets out of the hospital, we are going to ship his ass off to the States for a section eight discharge." Of course, the adjutant had never spoken to the young Marine and knew nothing of his problems, but with the company commander in the field at the time, I wanted a chance to explain the situation to the battalion commander. My request to speak with Lieutenant Colonel Leftwich was granted.

I told the colonel my story and explained the conversation I had with the young Marine. The colonel thought for a moment and then said, "First Sergeant, if you feel that strongly, I understand. And, although I don't want to go against my own adjutant, I will grant your wish not to pursue a medical discharge in the case, as I think that you know this Marine better than the rest of us." From that day forward I knew that Lieutenant Colonel Leftwich cared greatly for the Marines in his battalion.

Not long after that incident, Bravo Company conducted a change of command. First Lieutenant Allard returned to the States and 1st Lt. Mike Fallon took command. Lieutenant Fallon came to us from D Company, where he had served with distinction as a platoon leader. He was on an extended tour of duty.

As the winter rainy season began to close in, the need for increased patrolling was evident. With long periods of limited visibility denying us use of aerial observation, the encroachment tactics of the NVA were sure to affect the TAOR surrounding Da Nang.

Because fewer battalion recon teams were available and operations in the mountains were restricted by the fall-winter monsoon, we concentrated patrolling efforts in the Que Son Mountains west of Da Nang, sending out patrols from our company's small patrol base. Marines who were not assigned to the patrol base underwent training either at Camp Reasoner or at a nearby ARVN training site. At the ARVN training camp we were able to "fam-fire" all our organic weapons. That was also where I taught our new joinees how to properly use high explosives. Once trained in reconnaissance techniques, the new men were allowed to participate in the saturation patrolling from the platoon patrol bases in the mountains.

The battalion had set up the first of those patrol bases on 5 October on Hill 845 in the Que Son range. Three teams used the hill as a CP, radio-relay site, and a resting place. Remaining for up to thirteen days, they fanned out, on foot, on assigned patrols. While one team usually rested at the patrol base, constituting a small reaction force, the other two teams were deployed. From then on, the battalion maintained a patrol base continuously in the Que Sons and periodically established bases on Charlie Ridge and in Elephant Valley. Patrolling from the CP on Hill 845, when weather restricted helicopter operations, our teams could remain longer in the field and reinforce each other in the event of a major contact. By patrolling into their TAORs on foot, the teams also gained the advantage of surprise, since no helicopter activity except for that which involved setting up the patrol bases, signaled the entry of recon teams into the enemy's operating areas.

On the afternoon of 18 November, great tragedy struck our battalion, and in particular Bravo Company. A seven-man recon team, code-named Rush Act, was on an extended patrol from LZ Ranch House. One of its men was severely injured in a fall from a cliff, and the team had requested an emergency helicopter extraction. The radio call reached the battalion CP at Camp Reasoner just as a CH-46D from HMM-263 piloted by 1st Lt. Orville C. Rogers, Jr., landed on the pad after completing a mission. The helicopter was carrying Lieutenant Colonel Leftwich and six other Marines from the battalion, including 1st Lt. Butch Harvey, our company's extraction officer. Colonel Leftwich often flew on insertion and extraction missions, and that day he decided to fly along and observe as Team Rush Act was extracted using the SPIE rig system.

It was a difficult and dangerous mission. Heavy cloud cover had settled in around the team in the Que Sons, and it was getting late in the day. With no clear space near the team for a landing, the helicopter maneuvered to pick the team up after lowering the 120-foot nylon SPIE rig. In spite of the difficult conditions of weather and terrain, the CH-46 helicopter managed to pick up the team. With seven Marines dangling below, the helicopter climbed back into the clouds to return to Camp Reasoner. Instead, it smashed into a mountainside two miles southeast of Fire Support Base Rainbow. The next day, two reconnaissance teams from the battalion were inserted into the area and worked their way to the crash site. All fifteen Marines lay dead amid the wreckage.

A native of Memphis, Tennessee, William G. Leftwich graduated from the Naval Academy in 1953, having held the rank of brigade captain of midshipmen. He served his first Vietnam tour in 1965–1966 as adviser to Task Force Alpha of the Vietnamese Marine Corps. He won the Navy Cross for heroism during operations with the Vietnamese Marines in the Central Highlands. From Vietnam, he went to assignments with the Marine Corps Schools and HQMC, and from March 1968 to May 1970 was Marine Corps aide and special assistant to Undersecretary of the Navy John W. Warner. In June 1970, he returned to Vietnam to command 2d Battalion, 1st Marines, and in September took over 1st Reconnaissance Battalion.

From B Company we had lost:

1st Lt. Butch Harvey—Extraction officer
Cpl. J. Stockman—Patrol leader
Cpl. F. Villasana—Assistant patrol leader
LCpl. D. Delozier—Point man
LCpl. J. Hudson—Radio operator
HM-2 R. Daniels—Corpsman
LCpl. D. Tucker—Secondary radioman
LCpl. C. Pope—M-79 grenadier

The loss of so many dedicated young Marines was simply overwhelming. Lieutenant Fallon had been very close to Lieutenant Harvey and to the Marines who made up Rush Act. We posted a sign on the door of the company's supply hootch which read:

Not for fame or reward. Not for place or rank.
Not lured by ambition or goaded by necessity.
But in simple obedience to duty as they understood it.
These men suffered, sacrificed, dared all and died.
Let us not forget these men who died before us.
"Rush Act"
18 NOV 1970

Just before I left 1st Force Recon Company, I had gone to our administrative chief, Staff Sergeant Vanner, and asked him to type up an AA Form so that I could extend my time in Vietnam. In late November, the answer to my request came through loud and clear from Headquarters Marine Corps: No extension was to be granted; I could request to stay in the western Pacific, on Okinawa, when my tour date expired. I then requested that I be transferred to the ranks of the 3d Marine Division when my tour ended. To secure my future on Okinawa, and considering that I had not taken any R & R in eleven months, I took several days' R & R, flew to Okinawa, and after visiting with my wife for several days, I went to the office of the 3d Marine Division's sergeant major, at Camp Courtney, and requested that I be assigned to a rifle or reconnaissance company when I transferred to the division. He assured me that my request would be granted.

I returned to Vietnam in time to meet with our new battalion commander, Lt. Col. Bernard E. Trainor, who was checking into the battalion on the day that I returned from Okinawa. Under Lieutenant Colonel Trainor's fine leadership, our battalion continued to utilize the platoon patrol base concept in 1970 and during the first months of 1971. On both Charlie Ridge and in the Que Sons, infantry platoons took over the protection of reconnaissance patrol bases, while our recon teams did most of the patrolling. While I continued to accompany reconnaissance patrols as often as possible, I was the only jumpmaster still qualified to jump those Marines from 1st Force Recon Company who had been assigned to Alpha Company as a subunit. On the few occasions when we could make practice jumps, I was joined by my longtime friend, 1st Sgt. Art Torizzo, who was then on his second tour and assigned to 1st Reconnaissance Battalion.

One morning just after Christmas 1970, while I was having breakfast in the battalion's mess hall, a huge hand squeezed my shoulder, and I looked up to see another old friend from times past, Sgt. Maj. I. V. Long, who, when we had last seen each other, had been a gunnery sergeant. The sergeant major was now serving with distinction in the 3d Battalion, 1st Marine Regiment, and had stopped by just to let me know that he was in the area. It was great to see him and to learn that he had survived his first tour of combat, and as we sat and talked, we reminisced about those fellow Marines who would not be going home. The list of names had grown far too long.

During late 1970 and early 1971, reconnaissance sightings of enemy troops and reconnaissance-inflicted casualties grew steadily fewer. This decline reflected both reduced reconnaissance activity and the shift of most patrolling to areas closer to Da Nang. The low level of action also indicated an apparent decline in enemy strength and aggressiveness. In December 1970, the battalion sighted only 162 NVA and VC during 56 patrols, called in 10 artillery fire missions and three air strikes, killed 23 enemy soldiers, and captured nine weapons. In the same month, the battalion lost three Marines wounded in action and suffered seven nonbattle casualties.

Finally, on 15 January, I left Bravo Company and the cantonment of 1st Reconnaissance Battalion and was driven to Da Nang Air Base. I left behind a company of outstanding young Marines, and I felt downhearted because of it. But despite the problems common to much of the Marine presence in Vietnam, problems associated with low morale, an increase in drug use, and the problems associated with racial interaction throughout the services, the Marines of Bravo Company, and of 1st Reconnaissance Battalion, had not been greatly influenced by it all. In my opinion, they had remained professional, dedicated and always committed to the fight. That was all part of being a "Recon Marine."

I boarded a Marine Corps KC-130 aircraft and without much fanfare from passengers and crew, we flew away from Vietnam and on to Okinawa where I was to join the ranks of the 3d Marine Division. I had completed forty-three months of duty in Vietnam.

On 14 March 1971, 1st Reconnaissance Battalion began its Keystone Robin Charlie redeployment. On that day, the Headquarters and Service Company and Company B ceased operations against the NVA and VC. After a farewell ceremony on 19 March, those units left Da Nang for Camp Pendleton on the twenty-fourth with the battalion colors. Company A of the battalion, the reconnaissance element of 3d MAB, continued operations until 28 April, when it extracted its last two teams from Sherwood Forest, west of Da Nang, and from Elephant Valley. On 1 May, the company stood down; by 13 May the last reconnaissance Marines had left Vietnam.

CHAPTER 25

In Every Clime and Place—1971

After enjoying several hours of deep sleep aboard the KC-130, I was awakened by the captain's instructions to buckle up prior to landing. We were taken by bus from Futema to Camp Hague, where all the other passengers were to begin processing for return home to the States. The only passenger not heading home, I was taken to the 3d Marine Division headquarters building at Camp Courtney. The new headquarters building had originally been built exclusively for the 3d Marine Division, but occupation by the division had been delayed over the years until the division was finally out of Vietnam.

I arrived at Camp Courtney just in time to find the division sergeant major, who was just about ready to secure for the day. I reminded the sergeant major that I had talked with him in November, and he invited me into his office to see what positions were available. Looking over his memorandum book he said, "Oh yes, I remember now. I'll be sending you to the 2d Battalion, 9th Marines, up at Camp Schwab. Outside the front door of the CP is a van that will take you up north, and you can report directly to your battalion without having to go through the regimental sergeant major. I'll call the sergeant major of the battalion; he'll be expecting you by the time you arrive."

Within an hour, I was being driven past the front gate

of Camp Schwab and brought directly to the command post of the 2d Battalion, 9th Marines. I went into the CP, and there stood the battalion sergeant major, waiting to introduce himself. "I am Sergeant Major Simmons, First Sergeant Jacques. Welcome aboard. I want you to know that you are arriving just in time to deploy with Echo Company. You have just three days in which to draw all of your equipment and your cold weather clothing 'cause on Monday you'll be headed to Mount Fuji, Japan."

I wasted no time in walking over to E Company to meet with the first sergeant whom I was replacing and to introduce myself to my new company commander. To my surprise my new commanding officer was none other than Capt. M. J. Evans whom I had previously served with on the drill field at MCRD San Diego, California. We talked for a very long time, telling each other where we had been and what we had done. I left the captain's office and went directly to the battalion supply area to pick up all of the clothing and equipment that I would need to help me survive the cold weather at our training camp on Japan's highest mountain.

I knew that by Monday morning I would be walking aboard the USS *Tom Green County*, a navy LST, and I had to prepare for that event. After spending the remainder of the weekend with my wife, I returned to Camp Schwab on Sunday afternoon and watched the Marines of the company stage the equipment in preparation for the following day's movement. Early on Monday morning, we boarded trucks and were taken to Red Beach, near Camp Hansen, the island's central training area, and went aboard the waiting LST, where we were joined by a handful of Marines from the battalion's H&S Company and the Marines attached to the tank platoon designated to accompany us to Mount Fuji.

Our ship sailed at 1000 for Numazu, the seaport closest to the most prominent geographic symbol of Japan. Our arrival was not without notice as the local chapter of the Communist party and their hired crowd had planted huge red banners around the beach protesting our presence and

had organized a ceremonial dragon-dance to call attention
to our landing on Japanese soil. To help complicate the
ship-to-shore off-loading of our tank platoon, several of
the protesters, fueled by liberal amounts of sake, tried to
lie down in front of our tracked vehicles. The Japanese
police, who had absolutely no tolerance for such antics,
came to the scene and removed the group. To help ease
the situation, the Japanese government had provided
twenty low-boy trucks to help the embarkation specialists
move the tanks inland, and within an hour, buses brought
us to our training area on the slopes of Mount Fuji.

As we arrived, we were greeted by the sight of row
upon row of canvas tents, which would be home for the
battalion during the training period, and columns of dark
smoke rose from the small heating stoves in the community of tents. When I stepped down and away from the
warmth of the bus, I realized just how cold it was. The remainder of the Marines from the battalion had preceded
us, coming by air to Mount Fuji, but enough tents had
been reserved to accommodate our company. As soon as
we arrived, the company gunnery sergeant took charge,
broke down the company by platoons, and made the tent
assignments—one squad in each tent, one row of tents per
platoon, and one tent designated the company office.

In 1971, Camp Fuji was a primitive training site. There
were only half a dozen permanent structures—a mess hall,
two clubs, a small sick bay, a supply building, and a modest exchange. The training camp called North Camp Fuji,
had originally been built for use by the 3d Marine Division during the Korean War. To our south was a larger
camp used as a headquarters and training area for the Japanese Self-Defense Force, formerly known as South Camp
Fuji. Both the camps and their surrounding training areas
were built on a lava flow, and all of the connecting roads
were constructed of crushed lava rock.

After stowing my gear in my tent, I joined the company
commander to meet with those officers and SNCOs of the
battalion I had not met when I first reported in for duty.
Our first stop was at the tent of the battalion's command-

ing officer, a Lieutenant Colonel Johnson, who had come from Parris Island, South Carolina, where he had been the commanding officer of a recruit training battalion. Our meeting was pleasant, but short, and we left to meet with the commanding officers and first sergeants of F, G, H, and the Headquarters and Service Company. By the time I had finished meeting everyone, I realized I had joined a rifle battalion served by well-trained and capable career Marines.

Within two days, we began the training schedule, and Echo Company was first to begin the tank-infantry training, which had been scheduled long before I joined the command. By the time we moved to our training area, the weather had changed, and it began to snow—and continued to do so for the next two days. The freezing weather made riding on the top of our tanks just a bit difficult, and those Marines who took the chance and lost their balance found themselves scrambling in the snow to avoid getting crushed by twenty tons of armor. We completed our first week of training with only a few sprained ankles.

During the second week, we were pitted against another rifle company, each company having three tanks attached. Tank-infantry training, new to most of the younger Marines in the battalion, was particularly valuable, as Mount Fuji was the only training area in the western Pacific where our tanks could operate without restriction. For training on Okinawa, the rules of engagement prevented the use of tanks in support of infantry and additional political restrictions on nighttime training and the use of artillery were soon to be realized. The third week of training was devoted to sharpening our battalion tactics as a rehearsal for the fourth and final week, a battalion tactics test. Our real enemy that week was the weather. The first day in the field was encumbered by a heavy snowstorm, but the second day brought warmer temperatures, and the snow turned to a heavy relentless winter rain. The lessons learned that week about staying dry and warm and keeping one's equipment clean and dry would serve the Marines of the battalion for a very long time. When we returned to the base camp, a big surprise greeted us. Our company commander was a "temporary" officer, commissioned during the Vietnam War. But with the massive postwar reduction in troop strength or rifs (reductions in force) came a reduction in the size of the Corps' officer ranks. Many of the senior staff noncommissioned officers who had been selected for commissions found themselves once again senior enlisted men. That was the fate of Capt. M. J. Evans, who received notification that he had become a master sergeant. His departure opened the door for one of the company's platoon leaders to take the position as the new E Company commanding officer.

After four weeks in the field, the battalion was given liberty from Friday until the following Monday at 1300. It didn't take long for the battalion area to resemble a ghost town. My new company commander came to my tent and invited me to join him in a trip to the closest town, Gotuba, to enjoy a steam bath and a good meal at a Japanese restaurant.

We selected a Japanese bar, and once inside were surprised to be welcomed by a roomful of Japanese Army officers from the nearby Self-Defense Force. Most of the men were company-grade officers, well-educated men who spoke fluent English. One of them was commanding officer of a Japanese reconnaissance company. Seeing my jump wings, he introduced himself and asked the lieutenant and myself to join him. He was extremely curious about my years in Vietnam, and we spent hours talking about our tactics in the jungles of Southeast Asia. A former Imperial Army colonel was present, and he was an extremely interesting individual. He had been a young lieutenant during World War II, had fought the British in Burma, and had fought against the Americans, too. He regaled us with remarkable stories of his experiences as a seasoned jungle fighter. When I glanced at my watch, I was surprised to see that it was nearly 0900. We had kept the bar open through the night, but, as was the custom in Japan, the proprietors would not have dared to suggest we leave. When it was time to go, we ended the evening shaking hands and wishing one another good luck.

Once outside the bar, it looked as though we were in for another snowstorm, but wanting to take advantage of our liberty, the CO and I returned to the base camp; each of us packed an overnight bag and headed for the train station in Go Temba, where we purchased tickets for Tokyo. After arriving in Tokyo, we visited the more famous tourist attractions such as the Tokyo Tower, the Imperial Palace, and the notorious Ginza district. To satisfy the lieutenant's curiosity, we bought tickets for Japan's latest transportation wonder, the bullet train, which we rode from Tokyo to Osaka, traveling across Japan at speeds in excess of 120 miles per hour. The weekend seemed to go by as quickly as our train ride, and late on Sunday afternoon, we arrived back at the battalion area in time for the evening meal and learned for the first time of a startling incident that had occurred while we had been gone.

During the weekend, while the majority of the Marines in the battalion had been away on liberty, a racial incident had taken place within the camp. Ten black Marines, fueled by ignorance and animosity, had charged through the rows of tents and attacked dozens of Marines who were asleep in their sleeping bags. They carried entrenching tools with them and had struck at every white Marine within their reach. By the time they had gone through nearly twenty tents, they were finally surrounded in one tent by members of the battalion's interior guard force, commanded by our company's executive officer. The interior guard force had been given orders to "lock and load" with live ammunition, and with no chance of escape, the entire group was apprehended. By the time their vicious rampage had ended, nearly a dozen Marines required hospitalization for injuries ranging from cuts and bruises to broken bones. Fortunately, no one had been more seriously injured or killed. To my surprise, four of the Marines who had taken part in the incident were members of E Company, including the ringleader, a Marine with a spotless record who had only recently been meritoriously promoted to the rank of sergeant. Wearing shackles and under armed guard, the group of offenders was taken from Mount Fuji to stand trail.

The 3d Marine Division commanding general, MGen. Louis Wilson, learned of the incident and demanded swift and uncompromising justice. Courts-martial for the offenders were ordered, and within three days the trials were over. All ten were convicted; nine were awarded bad conduct discharges, and the ringleader received a stiff two-year prison sentence and was ultimately given a dishonorable discharge.

Our battalion's tactical test was delayed for four days because of the trial, and when we did manage to get to the field, the weather taxed our abilities to maneuver. It snowed and rained intermittently, making the movement of our six attached tanks all but impossible and adding to the difficulty, but our battalion did receive a noteworthy grade for readiness. When we returned to the base camp at the end of the week, we learned that Echo Company would be flying back to Okinawa while the remainder of the battalion would return by ship. Bussed to the U.S. Naval Station at Atsugi, Japan, we boarded one of the navy's Constellation aircraft and returned to Okinawa.

Shortly after we returned from Okinawa and while we were preparing to go aboard ship for a three-month deployment as an SLF (special landing force), a first sergeant by the name of Mitchell paid me a visit. Mitchell, who was assigned to 3d Reconnaissance Battalion, was very much interested in joining an infantry unit afloat. He had already spoken with the division sergeant major who had given his initial approval to our swapping assignments if the battalion commander and our battalion sergeant major approved. My wife's living on the island was, of course, an additional incentive to my making the swap, so on 26 March 1971, permission was given for me to stand detached from the battalion and joined to B Company, 3d Reconnaissance Battalion, for duty.

At 3d Reconnaissance Battalion, I was placed on the

rolls as a scuba diver and would receive an additional sixty-five dollars per month once I had completed my required requalification dive. I was notified that all of the battalion's divers would soon be going aboard the USS *Grayback*, a submarine considered as special because its keel had been laid as a launching platform for the Polaris missile. Its new capability allowed for twenty-five scuba divers to move into a compartment known as the launching tank. When flooded, twenty-five internal hookah-rigs provided oxygen to the divers prior to launching. When the large compartment door was hydraulically opened, two dozen pairs of divers could swim away from the submarine virtually undetected and move toward multiple objectives. Not long after we returned to the battalion area from the *Grayfish*, we were notified that all of the battalion's divers had been given a two-week operational mission to help mark a channel through the coral reef offshore Camp Schwab. The channel markers had to be anchored into the coral reef with steel pitons and cable, and the job proved to be so time-consuming that the two-week job required an additional week of underwater work.

When finished, we returned to Camp Schwab only to learn that within several weeks the entire battalion would relocate to the western side of Okinawa at a former air force installation known as Onna Point, which proved to be the best possible location for the reconnaissance battalion. The camp, which bordered on the East China Sea, had its own helicopter landing zone, and that feature enabled us to begin a training program not unlike the one we had conducted in Vietnam. With our COC located at Onna Point, and a radio-relay site located at the island's northern training area (NTA), we began conducting reconnaissance patrols all around the NTA, with seasoned observers accompanying each of the teams. Our aggressive training program stressed the significance of land navigation, communications, and live-fire exercises. By maintaining this continuous rigorous program, we believed that our reconnaissance teams were kept physically and mentally prepared for immediate deployment anywhere in the Far East.

Duty at Onna Point was not without its share of fun. I was often joined by 1st Sgt. Art Torizzo, now stationed with the 1st Marine Air Wing at the Marine Corps Air Facility (MCAF) Futema. As diving partners with access to an unlimited compressed-air supply, Art and I spent our weekends diving on the reef heads at Onna Point, Moon Beach, and Imbu Beach, all known for their phenomenal underwater beauty. On those occasions when we speared fish, nothing was wasted as I would return from our diving and present my mother-in-law with nylon laundry bags full of fresh fish, and Okinawans love to eat fish.

In June 1971, I received permanent change of station orders directing that I leave Okinawa and proceed to the 1st Marine Brigade, located in Hawaii, at Kaneohe Bay, to begin a four-year tour of duty. Wanting to take advantage of the reduced prices of automobile sales overseas, I decided to buy a new 1971 Mustang. I purchased the model that I wanted and made arrangements to pick the car up in San Diego, for further shipment to Hawaii. To complete the plan of moving the new car and myself from San Diego to Hawaii, I flew to California and headed for Camp Del Mar, where I was able to stay for several days at the 21 Area SNCO club BEQ. When the necessary paperwork arrived, I went to 1st Force Reconnaissance Company, located on the beach at Del Mar, and solicited the help of Sgt. James Christopher, who followed me to Long Beach, where I was able to arrange for the shipment of my new Mustang to Hawaii. I then went to the Camp Pendleton transportation office and purchased a plane ticket for Hawaii, reporting in at the brigade headquarters on 30 July 1971. There I was greeted by the brigade sergeant major, Sergeant Major Planer, who had been the regimental sergeant major of the 1st Marine Regiment during my third tour in Vietnam. His plan for my next assignment came as a surprise.

I had asked him for the opportunity to go to a rifle company or to a reconnaissance company, but he looked me straight in the eyes and said, "First Sergeant, we have a unique situation, here in the brigade. The 7th Marines, with all their attachments, came out of Vietnam about four months ago and relieved the 3d Marines at Camp Pendleton. The regimental colors of the 3d Marines were transferred to Hawaii, but very few men came along. The 3d Marines have only two active battalions with A, B and H&S companies in the 1st Battalion, and E, F and H&S companies in the 2d Battalion. All of these companies are under strength. A Company, 3d Recon Battalion has only *six* Marines. The company that I am sending you to just arrived here from Vietnam, one week ago, and is at 75 percent strength. So be it."

Since I had become a first sergeant, this was my first assignment to a non-FMF (Fleet Marine Force) organization, but I understood the reason for Sergeant Major Planer's decision. I told him that I would do the best job I knew how, and he promised that he would transfer me to an infantry unit when he could. We shook hands, and as I left his office I told him that I felt fortunate to serve with him once again, and I meant it.

I went down to the brigade's Communications Support Company and checked in. The first Marine I met was the company's administration chief, a gunnery sergeant, who seemed very happy to see me as the company had not had a first sergeant for weeks. With a great smile secured to his face, the gunny took me down the hall and introduced me to the company commander, Major Hendricks. The major had brought his company out of Vietnam, and our initial meeting convinced me that he was a competent and experienced officer. In a matter-of-fact way, he said, "My approach is fairly simple, First Sergeant. I'm in command; you run the troops, and I'll back you all the way."

On my way out of the commanding officer's office, I met the company executive officer, Captain Godsail. The captain was a mustang (a former enlisted Marine) who had served in a number of interesting billets over the years and who enjoyed a reputation as an effective leader. The XO, in turn, introduced me to the company's operations chief, a Master Sergeant Mitchell, who was also assigned as the company gunnery sergeant. It was Master Sergeant Mitchell who helped me get settled into the company's routine and taught me how a communications company worked best. We soon became friends, and I looked forward to each noon hour when the Top and I scheduled time to run with the entire company.

In August 1971, the Communications Support Company worked like this: A headquarters platoon managed the company's administrative needs, followed by a radio platoon, a radio-relay platoon, and a wire-construction platoon. The company consisted of two hundred officers and men and was supported by dozens of jeeps, trucks, and vans necessary to move men and all of their communications equipment to the field.

My wife had agreed to remain with her family on Okinawa until I was able to secure government quarters, and while I waited, I lived in the SNCO barracks and spent the majority of my off-duty time working out in the gym and getting to know the Marines in our company.

When I joined the company, most of the young Marines had not been home on leave since returning from duty in Vietnam, and the company was kept very busy performing countless hours of maintenance and the cleaning of tons of communications equipment after years of use. With many Marines from the company going home on leave, the workload was severe, but the time I spent observing the Marines at work enabled me to learn a great deal about them and their specific jobs. I quickly came to appreciate what it took to become a good communications Marine.

Not until 27 August 1971 was I notified that government quarters aboard the base had been made available to me. I was fortunate to have been given quarters at 2046-A, on Brown Drive; a two-bedroom house located only a short distance from the ocean. The vegetation surrounding the house provided a fragrant, lush green setting, and the slight breeze from the island's trade winds made us feel like the house was located in the garden of Eden.

Best of all, I knew that my wife would really enjoy it. On 2 September 1971, I went to the Honolulu International Airport and met her flight from Okinawa. After I picked her up that afternoon, we drove directly to Pearl City, where I was able to claim my new car, which had arrived safely from Long Beach. Life was good that day; not only to have been reunited with my wife, but to be able to show her our new home, as well.

By October, the majority of the Marines in the company had returned from leave, and as a surprise, Captain Godsail decided the company should have an organized field meet. I was tasked to get together with the company's staff noncommissioned officers and find some special talent. We had one staff sergeant who had wrestled in college, and he helped set up matches. I volunteered to referee the boxing matches, and an all-ranks softball game rounded out the day's events. We finished the day with barbecued steaks and beer, all as a "Welcome back from Vietnam" party for the company. It was just what the men needed.

From the day I arrived, I had made a habit of inspecting the company barracks, but with rooms on three floors to inspect, the routine took up a large portion of the morning. When I first began, the barracks looked like a hog's wallow, and I held the SNCOs responsible for not supervising. Within a few weeks, the men got my not-so-subtle hint, and life for them became better in direct proportion to how well the barracks looked. Soon, the company commander began to inspect weekly. His inspections of the barracks, individual weapons, work spaces, and company personnel were not taken lightly, and the Marines of the company did their very best not to disappoint him. Their pride was infectious.

In November 1971, the promotion board for sergeant major was to convene, and prior to the commencement of that board, Headquarters Marine Corps published a list of the names, promotion dates, and each man's standing as either above the promotion zone, in the zone, or below the zone. When I read the list, I saw that there were Marines listed who had the same date of rank as myself, but what I did not see was my name on the list. I went in to see Major Hendricks and explained my concern. The CO fired off a message to Headquarters Marine Corps requesting an explanation, and four days later a message came back to the brigade stating it was because of "an unfortunate oversight" that my name had been left off the promotion list, but I was now in the zone for promotion. On 1 December 1971, the promotion board published the official list of selectees, and I learned that I had been selected to the grade of sergeant major of Marines! I had been in the Corps for twenty-three years!

On 2 December, I was summoned to the office of the brigade commanding general, Brigadier General Armstrong. Accompanied by Nobuko and by my company commander, I was promoted to sergeant major. General Armstrong gave quite a speech that morning. He said that I had achieved a rank which only a very few Marines would reach and that my service record was a reflection of hard work and commitment that set me apart from other Marines. It was a proud moment in my life.

On the way out of the brigade headquarters building, Sergeant Major Planer asked me into his office and congratulated me on my promotion. He said, "You did one hell of a fine job at Communications Support Company as is evident by having no UAs (unauthorized absences) during the last four months. When you came here, I promised that I would send you to an infantry unit, if I could. As soon as the sergeant major of the 2d Battalion, 3d Marines, leaves for the States, in February, you will relieve him. Welcome to the rank, Sergeant Major Jacques."

CHAPTER 26

Duty with the 3d Marines—1972-1975

On 24 February 1972, I was transferred from the Communications Support Company and joined to the rolls of the 2d Battalion, 3d Marine Regiment, relieving Sergeant Major McLearnie, who was retiring after thirty years of service. McLearnie had joined the Corps in 1942 and had seen combat as an infantryman on Guadalcanal, Tarawa, Saipan, and Okinawa while serving with the 2d Marine Division. During the Korean War, he had participated in the landing at Inchon, in the recapturing of Seoul, and the Chosin Reservoir campaign. During the war in Vietnam he had served with the 3d Marine Division. I knew that I would be filling the shoes of a man well respected for having spent the last three decades of his life in faithful service to his country.

After checking into the battalion command post, I went to meet my battalion commander, LtCol. Robert J. Modrzejewski. The colonel had a great reputation as a strong leader who took exceptional care of his Marines. His famed personal courage was a matter of record—he had won the Medal of Honor while serving as the commanding officer of K Company, 3d Battalion, 4th Marines, in Vietnam in 1966. Lieutenant Colonel Modrzejewski welcomed me aboard and wasted no time explaining how he viewed my role as his battalion sergeant major, his ideas about training, and where the battalion was headed as part of that training plan.

At the time I joined the battalion, the regiment was in the process of growing—the 1st Battalion consisted of A and B Companies, a Headquarters and Service Company, one 81mm mortar platoon, and a 106mm recoilless rifle section. My 2d Battalion also had a Headquarters and Service Company, and E and F Companies, with the activation of C and G Companies planned for within six months.

In 1972, the brigade was uniquely organized. On the air side of the house we had both A-4 Skyhawks and the F-4 Phantom. We also had one CH-46 helicopter squadron, one CH-53 squadron, and additional Cobra gunships and Huey helicopters. On the ground side, the 3d Marines had: A Company, 3d Reconnaissance Battalion; 1st Battalion, 12th Marines, providing 105mm howitzer support; one engineer company; a motor transportation company; and one amphibious tractor company. Our additional logistical needs were met by a supply battalion designated as PSB.

In those days, before orders to Hawaii could be cut, Marines in the grades of private through corporal needed twenty-four months of remaining obligated service. For sergeants who were single, twenty-four months of remaining obligated service was necessary. But for married sergeants and staff noncommissioned officers who had dependents, three years of obligated service was required. These requirements of "time to serve" guaranteed such a high degree of unit cohesion within the battalions that training, morale, and overall combat readiness were enhanced significantly. Unlike the Stateside infantry battalions of the 1st and 2d Marine Divisions that suffered from high turnover rates of enlisted personnel, we enjoyed a level of continuity that we felt was second to none. A young private first class could find himself leading the first fire team he had joined, and with his second year in the regiment he might become a squad leader within the same platoon. Having served with infantry units within the divisions and with those of the brigade on Hawaii, I can say without hesitation that the Marines of the brigade who participated in the Corps' annual "Supersquad" competition always fared better than the other infantry organizations.

One other element of abnormality was the fact that the 1st Marine Brigade had both helicopters and fixed-wing aircraft assigned directly to the parent organization. Coming from the same base and being personally and professionally familiar with their counterparts on the ground, those pilots had a special type of pride. Their efforts in support of our training operations were nothing short of superb.

In April 1972, our battalion was making its first deployment as a BLT (battalion landing team) to the "big" island of Hawaii and to the Pohakuloa training area, which was jointly used by the U.S. Army's 25th Infantry Division and the 1st Marine Brigade for live firing within a regimental-size maneuver area. That training area was the only place in the Hawaiian Island chain large enough to accomodate large-scale military organizations. We were taken in a series of U.S. Air Force flights from Kaneohe Bay to the big island, where chartered civilian buses brought us and our equipment to Hilo. The battalion landing team consisted of our battalion, A Company from the 1st Battalion, B Battery, 12th Marines, 1st Platoon, 3d Amtracks, one platoon from battalion recon, and additional support from elements of the brigade's engineer and motor transportation battalions. Our air assets consisted of three CH-53s, six CH-46s, three Cobra gunships, and three Huey helicopters, rotating from squadrons assigned to Kaneohe Bay.

We quickly discovered that even in late April, and particularly at night, the temperature at Pohakuloa dropped enough to require the use of camp stoves to provide a little additional warmth. It got cold enough to freeze the water stored in our water buffaloes, and field jackets were worn until well after the morning sun had risen in the sky.

The first two weeks of our training program were live-fire exercises run by the battalion's S-3 (operations and training section). The firing ranges were located throughout the training area, and we encountered difficult terrain, particularly the areas where exposed lava flows made the place look more like a moonscape than a tropical island.

The battalion commander and I visited each of the live-fire ranges, and on a few occasions participated in the shooting. I recall one day when I asked to shoot the 106mm recoilless rifle. I was no stranger to the weapon, but I asked for a short refresher course before I embarrassed myself in front of Marines who had been using the rifle all day. I asked them to point out a distant target, and they selected a metal wall locker standing upright nearly two thousand yards away. Firing one round from the .50-caliber spotting rifle, which was used as part of the recoilless rifle system, I knew I was on target, and when I fired the 106mm round at the wall locker, I kept my fingers crossed. When the smoke around the target finally cleared, no wall locker was to be seen, and I walked away from the group of observing Marines, having made the shot look easy. Of course, the truth is that I could not have been any luckier, but I never let on, wanting to savor the moment for myself and for them.

For two weeks, the battalion fired its crew-served weapons, concentrating on improving techniques of overhead fire. Having learned important lessons, still fresh in the minds of our Vietnam veterans, we knew that the dense, triple canopy of the jungle could do much to influence the accuracy of impacting rounds, and we wanted that lesson driven home to the new mortarmen and machine gunners. At the end of the two-week firing exercise, our machine gunners had practiced night firing and then went on to shoot for record. Having an artillery battery in direct support of our battalion, our 60mm and 81mm mortar crewmen benefited from classes taught by the artillerymen. They learned how the FDC (fire direction center) operated, and became quite proficient in the ability to call and to adjust mortar and artillery fire.

At the conclusion of the two weeks of training, Colonel Modrzejewski authorized a forty-eight-hour liberty call. At that time, it was a former Marine named Gonzales, a veteran of the Korean War, whose generosity and sincere belief that "Marines take care of their own," really came to the aid of the battalion landing team. Mr. Gonzales owned a company which provided security for the major hotels on the big island. Wanting to help our Marines enjoy their two days' liberty within an expensive area of Hawaii, he arranged reduced-cost hotel rooms for them at Hilo and Kailua Kona. He had also arranged "no-cost" bus transportation for all of our Marines and corpsmen. On the advice of Mr. Gonzales, Colonel Modrzejewski and I were urged to visit with the city fathers of both of these resort areas to let them know our plans to "police our own problems" and describe our ability to take care of any such problems which might arise from young Marines on liberty. Mr. Gonzales arranged the time and place for each of the meetings. The following day, having requested the use of an army sedan, I checked the car out of the motor pool and drove the colonel to the Hilo Yacht Club, where we attended a luncheon given in his honor.

At 1000, on the first day of liberty, the buses we had requested arrived from Hilo and Kona; by 1300 we were headed to town. The majority of the BLT's officers and senior staff noncommissioned officers had elected to stay at the famed Hilo Lagoon resort, where we paid only sixteen dollars per night to enjoy the accomodations. The hotel provided an extensive tour of the surrounding area followed by a great laughs-show, which was attended by Marines and guests of the hotel. One of the older couples present at the party took me aside and told me that I should be very proud as they found our Marines to be polite, courteous, and respectful. They were correct, and shortly after we had returned to our training area, the battalion commander received telephone calls from the mayors of both towns saying that 2d Battalion, 3d Marines, was welcome back any time. For the battalion commander and this sergeant major, those words of praise from the civilian community were most welcome and, in my opinion, reflected the high quality of officers and noncommissioned officers who were doing their job.

The BLT spent the next eight days back in the field overseeing company operations, which used amphibious assault vehicles, numerous troop displacements using helicopter support, and walking mile upon mile from one objective to another. We had requested umpires to help grade the overall success of the week's work, and by the time the last training objective was taken, the BLT received a grade of "noteworthy." The timeliness of our graded readiness proved to be important, for no sooner had our battalion returned to Kaneohe Bay when we learned that Lieutenant Colonel Modrzejewski had received orders and would be relieved of his battalion by LtCol. D. R. Timmons. Colonel Timmons and I had served together when he was the executive officer of 1st Reconnaissance Battalion in Vietnam. He had an extensive background as an infantry officer, beginning his career as a platoon leader in B Company, 1st Recon Battalion, in 1957. He had come to our regiment with an outstanding reputation, and I was looking forward to serving with him once again.

Lieutenant Colonel Timmons took a great deal of interest in training, and it was his announced policy that he and I would visit as much of the battalion's training as possible, which oftentimes meant our personal involvement as observers or participants. It was not unusual for us to spend several nights in the field to get a better understanding of a particular company commander's method of operation. Our presence in the field was never viewed as detrimental to the scheduled training, and we learned about the Marines who made up our battalion. These were, without doubt, the most profitable hours we would spend with the battalion.

On one such visit, we were observing Fox Company during a live fire-and-maneuver exercise on the big island. During the first day, the Marines of the company had dug out a six-foot-deep garbage pit for the company's use. Just after dark a wild pig, drawn by the smell of leftovers, fell into the garbage pit. Its squeals and grunts could be heard for quite a distance. Without hesitation, armed only with his K-bar knife, a young corporal from Texas jumped into the pit and, within a few minutes, the lethal wrestling match between pig and Texan ended. A victorious Marine NCO was offering roasted Kalua pig to the company on the following night.

Two months after Lieutenant Colonel Timmons took command of the battalion, a new operations officer checked in. Maj. R. B. Trapp had come from duty as aide to LtGen. Louis H. Wilson. Major Trapp brought with him a number of good ideas about operations and training, and in my last year with the battalion, he would become our battalion commander. I had a great deal of respect for him because he was a straight shooter who was never afraid to "tell it like it was."

As the battalion sergeant major, I was also a member of the command's meritorious promotion board. This board was tasked with selecting the very best lance corporals and corporals from within our battalion for the next higher grade. I had long thought that a practical application test should be a part of the selection process for several reasons. First, members of the promotion board could learn more about the Marine as an individual, than by just studying his service record book, and second, I thought that any Marine who was to be selected above his peers, particularly a young noncommissioned officer, should be able to demonstrate confidence as well as ability. Fortunately, my views were shared by Lieutenant Colonel Timmons, and I was able to put my plan into action, ensuring that those Marines selected for meritorious promotion from our battalion would be as competitive and as worthy as any other Marine in the regiment.

From the day that I joined the Corps, and at the time that I was an infantry battalion sergeant major, the art of becoming a fire-team leader, a squad leader, and a platoon sergeant was usually learned the hard way—rote memory, trial and error, and watching and learning. In the old days, infantry squad leaders were poorly educated but physically tough—they could whip anyone in their squad, and their fire-team leaders followed suit. Well-educated Marines were held in contempt by those types of individuals, and it took decades before brains overcame brawn. I hoped that my practical application test would be an equalizer in cases such as these.

The test, conducted several days before the promotion board was seated, was based upon five subjects—infantry tactics, land navigation, first aid, issuing a patrol order, and conducting a rifle inspection. With the assistance of several volunteers, the use of some training aids, and several SNCOs as graders, I relied upon three gunnery sergeants for additional expertise. Gunnery Sergeant Dyer, Gunnery Sergeant Browning, and Gunnery Sergeant Maloy were three of the best in the business. All of them came from E Company, and they helped make the experience an educational event.

The first test, conducted by Gunny Dyer, who had furnished a squad of three fire teams, was on tactics and maneuver. Each candidate was given a card instructing him to conduct several specific events: He was required to move a fire team or the squad in different formations, he was required to use only hand-and-arm signals, and he was required to move his fire team or squad by leaps and bounds on a frontal attack in an open area.

The land navigation portion of the test had five events. Intersection, resection, estimating distance using the map, understanding symbols, and map orientation separated those who knew from those who did not. The senior corpsman of the battalion aid station provided five "injured" corpsmen, representing a broad spectrum of injuries. Each candidate had to perform emergency first-aid based on what he encountered when he approached each victim. The ability of each Marine to properly issue a patrol order and the conducting of a rifle inspection seemed fairly easy events to grade considering the number of former drill instructors we had within the battalion.

After the candidates had gone through all five events, a

grade sheet indicating a rating of outstanding, satisfactory, or unsatisfactory was made a part of each Marine's package before the board. An example of the degree of competition for meritorious promotion is reflected by the example of one Marine. We had a lance corporal who had nine months in the Corps. His conduct and proficiency marks were outstanding. He received an overall grade of outstanding for the practical application portion of the test, and he had presented himself extremely well before the members of the board. Two other Marines were nearly as good as he, and could have been selected for meritorious promotion, but the other two battalions each sent two Marines equally well qualified. Of the seven candidates for meritorious promotion to the grade of corporal, one was selected—ours.

Duty on Hawaii was not all work and no play. After driving around the island of Oahu with my wife and swimming in its celebrated surf, I was again bitten by the bug to go beneath the waves and take up scuba diving. I joined the Kaneohe Bay diving club, known as the Aku Marines, and the club set up a dive each weekend. We would dive at Maunalua Bay, where the underwater park offered spectacular opportunities for photographing the local sea life. When we wanted to spear fish for dinner, we would dive at Makapu Point for snappers, jacks, and the most elusive prize of all, ulua.

In the summer of 1973, during a battalion staff meeting, Lieutenant Colonel Timmons surprised us when he announced that one rifle company from our battalion would be sent to Australia as aggressors against a regimental landing team from the 3d Marine Division. The lucky company would be in Queensland for five weeks, and that news made quite an impression on the Marines in the company. The competition was immediately narrowed down to E and F Companies. G Company had begun to form in June, and its ranks were filled by a majority of young Marines fresh from boot camp who had not been able to attend the infantry training school because of the Corps' budget limitations. Our battalion had been tasked with conducting its own field skills training (FST) for those young Marines to bring them up to speed as quickly as possible.

A week after making his announcement, the colonel asked me, if given the choice, what company I would send to Australia. The decision was difficult; both were top-notch rifle companies, but I told him that if it were up to me, Fox Company would be rewarded with the trip down under. The colonel, surprised at my response, asked why, since E Company had scored higher during their recent tactical test. In my opinion, the Marines of Fox Company had better discipline. I then went on to explain that less than a week before, Fox Company had held a party at Fort DeRussey and, following the party, had ridden in buses through Waikiki without a single catcall being uttered or any incidents being recorded. I said that this was a great example of NCOs doing their job and that was discipline in its better form. I thought that Fox Company would represent our country and Corps well. At the following week's staff meeting, the colonel announced that Fox Company would represent the regiment in Australia.

In September 1973 our battalion deployed to the island of Kauai. With Fox Company still gone, we sent our 81mm mortar platoon to participate in a live-fire shoot on the island of Oahu, and sent our 106mm recoilless rifle platoon to the island of Kahoolawe. The objective of the training for the rifle companies was patrolling in dense vegetation and mountainous terrain. Company patrol bases were set up on a plateau known as Kapoki, located above a rugged canyon on Kauai known as the Grand Canyon of the Pacific. I could not believe how difficult the island's terrain was. The entire training area was heavily vegetated with a triple canopy so dense that no sunlight could penetrate to the jungle floor. While the companies ran patrols against each other, it rained constantly.

The battalion commander and I left Kaneohe Bay, using a Huey helicopter, and flew to Kahoolawe to first observe our 106mm recoilless rifle platoon. We stayed with the 106mm recoilless rifle platoon and watched them fire their weapons that night under a full moon. They had benefited from the training and showed a great improvement in their ability to rapidly select targets and hit what they were aiming at. The following morning, we flew to Schofield Barracks, where our 81mm mortar platoon fired in competition against a U.S. Army mortar platoon of the 14th Infantry, with judges provided by the 35th Infantry. The judges acted as forward observers, and all calls for fire were graded, based upon the number of rounds it took each mortar team to get on target and the efficiency of the FDC (fire direction center). Under the direction of GySgt. J. Johnson, our 81mm mortar platoon won by a narrow margin.

Returning from Kauai, we found our Marines of Fox Company had returned from training in Australia and along with them came messages of praise from the Australian Army and Navy. The Fox Marines had impressed our Australian allies and had made many friends along the way. Many were invited into the homes of local Australian families. Their demonstrated professionalism and good conduct helped open the door for other Marines within the brigade, and within several years battalion-size Marine units were being welcomed at Perth for joint operations.

Following a battalion staff meeting in February 1974, our CO passed the word that the battalion would once again be deploying to the big island, Hawaii, to participate in some new training. The colonel mentioned that one battalion from the 4th Marines had marched from Hilo to Pohakuloa. This difficult route had never been tried by any other battalion, until now. The colonel had offered us, the Marines of his battalion, a challenge, and we accepted.

Our plan to complete the forced march was simple, requiring only commitment and a lot of guts. We would fly from Kanehoe Bay to Hilo, using air force C-141 cargo jets. With the exception of one ambulance and the "mules" with their attached 106mm recoilless rifles, all of the battalion's rolling stock would be driven to the training camp. All weapons organic to the battalion would be carried, including the 81mm mortars. To help set the pace, the 81s would be the point element in the battalion's order of march, and we would begin from the Hilo airport and march all the way to Pohakuloa with only three rest stops planned along the way.

It was mid-February when 2d Battalion landed at Hilo. With the exception of one platoon of reconnaissance Marines from A Company, 3d Recon Battalion, which would move with our Headquarters and Service Company, the battalion commander released those Marines attached to the command. At 0700, the commanding officer and I, walking ahead of the 81mm mortar platoon, stepped off toward Pohakuloa. A feeling of excitement was generated when riflemen from the companies ran forward to temporarily relieve the mortarmen of their heavy base plates and mortar tubes as we marched.

By 1900 on that same day, the last Marine in the battalion walked through the main gate at Pohakuloa. We had completed the march suffering only two casualties, two Marines who were picked up by the ambulance because their feet had started to bleed. We had begun at sea level and crossed the seven-thousand-two-hundred-foot level at the end of our twenty-mile walk. The temperature was eighty-nine degrees when we started, and when we finished, it was a chilling twenty-three degrees. Our training operation went very well—the live firing of all our organic weapons and crew-served weapons lasted for five days. We displaced our command post without any interruption of our radio communications, and that was, in itself, a significant accomplishment.

Upon our return to Kanehoe Bay, the battalion commander and Major Trapp asked me if it was feasible to start a noncommissioned officer's leadership school within our battalion. The battalion commander did not want a school similar to the brigade's, where close-order drill, map reading, and topics of military instruction (TMIs) were the order of the day. Lieutenant Colonel Timmons wanted leadership skills taught to Marines who needed them most, and he wanted examples of leadership that dealt with garrison problems as well as with combat situations.

I thought that with the wealth of senior SNCO talent we had, and officers, there was no reason we could not put together a well-run course.

I assembled the senior Marines who I thought would help best to design the NCO leadership course, and we selected subjects we thought would make the course most challenging: teaching the definitions, traits, and principles of leadership; human behavior; problem solving; teaching the Leader's Code. Our final subject was leadership in combat.

The classes were assigned to our SNCOs, who were encouraged to use training aids, personal experiences, and even skits to help get the message across. We had designed a ten-day course of instruction, offering it to our fire-team leaders, squad leaders, and machine-gun-section and mortar-section leaders. Getting our young NCOs to believe in the Leader's Code (found in a leadership pamphlet published by FMFPAC) was the key to our success:

The Leader's Code

I become a leader by what I do. I know my strength and my weakness and I strive constantly for self-improvement. I live by a moral code, with which I set an example that others can emulate. I know my job and I carry out the spirit as well as the letter of orders I receive.

I take the initiative and seek responsibilities, and I face situations with boldness and confidence. I estimate the situation and make my own decision as to the best course of action. No matter what the requirements, I stay with the job until the job is done. No matter what the results, I assume full responsibility.

I train my men and lead them with tact, with enthusiasm, and with justice. I command their confidence and their loyalty. They know that I would not consign to them any duty that I myself would not perform. I see that they understand their orders and I follow through energetically to ensure that their duties are fully discharged. I keep my men informed, and I make their welfare one of my prime concerns. These things I do selflessly in fulfillment of the obligations of leadership and for the achievement of the unit goal.

Twice a year the battalion conducted "adventure training," which took place in the Schofield training area known as Kutree. That type of individual training involved a slide for life, where each Marine slid down a 150-foot cable—dropping from a height of thirty feet at forty miles per hour—into a freshwater lake; learning to rappel from a forty-foot tower, crossing streams using rope bridges, and having to swim across a lake while carrying a full combat load of equipment. This training helped to maintain a level of confidence that most Marines welcomed.

In mid-October 1974, our battalion was transplaced to Camp Pendleton, California, for a month of training. We were taken to Camp Pendleton aboard the navy's USS *Fredrick County*, an LST large enough to accommodate our entire battalion, including attachments. The LST delivered us to San Diego on 23 October, and we were taken by bus directly to Camp Telega at the northern end of the base. The battalion's training and operations section (S-3) had locked on the use of many of the firing ranges at the Infantry Training School, and we gained particularly valuable expertise by utilizing the school's combat town. Training for combat in a built-up area was something we had not been able to do in the brigade, and we welcomed this type of new experience. Camp Telega brought back a flood of memories for me. I had been stationed there during the 1950s, and now in 1974, with the war still going on in Vietnam, our battalion's training became even more important.

Even though there were few Americans left in Vietnam in early March 1972, the North Vietnamese offensive to try and capture the two northernmost provinces of South Vietnam caused the 1st Battalion, 3d Marines and two squadrons of fixed-wing aircraft to deploy to the Far East. We knew that if the brigade were called upon to send Marines to Vietnam, we would be one of the battalions to go. And that was why training at Camp Pendleton was so important to us. I believed that if we were ordered into combat, we were as well trained as any battalion in the Corps. We returned to Kanehoe Bay just in time to enjoy Thanksgiving and then slowed the tempo of our training schedule to benefit Marines who were taking leave during the holidays.

Early in 1975, Lieutenant Colonel Timmons received orders directing him to return to the mainland, and he was replaced by LtCol. Philip Shaw, who had been the regimental operations officer. Colonel Shaw was a well-decorated veteran of the Vietnam War and had a particular interest in tactics. During late January, our battalion participated in an amphibious operation on the island of Molokai. Using the concept of vertical envelopment in combination with LVTs as part of the amphibious assault, we were able to reduce the amount of time it took to get our battalion ashore. The battalion CO was pleased with the results of the training and went out of his way to let the Marines of 2/3 know how pleased he was with their support.

April 30, 1975, was one of the most disappointing days of my life; that was the day the government of South Vietnam fell to the Communists, and our government did little to aid the South Vietnamese. My feelings were magnified by the thought that there I sat as a member of one of the best infantry battalions in our Corps, and we could do nothing for a people we had assisted for the last twelve years. I thought of the names and faces of all of the Marines I had known who had died in Vietnam. And now it seemed that they had died for nothing. In my opinion, our political leaders had given in to the antiwar cowards who had influenced the media. I was heartbroken.

Shortly afterward, Lieutenant Colonel Shaw was relieved by our operations officer, Major Trapp, who had been selected for promotion. Colonel Shaw had received orders back to the mainland, and Lieutenant Colonel Trapp did a superb job as our new battalion commander. There was no wasted effort in maintaining our state of readiness, and we continued to go to the field and train as though we were headed for war the following day.

In August 1975, I received orders directing me to return to the 1st Marine Division for duty at Camp Pendleton. With a date of rank of December 1971, and having spent four years as the sergeant major of an infantry battalion, I set my sights on my next goal: regimental sergeant major. My wish was granted after the 1st Marine Division sergeant major, Sgt. Maj. Jess Wise, called and told me that I had been selected to be the sergeant major of the 1st Marine Regiment.

I left the brigade in Hawaii knowing I had tried to make a positive difference in the lives of more than a few Marines. I believe I succeeded. Now, I looked forward to applying what I had learned at the battalion level to the 1st Marine Regiment. For this sergeant major, life in the Marine Corps was excellent.

CHAPTER 27

Sergeant Major, 1st Marine Regiment—1975–1976

My wife and I departed Honolulu International Airport at 2330 on 24 July 1975, arriving at Norton Air Force Base at 0500 the following day. After talking a cabdriver into taking us to Long Beach, we picked up our Mustang, which had been shipped ahead of us, and continued south to Oceanside.

We had worked to save some money during our previous four years on Hawaii, and we had intended to buy a home not too distant from Camp Pendleton. After only a few days of searching, we were able to find what we had been looking for. The three-bedroom, single-story house was still under construction, so while we waited for the house to be finished, Nobuko and I set up temporary housing in an efficiency apartment until we were able to settle into our new home in late September. My next move was to check in with the senior enlisted man of the 1st Marine Division, Sgt. Maj. Jess Wise. I hadn't seen the sergeant major since May 1965, when he was the assistant director of the 3d Marine Division schools, which was just before I departed for my first tour in Vietnam. Jess Wise had always been a man whom I could trust, and I respected his position. A veteran of World War II and Korea, and with several tours in Vietnam, he certainly was familiar with the Marines of the reconnaissance business,

401

having been a charter member of 1st Force Recon Company during the 1950s and 1960s.

After a long discussion with the division sergeant major, I drove north, across Camp Pendleton, to Camp Horno, the home of the 1st Marine Regiment. On 31 July I met with Sgt. Maj. Charlie Otto, another three-war, thirty-year veteran whose duties I was about to assume. Sergeant Major Otto had decided that thirty years of honorable and faithful service to Corps and country was enough, and we planned for the ceremony known as "Post and Relief," which would allow for him to retire and for me to assume the position as the senior enlisted Marine of the 1st Marine Regiment. Sergeant Major Otto then introduced me to the 1st Marine's regimental commander, Col. Ed Snelling. Colonel Snelling had a reputation as a truly outstanding officer. A veteran of the Korean War, he had distinguished himself in combat, winning the Navy Cross, in 1951.[1] I considered it an honor to be serving with a man of his caliber, and our association would be one of the highlights of my own thirty years of service. After meeting with the regimental commander, I was introduced to his executive officer, another outstanding Marine officer with a great reputation, LtCol. Eldon L. Erickson. I could not have been more pleased in knowing that as the regimental sergeant major I would have the experience, maturity, and wisdom of two of the Corps' finest officers to help me.

Within a week, Sergeant Major Otto and I had completed plans for the turnover, and the reins of responsibility as regimental sergeant major were bestowed upon me. Ironically and unfortunately, the Marine Corps had begun to enter into one of the most difficult periods in its history, and the leadership problems that presented themselves to every aspect of life in the Corps tested the character and courage of virtually every Marine officer and staff noncommissioned officer worth his or her salt.

While serving with Colonel Snelling in the 1st Marine

---

1. Citation for Colonel Snelling's Navy Cross.

Regiment, the principles of leadership that have served as the backbone of our Corps were practiced on a daily basis. In my opinion, at that time the quality of young recruits who were being allowed into the Corps was for a large part, poor, and the lack of discipline, particularly at the small-unit level, created many problems. The first time that the colonel and I went to the field to observe training serves as a prime example.

The 2d Battalion, 1st Marines, was training at the Marine Corps' Cold Weather Training Center, in the Sierra Nevada range near Bridgeport, California, and was under the command of LtCol. Pony Baker. The battalion was undergoing guerrilla, counterguerrilla, and survival training during the best time, weatherwise, of the year. And it was during this time that Colonel Snelling told Lieutenant Colonel Baker that he wanted to personally participate in the training and that both he and I would temporarily assume the roles of private first class and private, respectively, to better observe the quality of training.

We were joined to the rolls of a platoon in Echo Company, and with a corporal as our squad leader, we became riflemen in his third fire team. We were taken by truck and inserted into the Wolf Creek training area, simulating that we had survived a helicopter crash. We were now in Indian country and would have to make our way to friendly lines. The Marines of the battalion's Fox Company were serving as aggressors during the training, and that made the event more interesting. Fox Company was under the command of Capt. Sans Robnick, who had served as a platoon leader in 1st Force Recon Company during my third tour in Vietnam. He, of course, wanted his Marines to capture his former company first sergeant and offered as bounty, a forty-eight-hour pass, to anyone who managed to corner either Colonel Snelling or myself. We spent three days with that squad and traveled over thirty miles of heavily wooded, mountainous terrain without getting captured. We carried a minimum of chow, and did not interfere with the plans of our young squad leader. When we crossed back into friendly territory, both the colonel and I had a great deal of respect for that young corporal. The principles of leadership gleaned from our three days in the field were: one, know your men and look out for their welfare; two, set the example. By quietly assuming the role of two riflemen and having to operate under the same conditions as every member of the squad, we learned, in a short period of time, a great deal about Marines of Echo Company.

The colonel made a habit of participating in some form of training as often as possible. As members of the regiment's Headquarters Company, the colonel and I participated in that company's physical training program, led by First Sergeant Barron. Each training day would begin with at least one hour of pull-ups, sit-ups, and calisthenics and was finished with a five-mile run. Again, our participation guaranteed that we became familiar with every Marine assigned to the Headquarters Company element.

During mid-September 1975, Colonel Snelling and I drove from Camp Pendleton to Bridgeport to observe the training of 3d Battalion, 1st Marines, commanded by LtCol. Alex Lee, who, in my opinion, was unquestionably the best of Colonel Snelling's three battalion commanders. A decorated veteran of several tours in Vietnam, with an extensive knowledge of infantry and reconnaissance operations, Lieutenant Colonel Lee was a master of small-unit tactics. Assisting Colonel Lee was his executive officer, Maj. Jon Rider, and the battalion's operations officer, Maj. Jack Kelly. Colonel Snelling often said that with a core of "warrior" officers second to none, 3d Battalion, 1st Marines, was the best-led battalion in the Marine Corps. The battalion's training would consist of basic mountaineering techniques, obstacle crossing, and combat in mountainous terrain, which culminated in a five-day war above the seven-thousand-foot level.

Just as we had done with the 2d Battalion, Colonel Snelling and I participated in training with the "Thundering Third," climbing several cliff faces, mountain walking, and attempting to cross several mountain streams using a two-rope bridge system. While attempting to cross the west fork of the Walker River, I lost my balance and fell into the stream. Seeing the regimental sergeant major in waist-deep, ice-cold water caused more than a few smiles, but the experience was the same for me as for the most junior Marine in the battalion. The colonel and I enjoyed our time in the field with 3/1, but we had to return to Camp Horno to finish the planning for the activation of the regiment's 1st Battalion. Just after our return from Bridgeport, I received word that our new home was ready for occupancy. I had saved nearly every cent of combat pay during my forty-three months in Vietnam, and that money certainly came in handy as I applied it to the house, but the money was well invested in my part of southern California. My wife and I planned to make the house a permanent residence for the two of us, in the country that I loved so dearly and had served for three decades.

When I joined the 1st Marine Regiment, two battalions were up to strength, but our 1st Battalion had been in a cadre (reduced) status, since the regiment left Vietnam, but with a redesigning of the Corps' assets, new men were being assigned to enhance the 1st Marine Division's fighting capability. The 1st Battalion, under the command of Lieutenant Colonel Carney, was activated with a majority of veteran staff NCOs and company-grade officers.

During the first week of October, Colonel Snelling talked to me about setting up a Marine Corps birthday ball for all of our Marines in the regiment in the grade of sergeant and below. This birthday ball was to include a sit-down, roast beef dinner, entertainment, and a formal dance. I assured the colonel that I would be able to plan such an event and immediately sent for the three battalion sergeants major to help me keep my promise.

I can recall that birthday ball just as though it happened yesterday. The event was held in the Camp Horno gymnasium on 10 November 1975, the two-hundredth birthday of our Corps. The gym had just been built, and it had more than enough floor space to accommodate all of the regiment's sergeants, corporals, and non-NCOs. The guest of honor was the assistant division commander, and seated with him at the main table was the regimental commander, his three battalion commanders, and their ladies.

The first event of the evening was the traditional cake-cutting ceremony. The birthday cake, baked in one of the battalion's mess halls, was escorted by four pairs of side boys marching in order of sergeant to private, followed by the oldest and youngest Marines in the regiment. Following in trace of the cake came an unexpected surprise, the 1st Battalion's mascot, an English bulldog riding on a separate cart. As the dog's cart moved past the head table, the Marine pushing the cart executed an "eyes right," and so did the dog. The assistant division commander was impressed and asked half a dozen times throughout the evening how we had managed to train the dog to do it. Following the traditional cake-cutting ceremony, where the first piece of cake is served to the oldest Marine present and the second piece is served to the youngest, the evening's entertainment began. Seven Marines from Fox Company, all American-Samoans, performed a knife-fire dance, a traditional dance of the islands, in which long-blade knives, ablaze at both ends, were tossed back and forth by the dancers. I had seen similar dances performed on Hawaii by professionals, but my Marines were just as good, perhaps better.

Following the fire dance, dinner was served, and Gunnery Sergeant Patterson, the SNCOIC of the regiment's 1st Battalion mess hall, and his messmen had really outdone themselves. A former chef from New Orleans, Gunny Patterson presented one of the best roast beef dinners any of us had ever had at a birthday ball. Following dinner, the 1st Marine Division band provided the music to round out a great evening of comradery and fun. It was an evening that made a great and lasting impression not only on those young Marines who were attending their first birthday ball but also on those of us who were veterans of many years of service.

One of the saddest days of my life came on Saturday, 16 February 1976, when I was visited at home by Lieutenant Colonel Erickson, who had come to inform me that my beloved mother had passed away after many years of suffering from the effects of diabetes. The colonel offered his heartfelt condolences, told me that my place was back in Lawrence, Massachusetts, and instructed me to take all the time I needed. I left California the following day and arrived at Boston's Logan Airport, where I was met by my brother Ted, who then drove us to the funeral home where the rest of my family was waiting. Asking only to be left in her presence, I went to the prayer railing beside my mother's casket and looked at her lying there, free from pain and suffering and at eternal peace. I wept openly as the memories of my mother flooded back across my mind. She had always been there for us when we were growing up, and I had tried always to keep her informed about my life in the Corps. I only regret that she had not had the opportunity to see me wearing the uniform of a Marine sergeant major, for I know that she would have flashed her great smile, as only she could do, the unmistakable smile of a mother so proud of her son. She had raised three sons and a daughter, all who loved her dearly, and we would miss her greatly. A week later, I returned to Camp Pendleton, ready, once again, to resume my duties.

It is my opinion that by 1976, 30 percent of our enlisted Corps were men unworthy to wear the uniform of a United States Marine. I had seen that percentage grow slowly but steadily over twenty-eight years, and wondered what it was that we were doing wrong that allowed such individuals to invade our Corps like a cancer. I can only imagine that if a graph was drawn indicating the overall quality of enlisted Marines from the end of the Korean War until 1966, it would depict a line of steady improvement. But, after 1966, the quality of our Marines went steadily downhill, bottoming out during 1977 and 1978.

Why? The answer is simple. The moral corruption which the United States civilian population was experiencing during those years—increasing drug use, lack of respect for authority, and the idea that young men over the age of eighteen were owed a living by the government were brought directly into our Corps. Our ability to deal with these problems, particularly at the first line of defense, our well-disciplined NCOs and SNCOs, had been lost to the Vietnam War. Those NCOs and SNCOs who showed ability and leadership on the battlefield were often offered temporary commissions, and that situation, not unlike World War II and the Korean War, created a great vacuum within the noncommissioned officer ranks. Second-rate noncommissioned officers were placed in positions of responsibility and authority although they could barely take care of themselves. In addition to that situation, the draft system came to its conclusion. The Marine Corps had received a large portion of its inductees from young men who wanted to avoid the draft, but who chose to volunteer for duty in the Corps rather than face duty in the U.S. Army or the navy. During the late 1970s, the challenge to effective leadership and applied discipline was unequaled in the history of our Corps. Not only was it difficult to purge our ranks of those who should not have been there to begin with, but it was equally difficult to retain those "few good men" who wanted to make the Marines a way of life. The old quote that "90 percent of our time was being wasted on 10 percent of the ne'er-do-wells" was unfortunately a reality.

My tour of duty as regimental sergeant major of the 1st Marines was a wonderful experience because I was able to work and learn from some of the finest officers and enlisted men I had known in twenty-eight years of service. My three battalion sergeants major were each seasoned combat veterans, highly regarded by their battalion commanders. One who stands out as a truly remarkable Marine was Sgt. Maj. Bill Gribben, from 3d Battalion, 1st Marines. Bill Gribben had gone from private to sergeant major in less than seventeen years, making him the youngest sergeant major I knew of in the Corps. His commanding officer, LtCol. Alex Lee, had nothing but high praise for his young sergeant major, and praise from Alex Lee had to be earned.

There was another Marine, also serving in the 3d Battalion, and I was extremely proud when I found out that he was assigned to our regiment. Bruce H. Norton had served with me in Vietnam when I was the first sergeant of 1st Force Reconnaissance Company during 1970. At the time, he was a navy hospital corpsman with a fine reputation as a recon team leader; he also served as my diving partner when we checked bridges and sunken boats for hidden explosives. The last time that I had seen Doc was at the naval hospital in Da Nang after he was wounded while on Hill 510. After he finished his enlistment in the navy, Doc graduated college, joined the Marine Platoon Leader's Course (PLC) and was commissioned a second lieutenant infantry officer in December 1974. Alex Lee, Doc's company commander during his tour in Vietnam with 3d Force Reconnaissance Company, was now Doc's battalion commander. From time to time, I would ask Colonel Lee how the Doc was handling his platoon, and I always got the traditional thumbs-up sign of approval from his CO.

Colonel Snelling and I spent numerous days in the field with each battalion at Camp Pendleton, at training areas in the mountains near Bridgeport, the desert environment of Twenty-nine Palms, and on San Diego's Silver Strand, where the Marines of our regiment attended amphibious training and planning courses. One particular operation was a division-size deployment during the first week of March 1976. That date was etched in the memories of every Marine in the field. We awoke to find the training areas of Camp Pendleton covered in several inches of snow. It was the first time that any of us had seen measurable snow accumulate at elevations beneath the one-thousand-foot level in southern California. By noon, barely a trace of snow was visible.

During May 1976, the 1st Marine Division witnessed the departure of Sergeant Major Wise and the arrival of his replacement, Sgt. Maj. John R. Massaro. The new sergeant major had come to the division from Headquarters Marine Corps, where he had served as the sergeant major of the commandant's inspector general (IG) team. He was a pioneer in the world of Marine reconnaissance, having served in division recon company during the Korean War, and was one of the early members of 1st Force Reconnaissance Company in 1957. The last time that I had seen John Massaro was when he had come to Hawaii to inspect 2d Battalion, 3d Marines in 1973. Now he was the senior enlisted Marine of the division and, not surprisingly, in later years would become the sergeant major of the Marine Corps. I could not have been more pleased for him and for the Corps.

In June 1976, Lieutenant Colonel Erickson was selected for promotion to colonel and was transferred to Headquarters Marine Corps in Washington, D.C. During the time that I served with him, I benefited from watching him as he applied leadership by example and helped to make the regiment a challenging place for every Marine. The division needed more men like Colonel Erickson, for in 1976 the Corps was in trouble. The Marine Corps' budget had been reduced significantly, and we were suffering because of it. Without money, training from the fire-team level up was a pitiful experience. Rifle companies went to the field with less than fifty men. There was no blank ammunition to be had, and infantry Marines were humiliated, having to shout "bang, bang, bang" to simulate the sound of firing their M-16 rifles. Battalion-size operations were frequently canceled for lack of fuel, and joint exercises with the wing suffered due to a lack of aviation fuel. "Innovative" (cost-free) training became the mark of those company and battalion commanders who managed to make training a learning experience. A better example cannot be found than 3d Battalion, 1st Marines' preparation for a command post exercise (CPX). The battalion, under the command of Lieutenant Colonel Lee, set up tents on the lawn that bordered the battalion's command post and simulated the battalion's staff being in the field for a period of ten days. That kind of innovative thinking would help to maintain combat efficiency during the days of the declining dollar. One of the officers responsible for keeping the 3d Battalion combat-ready, was Major Jack Kelly, the battalion's operations and training officer. Major Kelly had earned a great reputation for motivating young Marines with athletic field meets, competition in arms, and a unique style of leadership. His talent was not wasted during the two years he served in that battalion.

In August 1976, Colonel Snelling left the regiment and was transferred to the division's G-3 section. The regiment went through a complete turnover in staff, gaining a new regimental commander, regimental executive officer, and for the most part, a new regimental staff. It seemed as though the Marine Corps was shattering one of the most effective regiments it had. Not long after the regimental change of command, I received a telephone call from the division sergeant major. He asked me how I liked airplanes, and when I answered that I liked to jump out of them, he replied that I had better like them a lot more than that, because I was about to receive orders to the 1st Marine Air Wing, Okinawa.

In October 1976, I was relieved as the regimental sergeant major of the 1st Marines, by Sergeant Major McFarland, and after a short turnover to make sure that he had a grasp on what was required of him, I checked out of the regiment and took several weeks of annual leave before heading to Okinawa.

My tour of duty as the sergeant major of the 1st Marine Regiment was an experience I shall never forget, if only for the reason that I was used correctly as a sergeant major by the regimental commander, Col. Ed Snelling. He asked my opinion on many issues, and I offered it without fear of retribution, ever. We worked as a team: He kept me informed as to what he wanted, and I offered my views based on twenty-eight years of service. I had never served in any Marine aviation section, and I honestly was not looking forward to my next tour of duty. But I thought that I had learned enough about leadership and the management of Marines to help me with my next assignment. I had no idea how wrong I could be.

CHAPTER 28

A Short Swing with the Wing—1976–1977

My wife drove me to Norton Air Force Base, and after saying our good-byes, I departed California on a civilian charter flight that would first take me to Anchorage, Alaska, for a brief stop before heading on to our final destination: Kadena Air Base, Okinawa, on the day before Thanksgiving. After being administratively processed at Kadena, I was taken by bus to the 1st Marine Air Wing's new headquarters, which was located at the U.S. Army's old island headquarters building. In 1976, the 1st Marine Air Wing was actually located in two places—on the island of Okinawa, where all of the helicopter assets were located, and at Iwakuni, Japan, which the fixed-wing fighters called home. After being dropped off in front of the wing's headquarters building, I was directed to the office of the sergeant major of the 1st MAW, Sgt. Maj. Gene Mills, a Marine I had known for a very long time.

I had first met Gene during my first tour in Vietnam when he was serving as the company gunnery sergeant for B Company, 1st Reconnaissance Battalion. We met again in 1966 at Chu Lai, when Gene was first sergeant of Fox Company, 7th Marines. Now he was about to be my boss. Sgt Maj. Gene Mills was a very colorful individual who had seen more than his fair share of combat, first in Korea and then two tours in Vietnam. He had a reputation as a straight shooter and always went to bat for his Marines. I was looking forward to serving with him, and he assigned me to a unit that was located close to the headquarters, Marine Wing Headquarters Squadron One (MWHS-1).

The composition of this squadron was unique, consisting primarily of the Marines who were assigned to the headquarters' G sections, those Marines assigned to maintain and pilot the commanding general's aircraft, the assorted "dogs and cats" who maintained and flew the C-47 aircraft, and those "unsung" Marines assigned to the Armed Forces Radio and TV station, the post office, and the cooks and bakers assigned to run the general's mess.

After leaving the sergeant major's office, I was shown to my new quarters in a building known as BOQ #6, where I had a bedroom and an efficiency kitchen, and I shared a living room with another sergeant major, who just happened to be Sergeant Major Mills. The sergeant major I was replacing had been kind enough to leave all his kitchen utensils behind, along with a television set. And, as this was an unaccompanied tour of duty, I could not complain about the quality of the bachelor quarters that I was to call home for the next year.

On Okinawa, with November came the rainy season, and that Thanksgiving Day was spent unpacking my gear and settling in. As it was a holiday, I was unable to check in at my new squadron, but I did enjoy the Thanksgiving meal in the mess hall, and I was later taken on a walking tour of the squadron by the sergeant major I was relieving. I was surprised at the size of the squadron, as its manpower nearly equaled that of a regiment, three-fourths of it based at Zukeran, Okinawa, the remainder in Japan at Iwakuni.

The day after Thanksgiving, I checked into my new squadron and was introduced to the squadron commander, a lieutenant colonel named Clark. The CO had two primary duties—first was commanding officer of the squadron, the second was as one of four pilots qualified to fly the commanding general's Learjet. The CO would fly every other day, and if the Lear wasn't being used by the wing commanding general, then the 3d Marine Division commander had first use of the small jet.

Following my introduction to the squadron CO, I met with the XO, a Major Black, who flew on the same aircraft as the commanding officer. Later, I walked through the headquarters building, meeting the adjutant, the administrative chief, and all the clerks assigned to help run the squadron. I had less than eight days to get accustomed to my new job before the current sergeant major departed for the States. We spent five days visiting all of the squadron's satellite units on Okinawa and less than three days to pay the Marines at Iwakuni a visit.

My duties as the squadron sergeant major were much different from what I had become accustomed to with the infantry over the past twenty-plus years. There was no field training, and the idea of doing anything that didn't relate to aircraft or administration was foreign to the vast majority of my Marines. Helping to complicate matters was the fact that my predecessor had come up through the ranks with the MOS of 0100 (administration specialist), and had given himself administrative responsibilities, removing himself from any position of leadership and keeping himself anchored to his desk.

After a short period of observing how the command functioned and taking notes on what I had seen, I prepared a short-term plan to correct the immediate problems, and a long-range plan to gradually give responsibilities back to those Marines who were accountable. My plans were designed not to disrupt the functioning of the sections, but to make changes that I knew would benefit the command.

My responsibility as the squadron sergeant major offered me access to many doors, and I looked behind each and every one of them, making my presence felt. I knew that there was no substitute for getting out from behind my desk to inspect the facilities that supported the Marines of the squadron. I set up a schedule to walk through all working areas at least once a week. I ate at the mess hall as often as possible and encouraged the staff NCOs to do the same. I visited the warehouses and storages areas just to see what was in them and insisted on having the individual Marine responsible for the area present to guide me around and answer questions.

I was surprised to learn that it had been the duty of the previous sergeant major to prepare the duty NCO roster—a job normally handled by the senior administrative chief. The issuing of military identification cards to Marines who had been promoted or who had lost their cards had also been the job of the former sergeant major. That responsibility I also gave back to the admin chief. I kept Lieutenant Colonel Clark well informed of my observations and of my plans to make what I believed were corrections that would improve efficiency. He listened to what I had to say, agreed with me, and backed me up, so that I was able to visit the different G sections, spend time with the Marines who worked there, and learn about their various jobs.

One of the first changes I made was in getting the barracks squared away. The Marines who lived in the barracks at Zukeran worked in the wing headquarters, but their staff NCOs had never made it a policy to check on the living conditions of the Marines in the various sections. I called a meeting of the SNCOs from the different G sections, told them what I expected from them, and that there was a new sergeant major on board. The response I wanted was actually not long in coming. Those SNCOs who took responsibility for their Marines, *and how they lived in garrison*, had no trouble from me. But for those individuals who were slow to act, life became increasingly difficult.

My specific areas of interest for the commanding officer included:

a. The personnel assignments of SNCOs.
b. Transfers.
c. Promotions.

d. Leave and liberty.
e. Morale and welfare of the Marines and their families.
f. Awards and punishments.
g. Reenlistments.
h. SNCO and NCO development training.
i. School quotas.

My duties as the commanding officer's senior enlisted adviser were:

a. To keep him informed about the daily running of the squadron.
b. To ensure that I knew exactly what he expected from me.
c. To be clear on his standards and policies.
d. To have at least one formal visit with him each week and update him on what was going on.
e. To invite him to all significant events within the squadron.
f. To speak frankly and candidly about all problems and issues.
g. Not to hold back bad news. Bad news never got better with age.

My goal, even though I was assigned to a wing squadron, was to prepare Marines to fight and to win the next battle. To accomplish such a goal would require the total support of the SNCOs and NCOs of the squadron. There is no secret handbook given to commanding officers or sergeants major that tells us how to accomplish such a lofty goal, but there are time-tested experiences, which when explained and accepted, can go a long way toward the success of any unit.

Strong leaders are the key to success. Successful organizations have successful leaders. They put into practice these leadership traits, characteristics which are usually found in Marine Corps units that are successful in peacetime and at war:

a. They lead by example. They do not ask any Marine to do something they can't or would not do. They share hardships and successes with their Marines.

b. They get involved. Good leaders make it their business to know what is going on, all of the time. They do not spend a great deal of time sitting behind their desks. They get out, move around the area, and talk to their men. They listen to their Marines and are at ease in their presence.

c. They delegate. They know they must operate today just as they will be forced to operate on the battlefield. They cannot make every decision themselves; they develop initiative and good judgment in their subordinates.

d. They are competent. They are technically, tactically, and administratively competent. They do make mistakes, but that doesn't stop them from taking a risk. They study ways to improve their knowledge and their skills.

e. They are good teachers. They have an ability to convey knowledge, experience, and professionalism.

The best Marines in the squadron were the two officers and forty enlisted men who maintained and flew the C-47, commonly known as a DC-3, the oldest aircraft in the Corps' inventory. Their small unit was based at MCAF (Marine Corps Air Facility) Futema, where they maintained eight DC-3s. The officer in charge was an old mustang who had been flying the aircraft since the Korean War. His maintenance officer was another old-timer, a warrant officer who knew his job and knew his Marines. He was assisted by a master sergeant who was a good troop leader. Their barracks were always spotless, and their morale was always high. They worked as a team, and that was how they managed to get things done. It was always a pleasure for me to visit with them, and because they knew I was genuinely interested in them and what they did, I was frequently invited to accompany them on flights all over the Far East.

A small section of only eight Marines who also caught my attention as being squared away, were those men with various MOSs who maintained and flew the general's Learjet. Those Marines were handpicked from squadrons within the wing. Living at the Kadena Air Base and led by a gunnery sergeant, three sergeants were crew chiefs while the remaining four Marines were maintenance specialists who kept the CG's aircraft polished and ready to go. Being competitive by nature, those Marines made the CG's jet stand out against the other jets, which were owned and operated by the air force at Kadena.

During the early part of February 1977, I was invited by one of the operations officers, a Captain Hayden, to go to Korea in the commanding general's jet. After getting permission from the colonel, I went by jeep with Captain Hayden to meet the rest of the crew at the flight line at Kadena. After the preflight inspection, we took on fuel and, with a second captain as copilot, we left Okinawa for the two-and-a-half-hour flight. The commanding general was in Korea, and we were instructed to pick him up and return with him to Okinawa, but we would have at least four hours of downtime at a place called Osan before he would meet up with us. During the Korean War, Osan had been known as K-55 and had remained an air base since 1953.

After an hour in the air, Captain Hayden came back into the passenger cabin for a cup of coffee and asked if I had ever flown in an aircraft such as that one. I told him that I hadn't, and he then invited me to come forward into the cockpit to show me how the plane operates. I was surprised to learn that the Learjet could practically fly by itself. I returned to my seat prior to landing, and once we were on the deck, we taxied over to the operations center and shut down the engines. A fuel truck pulled up and quickly topped off the jet's tanks for our return trip.

We had at least four hours of downtime before the CG arrived, and not being shy about going out on liberty, Captain Hayden asked me if I would go with him into Osan. Hayden had commented that the ribbons I wore indicated I had served in Korea and that the local merchants would take care of any Marine who had come to their country to fight against the Communists. The good captain had gotten his hands on a jeep, and within a few minutes, we were going out the main gate and headed into the center of the town.

We stopped first at a leather-jacket store, and as soon as we walked inside, we were met by the store's owner, who looked at my ribbons and noticed the Korean Presidential Unit Citation. He smiled and asked if I had been in Korea during the war. I told him that I had indeed been in Korea in 1952–1953. The shop owner shook my hand and said that he had been an ROK soldier during the war. From that moment on, I had a friend in Osan.

We bought several jackets at a hefty discount, and the shop owner then joined us as an escort. He showed us around the town, bought us lunch, and took us to the better stores in the town. Before we returned to the base, he gave each of us his business card and said that when we came back to Osan to please look him up. We made it back to the base before the general arrived, and as soon as the general climbed aboard, we taxied into position and left Korea for Okinawa.

In June 1977, Lieutenant Colonel Clark received orders directing him back to the States. The billet of commanding officer of the squadron was changed and would henceforth be filled by a colonel. Lieutenant Colonel Clark was replaced by Col. J. J. Reddy, who came from the 2d Marine Air Wing where he had served as the wing's chief of staff. The colonel was an old fighter pilot who had flown an F4U-4B Corsair (i.e., a propeller-driven aircraft) during most of the Korean War. He was also one of the most senior colonels in the 1st Marine Air Wing. Colonel Reddy had been around the block more than once, and I looked forward to our association. After the change of command ceremony, the colonel and I had a long discussion. It was his opinion that a sergeant major was an adviser to the commanding officer in all matters pertaining to enlisted men. He said that he expected me to be able to clearly state any leadership problems which affected the men of the command. I told the colonel about the types of problems that I had encountered when I first joined the squadron, and he made it quite clear that "his sergeant major" would not be hog-tied to a desk. He wanted me to travel with him because that was how I could best advise him. The colonel certainly did make my tour with the wing a memorable event. We spent a great deal of time visiting with the Marines of the squadron, and his concern for his Marines was always genuine. Because of Colonel Reddy's age, he was not qualified to fly the rotary-wing aircraft within the squadron, but that certainly did not prevent him from climbing into the cockpit of a C-47 and spending time behind the stick.

In June 1977, I learned that one of my former company commanders from Echo Company, 1st Reconnaissance Battalion, Capt. Doc White, was now the commanding officer of 3d Reconnaissance Battalion. Now a lieutenant colonel, Doc White's recon battalion was located on Okinawa's west coast at Onna Point, a former Japanese Self-Defense Battalion encampment. I made a point of going out to Onna Point to visit him because the last that I had heard about him was that he had been badly wounded while commanding a rifle company in Vietnam. Miraculously, he had survived a terrible head wound, and several years of intensive rehabilitation had enabled him to regain his strength, and he was returned to full duty.

Lieutenant Colonel White offered me the opportunity to make a number of parachute jumps with the Marines of his battalion. Within a few days, I had obtained the required orders and enjoyed jumping from the OV-10 Bronco, CH-46, and CH-53 helicopters, and several C-130s. On one occasion, Colonel Reddy was at the controls of a C-47, while we jumped onto the Yomatan drop zone, which was normally reserved for the U.S. Army's 173d Airborne Brigade.

In September 1977, we learned that the 1st Marine Air Wing was going to participate in one of the largest amphibious operations since World War II. Dubbed BALA-

KATAN FORTRESS the operation would include nineteen navy ships and required that the wing's headquarters element go aboard ship—something that had not been done since World War II. The amphibious landing was to take place on the Phillippine island of Mindoro, with elements of the wing also going ashore.

There was a great deal of work to do in preparation for the deployment. Not only would the wing headquarters need to get its mount-out capabilities up to date, but every Marine would need to learn how to pack his gear for duty aboard ship. Once ashore, we would be living out of tents, and the Marines of the wing's G sections didn't know how to erect a CP tent, let alone how to live in the field. Classes were scheduled for every Marine assigned to the deployment, and with the help of two gunnery sergeants who had just arrived from the 2d Marine Division, the secrets of living in the field were revealed to the Marines of the wing. The majority of the Marines in the wing did not have any 782 gear, which would be required to achieve any degree of comfort in the field. Once the necessary equipment was issued, additional classes were required to teach the wing's Marines how the gear was to be worn properly and comfortably.

During the first week of October, we boarded the USS *Juneau* and left Okinawa for a five-day cruise south into the Phillippine Sea to the shores of Mindoro. On the sixth day, we went ashore, landing on a strip of beach not too distant from an existing auxiliary airfield, and set up our wing command post. The operation lasted only five days, and it was on the final day, after the war had come to an "administrative ending," that tragedy struck. The pilot of one the CH-53 helicopters that had picked up a platoon from the 3d Battalion, 9th Marines, had decided to pick up an external load, a "water buffalo." As the CH-53 began to lift off from its hilltop landing zone, the helicopter could not sustain the lift and began to oscillate. It nosed over and slammed into a steep hillside covered by dense jungle canopy. The rugged, steep terrain made the initial attempt to rescue survivors all but impossible. The first

Marines to reach the scene of the crash were in a platoon from 3d Reconnaissance Battalion. Most of them had never seen anyone dead before, and this added to the intensity of the situation. First reports indicated many causalities, and within minutes, helicopters started to pick up survivors and the dead, delivering them to our airstrip for further evacuation to the hospital at Clark Air Base.

I was part of the ground crew that helped carry the injured to a C-130 for the flight to Clark. Then came the body bags carrying the dead. We set them in an empty tent until one of our C-47s flew in and took the bodies to Subic Bay. In all, thirteen Marines died in the crash, one of the largest losses of United States Marines since the Vietnam War. Colonel Reddy and I were two of the last Marines to leave Mindoro, departing in another C-47 for Subic Bay. It was a tragic end to what was otherwise a flawless operation. The loss of those thirteen Marines was deeply felt throughout the division and the wing, and cast a dark shadow on the amphibious operation. While I was at Subic Bay, I learned about the arrival of orders which would transfer me from Okinawa back to the 1st Marine Division during the month of November.

After returning to Okinawa, we celebrated the Marine Corps' birthday. However, due to the helicopter crash the celebration was a much more somber event than in years past. After a turnover period of only several days, I was relieved of my duties as the squadron sergeant major and departed Kadena Air Base for return to California. I landed at Norton Air Force Base on 17 November 1977, and as I was passing through customs, one of the agents looked me up and down, finally focusing his stare on the ribbons and gold jump wings, which I wore above my left breast pocket. He shook his head and said, "Marine, this must be your last trip." And as I picked up my seabag and swung it over my shoulder, I said, "You've got that right, buddy. It's sure good to be home."

CHAPTER 29

Back to where it all began; the 5th Marine Regiment— 1977–1978

After passing through customs at Norton Air Force Base, I was greeted by my wife, who was just as anxious as I was to leave the base and head back home to Oceanside. My being gone for a year not only meant a period of readjustment for the both of us, it meant that I also had to face a long list of "honey-do's," which probably began the day after I had left for Okinawa. Nonetheless, I was glad to see that she was in fine health, was happy to see me, and had managed to get along—with the help of a number of close family friends who looked out for her while I was gone. After two weeks at home, I reported in to the 1st Marine Division headquarters building, at Camp Pendleton, and went directly to the office of Sgt. Maj. C. W. Gamm, the sergeant major of the division. After a brief but friendly meeting with Sergeant Major Gamm, I was assigned as the regimental sergeant major of the 5th Marine Regiment, and left the division CP with a grin from ear to ear; I was about to be posted as the sergeant major of the first regiment I was assigned to after I left boot camp at Parris Island in 1948, the famous "Fighting Fifth Marines."

The activation of the 5th Marine Regiment dated back to 8 June 1917, just prior to embarkation to France during World War I. It was there that the regiment won its nickname of the Fighting Fifth. So fierce was their effort in the battle of Belleau Wood and subsequent victories, that the French government awarded the regiment the distinguished Croix de Guerre. Today, Marines serving in the regiment wear the fourragere (braided rope) on the left shoulder of their uniform coats.

With the advent of mail trains in the 1900s came bandits, and the mail service suffered. After having been reactivated in July 1920, elements of the 5th Marines became mail guards. While they were on the job, not one Marine was killed nor one piece of mail lost to the bandits. In March 1927, the regiment moved to Nicaragua and fought rebels there until April 1930.

Troubled times again caused the reactivation of the regiment on 1 September 1934, and after service in the United States and Guantanamo Bay, Cuba, it was deployed to New Zealand in 1942. During World War II, the regiment saw action at Guadalcanal, eastern New Guinea, Peleliu, and on Okinawa. Postwar, the regiment was in northern China until May 1947, then Guam, and subsequently Camp Pendleton until August 1950.

The country called again, and in August 1950, the 5th Marines found themselves in combat along the Pusan perimeter in Korea. During the next three years, the regiment saw action at Inchon, Seoul, the Chosin Reservoir, the east central front, and the western front. The 5th Marines returned to Camp Pendleton in March 1955 and remained there for eleven years before once again answering the call to arms. May 1966 found the regiment in the Republic of South Vietnam, where it remained until April 1971. The names of Rung Sat, Chu Lai, Phu Loc, Phu Bai, Hue, Que Son, An Hoa, Tam Ky, and Da Nang are still remembered by members of the regiment. The Presidential Unit Citation was awarded—the tenth time since Guadalcanal—upon the regiment's return home to Camp Pendleton.

The 5th Marine Regiment is the most highly decorated regiment in the Marine Corps, and the privilege of being assigned as the regiment's sergeant major marked a high point in my military career.

I went into the sergeant major's office and met Sergeant Major Vega, who had been filling in as the acting sergeant major since the retirement of the former incumbent. Vega, who was assigned to the regiment's 3d Battalion, took me to the office of the regimental commander, Col. R. R. Burritt, whom I had known in Vietnam as the commanding officer of 3d Reconnaissance Battalion.

After a lengthy discussion with the colonel, I had more than a fair understanding of the regimental commander's plans for training and which operations were planned for the future. The colonel escorted me to the office of his executive officer, LtCol. J. D. Beans. The regimental XO had served as a platoon leader at Camp Lejeune's 2d Force Recon Company, and during the time that I served as the regimental sergeant major, Lieutenant Colonel Beans took command of the regiment's 1st Battalion. Years later, he would distinguish himself, attaining the rank of Marine major general.

Colonel Burritt informed me that he wanted a monthly lecture presented to every new Marine in the grade of sergeant and below who had joined the regiment. Included in this lecture would be the history of the regiment, what local services were available to Marines and their families at Camp Margarita and in the nearby town of Oceanside. Marines newly joined to the regiment would also be required to attend a briefing presented by the commanding officer, welcoming them aboard, and they would receive an information booklet that defined the regimental policy on frequently addressed issues such as request mast, unauthorized absence, emergency leave, grooming standards, uniform regulations, and the liberty limits for overnight liberty, forty-eight-hour liberty, and seventy-two- or ninety-six-hour liberty.

I joined the 5th Marines just before the holidays, and the training tempo was traditionally eased during that time of year to allow Marines to go home for Christmas and New Year's. During that slack time, I had the opportunity to meet with many old friends who were now calling the regiment home. I was surprised to find many of them; the regiment was the better for their being there.

Just after the holidays, Colonel Burritt received orders directing him to join the division headquarters, and he was replaced by Col. William J. Masterpool. The new colonel was a very charismatic and well-known individual. An enlisted man during World War II, he had come up through the ranks, attaining the rank of first sergeant before being commissioned a second lieutenant in June 1948. He found himself back in combat shortly thereafter, in Korea for the Inchon Landing, Chosin Reservoir battle, and subsequent operations in the spring and summer of 1951. He was awarded the Silver Star for gallantry in action and the Bronze Star with combat V for heroic achievement during this period with the 1st Battalion, 1st Marines. Following the Korean conflict, Colonel Masterpool served in various billets in the infantry as well as the tank and amphibian tractors fields, Stateside and abroad.

Stateside duty stations during his service included tours at Parris Island, South Carolina; Camp Lejeune, North Carolina; Camp Pendleton, California; Quantico, Virginia; Landing Force Training Command; Coronado, California; and Washington, D.C.

With the outbreak of hostilities in the Republic of Vietnam and subsequent Marine Corps involvement, Colonel Masterpool was ordered to the II Marine Amphibious Force and commanded successively the 3d Battalion, 4th Marines, and the 2d Battalion, 26th Marines. He distinguished himself again in combat and was awarded the Legion of Merit with Combat V, his second Bronze Star, a second Purple Heart for wounds received in action and, from the Republic of Vietnam, two Crosses of Gallantry with Palms.

Subsequently reassigned, the colonel reported to the faculty of the Canadian Land Forces Command and Staff College in Kingston, Ontario, Canada. In June 1970, the colonel reported to the Basic School at Marine Corps Base, Quantico, Virginia, for duty as the executive officer.

Subsequent assignments found Colonel Masterpool assigned as chief of staff, 3d Marine Division; deputy chief of staff, and chief of staff Fleet Marine Force, Pacific; and chief of staff, 1st Marine Division. During his thirty-five years of active service, covering three major conflicts, he had commanded every Marine Corps unit from the fire team to the regiment, and had commanded units in five of the six Marine divisions.

I had met the colonel before, when I was assigned to the 1st Marine Brigade, and I was impressed with his friendliness. I considered myself extremely fortunate to have been given the opportunity to serve with him during what was to be my last year of service in the Marine Corps.

Just a few weeks after Colonel Masterpool took command of the regiment, Lieutenant Colonel Beans was transferred to the 1st Battalion as the battalion commander. First Battalion, 5th Marines, began an intensive training program in preparation for that battalion's selection as the second battalion to deploy to Okinawa, replacing a battalion from the 1st Marine Regiment. The use of "transplacement" battalions was not new; the practice dated to the years before Vietnam, but the idea of deploying overseas as a battalion also initiated a great deal of unit pride and seemed to bring a much-needed shot of stability to the battalion.

Our new regiment executive officer was LtCol. J. M. Nolan, an outstanding Marine infantry officer with a great deal of experience. A native of Boston, Massachusetts, he had a Yankee accent so thick it could be cut with a knife. I spent a great deal of time talking with the XO and enjoyed listening to his opinions on the direction the Marine Corps was taking. As direct representatives of the regimental commander, the XO and I worked together on many meritorious promotion boards and numerous inspections.

During March 1978, 75 percent of our regimental command post deployed to the Marine Corps base at Twentynine Palms, California, to support the 1st Battalion in a live-fire CPX (command post exercise) in a narrow desert area known as the Delta Corridor. The corridor was twenty miles long, flanked on both sides by rugged, worn mountains. Filled with the rusting hulks of amtracks, tanks, trucks, and jeeps, these targets had been strategically placed to represent a motorized enemy formation. The 1st Battalion had established its command post on one mountaintop while the regimental CP was positioned on another several kilometers away. Following a written script, and with no actual Marines within the corridor, the battalion moved east through the corridor "on paper," calling for artillery and air strikes as it made progress. The battalion staff was able, through observation, to see its targets and adjust its calls for artillery fire and close-air support.

From the day we departed Camp Pendleton, it had rained. The accompanying wind was so severe that we had to anchor our tents with large rocks. At night, the temperature was near freezing, and during those cold nights in the field I really got to know Colonel Masterpool. He ran the operation smoothly, not making any hasty decisions, and using his staff properly. His knowledge of supporting arms was extensive, and he educated his staff as we continued with the problem. It was one of the few times that I was able to witness the "teacher-student" environment that Marine officers are encouraged to use. After two weeks in the field supporting the 1st Battalion, the regiment's 2d Battalion, commanded by Lt. Col. W. A. Tilley, took its place. Accompanied by Sergeant Major Holland, Lieutenant Colonel Tilley and his staff also performed well in the field, learning the complexities of fire-support coordination. After spending two weeks in the Delta Corridor, we returned to Camp Pendleton, but had not managed to leave the rain in the desert. In fact, 1978 proved to be one of the wettest years on record in southern California.

During May, we again returned to Twentynine Palms and participated in one of the largest regimental operations since Vietnam. We were used as part of a plan to test and prepare the Marine Corps for a new concept—the rapid deployment force.

The National Security Act of 1947 assigned the Corps numerous missions, among which were providing detachments for service on armed vessels of the navy, and security detachments aboard naval stations/bases and other governmental installations; to develop in coordination with the army and the air force those phases of amphibious operations that pertain to the tactics, techniques, and equipment used by landing forces; and to perform other duties as the president may direct—thus permitting the president to call upon Marines as the nation's "force-in-readiness" in times of crisis.

Designed as a Marine expeditionary brigade (MEB)-type operation, Headquarters 5th Marines, our 2d Battalion and 3d Battalion, and the 2d Battalion, 2d Marine Regiment, from Camp Lejeune, made up our composite infantry regiment. Our armor, tanks, and amtracks were provided by the 1st Tank Battalion and 3d Amtrack Battalion, respectively. All the tracked vehicles had been moved overland by rail and on low-boy trucks from Camp Pendleton to Twentynine Palms.

The 3d Tank Battalion, from Twentynine Palms, acted as the aggressor force armor, while the 1st Battalion, 4th Marines, provided the ground aggressor force. The artillery support for the operation, 105mm and 155mm howitzers, came from the 2d Battalion, 11th Marines. Additional support, in the way of 8-inch self-propelled guns and 175mm self-propelled guns, was provided from Force troops stations at Twentynine Palms. To test the logistical support required for a Marine brigade in the field, the FSR had deployed from Camp Pendleton to the Twentynine Palms staging area known as Camp Wilson.

The air wing's participation in this operation began when a section of the wing's headquarters deployed to the expeditionary airstrip near Camp Wilson. Helicopter support—CH-46s, CH-53s and helicopter gunships—were the first aircraft to arrive. The fixed-wing assets came in the form of one squadron of AV8 Harriers and a squadron of A-4s from El Toro and Yuma.

Command and control was managed by the 1st MEB, commanded by the ADC (assistant division commander) of the 1st Marine Division, who was accompanied by his sergeant major, Crow Crawford. I had served with Sergeant Major Crawford during my last tour on Okinawa, and we would see a great deal of each other during our stay with the MEB. Soon after that, Sergeant Major Crawford learned of his selection to the position of sergeant major of the Marine Corps!

We spent the first ten days in the field as a brigade, conducting live-fire shoots for all of our infantry and supporting arms units. Included in these firing exercises, and of particular interest to me as a former combat engineer, was the appearance of the new antitank "Dragon" platoon. The Dragon, technically known as the M-47, was a surface-attack guided missile system, a shoulder-fired, recoilless, tube-launched, medium antitank weapon. It was making quite an impression on the Corps. The system is a one-man portable weapon characterized by a rugged design that allows for operation in all weather conditions where the target can be seen. The Dragon has two major components, the round and the tracker. The antitank round is expendable and discarded after use. It consists of two subcomponents: the launcher and the missile. The tracker is designed to attach quickly to the round and is the eye and brain of the missile. With a total weight of thirty-one pounds, and a maximum range of one thousand meters, this weapon would have been greatly appreciated during the Korean War, and I couldn't help but think what a difference it might have made in 1950 when the North Koreans headed south across the border.

In 1978, the Dragon was found in the weapons company of the infantry battalion. Organization during wartime placed thirty-two trackers, organized into four sections, in the Dragon platoon. During wartime, the platoon is commanded by an infantry lieutenant with four staff sergeants, one heading each section. During peace-time only half of a section is manned.

Observing one of these live-fire demonstrations, we visited the 2d Battalion, 2d Marines. I was particularly impressed with the rifle battalion because of the men's gung-ho spirit—their enthusiasm was apparent in everything they did. After mentioning this to the battalion sergeant major, I learned that the regimental commander of the 2d Marines was Col. Gene Turley, whom I had served with years earlier when he was the executive officer of 1st Force Recon Company. I learned that he was coming from Camp Lejeune, North Carolina, to visit with his battalion, and I made it a point to visit with him when he arrived.

Following the preparatory live firing and rehearsals, the operation began. Our CP was divided into two elements—the Alpha command group, headed by Colonel Masterpool, and the Bravo command group, led by Lieutenant Colonel Nolan. Mobility and our ability to communicate with our subordinate commands were to be the lessons learned from this exercise. To accomplish that, our Alpha command group operated out of an LVTC-7; an amphibious vehicle operated by a three-man crew, with room for five radiomen and four spaces for the commander and his staff. The LVTC-7 gave us the speed, mobility, and, to some degree, the protection we needed in a desert environment. The weather was a key factor during the operation as it rained continually during the time we spent in the field. The operational tempo was extremely fast-paced: Colonel Masterpool had to control his three fast-moving battalions while pitted against an aggressor force that knew every square inch of the surrounding terrain.

I recall one night when we had moved to the eastern boundary of Twentynine Palms and had stopped in a small canyon, which offered us a good defensive position. But at 0400 the next morning, the 1st Battalion, 4th Marines, hit us in a well-executed envelopment and was hoping to capture the regimental commander. They hit us so quickly that Colonel Masterpool and I, dressed only in long-john underwear and armed only with our .45 automatics, had only enough time to move away from our LVT and move to the top of a nearby hill. It was a moment I would never forget, and I could see why Colonel Masterpool had the well-deserved reputation for being a warrior. He took the attack just as though it were the real thing, all for the sake of the exercise.

When the CPX ended, the Marines of the regiment returned to Camp Pendleton while the regimental, battalion, and company staffs were required to remain and attend a four-day presentation by the Marine Corps Air Ground Combat Center (MCAGCC) on the latest Soviet air and ground threat. It was apparent that the Soviets had come a long way in the military and technological advances, but they had not seen combat since World War II, although it was in 1978 that they sent their troops into their own "Vietnam," Afghanistan.

The presentation was a success and well worth the four extra days at the Combat Center. On our fourth day, we boarded CH-53 helicopters for the flight back to Camp Pendleton. Much to our surprise, we found that the weather we were subjected to had also affected Camp Pendleton. The last spring torrential rains had destroyed many of the hard-surface roads aboard the base, and Camp Margarita was now cut off, remaining so for seven days.

During one of his walks around the regimental area, Colonel Masterpool decided to adopt a tradition he had encountered while attending the Canadian Land Forces Command and Staff College. The colonel wanted to display all of the regimental and battalion colors in the regimental chapel. He had ordered replacement colors for each of the battalions, to include company guidons, before we had deployed to Twentynine Palms, and they had come in. The colonel handed me a number of photographs of several Canadian military chapels and instructed me to use our new colors to create a similar atmosphere. When I had completed the job, the colonel was invited to the chapel to see the final results. As he entered the chapel, the first colors displayed were the regimental color, and as he moved forward toward the altar, he moved past the colors of his three battalions on the right side of the chapel and the companies' guidons—beginning with Headquarters Company and ending with M Company 3/5—displayed on the left side of the chapel.

In June 1978, Colonel Masterpool received his retirement package from Headquarters Marine Corps. He would retire from active duty during the last week of July, but he did not want to have a standard retirement parade in his honor. Instead, the colonel wanted a redecoration of the 5th Marine's color, followed by his change of command with Col. Anthony Lukeman. Lieutenant Colonel Nolan and I were tasked with putting this colorful ceremony together, and when the day of Colonel Masterpool's change of command came, we had created and rehearsed a ceremony we thought was worthy of the man to whom we were saying good-bye.

Lieutenant Colonel Nolan had appointed himself the commanding officer of troops, and he called for the regimental color to come forward. Once in position, a narrator read a brief history of the regiment before each of the Marines carrying a battle streamer was summoned front and center. Since the Fighting Fifth Marines was the most decorated regiment in the Corps, it required twenty Marines to attach the battle streamers to the color. The order of march required that the most senior award, the Presidential Unit Citation with one Silver and four Bronze Stars, be attached to the color, first. Following the numerous unit awards came the regiment's campaign streamers, beginning with the World War I Victory Streamer. The announcement of this particular streamer caught the attention of many guests as many of them did not know of the regiment's involvement in World War I. What followed was the visual display of the regiment's incredible military history:

Presidential Unit Citation Streamer with One Silver and
Four Bronze Stars
World War II
Solomon Islands—1942
Peleliu, Ngesebus—1944
Okinawa—1945
Korea—7 Aug–7 Sep 1950
Korea—15 Sep–11 Oct 1950
Korea—27 Nov–11 Dec 1950
Korea—21–26 Apr 1951
Korea—16 May–30 Jun 1951
Korea—11–25 Sep 1951
Vietnam—27 May 1966–24 Apr 1967
Vietnam—25 Apr–5 Jun 1967
Vietnam—6 Jun–15 Sep 1967
Vietnam 16 Sep 1967–10 Feb 1968
Vietnam—3 May–22 Jun 1968
Vietnam—24 Jul–31 Oct 1968

Navy Unit Commendation Streamer
Korea—11 Aug 1952–5 May 1953, 7–21 Jul 1953

Meritorious Unit Commendation Streamer
Vietnam—25 Jul–23 Oct 1968

World War I Victory Streamer with One Silver Star
Army Occupation of Germany Streamer
Second Nicaraguan Campaign Streamer
American Defense Service Streamer with One Bronze
Star
Asiatic-Pacific Campaign Streamer with One Silver Star
and One Bronze Star
World War II Victory Streamer
Navy Occupation Service Streamer with Asia Clasp
China Service Streamer
National Defense Service Streamer with One Bronze Star
Korean Service Streamer with Two Silver Stars
Vietnam Service Streamer with Two Silver Stars and One
Bronze Star

French Croix de Guerre with Two Palms and One Gold
Star
Korean Presidential Unit Citation Streamer
Vietnam Cross of Gallantry with Palm

The colonel's guest list read like a who's who of the
Marine Corps and the navy. There were more Marine gen-
erals and navy flag officers than we had privates first
class escorts in one of the regiment's battalions. Following
the redecoration of color came the change of command.
When the narrator read that during the colonel's thirty-five
years of active service and combat in three wars, he had
led every unit from a fire team to a regiment, the guests
rose to give the outgoing regimental commander a standing ovation.

That evening my wife and I were invited by the colonel's wife Maida to join his family at a local restaurant
and celebrate his retirement. To say his children were "all
Marine" is an understatement: His oldest daughter,
Shauna, was a Marine first lieutenant assigned to headquarters, 4th Marine Division, New Orleans, and his three
sons, William, a corporal assigned to the division's 1st
Tank Battalion; Michael, a former Marine sergeant and
then a midshipman in the NROTC Program at Texas
A&M, and Jerome, a competitive skier who was living at
home.

My service with Col. Bill Masterpool marked one of
the highlights of my thirty years of service. And when I
compare colonels like Bill Masterpool and Ed Snelling to
all others, I regard them as two of the finest officers in
our Corps. And, though they were not selected to the
grade of brigadier general, it was, in my opinion, the Marine Corps that suffered.

During July my orders to retire on 1 September 1978
came to the regiment from Headquarters Marine Corps. I
was instructed to complete a physical examination and
have the results of that examination to HQMC before my
retirement date. Those orders were difficult to execute because I was still spending time in the field getting the new

commanding officer acquainted with the regiment. At the same time, our headquarters was involved in another CPX, and my relief was not due to arrive at the regiment until November. I asked Sergeant Major Vega to stand in for me while I took some time to get things rolling for my own retirement. Sergeant Major Vega and I discussed a retirement ceremony in the regimental area. At the time, the majority of retirement ceremonies for enlisted men were conducted at the division headquarters. Since I had marched in more than my fair share of ceremonies as a young Marine at Pearl Harbor, I decided that my retirement ceremony would be conducted by only those Marines who are the backbone of the Corps: Marines in the grade of sergeants and below.

My retirement came at 1400 on 31 August 1978, on the parade deck of the 2d Battalion, 5th Marines. Sergeant Major Vega had planned the event, and though I may seem more than a little biased, it was the best retirement ceremony I had seen in thirty years. My thoughts went back to when I had first joined the 5th Marine Regiment on Guam in 1948, and again during the Korean War in 1952. To have this regiment of Marines presented in my honor was a exceptional experience—one that only a handful of Marines could, or would, ever realize—and I wanted the moment to last a very long time, for soon I would have only those memories, those echoes of the Corps to sustain me.

My more somber thoughts that day where also of my mother and of those extraordinary Marines I had known during the years who had given their lives in the defense of our nation. It was their memories that created my feeling of accomplishment and that truly marked my thirty years of service to the Corps.

On the morning of 1 September 1978, I felt very peculiar. I had worn the uniform of a United States Marine every day; I had observed training in the field, inspected young Marines, and observed how they lived and how they worked. Now, there was no place for me to report, no inspections to conduct, and I had no problems to resolve. There was no more going to the field for me, and for the first time in my life, I felt empty. But I knew there was life beyond the Corps of Marines, which I so dearly missed, and I was more than a little determined to try my hand at something new. Believing still that education is the key that opens new doors, I enrolled at a local community college that same day, having set my sights on a new mission: to obtain a degree and apply what I learned toward a new career.

CHAPTER 30

In your opinion, Sergeant Major . . .

Having completed this biography—a twenty-month-long process—I thought it would prove valuable to today's Marines to ask Sergeant Major Jacques to comment on his views on those issues that remain as significant and as challenging today as they were forty-six years ago. The sergeant major's comments are written as they were stated.

Question: What characteristics made you a successful Marine?
Answer: On the day that I was promoted to corporal, I listened to a lecture given by our commanding officer, Col. Lewis B. "Chesty" Puller. He wanted those of us who had been promoted to know the significance of our having just become noncommissioned officers and how to develop those special qualities of leadership that he believed were the most important. His advice certainly served me well during my career in the Corps, and I'll try to paraphrase what he said:

1. Use yourself as a personal example. NCOs are looked upon to set the example.
2. Create and maintain high moral standards for yourself and your men.

3. Be patriotic; a love of your country is second only to God and to our Corps.
4. Keep your personal behavior above reproach.
5. Strive to better educate yourself.

Question: Which traits, in your opinion, make a competent NCO?
Answer: I believe that five traits help to make an NCO competent:

1. Proper military behavior
2. Decisiveness
3. Courage
4. Endurance
5. Judgment

Question: Which traits make a proficient staff noncommissioned officer?
Answer: In my opinion, integrity, knowledge, and tact are the marks of a competent staff NCO.

Question: What positive things have you observed in today's Marine Corps?
Answer: The most positive things that I have noticed are that today's Marines are extremely knowledgeable of their weapons capabilities, their tactics, and that they possess an attitude that reflects a personal pride in being a Marine.

Question: In your opinion, how does a Marine establish esprit de corps, and not come to view duty as a seven to four job?
Answer: I believe that esprit de corps is accomplished by a Marine taking pride: first, in himself, and then in his unit. The building of teamwork within the unit will help to create the necessary esprit de corps.

Question: Did being a Marine help to make you a better person?
Answer: There's no question about it; the Marine Corps

taught me to be a better citizen. By saying that, I mean that I care about my country. I take pride in the fact that I vote. I am proud to be an American, and I am proud to have been a Marine.

Question: What might you have done differently?
Answer: I don't regret a single day of my life as a Marine, and I don't believe that there is anything I would have done differently.

Question: In your opinion, what qualities should a young man or woman have to become a Marine?
Answer: I believe that anyone who wants to become a United States Marine should come to the Corps wanting to bring something into the Corps. The attitude of wanting to know what the Corps will provide is all wrong. Secondly, a person who is unselfish and ready to learn will do well. Last, but certainly not least, I would strongly advise anyone wanting to join the Marine Corps to come physically fit. For the young men and women foolish enough to arrive at MCRD San Diego, or Parris Island, out of shape, life as a recruit will not be fun.

Question: Why should anyone want to become a Marine?
Answer: The challenge and pride of serving with our country's finest fighting force still remains. Earning the title Marine should not and does not come easy. The Marine Corps is one of the last places in this country where *men* come to work. To have served honorably in the United States Marine Corps has, since 1775, been a mark of distinction among Americans.

Question: Of the many Marines with whom you have served, who best exemplifies the meaning of the word Marine, and why?
Answer: Beginning with my first squad leader, Cpl. Robert J. Mesa, and my first platoon sergeant, Sgt. Roy Pitman, while serving on Guam with the 5th Marines, I thought those two men—both decorated combat veterans

of World War II—exemplified what Marines were supposed to be like. The longer I stayed with the Corps, and with a few more stripes on my shoulder, I began to take notice of those special characteristics that set some Marines apart from the majority of others. There are a few standouts who immediately come to mind: GySgt. Billy Lyday, Sgt. Maj. Jesse Wise, and Sgt. Maj. Crow Crawford rank as three of the finest enlisted Marines to have worn the uniform. And, as I have stated in the book, Col. Ed Snelling and Col. Bill Masterpool had those leadership qualities that set them apart from all others. These men were knowledgeable and shared their knowledge with other Marines, freely. They were courageous men, but never spoke in terms of personal bravery. Perhaps, best of all, they had the natural ability to communicate with their Marines and they knew how to *listen*.

Question: Being retired since 1978, what do you miss about the Corps?
Answer: I still miss going to the field. The days spent firing the weapons which were organic to an infantry battalion was time well spent. I also miss the adrenaline rush from the anxious moments during parachute and scuba diving operations. And, of course, nothing gets one's attention focused quicker than being shot at, and missed.

Question: Do you believe you would welcome being in today's Marine Corps?
Answer: No, absolutely not! I doubt that I would last a day because I believe in a different style of discipline. I was raised in a Corps that subscribed to blind obedience to orders. That was probably all right for the Marines of my day, but it isn't the way things work today.

Question: In your opinion, should young married men or women be allowed to enlist in today's Marine Corps?
Answer: No. I was in agreement with the commandant, (General Mundy) when he commented on that issue last year. He said that today's Marines spend an inordinate

amount of time deployed, which adds to the stress of the young family environment. He recommended against it. If it were up to me, I would not allow Marines to marry until they were in the grade of corporal, or above, and had the joint approval of the Marine's platoon leader, company first sergeant *and* company commander.

Question: In your opinion, do you believe that women have a place in the Marine Corps?
Answer: Yes, but with conditions. Based upon my fifty-three months of combat, I do not believe that women should be allowed to serve in any combat operations. I believe that there are specific jobs which women Marines do better than men, but I would draw the line when it came to going into combat. Women in combat is not the best that the Marine Corps can do.

Question: What do you remember as your "best day" in the Corps?
Answer: My best day in the Corps was always on graduation day, when I was a drill instructor at the Marine Corps Recruit Depot, San Diego, California. The pride that I felt on being able to see what I had helped to create in the making of a basic Marine was very special to me. And I am sure that feeling is still very much alive on the parade decks at San Diego and Parris Island.

APPENDIX I

Remembering Ba To

1. Interview with former Lance Corporal Mike Brown, 1st Force Reconnaissance Company, 1965–1966. (May 1994)

I may ramble a little bit, but I remember some points of interest. I remember when they said that General Walt was coming in to brief us on the mission. On the previous mission we had been out and came across a reconnaissance drone out in the jungle. When we found it, we reported it, and then requested a satchel charge. We took a lot of the equipment out of the drone. As I remember, the camera was gone, but they indicated that it happened a lot of times; the camera self-destructed if the drone went down at the wrong time. But we took some communications and navigation modules out of it. In the course of that mission, Peter Pullas from San Francisco was the first one to get airlifted out. They were pulling us out in a harness, and they pulled him up into a canopy of trees. The helicopter was above the canopy in the wind, and it swayed a little bit. Peter went into some treetops, and he reached up to move a limb, and when he did, he slipped right through the harness and hit the ground six or eight feet from me, landing between two big boulders. He bounced off the ground, then just lay there with a great big hole in the side of his head. He went into shock,

443

breathing. We called for a medevac chopper and they medevacked Peter out. Doc Haston, as I recall, was the corpsman on patrol with us. Doc did a great job in stabilizing him. We loaded up the rest of the gear into the same basket that Peter went up in, and we hightailed it for parts unknown. The chopper took off with Peter, and he lived through his injuries, which really surprised me.

General Walt came in one afternoon. As I recall, he came in a Huey, wearing starched utilities—real sharp—pressed utilities. And I recall that there seemed to be a problem when he arrived because we were assembled in our mess hall, and we were not approved to have a mess hall. We had built the mess hall and a lot of the camp by "trading out" scuba gear and beach privileges, with the Seabees, for lumber and stuff. Our cook was supposed to be cooking with the MAG-16 cooks, and we were supposed to walk back and forth to MAG-16 every day to eat.

With what we could scrounge and barter, we had established our own little camp. We had a real tight perimeter. Unlike most of the other camps, we did not let any South Vietnamese in our camp. We had the laundry guy stop at the main gate and unload his stuff. One day he went ahead and ran the main gate, and Woo put two shots over his head. He stood the truck on its nose, backed up, and never tried that again. We thought it was funny.

Anyway, General Walt came in and walked through the platoon, talked to each one of us, congratulated us on a job well done. He said that because of our work he was sending us to a Special Forces camp at Ba To. They were looking for the remnants of the 198th Regiment of the 325B PAVN Division. They had attacked a Special Forces camp in the coastal region, it seems like it was Qui Nhon, but I'm not sure anymore. They had been in a pretty long engagement when the weather broke, and air strikes hit them pretty hard. They had gone up to a hospital R & R–type facility, in the central highlands. And we were to go up there looking for them. And we found them.

He promised us that we'd get in the thick of it, pretty much, as I recall. He also said that he'd provide air support and whatever else we might need because it was an important mission and he wanted to get them while they were down. We flew into Ba To, in Caribous I think, from Australia.

We landed in Ba To, and we were well received by the Special Forces guys there. In their main mess area they had a sign painted above their food area that read something like, "Ba To, home of 13 hilarious comedians, entertaining continuously." In very short order, we went out on a number of patrols. I remember them as being fairly small patrols of four, five, or six men. We had quite a few sightings, came under fire a few times, not too terribly often. It wasn't unusual, at great distance, to see lines of eight to fifteen PAVN soldiers in uniform moving about the area, especially as we got closer to the Vuc Liem Valley. Which I guess is where the underground hospital was supposed to have been.

The patrol we are discussing was a company-strength, South Vietnamese reconnaissance-in-strength patrol.

I remember we played poker the night before. I remember it very well because for one of the last hands of the night, I had aces over—a full house! I couldn't see how any of the guys there could beat me. It looked like there were a couple of other guys who had full houses, but kings over or queens over, something like that. I couldn't throw my money in fast enough. Then a Special Forces sergeant—Sergeant West—he stayed in the hand with two pair. It just so happened that both pairs were fours, and he won the last big pot of the night.

I remember that night well because I had to borrow some money from Stan Joy. I had to borrow fourteen dollars to call the last bet.

When we went to bed that night, things seemed a little funny. There was a feeling of restlessness, or something. It was like everybody was wondering if something was happening.

We left early, early in the morning, before dawn, and moved to the last checkout point. I remember that about ten o'clock in the morning, we took a break, and one of the sergeants, not a Montagnard (CIDG) solder but a senior South Vietnamese sergeant who had gotten really drunk the night before, was close to us and over on his hands and knees throwing up. He was in a strange state of mind. Maybe it was just me.

I remember Joy looking at me and saying, "Ya know, I've got a feeling, Mike, that this time we are gonna see some action. We are going to get into it." And I looked at him, and his eyes looked funny, and I said "You have a premonition, don't you?" And I say this because a lot of guys, or a number of guys, have said they *had* a premonition before something happened to them.

Merrell, whom we named our camp after, Lowell H. Merrell, Jr., was supposed to have had a premonition and packed up his stuff and gotten his affairs in order and sent letters and had done stuff like that.

Joy seemed to feel the same way. He had written a long letter to his wife, and he seemed to have gotten his stuff in order. Just a strange kind of deal. I made light of it at the time. At the time it was a hell of a lot funnier than it ended up being later.

Lieutenant Lenker didn't go out this patrol; he had gone back to Da Nang for a briefing. I guess [Operation] HARVEST MOON had just started or was just fixing to start, which ended up being a big operation that year.

When we got to the main area where we were going to set up our base camp, we saw some little thatched huts down in the bottom of the valley. That afternoon, Gunny Jacques sent six or eight of us down into that valley. I say six or eight, because this was a pretty good group of us, the biggest group that had gone out. It was pretty much the whole platoon with our corpsman, Doc Haston, but without Lieutenant Lenker, Daniel Constance, and a couple of other guys.

We went down onto that valley, drew a little fire as we went up the other side, and got into a brief firefight, but no real close action. It was at pretty fair distances, a little testing of each other. And we made our way back to the top of the hill where we had staked out our camp. I was surprised when I got there for a couple of reasons. First, Gunny Jacques split us up, but this is one of those things that I think was a mistake, with benefit of hindsight, which is, I guess the way you learn most things in combat. He and Sergeant West had set up a command post at the very top, and he had us scattered down the finger, and that would prove to be a problem later.

That night, after we had humped out of the camp in the morning and gone down into the valley, he decided to send a patrol toward the Vuc Liem Valley in the darkness. And it was absolutely pitch-black, one of the darkest nights that I remember. I remember thinking it was a pretty stupid thing to do. We couldn't see our hands in front of our faces, and we were trying to take off on patrol. I was thinking that Gunny Jacques was probably trying to impress Sergeant West with how much stuff we could do. It was real, real hard goin'. Then all of a sudden I remember hearing some racket and feeling that everybody stopped, and we kind of gathered up. Sergeant Blanton, who later became Charlie Clemence when his grandparents adopted him, said that Woo, who was our scout, had slipped and fallen down into a ravine. He made a hell of a racket. We took one of the little survival, single-cell-type flashlights and hung it over the edge and turned it on briefly and called out, "Woo." We could hear him say something back to us. We could hear him start crawlin' back up again. He was crawlin' up five steps and fallin' back four steps. And you could hear his rifle clinkin' and stuff, and then as he drew closer and closer, we turned on the little light and left it close to the edge. He always wore his utility cap with the brim stuck up, and I remember him sticking his head up over the edge and looking at us and then pointing behind him and saying, "Don't go that way, guys."

We decided that it was so bad that we were going to make camp there that night. And we were dog-tired. We had come out about ten clicks as the crow flies from Ba To, had patrolled that valley, and now another night patrol was just too much.

We got down there the next day, and I don't know if anyone has told this story, but when the sun came up, we didn't move. We called in sightings and said that we were in places that we weren't. We felt that we didn't have any business nosing around any more than we already had, especially with all of the difficulties we had the night before. Late that evening toward sundown, we headed back up to the camp where the company of Montagnards was, and when we got up there, we staked out the area where we were going to be. We did a little minor digging in, but nothing to speak of, because we had come in late.

There was a guy, I think his name was Wyman. He had been in the navy but had joined the Marine Corps because he was told that he could get into the Marine Corps' aviation program and have a better shot of getting into the Naval Academy, through enlisted deals, if he was in the Marine Corps. I guess he thought, like a lot of people, that all Marines were stupid.

But Wyman and I were talking when we heard a *duke-duke* sound. I looked at him and he looked at me, and I said, "Do you think that was what I think that was?" "It sounded like mortars to me," he said.

And then we could hear the whistle of the incoming. They seemed to hit on one side of the hill, and we kind of pulled over to the other end of the crest. And I think that they also knew exactly what we were doing, and they planned on us doing that because the "fire for effect" seemed to come right along the other side of the ridgeline where we had retreated to. They were coming fairly heavily, and I was on the radio reporting to Ba To that we were under attack. Sergeant Blanton, it seems like, sent somebody up to see if Gunny Jacques wanted us to rendezvous with him in his position. It was very dark. I recall that it was very foggy.

Blanton and Joy—those are the only ones I remember for sure were there—and I could see shadows moving up the mountain, in a crawl, with weapons. And I rolled very quietly over and aimed my weapon—I was carrying a carbine—and I pointed my weapon at the leading figure, and for some dumb-ass reason, asked, "Who is there?" It was Bob Moore—Cpl. Bob Moore. I don't know why I asked. Initial instinct would be to shoot.

Moore had seen the South Vietnamese mortarman, and one of his ammo carriers, beat feet for the bushes as soon as the first rounds started falling. He chased the little bastards down and dragged them back into camp. I am still in awe of that. I think his presence of mind was just incredible.

Whoever had gone over to see Gunny Jacques—I think it was Corporal Lynch; I don't remember—came back and said that the gunny wanted us to join him. I remember as we were going over a little bit of a rise, we heard another mortar round coming in, and we hit the ground. And when the mortar round hit, that separated us. The people who were ahead of us kept going and Moore, Corporal Lynch, Joy, and I were left behind.

We got up to move and came under fire. We were shoulder to shoulder, talking amongst ourselves, trying to figure out what was going on, and it seems as if it was Joy who yelled to the gunny that we were under fire from our own troops. There was a burst of automatic-weapons fire. I jumped back a little bit; I don't know what Lynch did. I looked up and there was a tracer lying there in the ground burning. Joy was moaning. I'm not sure of the time frame. Joy might have yelled again. There was more fire. I remember Lynch yelling that our own troops had us under fire and Joy was hit and we didn't know what to do. We didn't hear anything in response except more fire from where we thought our troops were. I jumped back again. Joy had stopped moving. I assumed Joy was dead. There was just a lot of weapons fire. You could hear grenades hit the ground and then later explode. There was still some mortar fire coming in, but I think that it had died down quite a bit. I don't know how long things went on, it seemed like forever.

One of the most poignant memories about it is that almost every sound we made seemed to draw fire. I remember I made sounds a couple of times and then something would hit the ground close to me. I would roll over a couple of times away from it and sure enough there would be an explosion.

Lynch had quit making noise during all of the explosions and the fire, but there was still rifle fire in our direction anytime there was any kind of sound. In the distance, over where Gunny Jacques and Sergeant West had their command post, you could hear intense fire in both directions, and yelling, and later bugles. There were also whistles. There was incredibly rapid automatic-weapons fire from what somebody later told me was a Swedish-K submachine gun. It sounded like a steady stream of fire, and I hadn't heard anything fire that fast before.

About this time, as dark as it was between the occasional muzzle flashes and explosions, when there was a little flash of light, I could see Joy—who I'd thought was dead—on one elbow undoing his combat bandage. I didn't want to say anything because every noise drew weapons fire, but I started to move up toward him, then there was another burst of gunfire, and I could hear the bubbling in his chest and the air go out of him and nothing come back in. And I remember lying there thinking, This is just incredible, our own troops' [the South Vietnamese CIDG] total lack of fire discipline. The South Vietnamese just shot like crazy at any thing and at any time. And that was all that was going through my head at that time—that these bastards have killed my buddy, probably both of my buddies.

I was a hell of a lot closer to Joy than I was to Lynch. Joy was from Abernathy, a little town outside my hometown, Lubbock, Texas. He was in the company when I came to it. He was older than I was, and he took me under his wing. He was a mentor of sorts. And I thought, Jesus, these assholes have killed my buddy and no telling how many others. I had no idea what the whistles or the bugles were. For all I knew, it could have meant that they were sounding retreat or whatever.

Things had died down quite a bit, and there was start-

ing to be some movement like the attack was over and
things were settling down and maybe the panic had sub-
sided. At that time, I started looking around. I couldn't
see much of anything, except a little bit of light at the top
of the hill. I couldn't see anything in the light except
some faces. I was really upset, and really angry, and I
stood up and started yelling, *"Toi la My, Toi la My,"*
which I had been told meant "I am an American, I am an
American." The guys at the top of the hill looked in my
direction, started shining lights my way, and smiled, then
waved and came down to greet me. And they were patting
me on the back. I just wanted to get to Gunny Jacques
and tell him what had happened to Joy and to Lynch; I
was really upset as you can imagine. Then I noticed one
guy was taking my weapon, and another guy was taking
my pack, and a guy who looked like he was the leader of
the group was joining us, and because of the additional
flashlights I could see that these were not South Vietnamese troops! These were North Vietnamese troops, and I
was really in a state of shock. They walked me back up
to the top of the hill, and at this time I thought, Jesus, I
have been a complete idiot, and I'm the only one alive. I
think we've been overrun and everyone is dead. I had no
reason to believe that anyone else was alive.

As I got to the top of the hill, they were stripping Joy's
body. They were stripping some other bodies, but I
couldn't see whose. One of the guys motioned for me to
put my hands in the air. Then another guy came up from
behind me, pulled my hands down behind my back, and
tried to tie my hands. The guy in front of me was trying
to take off my cartridge belt, but he couldn't figure out
the rectangular clip. He must have just worked with the
old World War II–style cartridge belt that had a simple
hole and a simple button, which you didn't have to twist
to put on or take off.

The other guy was starting to tie my hands up, and my
life really did pass before my eyes. It was like a high-
speed movie. It occurred to me that they probably intended to drag me around from village to village and

show me off until I got sick, and then they would either let me die or kill me. I decided that I would just as soon die up there with everybody else. I took a step backward and pushed the guy who was trying to tie my hands up away from me. The guy in front of me was kind of taken aback and looked straight up at me, and I hit him right in the chest and knocked him backward.

I took off running toward the crest where I had originally stood up, and I guess that took everyone by surprise. Number one, I'd stood up and identified myself, and after I did that they probably thought that I would be docile. I guess they assumed that I knew what I was doing. They had no idea that I was as dumb as I was.

I caught everybody by surprise. At first there wasn't any rifle fire or anything. They were just dumbfounded. Like I said, the only light was patches of light where they had flashlights on. A couple of rounds were fired in my direction, but I just jumped for that crest, literally, the way you would jump into a swimming pool. I tumbled head over heels down the hill. Then the rifle fire started to increase, and a grenade went off very, very close to me. I thought, Jesus, these guys can't shoot, but somebody can throw a grenade like crazy.

I stopped tumbling when things kind of leveled out, then I jumped forward again, and tumbled some more. When I quit tumbling, I took off running in the general direction of Ba To. I had no idea who was behind me or how close they might be behind me. As I ran, I came across a trail, and I'm running along the trail, and my mind is still going a thousand miles a minute.

The trail dropped off to the left, and as I ran along it, I began thinking that if the North Vietnamese knew about the trail, during their cleanup operations they would probably set up an ambush along it to pick up stragglers. So I decided to get off the trail. It went down to the left, so I kept going straight into the tall grass and the small brush on the hillside. I was haulin' britches. I wasn't waiting for anyone because I thought I was the only one alive.

I was running along for a while, and then I came onto

the trail again. I had just cut across to it. There were two good-size, cedar-type bushes on the trail, and as I parted them bushes I saw people on the side of the trail. And I thought, Jesus, I've just gotten out of one bad deal, and here I'm back in another one. And for some dumb-ass reason, again, I said, "Who's there?"

A voice says, "Brown?"

I said, "Jesus, I thought all you guys were dead."

Somebody said, "We thought you were dead." Then Charlie Blanton said, "You almost are dead." I looked down to see where the voice came from, and I was literally staring down the barrel of his rifle. It was that close. It was right under my chin. He later said that I had sounded like a whole platoon of North Vietnamese coming after them, and I don't doubt it. Hell, I wasn't trying to be quiet, I was trying to get the hell out of there.

I was amazed. Doc Haston was there. Blanton was there. Woo wasn't there. Charlie Lynch was there, which surprised me. I'd thought that Charlie was dead with Joy. I think that Lynch had probably just beat feet a long time before me. I told them that Joy was dead. We stayed there for the night and began to move out the next morning. I had no weapon, no radio, and was absolutely scared to death.

During the attack, when we were under fire, I was able to establish radio contact with Daniel Constance who was back at Ba To as our radio-relay point. I told him that Joy and I were under friendly fire. I'm not sure if that part got through or not. I remember that the Special Forces camp tried to support us with some mortar fire from the camp, but we were beyond their range, which was another mistake. When we went back to Ba To, later, they brought out a battery of 105s to support us. But hindsight is always 20/20.

It was just incredible how much Doc Haston was shot up. We had a couple of South Vietnamese just in terrible shape—broken legs from rifle fire. I remember, later in the day, as we were carrying them back to the camp, how they would scream anytime we moved them. The pain just had to be awful.

When we got back to the camp, we reported Moore and Session as missing. I remember them saying that Moore and Session had been killed on the hilltop when we were overrun. I knew that Joy was dead, I saw him there. Woo was missing in action. I was missing for a brief period of time, obviously, and I was reported to my family as MIA, which was interesting. I guess that much information got through before I linked up with the rest of the platoon and before we got back to camp.

During the night, when we came under attack, I guess they flew in a company of Chinese Nungs with Australian advisers.

After we made our way back to camp, I remember Woo's Chinese Nung came into camp crying, saying that they [he and Woo] had linked up, they had been in trouble twice, had linked up again, and had gotten away, but he was afraid that the North Vietnamese had gotten Woo, and he was just in tears. Three days later, late in the evening, they reported that someone was limping into camp on a rifle. We jumped in a truck and drove down to the checkpoint, and here comes Woo. We came screaming up in the truck, jumped out, and ran to him saying, "Goddamn, Woo, how are you? What the hell happened?"

Woo looked up and said, "Hi, guys, what's happening?" That's the kind of thing that I'll remember until I'm gone.

On listening to some of the earlier parts of the tape, I see that there are some things I missed. I missed Joy crying. The first time Joy was hit, he yelled, and then he started whimpering and crying, and there was more fire. The crying went away to nothing, and I assumed that he was dead.

That grenade that went off when I was rolling down the hill, well, I assumed that someone threw a grenade—when we got up the next morning and got ready to move out, somebody pointed to my cartridge belt. The spoon to one of my grenades was still in my belt, but the grenade was gone. The grenade that I assumed somebody had accurately thrown at me, had come from my own cartridge belt and went off very close to me.

The funny noises that were being made when I decided to stand up, was the North Vietnamese going around mopping up. You could hear them going around, checking bodies, shooting the wounded, and dragging bodies around. That was when I decided to stand up; I just didn't know who was doing the policing.

Years later, Charlie Blanton told me that he was sent back toward the hill to see what he could see, and he saw that I was captured up there, but I never really believed it. I don't know how he could have gone that far and gotten that close. Also, years later, Doc Haston said that when Joy got hit, he kind of lost it. He credited Gunny Jacques with getting him back in line, and Charlie Blanton confirmed it. That surprised me because Doc Haston was always supertough. He was as good or better than any Marine around him. Between bullet wounds and shrapnel wounds, he came off that hill with thirteen holes, and he helped carry down the wounded. Doc Haston has since died of lung cancer. Blanton was killed in a domestic squabble. I don't see how any good came out of Ba To, except for the fact that we learned the lesson that when we went out together, we stayed together. I don't think there ever was a situation where Marines were split up again and scattered amongst the South Vietnamese. We stuck together after that, and we didn't go outside our [supporting] weapons range ever again.

2. Interview with Edsil Young, USMC, (Ret.) (Spring, 1994)

I was with the 2d Platoon of 1st Force Reconnaissance Company, with Gunnery Sergeant Jacques and a South Vietnamese lieutenant. We approached the hill approximately three days after we went out, 16 December 1965. I approached the hill through a little saddle, and we received sniper fire, basically from the west, but we proceeded up the hill after the sniper fire stopped, and camped on top of the hill—bare ground—some grass around about the size of grass outside on the lawn. We stayed there for approximately three days.

At approximately 1900, we started receiving mortar fire. Approximately fifteen to twenty minutes later, the enemy had the hill. When the first round hit at 1900 hours, then Sergeant Baker and myself, with Lance Corporal Moore, got together and moved to the east side of the hill. Moving to the east side of the hill, Lance Corporal Moore got separated from Sergeant Baker and me. During the time that Sergeant Baker and I were together, I recall a strange thing happening during those ten or fifteen minutes. An aircraft appeared and dropped flares. I have never heard who called those flares down. But what they did was to assist the enemy in overrunning the hill. Yes, there was a flare ship. If I recall, it was a C-47, what we called Spooky, that just dropped the flares.

Sergeant Baker and I were on the east side of the hill, probably ten to twenty feet apart, hugging the hill, and we could hear gunfire, because basically, we did not know what was going on. About seven-thirty or so, the heaviest downpour came, which, in my mind, is what saved us. Sergeant Baker and I were able to move in the general direction of south, down to the saddle area on the trail. I remember that I had a compass and I was leading the way, but for some dumb reason I put my compass away, and we came to a fork in the trail and instead of heading southwest in the general direction of Ba To, Baker and I went down toward a low area. I don't know how far we moved, but we stopped at midnight. Early in the morning, we heard voices approaching, so we went back up to the trail and found the fork. Since it was getting light, Baker and I spread out until we could barely see each other. Because we had the problem of security, each of us had to cover 180 degrees.

If I remember correctly, we would switch off walking point. I do remember that Baker was ahead of me when he ran into Jacques and the rest of the people, and we found out who was missing. Baker threw one of the South Vietnamese Army personnel aboard his back and carried him all the way in. After we got back, something like three or four days later, Woo came walking in on his own. He had been out, and from talking to Woo, he had been captured and had got away, and he was exposed to the elements all that time. I remember that he was okay until they sat him down and he had time to reflect on what had happened.

I was an instructor over at LFTC (Landing Force Training Command) from 1969 to 1972. Sometime close to 1970, Woo had been promoted to sergeant, but when I saw him over there (at LFTC), he was a private.

I want to talk about 1st Force Recon, when I was still in the company. I was again out (in the bush) when a guy named Dowling was killed. Lieutenant Lenker was there. We had Dowling up in the tree, as a lookout. A couple of (NVA) watermen, or people, came down, and instead of Dowling being still and quiet, he started coming down out of that tree. He was like a big rock ape coming out of that tree, making so much noise that instead of us ambushing them, we got ambushed. Lieutenant Lenker, myself, Solovskoy and Dowling, a four-man team—that was what we started doing when we were over there the first time— just four men, which after time progressed onward, we knew it didn't work because it was too small. My second tour, they increased it to eight men and nine men. But Dowling came out of the tree, so we started getting fire and once again running and trying to pack our packs, and you know. But I remember that Solovskoy got shot through the leg, so we moved down the hill. Another dumb thing—we stopped by a running stream. Because of the noise, we couldn't hear anything. I put Dowling up front to watch and I was sitting in the open; I can't remember where Lieutenant Lenker was. But instead of Dowling being on guard, he was on his back, and the North Vietnamese almost stepped on him. Evidently, they alerted and filled him full of holes where he lay. So, here we go again.

I had an M-2 carbine. I tried to fire that thing, but the barrel just went to pieces. I must have got it plugged, or something. I think our radio operator had gotten a call in, because a helicopter was there, but the three of us were separated. I popped my day-night flare, but couldn't get the helicopter down. Then I got my thoughts together and popped yellow smoke, and we got helicopters down. I can't remember if I was aboard first, or the radio operator, but we had to get the helicopter across the rice paddy and all the way over to the ridgeline, before we could pick up Lieutenant Lenker.

3. Interview conducted with Colonel Wheeler C. Baker, USMC, Chief of Staff, 1st Marine Division. (May 1994)

Based on the background information you have given me, there are a couple of key things that I want to stress about what happened at Ba To. First, the weather saved us. Sergeant Major Jacques is 100 percent right, when he says that had it not been for the torrential downpour that night, we would never have gotten out of there alive. Secondly, the concern that we Marines had about the main body remaining in position on that hilltop for too long, is entirely correct.

I don't recall how my recon team actually got into that huge village located south of the hill, but we did find ten or twelve big huts down there. We called it a way station and it was located down in the riverbed. We didn't even see it at first—we smelled it—smoke from their cooking fires. We could *feel* that the NVA were down there, but we didn't see anyone as we moved throughout the area.

I was monitoring the radio around noontime on the day of the attack, and I knew that we had to move up onto the hill that day, but since we were only a thousand meters from the hill, I figured that we could make it back within a couple of hours. We were hidden in the thick, triple canopy, where the village was, but I know we could have broken out of there and made it to where Gunny Jacques was within a couple of hours. I did not want to go back to that hill, and I'll tell you that right away. I called Gunny Jacques on the radio and told him that because of what we had found, we thought they should leave the hill, and that we could be on their flank and could scout for them on their way back to Ba To.

I could also hear Sergeant Blanton talking to Gunny Jacques on the team's radio, and he was saying the same thing as I was. Sergeant Blanton didn't want to move back up to that hill, either. We wanted to persuade Jacques to convince that Vietnamese lieutenant to start moving back in toward Ba To. We told him that we would even parallel his movement until we got close enough, and then we'd link up with them. The lieutenant refused to listen. It was really bad to hear that they were going to spend the night there. We thought that was a major mistake.

With that said, especially with all of the enemy sightings we had made, we did not want to move back to the hilltop during daylight and run the chance of bringing the enemy in with us.

I held off moving my team until the very last minute— until Gunny Jacques called me on the radio and told me to get my team back to his position on the hill. We moved up on the south end of the hill, and I was really upset when I got there. I believe that Sergeant Blanton had gotten there just before me. I remember leaving my teammates on the side of the hill and removing my gear just as I got to the top of the hill. I shucked off my rucksack and threw it down on the ground. I was really mad, and I went over to the gunny's position and said, "Okay, we have got to get off of this hill."

If I remember right, I hadn't been there for more than thirty seconds when the first mortar round landed right in the middle of the command post and killed the lieutenant and wounded several others.

The NVA didn't attack the hill—they were already there. They just stood up. They were on three sides of us. How we missed them, coming up from their village along this one finger, I don't know. They must have crawled through the grass and stayed hidden, but I don't know how we missed seeing them on our way up the hill. They must have come up from a different angle, and they were on us before we had any time to react.

As I said, that first mortar round landed right on the command post. I was only a few feet away from it, and I don't know how I missed getting hit. Instantly, there was lots of noise, and small-arms fire was coming from the grass, everywhere. Looking back on it, I know there were several hundred enemy soldiers moving on line toward us. Their numbers would constitute a North Vietnamese battalion. They were not at the base of the hill trying to maneuver up to attack us, they were already at their final coordination line. They just stood up and started, basically, to attack the topographical crest of the hill. There was max confusion, and it could not have been timed more perfectly. Just seconds after the first round hit, we went into total darkness. The darkness was on us as quick as those huge rain clouds came over us.

What I do remember vividly was that after that first round went off, most of the CIDG members went running off the hill. There was no organization, just total chaos, and they were running off the hill. The volume of returned fire was none to negligible toward the oncoming North Vietnamese. Instinctively, I ran back to my team. We got our gear on, and we began to maneuver back to where Gunny Jacques was located. I guess that "maneuver" might be a bad word—we were crawling, shooting, and trying to get some sort of organization going. The thought that came through my mind was to get organized so that we didn't shoot each other. I think that I had all but given up on our Vietnamese friends. I want to say that they were gone, but I can't honestly say that, because it was very dark, and I couldn't see where they were. I know that they were not standing there fighting alongside of us.

Then it started to rain so hard that it reminded me of an East Coast thunderstorm. It just pelted down on us, almost a horizontal rain, and I think that was what saved us. I remember, clearly, being with my four-man team. Corporal Young was my assistant team leader and Lance Corporal Constance was my radio operator. Corporal Moore was my point man. We tried to move over and link up with Jacques, but the heavy volume of fire made that impossible. The incoming fire at this time was greater than anyone can imagine. We were getting hit by mortar fire, rifle fire, recoilless-rifle fire, and automatic-weapons fire. It was like one of our "midnight-madness" fire demonstrations. There was a swarm of North Vietnamese running around, and I could hear a difference in the commands being given by those North Vietnamese. These were orders given with authority. I remember telling Ed Young that these were the NVA we had been looking for all this time. But we couldn't tell who the players were at this stage, and I knew that some of those CIDG soldiers who were with us on the hill must have spotted for that mortar round and let the NVA in on top of us. It was too well planned. In fact it had to have been rehearsed at some earlier point to be so effective.

I remember that Jacques was trying to get some mortar fire going out at this time, and that was the last I saw of Moore. He crawled off to help Jacques fire the mortar, and I never saw him again. I can remember pushing and hitting several NVA soldiers as they came running by in the darkness, and I remember hitting an NVA soldier who came running by me carrying a BAR. I knocked him down, tried to shoot him, but I don't think that I hit him. We had moved down to a small finger on the side of the hill by this time, and I remember Jacques saying that "we have to get out of here," but Gunny Jacques had not been hit at this time. I realized that we couldn't hold the hill; we were down to eight or ten men and there were hundreds of NVA still moving around above us. As we started to move off the hill, we drew a heavy volume of fire, and Corporal Young and I took cover and became separated from our column. Suddenly, we realized that we were alone. I saw some people coming toward us in the rain, and let them come up on us, until we saw that they were NVA. We weren't twenty feet away from them. I told Ed to follow me, and we ran like hell down and away from the hill. As we ran, I suddenly came onto an NVA sentry, and I hit him in the chest the way a football player would smash into a tackling dummy. I knocked him ass over teakettle toward the bottom of the hill, and we kept on moving. There were ten or fifteen NVA still trying to shoot at Young and me. I don't know why they didn't chase us down the hill. If they had, there is little doubt they would have caught us.

The sounds of the enemy's heavy concentrated firing had stopped, but there was still sporadic firing up on the hill. Young and I worked our way around the northwest side of the hill, and knowing that we didn't want to head back toward the village, we started to head west, back toward Ba To. But in the darkness, Young and I made a near-fatal mistake—we found ourselves right back on the hill we had just left. Then we heard voices of the approaching NVA. We could hear them shooting and killing the wounded on top of the hill. Young and I talked briefly about the situation we were in, and again, we ran back down and away from the hill. The NVA heard our movement and again fired a few shots in our direction, but failed to hit either Young or myself.

We decided we would execute our E & E plan (escape and evade) to get back to Ba To. There was nothing else we could do. The emotional side said we had to get back up on the hill to help with the wounded. We felt we should do something, but then reality set in; there was only the two of us.

We had hoped that some type of support would come out during the night, but the visibility and ceiling were zero/zero, and the rain kept any chance of air support on the ground. The rain did not let up all night long, and as I have said, that was what helped us get out of there alive.

Edsil Young and I had been moving on our own since nine o'clock that night. We had come upon a well-used trail and wanted only to get back to Ba To, to get help and to alert the Special Forces camp to the size of the NVA force so close by. Now, as we moved along the trail, we heard movement ahead of us, and we jumped off the trail and took cover. The bamboo on either side of the trail was extremely thick, and we knew that we were passing through the NVA assembly area, but our aim was to get back to Ba To as fast as possible and avoid enemy contact. We had tried, earlier, to move through the thick bamboo, but it was like trying to get through an iron cage.

The bushes came to life, and that was when we spotted one of the CIDG personnel. I leaned forward and took aim, ready to shoot the guy, when Gunny Jacques jumped up next to him. Jacques now wore a bloody bandage around his throat, and Young and I were relieved to have finally linked up with him. I told Jacques what had happened and that the last time I had seen Constance or Moore was back on the hill. That was when I learned that they, along with Joy, had been killed by the NVA.

With our arrival, Young and I had brought two weapons into the fight. I remember looking over the wounded in the group to see what condition they were in, and what I saw wasn't good. I took up the position as point man as we moved back to Ba To.

The mission we originally had was briefed to us by then-Major P. X. Kelly, the division's G-2 officer and later commandant of the Marine Corps. He said that we were going out to locate the 325B NVA Division, which was coming north, down the Ho Chi Minh trail. Elements of this division had already attacked a U.S. Army Special Forces camp inside the A Shau Valley, and it was believed to be heading our way to take out [the Special Forces camp at] Ba To. It seemed to me that if this NVA force was moving to attack Ba To, and they certainly had enough soldiers to do it, [they had made a mistake] since they had hit us first and they had committed their forces for all the wrong reasons. We had discovered their battalion, and they never did attack Ba To.

It took us until late that afternoon to finally reach Ba To. We didn't have any radios with us so once we left the hill, we were without any means of communications. We were hoping that bird-dog aircraft would come out to help us, but they could not have done anything. I don't have a clue as to what they knew back at Ba To. There was no doubt in my mind that somebody was on the inside and had to have set the whole thing up. We didn't trust the CIDG—we held them in low regard. You hate to make general statements about something like this, but that's the way it was. Those CIDG soldiers were carrying M-1 Garands, carbines, M-79 grenade launchers, and they carried a mortar. They never fired them.

I was a sergeant at the time, and my vote power was very low, but I did not like the idea of having a South Vietnamese lieutenant lead us out there. I didn't like the idea of patrolling after first light. I thought that the original plan was that we were going to drop off from the main body and that it was going to return to the Special Forces camp at Ba To. Then, after my team had slid off into the bushes, we would conduct our reconnaissance patrol and link up with the main body, later on.

The things which surprised me were, first, I was stunned to discover that the main body had not returned to Ba To as was planned. Secondly, the NVA unit that hit us was a well-trained, front-line unit. They were armed with AK-47s, SKS rifles, and mortars, and they responded well to orders. This was no irregular VC cadre force.

Lessons learned: following Ba To, we always went out "heavy"—well armed and ready to fight. The South Vietnamese lieutenant was not the most aggressive guy we had ever met, and I had mentioned this to Jacques, but what could we do? He was the officer in charge. That policy later changed, too.

There is no doubt that Gunnery Sergeant Jacques saved the lives of Marines and CIDG soldiers that night. Despite having been shot in the throat, he remained in command, managed to keep our group intact, and was responsible for leading us safely back to Ba To. We could not have had any better leadership than that Gunnery Sergeant Jacques provided to us at Ba To.